Rebounding Identities

Rebounding Identities

The Politics of Identity in Russia and Ukraine

Edited by
Dominique Arel and Blair A. Ruble

Woodrow Wilson Center Press
Washington, D.C.

The Johns Hopkins University Press
Baltimore

EDITORIAL OFFICES
Woodrow Wilson Center Press
Woodrow Wilson International Center for Scholars
One Woodrow Wilson Plaza
1300 Pennsylvania Avenue, N.W.
Washington, D.C. 20004-3027
Telephone: 202-691-4010
www.wilsoncenter.org

ORDER FROM

The Johns Hopkins University Press
Hampden Station
P.O. Box 50370
Baltimore, Maryland 21211
Telephone: 1-800-537-5487
www.press.jhu.edu/books/

2 4 6 8 9 7 5 3 1

A version of chapter six was published in *Sacred Stories: Religion and Spirituality in Modern Russia*, edited by Mark D. Steinberg and Heather J. Coleman © Indiana University Press, 2006

Library of Congress Cataloging-in-Publication Data

Rebounding identities : the politics of identity in Russia and Ukraine / edited by Dominique Arel and Blair A. Ruble.
    p. cm.
Includes index.
ISBN-13: 978-0-8018-8562-4 (cloth : alk. paper)
ISBN-10: 0-8018-8562-0 (cloth : alk. paper)
    1. Political culture—Russia (Federation) 2. Political culture—Ukraine. 3. Group identity—Political aspects—Russia (Federation) 4. Group identity—Political aspects—Ukraine. I. Arel, Dominique, 1959– II. Ruble, Blair A., 1949–
    JN6699.A15R35   2006
    306.20947—dc22

                                                    2006023459

Woodrow Wilson
International
Center
for Scholars

The Woodrow Wilson International Center for Scholars, established by Congress in 1968 and headquartered in Washington, D.C., is a living national memorial to President Wilson. The Center's mission is to commemorate the ideals and concerns of Woodrow Wilson by providing a link between the worlds of ideas and policy, while fostering research, study, discussion and collaboration among a broad spectrum of individuals concerned with policy and scholarship in national and international affairs. Supported by public and private funds, the Center is a nonpartisan institution engaged in the study of national and world affairs. It establishes and maintains a neutral forum for free, open and informed dialogue. Conclusions or opinions expressed in Center publications and programs are those of the authors and speakers and do not necessarily reflect the views of the Center staff, fellows, trustees, advisory groups, or any individuals or organizations that provide financial support to the Center.

The Center is the publisher of *The Wilson Quarterly* and home of Woodrow Wilson Center Press, *dialogue* radio and television, and the monthly newsletter "Centerpoint." For more information about the Center's activities and publications, please visit us on the Web at www.wilsoncenter.org.

Contents

Tables and Figures

Tables

ix

Figures

Acknowledgments

This volume is the product of three workshops on multicultural legacies in Russia and Ukraine hosted by the Kennan Institute of the Woodrow Wilson International Center for Scholars in Washington, D.C. The workshops, which were held in March 2002, November 2002, and November 2003, brought together an interdisciplinary group of scholars to discuss the historical legacies and contemporary consequences of cultural identity in Russia and Ukraine. The workshops allowed scholars from different backgrounds to share their diverse research and discover common themes in the role of identity politics in the former Soviet Union.

The Kennan Institute has sponsored fifteen similar topic-specific working groups and workshops since 1996. Each group was designed to bring together scholars engaged in a related area of research from varying perspectives. These multidisciplinary, multinational, and multigenerational sessions have explored such topics as civil society, social capital, and development in Eurasia (1996–98); urban civic cultural and democratic transitions (1997–2000); regional Russia (1998–99); rural Russia (1998–2000);

Russia's and Ukraine's experience of economic and political transformation (1999–2001); marketization and democratization in Russia (2000–2001); the role of women in postcommunist transitions (2001–2); integrating Russia into Europe (2001–3); contemporary and historical perspectives on conflict in the former Soviet Union (2002–3); migration and diasporas in Eurasia (2003–5); Russia and the world (2005); diverse cultures in contemporary society (2005–6); state and society relations in transitional societies (2005–6); religion in post-Soviet societies (2005–6); and civil society and democracy in Ukraine (2006–7). The general format has been for researchers to present their previous research as a way of posing shared issues for further discussion. That discussion becomes the basis for the plan of a book, with participants returning home to write original papers on the new topics before convening once again for a final manuscript review.

This format challenges each participant to prepare new work that is substantially different from what he or she has published before. It produces a collective voice that rises above the sum of its individual parts. This process thus achieves two important goals. First, it produces a publication of lasting value. Second, it encourages the formation of a thematic "invisible college" that takes on a life of its own as the group disperses.

Funding for the multicultural legacies workshops was provided by the U.S. Department of State Program for Research and Training on Eastern Europe and the Independent States of the Former Soviet Union (the Title VIII Program), and by the Kennan Institute's George F. Kennan Fund. Kennan Institute staff members Muhitdin Ahunhodjaev, F. Joseph Dresen, Margaret Paxson, Nancy Popson, and Erin Trouth Hofmann were all involved in making the workshops a success.

We are very grateful to the funders of the workshop, the Kennan Institute staff, and all the participants in the multicultural legacies workshops for making this volume possible.

Rebounding Identities

Introduction: Theorizing the Politics of Cultural Identities in Russia and Ukraine

Dominique Arel

The demise of the Cold War has brought about a paradigmatic shift in social science research. Scholars who had long been preoccupied with the role of class, or more generally with economically induced social identities, began to turn to the more elusive variable of culture to explain social action and political choices. The shift mirrored a change in the currency of mobilization worldwide, with the rhetoric of revolution increasingly ceding ground to that of national sovereignty and religious purity.[1] Scholarship is reactive. How movements or states frame their actions is bound to affect how scholars frame their research. In that respect, the Yugoslav wars and the September 11, 2001, terrorist attacks on the United States have become the defining moments of the postcommunist era.

The shift is felt throughout disciplines, which is to say that the study of culture as a central concern is no longer confined to anthropology, and it also cuts across areas of investigation, beginning with the territories of the former Soviet Union. The "nationality" question in and east of Germany had captured the imagination of researchers since the mid–nineteenth century, but it did not recover well from the human catastrophes of World War II. The relatively abundant postwar literature on ethnonational, linguistic, and religious problems in the Soviet Union tended to be kept on the sidelines and looked upon as a descriptive, if not militant, genre. The cohort that came of age in the 1970s and 1980s did offer a number of first-rate social science analyses on nationalities,[2] but their impact on Soviet studies remained minor. The Soviet Union had proclaimed that the national question had been "definitively" solved; and on the whole, Sovietologists, as they were then called, accepted the premise. Again, this reflected a dominant assumption in academia, namely, that global trends—in the so-called First, Second, and Third Worlds—favored nation building, understood as the acquisition of state-based identities. The "nation-destroying" admonition of Walker Connor took another two decades to undermine received wisdom.[3]

The delegitimization of applied socialism and the unleashing of grievances using the idiom of the cultural nation redefined the research agenda in the 1990s. In Imperial Russian and Soviet history, the near hegemonic social history practiced by the baby-boom generation was overtaken by a slew of studies privileging cultural factors. The veteran social historian Ron Suny led the way by demonstrating how the "revanchist" nations, which seceded from the Soviet Union, owed much of their existence, or "construction," to the Soviet experience itself. Terry Martin, inspired by the pathbreaking work of his mentor Sheila Fitzpatrick on the class-based social mobility of the Stalin era, conceived of the early Soviet Union as an "affirmative action" empire simultaneously promoting ethnic-based mobility. Among students of contemporary processes, Rogers Brubaker showed how the institutions of Soviet republican governments, defined according to the nationality principle, and yet relatively empty shells under the hypercentralized Communist Party, unintendedly provided the arenas around which groups contested political power. The comparativist David Laitin, migrating from African and Catalan studies, provoked us to think of the myriad ways in which socially and politically significant identities can be formed, and re-formed, in the crux of the post-Soviet transformation.[4]

The revival of the cultural perspective in social science brought to the fore the variable of *identity.* The use of this variable, in fact, became so pervasive that some diagnosed it as an overstretched and analytically fruitless concept.[5] Most scholars, however, beg to disagree and approach identities as critical categories of self-understanding.[6] How people conceive of themselves in relation to others, how they come to acquire this conception, and how their self-understanding affects, or is affected by, processes of collective action and state policies are the core questions raised by an interest in what came to be called identity politics. Rather than discarding identity as a tool of analysis, Chandra and Laitin propose disaggregating it into three components: attributes, categories, and dimensions.[7]

Attributes are the building blocks of identities, the cultural markers that provide contents to a proclaimed identity: speech, religious practices, skin color, or dress, for instance. Attributes can be socially constructed, as in speech, or acquired at birth, as in skin color. *Categories* are how people define themselves, as in "Ukrainian," "Russian speaker," "Orthodox," or "Cossack." They are, by definition, socially constructed. *Dimensions* refer to families of categories and their degrees of saliency in a given society at a given time. An individual can describe himself as a "Ukrainian" along a dimension of "nationality" (understood as a descent-based cultural identity), in a repertoire of several competing identity options, such as "Russian," "Polish," or "Romanian." Nationality has high saliency in post-Soviet Ukraine. In France, to give a counterexample, descent-based nationality is ascribed no saliency in social and political discourse. An immigrant from Ukraine to France will hardly have any socially significant opportunities to describe himself as a Ukrainian. Dimensions are also, by definition, socially constructed.

The politics of identities thus operate on many levels. Notwithstanding a tradition that endures among post-Soviet scholars, despite its theoretical discrediting in the West, identities are not kernels that are waiting to be "revealed" but rather labels that are fought over by state agents and nonstate entrepreneurs. How to name identities and make discrete categories prevail over others is a political, not a teleological, process. More often than not, it is a process that is fiercely contested. A similar battle can be waged over the proper combination of attributes that comprise a category. Identities— the categories that people use to describe themselves—can be based on an expansive set of attributes (e.g., speakers of a language, loosely defined), or more restrictive ones (e.g., speakers of a standardized language, who at the same time profess a certain form of religion). What makes an identity can change over time. The attributes themselves can change, within a lifetime or across generations, as people acquire languages, convert, alter the way they dress, and so forth. This process of cultural change is conceptually distinct from the configuration of attributes into categories (identities). The social and political import of these categories is also a distinct unit of analysis.

The three components of dimensions, categories, and attributes form a framework for understanding identity change. Change can be observed in how attributes, or cultural markers, evolve; how categories, or named combinations of attributes, arise; and how families of categories, or dimensions, acquire or lose social and political significance. Chandra and Laitin ambitiously aim at developing an all-encompassing theory of identity change, while in the process inviting us to reflect theoretically on more concretely delineated domains of identity formation. Their advice is most fruitful, as much of the research on culture and politics in the post-Soviet area does operate on these three levels of analysis. The Chandra and Laitin framework brings conceptual order to an exciting and ongoing field of investigation.

This book presents the research of ten young scholars, from four disciplines, examining aspects of the politics of cultural identities in Russia and Ukraine. The contributions by the authors can be regrouped in a number of ways (national or linguistic vs. religious dimensions; state vs. societal approaches; Tatarstan vs. Ukraine as fields of research). A more interesting perspective, in our view, is to highlight what their research has to offer to the literature on identity formation along the three components specified by Chandra and Laitin. Remarkably, the contributions in this volume are distributed almost equally not only across components but *within* them as well. Four chapters focus primarily on the politics of saliency (dimension), three on the politics of category formation (identity), and three on the politics of what make cultural traits (attributes) change. Within the dimension component, each of the four chapters is devoted to a distinct dimension (national, linguistic, religious, and civic). Within the category component, each of the three chapters revolves around a category belonging to a distinct family (national, linguistic, and religious). Within the attribute component, the three chapters cover the two cultural markers of speech and religious practice, the two main markers in modern societies. Collectively, these chapters offer a compelling sample of the range of theory-driven research being carried out on aspects of cultural politics in Russia and Ukraine.

The Saliency of Cultural Cleavages

In the age of mass politics, the cultural nation has become a pivotal lever of political organization. The personal principle of sovereignty, embodied in individual descent from a dynastic family, came to be replaced by a collective principle: that a group of people, sharing *common* descent, have a natural right to sovereignty. European policymakers called it the "principle of nationality." The claim of common descent was accompanied by a claim of identification. The putative members of the group united by common descent were deemed to share cultural markers. European discourse, going back to the writings of the German Romantics, privileged language as the core marker of a nationality. In this deceptively simple view, every language concealed a nationality—or ethnic nation—to distinguish it from the territorial nation invented by the French Revolution; and every nationality, by the mere fact of its existence, had the right to sovereignty.

The principle of nationality, however potent as a mobilizational force, is deceptively simple for two reasons. The first, to be taken up later in this chapter, is that the "identification" of a discrete nationality is a contested process, rather than an act of discovery. Were the "Ruthenians" in nineteenth-century Ukraine an ethnic group destined to be assimilated by the Polish group, a subgroup of the Russian group, or a nationality of its own standing? The Ruthenians themselves, through individual behavior and public debates, could not for a long time agree on a common position; and the Austrian, Polish, Imperial Russian, and Soviet states had distinct views on the question. At a time when the dimension of nationality became salient in Eastern Europe, political battles raged over the identification, or recognition, of specific *categories,* such as "Ukrainian," within the family of nationalities.

The second reason has to do with the variability of national mobilization. Even when the categories become more "settled," when contestation over how the group should be called is marginalized, this does not necessarily mean that group members will mobilize according to the nationality principle. In post-Soviet Russia, the Tatars of Tatarstan are faced with a challenge by a small group of Tatar-speaking Christians (the Kryashens) demanding recognition as a separate nationality. The vast majority of Tatars, however, do not question their nationality. Does that make them automatically nationalist, that is, prioritizing demands of sovereignty, based on cultural distinctiveness, over anything else? An affirmative answer to the question is often implicit in the literature, argues Elise Giuliano in chapter 1 of the present volume, and its main effect is to overpredict nationalist mobilization. Nationalist mobilization is not constant, but variable. In Tatarstan, Giuliano's original site of investigation, nationalist mobilization peaked in the early 1990s, before dwindling in the latter part of the decade. In order to understand why people mobilize along nationality lines, we have to understand why they do so at certain times but not others.

This brings us to the notion of salient dimensions. As Lipset and Rokkan established in their classic article on cleavage structures, there is only a finite number of axes along which political preferences can be distributed in polities.[8] A polarization of preferences creates a salient cleavage, a critical division in opinion. Lipset and Rokkan identified four such "critical lines of cleavage": (1) between the centralizing state and a territorially concentrated population invoking common descent or regional attachment; (2) between the secular state and the church; (3) between landed interests and urban industry; and (4) between owners and workers. Thus, for these scholars, in the modern era nationality is only one of four cleavages—along with religion, the urban/rural divide, and class—that have the potential to polarize opinion.[9]

These lines of cleavage operate in a hierarchy. Any concrete polity, at any given time, can be characterized by political divisions along several of these axes, if not all four. The question is which of these cleavages is the most polarized, that is to say, the most politically determinative or salient. Lipset and Rokkan's research showed great variation in the hierarchy of cleavages, not only across cases but also within cases over time. Yet, they cautioned that we know relatively little as to what causes cleavages to become more, or less, salient: "The conditions for the softening or hardening of such cleavage lines in fully mobilized polities have been poorly studied."[10]

Giuliano examines a period of high nationalist mobilization, between 1990 and 1994, in several republics of the Russian Federation. During that time, republican leaders challenged the center by electing presidents, proclaiming state languages, disregarding federal legislation, and organizing referendums on sovereignty. Chechnya, Tatarstan, Bashkortostan, and Tuva made the boldest steps by either boycotting or rejecting the 1993 Russian Constitution. In all cases, the challenges to the center were framed in nationalist terms, as the right of the titular nationality (e.g., Tatars) to exercise sovereignty in its historic homeland (e.g., Tatarstan), and had mass support. In Tatarstan, research has suggested that the support ran essentially along ethnic lines, with the Tatars and Russians, whose proportion of the population was nearly equal, polarized on the issue.[11] After 1994, however, elites in these republics, with the important exception of Chechnya, shifted to a strategy of accommodation, and nationalist grievances lost their urgency. In the Lipset and Rokkan framework, the nationality cleavage, which dominated center–periphery relations in the early 1990s, lost its primacy later on. The masses no longer mobilized to demand more powers from Moscow. Why?

Giuliano adeptly reviews four theories that attempt to explain nationalist mobilization and finds them wanting. Two theories focus on elites. The historical-institutional school states that Soviet republican institutions, which symbolically empowered nationalities while depriving them of real influence—the empty shell argument mentioned above—provided incentives for elites to play the nationality card with the demise of the Communist Party. The economic-structural school, conversely, puts the emphasis on economic resources. Elites with the most resources at their disposal were those with the greatest incentives to play the national sovereignty game. Both theories assume that elites act according to their interests. Both, however, make the questionable assumption that the masses reflexively follow their elites. Giuliano, following Horowitz,[12] does not buy it: "Such a distinction between crafty leaders and credulous masses rings false and is also empirically inaccurate insofar as local populations and nationalist movements did not allow republican leaders to direct their political behavior."

The two theories presenting a "bottom-up" perspective do not fare much better in Giuliano's analysis. The ethnodemographic explanation correlates numbers with behavior: The greater the proportion of a nationality on a territory, the greater the propensity for nationalist mobilization. Though the explanation works at a basic level, because it is obvious that some critical mass is necessary to make mobilization a viable project, in the Russian case it fails to explain variation past the threshold. In Russia, republics with the highest proportions of titulars (members of the nationality after which a republic is named) were among the leaders (Chechnya) and the laggards (Chuvashia) of mobilization, and a very small proportion of titulars (22 percent) did not prevent Bashkortostan from a being a strong challenger. Numbers, cautions Giuliano, tell us nothing about the intensity of preferences. Put differently, identifying with a category ("Tatars") does not necessarily make the dimension to which the category belongs a salient one.[13]

The cultural explanation, finally, emphasizes the content of, and emotional attachment to, an identity. Commonly known as primordialism, it has little currency in social science. Emotional attachments do matter, of course, and are not sufficiently taken into account in theories of nationalism. Yet they in themselves cannot explain change. Tatars in 2004 did not feel less attached to their national identity than they did in 1994. But national identity does not appear to act as a lever of mobilization as it did before. In the hierarchy of cleavages, nationality has dropped a notch. Giuliano's own explanation does not assume that elites autonomously determine the political saliency of a dimension. Elites have the capacity to frame the political agenda, by emphasizing certain issues at the expense of others, but their appeals have to strike a chord in order to translate into mass support. In her argument, grievances will resonate only if they allow individuals to make sense of their own experiences.

In the waning years of the Soviet Union, the two critical trends were the contraction of career opportunities and the weakening of central power. With the rapid decline of the Soviet economy, members of all ethnic groups, including Russians, were facing bleaker prospects of upward mobility. In a political environment where the public airing of ethnic grievances was now tolerated and where government elites for the first time had to get themselves elected, elites blamed economic problems on Russians, a stance which the Tatar workers found credible. In rejecting the standard economic explanation to ethnic mobilization, Horowitz demonstrated that direct job competition among ethnic groups is actually very rare.[14] Giuliano's point, however, is not about empirical evidence but perception. Ethnic Russians suffered as much as ethnic Tatars from the economic downturn, but the Tatars were nevertheless vulnerable to a discourse that rang true. The saliency of the national dimension was thus dependent on structural conditions. With the privatization of a large sector of the economy in the 1990s, opening up avenues of mobility for titulars, these conditions were no longer in place and national mobilization waned.

In chapter 2, Alexandra Hrycak is concerned with variation in the political saliency of a cleavage not over time, as with Giuliano, but across public domains. A debate has endured among students of Ukraine over the primacy of the language cleavage in electoral contests.[15] A key argument in this debate is that whenever a presidential candidate or parliamentary party in Ukraine is perceived as "nationalist," which happened in most but not all contests since 1990, voting support largely falls along the language of preference, namely, the language that people prefer to speak when given the choice. In other words, language tends to act as the most significant cleavage of Ukrainian electoral politics.

The puzzle is that this polarization does not carry over to public policy on the most sensitive aspect of language politics—the language of instruction in schools. The basic nationalist premise, that the language of instruction is not a matter of choice but of heritage, has quietly prevailed since independence with hardly any debate in parliament, and the proportion of students enrolled in Russian-language schools shows a steady decrease.[16] This despite the fact that, according to surveys cited by Hrycak, only half of ethnic Ukrainians prefer to have their children taught in Ukrainian. School policy can induce major political conflicts, as in Belgium in the 1960s and Quebec in the 1960s and 1970s.[17] Why does a linguistic cleavage that is enduringly salient in electoral contests and public opinion surveys go under the radar in day-to-day politics in Ukraine? What makes an issue salient in some domains of public life, such as electoral contests, but not others, such as the implementation of school policy?

Hrycak's explanation focuses on the intensity of preferences. Ethnic Ukrainians form nearly three-fourths of the population in Ukraine, yet the proportion of those speaking Ukrainian as a language of preference is closer to 50 percent.[18] The Language Law, passed in 1989 at a time when public preferences were not expressed in open electoral contests, was never amended. Its key article on language in school unambiguously stated that "freedom of choice in the language of instruction in [elementary and secondary] schools is an inalienable right." The law has been disregarded by the Ministry of Education since the 1990s. The ministry bases its own policy not on parental rights but on the principle that native language determines the language of instruction.

"Native language" (*rodnoi iazyk* in Russian; *ridna mova* in Ukrainian) is a category that goes back to the second half of the nineteenth century, in both the Austrian and Imperial Russian parts of what is now Ukrainian territory, as Hrycak demonstrates at some length. Subsequently, Soviet citizens and nationalist entrepreneurs have tended to interpret it to refer to the language native to the *group* to which the individual feels he belongs, rather than to the individual himself. Someone identifying as Ukrainian, whose first language in childhood was Russian, could still claim Ukrainian as his "native" language, in the sense of being the language of his native group. Most Ukrainians who grew up speaking Russian claimed Ukrainian as their native language in Soviet censuses and continued to do so in the 2001 Ukrainian census.[19] The Soviet Union had co-opted the nationalist idea that nationalities owe their distinct existence to a distinct language. A nationality *had* to have its own language. In practice, the public use of titular languages was often frowned upon, and that was certainly the case in Ukraine. Yet at the same time Ukrainians were socialized into identifying with a language that they preferred not to speak, and a similar phenomenon could be found in non-Russian territories outside the Baltic republics and the South Caucasus, as Dmitry Gorenburg points out in this volume. It is this ambivalence over language, for Hrycak, which accounts for the lack of saliency of the language question in schools.

Russian speakers, understood here as those who prefer speaking Russian when given the choice, irrespective of their claimed native language, have not organized over language policies. Parties or electoral blocs primarily promoting language rights have remained marginal. The native language school policy of the Ministry of Education has encountered little opposition in Russian-speaking Ukrainian areas, except in the Donbas and Crimea, even if a large proportion, and probably a majority, of these Ukrainians prefer a Russian-language education for their children. Russian speakers prefer the status quo, but their ambiguous stance vis-à-vis Ukrainian, which after all is the language that defines their ethnic identity, according to a central tenet of Soviet nationalities policy that they have thoroughly internalized, makes them unable or unwilling to positively demonstrate to resist changes to the status quo. Russian speakers tend to side with ethnic Russians during elections, as was noted above, but when it comes to matters that require group organization, they are no match for Ukrainian speakers. Giuliano's point about numbers not mechanically translating into political action is well taken. Russian speakers and Ukrainian speakers may split down the middle according to surveys, but the intensity of preferences over language is clearly on the Ukrainian-speaking side.

At the level of high politics, argues Hrycak, the decision not to confront the issue since the passing of the Language Law in 1989 creates an opening for bureaucratic actors to autonomously conduct policy. In divided societies, when the intensity of preferences is asymmetrical, nationalist actors tend to capture the educational apparatus, their opponents having neither the talent nor predisposition to offer their own team.[20] This creates a schizophrenic situation where actual policy jars with what is formally in the books. Hrycak grounds her analysis in an institutional argument of Theda Skocpol, according to which the ability of state bureaucracies to act in pursuit of their autonomously defined policy goals depends on expanding their control over organizational resources at times of deep political division among elected officials. In the Ukrainian case, nationalist-minded bureaucrats, who control the educational sector for lack of an alternative, are able to take advantage of the unwillingness of parliament to act and of the passivity of Russian speakers to defuse the saliency of the language dimension in school policy. The native language rule prevails, and children of Russian speakers are learning more Ukrainian than Russian, an outcome that is bound to have important repercussions for the saliency of language in Ukrainian politics over the next generation.

Defusing the saliency of a dimension is also at the heart of chapter 3, by Katherine Graney. The cleavage in question is religious, specifically, over Islam. Graney explores attempts by elites, Muslim and non-Muslim alike, to make the Islam practiced in Russia an integral part of society rather than a security problem, or a culture perceived to challenge the fundamental values of the Russian state. Contrary to Giuliano's study of nationalist mobilization and Hrycak's case of linguistic polarization during elections, the evidence for the saliency of religious cleavages in Russian politics is fragmentary. The state, after all, does not gather data on religious affiliation. Reports of hostile attitudes or actions against Muslims abound in the press, but the targets are often framed as "peoples of the Caucasus" or "illegal migrants," in both cases not always Muslim. Radical Islamic symbols displayed by Chechen terrorists, however, run the risk of associating Islam, in popular sentiment, with anti-Russian behavior. In the post–September 11, 2001, world, the hardening of a religious cleavage, to use Lipset and Rokkan's terminology, is not implausible in Russia. Graney notes that "the question of how the Muslim minority 'fits' in the new Russia has perhaps replaced even Russia's eternal and destructive history of anti-Semitism as the most contentious and potentially violence-provoking religious problem facing the country."

Graney looks at the efforts of the elites of Tatarstan, the most powerful Muslim republic in the Russian Federation, to forestall this hardening. At stake is the relationship of Islam with modernity. Radical Islamists do not distinguish the temporal (political affairs) from the sacred, and they privilege faith-based over skill-based education. Their rejection of the secularism underpinning the Western political and educational systems is existential. To counter the radical Islamic vision, embraced by communities in the Caucasus claiming to be followers of the Saudi Wahhabist sect, or bellowed by Chechen rebels, Tatar leaders seek to resurrect the prerevolutionary Jadidist project.

Jadidism was an indigenous movement of Muslim intellectuals in late-nineteenth- and early-twentieth-century Imperial Russia who believed that social backwardness in Muslim society could be overcome by emulating Europe and Russia—Westernizing Russia, that is—as models of civilization. In the postcolonial world, Muslim secularists no longer pose the problem as one of civilizing influence, and they couch their program in the language of national equality and dignity, but they see their future as one *with* Europe, rather than in opposition to its values.[21] The model here, explicitly endorsed by Tatar leaders, is Turkey, which has combined a strong nationalism intolerant of minority claims—evidenced by its violent struggle against Kurdish nationalism—with a resolute orientation toward the West.

The Tatar project to present Russian Islam as neojadidist, instead of *jihadist,* faces a number of obstacles. The first is disunity among Islamic religious elites in Russia. The collapse of the Soviet Union and the rise of sovereignty movements in republics of the Russian Federation has brought about a multiplication of Islamic organizations, known as Spiritual Boards, whose spokesmen are regularly at loggerheads. Graney tells of the rivalry between two muftis, one based in Bashkortostan who heads a Spiritual Board that nominally oversees the entire Islamic community, and another based in Moscow who challenges this supremacy. The former accused the latter of "Wahhabism," until the latter, incensed by the invasion of Iraq in the spring of 2003, called for a "jihad" against the United States, for which he was promptly "excommunicated" by the former. Routine accusations of radicalism by religious rivals could have the effect of increasing, rather than decreasing, the saliency of religion in Russian society.

A second obstacle is nationalism. Policies to promote the ethnic distinctiveness of predominantly Muslim republics can call into question their desire to integrate into Russia. A case in point is the law reintroducing the Latin script in Tatarstan, passed by the Tatarstan parliament in 1999 and challenged by a federal law on languages in 2003.[22] The Tatar law is about ethnic symbolism and is not construed as a religious or civilizational challenge, because it is modeled on pro-Western Turkey's latinization drive in the 1920s. In popular consciousness, however, an ethnic identity defined by language (Tatars) but reinforced by a religion not exclusive to the group (Islam) is difficult to distinguish from a religious identity.

The third obstacle is elite limitations in framing public discourse. Elites strive to provide a paradigm for public debate by emphasizing certain issues and marginalizing others. But as Giuliano reminds us, their appeals must resonate with the population to obtain primacy in social life. It could very well be that a neojadidist discourse will find roots among Muslim communities in Tatarstan and the Volga region, but it is far from clear that a similar appeal will be found in the North Caucasus. The saliency of the religious cleavage in Russia remains an open question.

In chapter 4 of this volume, Mikhail Alexseev addresses the saliency of cleavages by focusing on the fear of Chinese migrants in the Siberian borderland of Primorskii, off the Pacific coast. The specter of a takeover of Siberia by Chinese settlers—an old theme in Russian dissident literature[23] —was regularly raised in the 1990s by the media and politicians, including the local governor. Dire predictions that the 2002 census would uncover "millions" of Chinese were common. The facts, however, are more sober. The number of Chinese counted in the census was 35,000, and there is no documented evidence of a massive undercounting of Chinese illegals, that is, without proper registration, but actually living in Russia.[24]

In Primorskii proper, Alexseev estimates that the maximum number of

Chinese working in the late 1990s was 10,000, with perhaps up to twice as many tourists, a small quantity in a population exceeding 2 million. And yet the average Primorskii resident thinks otherwise. In surveys administered by Alexseev, nearly half see "Chinese 'peaceful penetration' as threatening Russia's sovereignty," and more than half believe that the Chinese are stealing their jobs. A whopping 89 percent agree with the proposition that "illegal" Chinese migrants should be deported. Primorskii Russians appear to be distrustful of current and long-term plans of the Chinese settled across the border (where the density of the population is ten times higher than in Primorskii proper).

This latent hostility vis-à-vis the Chinese presence, however, has not translated into political mobilization. Support for political parties unabashedly promoting an antimigrant agenda has remained weak. Aggressive actions against migrants—such as attacks on settlements of the sort that are frequently reported in Krasnodar Krai at the outer edge of the Caucasus—have been few. The Chinese question is a sore point among the Primorskii Russians, but it has not crystallized into a salient cleavage. Alexseev seeks to figure out why.

Before assessing its findings, a discussion of the nature of the cleavage is in order. The conflict in Primorskii opposes two groups with distinct languages, religious traditions and, more generally, customs. Surveys suggest a fair degree of ethnic distance between groups, with only a tiny percentage of Russians open to the possibility of interethnic marriages. Ethnicity thus appears to be the main cleavage. However, in public rhetoric, the issue is primarily presented as the invasion of a foreign element into the Russian body politic. The Chinese are not just of another culture; they are of another country, and what is at stake in popular discourse is the legitimacy of their presence within the Russian polity. In that light, one could argue that the dimension that is highlighted in Primorskii, and throughout the Siberian provinces bordering China, is a civic one, that is, the criteria that make one a member of the Russian political community.[25] Of course, nationalist grievances are often directed at a group portrayed as "foreign" to the homeland, despite centuries of cohabitation. The Primorskii case, conversely, is about foreigners in the civic sense, namely, people without Russian citizenship. The fact that the Chinese settlers are migrants is what matters most.[26]

Alexseev argues that the migrant question has failed to become salient in Primorskii politics because it only proved meaningful in the daily experience of a small sector of society: the agricultural workers. People working the land most likely fear that privatization would bring in Chinese landlords. Blue-collar workers, by contrast, have few encounters with Chinese workers in their daily lives, because the Chinese have established themselves in socioeconomic niches, areas in which they excel (e.g., street markets) or that are shunned by local labor (low-paid construction jobs). These same blue-collar workers may believe that the Chinese are unfairly competing with them, as the surveys mentioned above indicate, but their stance vis-à-vis the foreign Chinese appears to have far less urgency than among people in the countryside. Once again, the intensity of preferences appears to be a factor accounting for the softening or hardening of a dimension, in this case, a civic dimension—citizens versus foreigners. Peasants sense the urgency, but their small number and low social status make them politically inconsequential.

Meanwhile, adds Alexseev, the Cossack paramilitary formations have the support of most Orthodox, but among those who feel the greatest urgency on the matter, only one-third of peasants declare themselves Orthodox. This leads Alexseev to conclude, using a variation of what is known in political science as the security dilemma, that the migrant question in Primorskii will acquire political saliency only if the Primorskii Russians feel that they have been abandoned by the center, through a breakdown of transportation or political paralysis at the national level, and if the Chinese demographic presence and territorial pretensions of the Chinese state become far more visible.[27] Saliency is contingent on structural conditions, per Giuliano, and it is these conditions that do not obtain in Primorskii, which makes people receptive to a polarizing discourse.

The Struggle to Define a Category

Categories are modes of identification. They are the labels that people use to identify themselves, the answer to a "Who are you?" probe. How people define themselves is context dependent. In Tito's Yugoslavia, a resident of Belgrade may have answered "Serb" or "Yugoslav" depending on who was asking the question, and where the encounter took place. Categories thus spring from self-assertion, but they also derive from "other"-assertion, the labeling that individuals or groups ascribe to the *Other.* Armenians routinely refer to ethnic Azeris as "Turks," the category used by the predecessors of the Azeris but no longer by contemporary Azeris. Armenians use "Turks" pejoratively. Derisive categories, however morally reprehensible, are standard in interethnic dynamics. How people name themselves and others, and in which situations, is scrupulously studied by anthropologists and ethnographers.

Categories are also units of political standing. In the modern era, states ascribe identities to their populations for purposes of security and/or public policy. Only some of the categories used in social life are recognized as official categories by the state. Much of the political controversies over identities revolve around this issue of *recognition*. The sites of political contestation over identities include censuses, maps, identity papers, museums, and constitutional and legal documents.[28] In chapter 5, Steven J. Seegel focuses on the use of maps, in the half century that preceded World War I, to represent ethnonational identities in the territories that now make up Ukraine. Maps, Seegel tells us, were the preserve of militaries and subject to censorship. This was particularly true in the autocratic Russian Empire, although one surmises that in an age when offensive wars were still accepted as legitimate acts of statecraft, topographical maps had restricted circulation in all states.

What interests Seegel is the shift in mapmaking from describing territories legitimated by their recognition from Great Powers to describing *peoples* within these territories. The shift paralleled the rise of a competing principle of state legitimacy in European politics—the nationality principle—which, as discussed above, declares that states are not the product of dynasties, conquest, or the alleged consent of a territorially defined population but of the cultural character of a population. To the common assertion, in late nineteenth century, that only peoples possessing "historic" states have the right to a contemporary state, the nationality principle rejoined that the mere existence of a nationality is a sufficient condition for statehood. From the 1860s, actors in Ukrainian territories were engaged in the project of ethnographically documenting a separate East Slavic group, but the conditions under which their work took place were starkly different according to regions. Ukrainian territories were then divided between the Austro-Hungarian and Russian empires. The Austrian wing of Austro-Hungary, or Cisleithania, was the first state to recognize the nationality principle, inasmuch as it granted nationalities the right to use their language in schools and local politics.[29] Austria recognized "Ruthenians" (Ruthenisch) as a nationality in its Province of Galicia, now Western Ukraine. Russia, conversely, considered "Little Russians" as a subcategory of "Russians" and their language a "dialect" of Russian. The group that became the Ukrainians was thus afforded opportunities for self-affirmation in one territory but not in the other.

The favorable conditions in Galicia impelled ethnographers to produce a first demographic atlas highlighting "ethnic" categories by the mid-1870s. Nationality entrepreneurs in Galicia, however, were still divided as to what to call their group. The category popularly used by East Slavs in Galicia, and from which Ruthenisch derived, was *rus'kyi,* or "from Rus'," the name of the medieval state that extended to Galicia. Ruthenian intellectuals were still unsure of their orientation toward Russia at that time, but by the 1880s a consensus that they were not Russians crystallized.[30] *Rus'kyi* was deemed too close semantically to *russkii,* the adjective connoting an ethnic Russian.

The category "Ukrainian" began to get the upper hand by the 1890s, as epitomized by the publication of the map "Rus' Ukraina and White Rus'," by two national activists from L'viv University in Galicia. Ethnographic mapmaking had a clear political purpose: to demonstrate that the Ruthenians/Ukrainians held a majority in Galicia, and therefore that Galicia *belonged* to Ukrainians. The claim was directed less at the Austrian state than at the Poles. The Poles, bereft of a state since the Partitions of the 1790s, continued to view Galicia as an integral part of their historic territory (Mala Polska, or Little Poland). Polish mapmakers had heretofore depicted Poland according to the historical principle, that is, the lands that historically belonged to the Polish-Lithuanian Commonwealth. Seegel notes that Polish maps gradually began to integrate the ethnographic principle, foreshadowing pitched battles on how to demarcate the Polish and Ukrainian nationalities, in an environment where cultural boundaries were fluid. In Russian Ukraine, meanwhile, the attempts by ethnographers from the Imperial Russian Geographical Society to surreptitiously record "Little Russians" was stopped dead in its tracks by Imperial order. The meticulous measurement of Ukrainian "ethnographic territory" from scholars based east of Galicia had to await the Soviet period.[31]

Seegel's chapter raises questions about the construction of categories. The nationality principle, first accepted by Austria, was progressively adopted by Polish stateless elites and eventually Imperial Russia. The political dispute hinged on the categories that were to be recognized and how to define these categories. The nationality principle, however, remained silent on religion as an identity attribute, and the Soviet Union, which went the furthest of any multinational state in its co-optation of the principle, categorically excluded religion as a criterion of nationality recognition.

Yet religion, as Paul Werth reminds us in chapter 6, was the critical criterion that defined public identities in the Russian Empire. Civil registration records—the so-called metrical books recording births, marriages, and deaths—were the preserve of religious communities in prerevolutionary Russia. Subjects of the empire were ascribed a "confessional" identity, which could prove decisive in matters such as inheritance rights, military conscription, and eligibility for state service. For certain groups, confessional identity could restrict their rights of residence (Jews, confined to the Pale of Settlement) or access to land ownership (Polish Catholics, in the Western Provinces). While Seegel examines mapmaking as a site of contestation for the recognition and definition of categories, Werth's site is the official confessional status. The state is all too prominent in the Seegel narrative, but nonstate actors did play an autonomous role, because the Ukrainian and Polish ethnographic maps printed in Galicia did not require state sanction. For confessional status, however, the state, irrespective of the nature of the regime, is the monopoly provider.

Werth's story is about the rigidity of religious categories in Imperial Russia. The idea that an individual could freely determine his confessional affiliation jarred with state principles of categorization, particularly with Orthodoxy. Individuals were ascribed a confessional identity at birth and had few recourses to change it in their adult life. The state accepted conversions *to* Orthodoxy but not *from* it. Some new denominations were recognized, insofar as they did not affect Orthodox communities, as with the Baptists or splinter Lutheran groups in the Baltic region. Communities whose leaders claimed to have been forcibly incorporated into the Orthodox confession were not given the legal means to exit.

A case in point was the Uniate Church, a Roman Catholic–oriented church of Orthodox rite, which was dismantled in 1839 in provinces now belonging to Western Ukraine and Western Belarus. The 1905 Manifesto promised "freedom of conscience" to the citizens of the empire, but as Werth makes clear, government officials interpreted it to mean a return to the confession of one's "ancestors." The category "Catholic" thus became permissible as the confessional status of those able to demonstrate Uniate ancestry, even if the implementation of this ruling proved terribly chaotic. The definition of "ancestors," however, was restricted to those kin who an individual "could have encountered while he was still alive," his parents or grandparents. Christian Tatars who claimed that their ancestors had been forcibly converted under Ivan the Terrible were not allowed to become Muslims. Ultimately, freedom of conscience was not interpreted to mean individual self-determination. The state continued to assert for itself the right to rigidly regulate transfers across confessional categories.

In the Soviet period, the state replaced religion with nationality as the cultural identity inscribed in personal identification documents (internal passports). Intriguingly, how the Soviet state approached the categorization of cultural identity in passports was in near perfect continuity with Imperial Russian practices. After a brief period in which individuals were allowed to freely select their nationality, when passports began to be issued in the early 1930s, the state ruled that heretofore nationality (ethnic affiliation) was a matter of lineage. A child's nationality was that of his parents. At the height of the terror, in the late 1930s, the secret police even issued a directive aimed at revealing the "true" nationality of suspected individuals. A Müller whose grandparents were German could not claim to be Russian. Nationality was thus equated with historical authenticity. An individual could not escape his or her past.[32]

Similarly, the reforms that were instituted in 1905 assumed that a "true" confessional identity could be revealed by examining documents of the (recent) past, rather than asserted as a matter of individual conviction. In both cases, state officials operated within a paradigm that greatly restricted the recognition of identity change. In the Imperial case, the reforms amounted to a rectification of, as Werth puts it, "the *inaccurate ascription* of certain subjects to Orthodoxy." In the Soviet case, the passport made assimilation into another nationality legally impossible. Though acculturation to another identity was important, principally linguistic shift to Russian, individuals could not change their legal identity.[33] Categories are often taken for granted in scholarship. Werth's chapter compels us to reflect on the politics, and philosophical assumptions, that lie beneath the nomenclature of categories in official modes of categorization, as well as the critical importance that these state-regulated identities can have in the life chances of individuals.

In chapter 7, Oxana Shevel raises similar questions in investigating the construction of the category of "refugee" in post-Soviet Russia and Ukraine. In the 1990s, millions of former Soviet citizens from the Caucasus and Central Asia migrated to Russia and Ukraine, driven by economic dislocation, a perception that ethnicity was impeding their career prospects, and violence. A significant proportion of these migrants were of the dominant nationality of their country of destination, because 60 percent of migrants to Russia were ethnic Russians, and 43 percent of migrants to Ukraine were ethnic Ukrainians. Shevel is struck by how differently these migrants were treated by their host country. Migrants to Russia were provided with state assistance, whereas those to Ukraine were not. Why? The answer cannot be reduced to economic factors, which on the whole were similar in these two post-Soviet states, even if the situation was relatively worse in Ukraine. Shevel argues that the differential outcomes were conditioned by distinct nation-building policies.

A nation-building project aims at defining the members of the nation, clarifying who forms the "us" in a community. In Russia, a consensus quickly emerged that the "us" consisted of former Soviet citizens, mostly Russian speaking, and mostly, but far from exclusively, ethnic Russians. As a result, the overwhelming majority of those receiving refugee status were former Soviet citizens. Ukraine, conversely, has vocal movements emphasizing the ethnic nature of the "us": Ukraine as the historic homeland of the ethnic Ukrainians. In domestic politics, however, this vision is countered by a neocommunist orientation toward the "unity" of the Russian, Ukrainian, and Belarusian peoples, a stance that calls into question the legitimacy of an independent Ukrainian state. In the 1990s, the collision of these two visions produced a legislative stalemate. Former Soviet citizens, including ethnic Ukrainians, were deprived of refugee status.

As we saw above, discussing Hrycak's chapter, the stalemate between the nationalist and antinationalist camps gave an opening to the educational bureaucracy to autonomously implement the nation-building policy of the nationalist camp, according to which the language of instruction is determined by descent rather than freedom of choice. In matters of migration, however, the bureaucracy played no such role. As a middle ground between the two polar views—Ukraine as the state of ethnic Ukrainians; Ukraine as a territory of a larger whole—the nation was defined territorially: Ukraine as the state of all those born on its soil and of their descendants. The citizenship law therefore privileged applicants whose family history hailed from the territories of Ukraine, broadly construed. But this policy did not translate into immediate assistance to those territorial Ukrainians "returning home." Contrary to Russia, there was no priority within the executive branch to provide aid to these newcomers. What this meant in practice is that while Russian and Russian-speaking migrants in Russia were quickly recognized as "refugees" and aided accordingly, the official refugees in Ukraine were mostly international migrants, primarily from Afghanistan. The construction of the "refugee" category was directly linked to the status of the nation-building project: consensual in Russia, and undecided in Ukraine.

The legislative stalemate, as variously narrated in Hrycak's and Shevel's chapters, thus produced strikingly different outcomes: ethnically based in the first case, territorially based in the second. What accounts for the difference? The two chapters, read together, have the virtue of formulating the question while coming short of an explanation. Two hypotheses are worth exploring. The first has to do with elite skills. In Hrycak's story, nation builders are able to formulate their own language policy in education as a result of their sustained ability to monopolize positions in the educational branch. Could it be that the cultural intelligentsia have no such comparative advantage when it comes to the implementation of migration policy? Or is the difference in outcome to be explained with access to resources? The Ukrainization of the educational sector, though no doubt hampered by insufficient resources (as constantly bewailed in the Ukrainian-language press), still operates within a large-scale budget. A redefinition of the category of refugees, to encompass "former residents of Ukraine" rather than "international" migrants, would have brought the number of eligible refugees from the low thousands to the hundreds of thousands. Nation builders, even if they had captured the migration agencies (which they may have), were unable to lobby for that kind of massive injection of funds. The legislative stalemate translated into a stalemate in resources.

The upside, argues Shevel, is that the nation-building stalemate in Ukraine produced a more liberal refugee regime favoring international migrants. For all intents and purposes, international migrants were barred from acquiring refugee status in Russia, while they accounted for most recognized refugees in Ukraine. The argument is interesting, but it rests on a slender statistical base, because the absolute number of recognized international refugees was very small in both cases—a few hundred.

More compelling is Shevel's analysis of how initially clueless the United Nations refugee agency (the Office of the UN High Commissioner for Refugees, or UNHCR) was in attempting to provide assistance. The UNHCR operated with a rigidly defined category of "refugee," which disqualified migrants eligible for citizenship. In the post-Soviet context, this meant that most of the migrants to Russia and Ukraine failed to qualify, even though the factors impelling their migration were identical to those of international migrants around the world, that is, economic and/or ethnic turmoil. The UNHCR assumed that a category such as "refugee" could be defined outside a domestic political context. What Shevel demonstrates is that one cannot understand refugee politics in Russia and Ukraine without examining how the very category "refugee" was a domestic construction.

Changing Attributes

Attributes are the cultural markers that serve as the building material of categories. A category of "Ukrainian" that includes "language" as one of its components presupposes that individuals identifying as Ukrainian have the Ukrainian language in their repertoire. A category is not sustainable politically without a base in measurable attributes. If no one spoke Ukrainian in Ukraine, a Ukrainian identity based on language would fail to garner support. Yet attributes do not have a linear relationship to categories. Categories are combinations of attributes that can change over time and across cases. For instance, scholars argue that religion (the Catholic/Uniate divide) was the critical attribute distinguishing Ukrainians from Poles in interwar Galicia.[34] With the ethnic cleansing of Poles and the postwar settling of Russians, language replaced religion as the core attribute of the category "Ukrainian" in Galicia. Once the number of Catholics slipped below a critical mass, it ceased to act as a category-defining attribute.

The last three chapters in this volume explore the causes and implications of a change in attributes. In chapter 8, Catherine Wanner sets her gaze on the religious revival taking place in Ukraine. The number of religious communities in this former Soviet republic grew almost fivefold in the 1990s, from 4,500 to nearly 20,000, according to a 2001 report that she cites. Parallel to this tremendous growth has been a proliferation of churches. Most Ukrainian citizens are of Orthodox heritage, but four churches are battling for their loyalty: the Orthodox Church–Moscow Patriarchate, the only one with official recognition in the Soviet era; the Orthodox Church–Kyiv Patriarchate, a creation of the 1990s; the Ukrainian Autocephalous Church, with strong roots in the diaspora; and the Greek Catholic (Uniate) Church, which despite its affiliation with Rome has been historically allowed to keep Orthodox rites, and therefore can be said to belong to the larger Orthodox family.

Wanner links the rise in religious practice to a change in political and economic regime. Politically, the postcommunist state ceased to have a hostile policy toward the church, creating an opportunity for individuals to embrace religion without fear for their career prospects. Economically, the rise of a volatile market, on the ashes of the planned economy, created enormous and highly visible economic disparities. Religion provides a moral compass for the losers during economic transformation. The winners are perceived as immoral, preying on a rapacious market impervious to social costs. Religion also offers a thick social network of community support.

The fastest growing churches, however, are the non-Orthodox ones, namely the evangelical churches, which now constitute approximately one-quarter of all registered churches in Ukraine. Wanner examines how this remarkable rise occurs at the microlevel, what makes individuals convert to these nontraditional (to the area) faiths, and the larger implications this holds for society. Conversion is a change in attributes—in this case, a change toward the beliefs and practices associated with a given faith. The change is not necessarily from one set of religious beliefs and practices to another but, more often than not, from a passive sense or religious heritage, or overt agnosticism if not atheism, to an active embrace of a religious experience. As one of Wanner's recent converts points out: "They were real believers and we were just Christians."

The rise of evangelical churches is a global phenomenon, not peculiar to Orthodox areas, and what generally prompts individuals to convert to nonestablished churches is a question that goes beyond the scope of Wanner's chapter. Yet Ukraine is the country in the post-Soviet region where the evangelical movement has encountered the most success, by far. For instance, Ukraine has more than twice as many evangelical missionaries as Russia, with three times less population.[35] Wanner argues that the fragmentation among Orthodox churches opens up a space for upstart churches: "When a single church cannot dominate and influence political policy, de facto there are greater freedoms for other faiths to exist and for individuals to worship as they choose." The extent to which churches compete within the dominant faith in Ukraine is unique to the region.

Wanner is theoretically most engaging when she reflects on the impact of mass conversion on national identity. In her view, the rise of evangelicalism in Ukraine is significant because it offers an alternative identity to the one promoted by the state and the dominant churches. "The Orthodox Church," she writes, including the Uniate "cousins" within its midst, "considers Orthodoxy an attribute of Ukrainian nationality, that is to say, a Ukrainian is by definition Orthodox." Evangelicals, conversely, are less inclined to think in ethnonational terms. In interviews she conducted in Ukraine in 2000–2002, she notes that, faced with open-ended questions, most evangelicals chose the categories of "Christian" or "believers" over that of nationality (or other competing categories). The fact that the rise of evangelical churches in particularly significant in areas, such as Southern Ukraine, where parties symbolized by the "national idea" are repeatedly striking out in electoral contests, invites us to think seriously about the long-term political consequences of the heretofore unheralded phenomenon of mass conversions in Ukraine.

Chapters 9 and 10, respectively by Dmitry Gorenburg and Helen Faller, for their part, focus on language attributes. Gorenburg revisits the literature on assimilation in the Soviet Union. As was stated at the outset, Western scholars who studied the nationality question during the Soviet period were at the fringes of their profession, but among them the dominant narrative was one of state-sponsored assimilation. The Soviet strategy, which was implemented in 1938 and went into overdrive after 1959, was to linguistically Russify its non-Russian nationalities.[36] After the Soviet collapse, however, the narrative changed. Scholars, now very much in the mainstream of their profession, argued that the Soviet Union created institutions that in fact *impeded* assimilation. The "breaker" of nations became the "builder" of nations.[37] Gorenburg believes that the new narrative has gone too far in downplaying assimilation. At the core of his analysis is the attribute of language. As was discussed above, the Soviet category of nationality incorporated the attribute of language as "native language," which came to be interpreted as the language of one's group. This seriously underestimated the proportion of non-Russians who preferred to use Russian privately.[38] Gorenburg cites evidence to that effect from the 1994 Russian "microcensus," which asked respondents about their native language *and* home language, something Soviet censuses never did. One-third of those non-Russians who claimed the language of their nationality as their native language spoke Russian at home.

For Gorenburg, the home language, or what this author calls the language of preference, was the most far-reaching attribute of the category of nationality in the Soviet period. The 1959 Education Law virtually eliminated titular schools in urban areas of republics (except in the Baltics, Armenia, and Georgia) and autonomous republics. The effects on the language spoken at home were huge. Had the Soviet Union continued for another generation, reckons Gorenburg, it is possible that certain nationalities would have become entirely Russophone, in terms of the language that they actually prefer to speak. To be sure, Soviet passports prevented them from changing their nationality, and most non-Russians continued to claim in large numbers the language of their nationality as their "native" language.

Yet the de facto adoption of Russian had one major effect on ethnic assimilation: Non-Russians acculturated to Russian were far more likely to marry outside their group, and their children were more likely to adopt

Russian nationality. Assimilation to Russian nationality was thus indirect but no less real. The more people spoke Russian at home, the more they married outside the group, and the more their children "became" Russian. The one major exception to that rule was in Central Asia, where marriage across the religious line (Muslim/Orthodox) was rare.[39] Gorenburg argues that it is precisely the changes in the attributes of language (the language that people prefer to speak), and not in the category of nationality (which remained fixed with native language) that were pregnant with long-term consequences. The stunning national mobilization that unfolded under Gorbachev cannot be reduced to a failure in the Soviet project of assimilation.

In chapter 10, Faller likewise concentrates on the attribute of language of preference, but from the ground up, so to speak. She observed the evolving use of the Tatar language in the public domains of Kazan, the capital of Tatarstan. During the period of high assimilation described by Gorenburg, titular republics were often unilingually Russian, with tiny islands of titular speech: the market, the writers' union, some programs on radio and television, and occasional state ceremonies. Low-status languages, as most titular languages were outside the Baltic republics, Armenia, and Georgia, were associated with the low-status peasantry. Moreover, the state discouraged any initiative to speak the titular language in formal settings. Speaking the titular language was politically correct if sanctioned by the state, which occurred less and less under Brezhnev. Unsolicited utterances in the titular language could risk branding the speaker with the infamy of "nationalism."

The situation has become far more fluid since the late 1980s. In Kazan, speaking Tatar in public is no longer politically dangerous, but it can bring discomfort to speakers of Russian, many of whom are ethnic Tatars, whose active knowledge of Tatar is rudimentary. Though social conventions still demand that speakers of Tatars switch to Russian in the presence of Russophones, the practice of code switching—speaking parts of a conversation in a different language—is making inroads in public domains. Faller cleverly demonstrates how the Russian language is associated with authority, whereas Tatars connotes intimacy. The use of Tatar, as a means of communicating at a level not attainable with Russian, can bring benefits to speakers of Tatar. This social incentive to use the titular language, writes Faller, "[has] created a great deal of uncertainty in Kazanians' everyday interactions." To the keen eye of an ethnographer, the attribute of language in contemporary Kazan is very much in flux.

The language that people actually prefer to speak, argues Faller, is consequential because it brings out competing world views, a perspective also known as "cognitive" in the literature.[40] She conducted an experiment by showing Western newspaper articles detailing atrocities committed by Russian soldiers in Chechnya to students from Russian-language and Tatar-language classes. The Russian class reacted with outrage at the criticism of Russian soldiers. The Tatar class was not surprised at the exactions perpetrated against Muslims. Interestingly, the main cleavage between the classes was not religious, because several Russian speakers were ethnic Tatars. Faller ascribed the difference to the different language worlds inhabited by the students. Russian speakers have access only to the Russian media, which is generally sympathetic to the soldiers' plight. Tatar speakers are bilingual and have access to a Tatar media whose perspective on the Chechnya war is radically different. The identity boundary between the groups, however, is not rigid. The Tatar language project is not to make Tatar speakers unilingually Tatar but to make Russian speakers bilingual. The acquisition of Tatar as a second language, at a level sufficient to follow broadcast in Tatar, could have the effect of bridging together the two competing world-views. We owe it to observers like Faller to reveal far-reaching trends that are easily buried by the hurly-burly of daily politics.

Conclusion

The end of the Cold War has brought the study of identities to the center stage of social science analysis. Western scholars approach identities with the paradigm of social construction but tend to conflate the various political aspects of this construction. Chandra and Laitin offer a compelling framework that delineates three levels on which identity politics operates: the politics that makes a cultural cleavage salient (dimension); the politics over the labeling and recognition of identities (categories); and the politics inherent in the development of cultural markers (attributes).[41] The framework has the virtue of bringing the best research on identity politics into a theoretically coherent whole.

This volume presents contributions from a new cohort of scholars studying the politics of culture in the territories of Russia and Ukraine. These scholars, from the disciplines of political science, anthropology, history, and sociology, collectively cover the entire conceptual field elaborated by Chandra and Laitin, not only in terms of the levels of analysis but also of the main variables at work for each level in the specific context of Russia and Ukraine. In that regard, the present volume offers a comprehensive treatment, akin to a "state of the field" for the up-and-coming generation of scholars, of the theoretically stimulating research taking place on the two largest states of Eastern Europe.

The chapters in this volume share several common analytical threads. One is the relationship between structural conditions and the saliency of cultural cleavages. Giuliano links nationalist mobilization in Russia to blocked mobility induced by economic decline, and the waning of mobilization to economic changes opening up new avenues of mobility. Alexseev explains the lack of xenophobic mobilization in Far Eastern Russia to political order: Notwithstanding economic hardship, the center holds the periphery in check and external migration (from China) has not passed the critical mass.

A second common thread among the chapters is the unintended consequences of a polarizing nation-building project. Hrycak shows how a legislative stalemate allows the education bureaucracy to nationalize the school in an extralegal fashion. Shevel points out how the same stalemate produces a refugee policy far more liberal than in Russia, but at the cost of leaving ethnic Ukrainian migrants to their own devices.

A third thread is the critical, but not hegemonic, role of the state in constructing identity categories. The contrast drawn by Seegel on the impact of Austrian and Imperial Russian policies on the mapmaking of Ukraine is striking. The rigidity of the Imperial system of categorizing confessional identities, painstakingly probed by Werth, and its strong, if unconscious, legacy for the Soviet categorization of nationalities, bears reflection. The attempts by Tatar and Russian state elites to construct Islam as a Russia-integrating, and Western-friendly, category, as adumbrated by Graney, merits close attention.

A fourth thread are the undercurrents that may prove more decisive than the trends that have greater visibility. Kazan may appear as a solidly Russian-speaking city to the casual visitor, but the gradual, if subtle, penetration of Tatar, as chronicled by Faller, could have far-reaching consequences within a generation or two. Despite the tension among the four churches of Orthodox rites, the nation-building project may appear to rest on a common Orthodox tradition, but the challenge of evangelical movements, not only to the churches but also to conceptions of national identity, could manifest itself in unforeseen ways. The stunning nationalist mobilization that swept through the non-Russian republics in the Gorbachev and early Yeltsin eras could be seen as a spectacular failure of "fusing" nationalities into a Soviet identity. Yet they mask, for Gorenburg, the advanced stage of a linguistic assimilation, and indirectly an ethnic assimilation, that had been taking hold for nearly two generations—an assimilation whose legacy, in post-Soviet states and republics, remains underestimated.

This volume started out as an investigation of multicultural "legacies" in Russia and Ukraine. It evolved into a critical examination of how the identities bequeathed by history are being transformed, or "rebounding," at the levels of attributes (the markers), categories (the labels), and dimensions (the cleavages). The contributors to the volume raise a rich array of questions that enhances our understanding of how identity politics operates across the spectrum. This, one hopes, will be the modest legacy left by the authors.

Notes

1. Rogers Brubaker and David D. Laitin, "Ethnic and Nationalist Violence," *Annual Review of Sociology* 24 (1998): 423–52. Reprinted in Rogers Brubaker, *Ethnicity without Groups* (Cambridge, Mass.: Harvard University Press, 2004), 88–115.

2. Edward Allworth, ed., *Soviet Nationality Problems* (New York: Columbia University Press, 1971); Brian D. Silver, "Social Mobilization and the Russification of Soviet Nationalities," *American Political Science Review* 68, no. 1 (March 1974): 45–66; Ralph S. Clem, "The Ethnic Dimension of the Soviet Union, parts I and II," in *Contemporary Soviet Society: Sociological Perspectives,* ed. Jerry G. Pankhurst and Michael P. Sacks (New York: Praeger, 1980), 11–62; Victor Zaslavsky, *The Neo-Stalinist State: Class, Ethnicity, and Consensus in Soviet Society* (Armonk, N.Y.: M. E. Sharpe, 1982); Barbara A. Anderson and Brian D. Silver, "Estimating Russification of Ethnic Identity Among Non-Russians in the USSR," *Demography* 20, no. 4 (November 1983): 461–89; Walker Connor, *The National Question in Marxist-Leninist Theory and Strategy* (Princeton, N.J.: Princeton University Press, 1984); and Rasma Karklins, *Ethnic Relations in the USSR: The Perspective from Below* (Boston: Allen & Unwin, 1986).

3. Walker Connor, "Nation-Building or Nation-Destroying?" *World Politics* 24, no. 3 (April 1972): 319–55.

4. Ronald G. Suny, *The Revenge of the Past: Nationalism, Revolution, and the Collapse of the Soviet Union* (Stanford, Calif.: Stanford University Press, 1993); Terry Martin, *The Affirmative Action Empire: Nations and Nationalism in the Soviet Union, 1923–1939* (Ithaca, N.Y.: Cornell University Press, 2001); Sheila Fitzpatrick, *Education and Social Mobility in the Soviet Union, 1921–1934* (Cambridge: Cambridge University Press, 1979); Rogers Brubaker, *Nationalism Reframed: Nationhood and the National Question in the New Europe* (New York and Cambridge: Cambridge University Press, 1996); David D. Laitin, *Identity in Formation: The Russian-Speaking Population in the Near Abroad* (Ithaca, N.Y.: Cornell University Press, 1998).

5. Rogers Brubaker and Frederick Cooper, "Beyond 'Identity,'" *Theory and Society* 29, no. 1 (February 2000): 1–47. Reprinted in Brubaker, *Ethnicity without Groups,* 28–63.

6. Rawi Abdelal, Yoshiko M. Herrera, Alastair Iain Johnston, and Rose McDermott, "Identity as a Variable," *Perspectives on Politics* 4, no. 4 (December 2006).

7. Kanchan Chandra and David Laitin, "A Constructivist Framework for Thinking about Identity Change," paper prepared for the conference "Modeling Constructivist Approaches to Ethnic Identity and Incorporating Them into New Research Agenda," Massachusetts Institute of Technology, Cambridge, Mass., December 2002.

8. Seymour Martin Lipset and Stein Rokkan, "Cleavage Structures, Party Systems, and Voter Alignments: An Introduction," in *Party Systems and Voter Alignments: Cross-National Perspectives,* ed. Lipset and Rokkan (New York: Free Press, 1967), 1–64. Reprinted in *The West European Party System,* ed. Peter Mair (Oxford: Oxford University Press, 1990), 91–138; this is the version cited here.

9. As will be discussed below, the number of identity dimensions, or for that matter, any level of identity politics, should not be thought in restrictive terms, and the contributions in this volume suggest a fifth, and perhaps even a sixth dimension.

10. Lipset and Rokkan, "Cleavage Structures," 100.

11. V. V. Mikhailov, A. A. Novikov, and I. T. Sultanov, "Tatarstan: Referendum—National'noe soglasie," *Konstitutsionnyi vestnik* 14 (1992): 56–63.

12. Donald L. Horowitz, *Ethnic Groups in Conflict* (Berkeley: University of California Press, 1985).

13. Chandra offers an ethnodemographic theory to explain the relative success of ethnic parties in India; Kanchan Chandra, *Why Ethnic Parties Succeed: Patronage and Ethnic Head Counts in India* (Cambridge: Cambridge University Press, 2004). In "patronage democracies," she argues, voters are more interested in having "their own" in power, than in supporting party programs, as they believe that co-ethnics benefit from the implementation of policies. A constant in the ethnic republics of post-Soviet Russia, however, is the electoral capture of state offices by the "titular nationality" (the ethnic group after which the republic is named), irrespective of the official proportion of titulars in the population, a phenomenon that has been traced back to the first election of the late Soviet period; Valery Tishkov, "An Assembly of Nations or an All-Union Parliament?" *Journal of Soviet Nationalities* 1, no. 1 (1990): 101–27. Under conditions where titular (over) representation is a given, the ethnodemographic argument fails to account for the variation in what makes nationality central (salient) across Russian republics, which is Giuliano's point.

14. Horowitz, *Ethnic Groups in Conflict,* 107–29.

15. Dominique Arel and Valeri Khmel'ko, "The Russian Factor and Territorial Polarization in Ukraine," *Harriman Review* 9, nos. 1–2 (Spring 1996): 81–91; Paul Kubicek, "Regional Polarisation in Ukraine: Public Opinion, Voting and Legislative Behaviour," *Europe-Asia Studies* 52, no. 2 (March 2000): 273–94; Lowell W. Barrington, "Examining Rival Theories of Demographic Influences on Political Support: The Power of Regional, Ethnic, and Linguistic Divisions in Ukraine," *European Journal of Political Research* 41, no. 4 (June 2002): 455–91.

16. Jan Germen Janmaat, *Nation-Building in Post-Soviet Ukraine: Educational Policy and the Response of the Russian-Speaking Population* (Utrecht: Netherlands Geographical Studies, 2000).

17. Dominique Arel, "Political Stability in Multinational Democracies: Comparing Language Dynamics in Brussels, Montreal, and Barcelona," in *Multinational Democracies,* ed. Alain-G. Gagnon and James Tully (Cambridge: Cambridge University Press, 2001), 65–89.

18. Arel and Khmel'ko, "Russian Factor."

19. Dominique Arel, "Interpreting 'Nationality' and 'Language' in the 2001 Ukrainian Census," *Post-Soviet Affairs* 18, no. 3 (July–September 2002): 213–49.

20. Charles King, "Moldovan Identity and the Politics of Pan-Romanianism," *Slavic Review* 53, no. 2 (1994): 345–68.

21. Graney's chapter is thus a detailed exploration of the politics surrounding the meaning of the category "Islam" in contemporary Russia. Nonetheless, since the neo-jadidist project of Tatar political entrepreneurs aims at preventing religion from becoming a salient cleavage, we felt that the placement of her chapter in our section on identity dimensions (cleavages) brings more theoretical coherence to the volume.

22. Valery Tishkov, "Yazyk i alfavit kak politika," in *Etnologiia i politika* (Moscow: Nauka, 2001), 215–22; *Gazeta.ru,* "Deputaty zapretili tataram izpol'zovat' latinskii alfavit," November 15, 2003, http://www.gazeta.ru/parliament/news/8044.shtml.

23. Andrei Amalrik, *Will the Soviet Union Survive Until 1984?* (New York: Harper & Row, 1971); Alexander Solzhenitsyn, *Letter to the Soviet Leaders* (New York: Index on Censorship and Harper & Row, 1974).

24. Tat'iana Smol'iakova, "Strana rabochykh i rant'e," *Rossiiskaia gazeta,* October 29, 2003.

25. The Russian language has two terms to distinguish the Russian political community (*rossiiskii*) from the Russian ethnic community (*russkii*). Both terms are translated as "Russian" in English, although "all-Russian" is sometimes used for *rossiiskii.*

26. This builds on Lipset and Rokkan by adding a dimension of citizen/foreign not envisaged in their fourfold repertoire of cleavages. One may ask whether the dimension of language, central to the Hrycak chapter, is also new to their initial repertoire. In our view, however, it is subsumed under Lipset and Rokkan's first dimension involving "a territorially-concentrated population invoking common descent," since language conflict necessarily presupposes a degree of territorial concentration.

27. The security dilemma is a "state of nature" argument, premised on the breakdown of central authorities. Left to their own devices, two groups will be prone to attack each other on the grounds that each cannot ascertain whether the other has aggressive or peaceful intentions. For a classic and nuanced exposition, see Barry R. Posen, "The Security Dilemma and Ethnic Conflict," in *Ethnic Conflict and International Security,* ed. Michael E. Brown (Princeton, N.J.: Princeton University Press, 1993), 103–24. Alexseev argues, here, that a breakdown of communication between Moscow and its outlying regions could make the fear of Chinese aggression central to political perceptions.

28. Benedict Anderson, *Imagined Communities: Reflections on the Origins and Spread of Nationalism,* 2nd ed. (London: Verso, 1991); Brubaker, *Nationalism Reframed.*

29. After 1867, Hungary had full autonomy on domestic politics and, in that respect, acted like a sovereign state.

30. John Paul Himka, "The Construction of Nationality in Galician Rus': Icarian Flights in Almost All Directions," in *Intellectuals and the Articulation of the Nation,* ed. Ronald Grigor Suny and Michael D. Kennedy (Ann Arbor: University of Michigan Press, 1999), 109–64.

31. The first Imperial Russian census, in 1897, did have an entry for "Little Russians." Though the category was not recognized as a nationality, the Little Russians were nonetheless counted separately.

32. Dominique Arel, "Fixing Ethnicity in Identity Documents: The Rise and Fall of

Passport Nationality in Russia," *Canadian Review of Studies in Nationalism* 30, nos. 1–2 (2003): 125–36.

33. The one important difference between the confessional and the nationality systems of ascription pertained to marriage. While individuals could not marry outside of their confession without converting (in cases where conversions were allowed), they could marry outside of their nationality. The children of interethnic marriages had the possibility to choose their nationality. As Dmitry Gorenburg argues, this created an avenue for assimilation.

34. Volodymyr Kubijovyc, *Western Ukraine within Poland 1920–1939 (Ethnic Relationships)* (Chicago: Ukrainian Research and Information Institute, 1963).The Uniate Church adheres to the Pope, while preserving Orthodox rites. The church was banned in 1946 and recognized anew in 1989. Many former Uniates and their children now identify as Orthodox; Omar Uzarashvili, "Plutaiuchy derzhavnu sluzhbu z Bozhoiu," *Demos* (Kyiv), no. 2 (1995). Because language assimilation to Russian is insignificant in Galicia, language has displaced religion as the critical attribute of Ukrainian nationality.

35. Wanner also adduces data on the depth of evangelical sentiment which places Ukraine first among all former Soviet and Central European states.

36. A 1938 Soviet law made the study of Russian as a second language mandatory in all non-Russian schools. A 1959 law based the primary language of instruction on the freedom of choice of parents. See Yaroslav Bilinsky, "The Soviet Education Laws of 1958–9 and Soviet Nationality Policy," *Soviet Studies* 14, no. 2 (June 1962), pp. 78–89. The fast disappearance of non-Russian schools in cities made the exercise of that choice illusory.

37. This is stated in reference to the book *Stalin: Breaker of Nations* by Robert Conquest (New York: Viking Press, 1991).

38. Arel, "Interpreting 'Nationality.' "

39. Brian D. Silver, "Bilingualism and Maintenance of the Mother Tongue in Soviet Central Asia," *Slavic Review* 35, no. 3 (1976): 406–24.

40. Rogers Brubaker, Mara Loveman, and Peter Stamatov, "Ethnicity as Cognition," *Theory and Society* 33, no. 1 (2004): 31–64. Reprinted in Brubaker, *Ethnicity without Groups,* 64–87.

41. Chandra and Laitin, "Constructivist Framework."

Part I

The Saliency of Cultural Cleavages

1

Theorizing Nationalist Separatism in Russia

Elise Giuliano

During the years that spanned the Soviet collapse and the founding of the Russian Federation, ethnic republics inside Russia began to challenge Moscow's authority by demanding political, economic, and cultural autonomy. Ethnic populations, living in territories designated "autonomous" by Soviet leaders decades earlier, joined nationalist movements, took part in street rallies, and voted for nationalist candidates in local parliamentary elections. As mobilization intensified, republican leaders began to defy federal authority by, among other things, asserting control over local natural resources and establishing republican presidencies. Some republican actors sought nothing less than independent statehood, believing in the nationalist principle that the rulers of a political society should belong to the same cultural group as a majority of the ruled.[1] Others simply wanted more control over their republic's political and economic life. These varied aspirations came together in campaigns for sovereignty that threatened to pull apart the Russian Federation along ethnic lines like the Soviet Union before it.

Why did the dimension of ethnicity become politically salient at this time and generate sovereignty campaigns in Russia's republics? This chapter considers several arguments put forward in the post-Soviet politics literature to explain this phenomenon. The arguments can be grouped into four categories; two of which—the "historical-institutional" and "economic-structural"—emphasize the role of elites; and two of which—the "ethnodemographic" and the "cultural"—emphasize the masses.[2] This discussion will show how certain arguments have advanced our understanding both of nationalist mobilization and of center–periphery relations during the late Soviet and early post-Soviet era by highlighting the role played by particular actors or processes, and by identifying mechanisms driving particular outcomes. I will argue, however, that existing approaches make critical assumptions about the relationship between mass and elite within Russia's republics, and that these assumptions tend to overpredict the saliency of ethnicity and thus the likelihood of nationalist separatism.

Nationalist mobilization should be distinguished from other forms of ethnic mobilization that have occurred throughout the former Soviet Union, such as a sudden outbreak of violence between two (or more) ethnic groups. The latter, which Lapidus and Walker label "horizontal" conflict as opposed to "vertical" conflict, often take place over a specific issue, such as ownership rights to certain property or territory. Although it is possible for horizontal conflict to eventually lead to nationalist mobilization against the central state, ethnic groups' goals in horizontal conflicts are generally much more limited. This chapter considers only the phenomenon of vertical, nationalist challenges to the legitimacy of the central state.[3]

The chapter begins with a brief review of events in Russia's republics, followed by discussion of four types of arguments addressing nationalist separatism. The arguments are analyzed in terms of whether they identify elites or masses as instrumental in driving nationalist separatism. The final section of the chapter introduces my own explanation of nationalist separatism, which addresses the relationship between mass and elite by linking structural economic conditions to peoples' perceptions of those conditions. I argue that nationalist elites were able to mobilize ethnic populations in certain of Russia's republics by constructing grievances around the issue of underrepresentation of titular ethnic groups vis-à-vis Russians in local economies. These issues resonated because titular ethnic groups were experiencing limits to their educational and professional mobility due to growing job competition in a contracting economy. In republics where nationalists articulated these issues—such as Tatarstan, Sakha-Yakutia, and Tuva—people supported nationalist programs calling for radical change or even secession from Russia. In republics where nationalists articulated other kinds of issues, such as Mordovia and Mari-El, nationalists attracted very low levels of popular support.[4]

Nationalist Mobilization in Russia's Republics

In the late 1980s, as the "parade of sovereignties" unfolded in the USSR's union republics, national revivals began to develop among ethnic populations in certain of Russia's autonomous republics.[5] After the Russian Soviet Federated Socialist Republic passed a declaration of state sovereignty in June 1990, republics within Russia began to reproduce this dramatic act. During the next twelve months, each of Russia's sixteen autonomous republics passed its own sovereignty declaration,[6] laying claim to natural resources and enterprises located on republican territory, and asserting the precedence of republican over federal law.[7] Later that year, several autonomous republics appealed to Mikhail Gorbachev to raise their administrative status from "autonomous" to "union" so they could share in the increased rights, privileges, and autonomy recently acquired by the union republics. Boris Yeltsin, as the newly elected president of Russia, supported demands made by several assertive republics as part of a plan to undermine the legitimacy of Gorbachev and the Soviet state itself. Yeltsin traveled to the Tatar and Bashkir Autonomous Soviet Socialist Republics in August 1990 and uttered the now infamous exhortation to "take as much sovereignty as you can handle."[8]

For several of Russia's republics, such as Mordovia and Mari-El, the early declarations of republican sovereignty represented the limit of their challenge to Moscow.[9] Other republics, however, took the opportunity presented by the Soviet collapse and establishment of the Russian Federation in 1991 to mount more fundamental challenges to Moscow. Republics such as Tatarstan, Yakutia, and Tuva began to act like independent states, electing presidents, passing language laws, and adopting constitutions.[10] The most rebellious republics challenged central state authority by boycotting or voting against President Yeltsin in the 1993 national referendum.[11]

Later that year, as Yeltsin tried to end Russia's constitutional crisis by dissolving supreme soviets in the regions, republican soviets ignored or condemned his decree. When he pressed his point by shelling the Federal

Duma, most republics agreed to hold new elections, leading to a shift in power from legislature to executive within the republics.[12] However, Yeltsin's victory over the Duma failed to force the most recalcitrant republics into line. Tatarstan and Chechnya boycotted the Yeltsin-sponsored vote on Russia's new constitution in December 1993, while Tuva and Bashkortostan rejected the new Russian Constitution.[13] Overall, the most autonomist, or separatist, republics during the period 1990–94 were Tatarstan, Chechnya, Sakha-Yakutia, Tuva, and Bashkortostan.[14]

Yet by the mid-1990s, secessionism was fading in even the most assertive republics as popular support for nationalism within the republics dwindled and incumbent leaders figured out how to co-opt the nationalist movements. Because the sovereignty campaigns took place in a period of massive state weakness, once Yeltsin managed to centralize power in 1994 and 1995, the entire institutional environment in Russia shifted, making it more difficult for republics to challenge the center. However, Tatarstan, Bashkortostan, and Sakha-Yakutia benefited enormously from their aggressive campaigns by signing bilateral treaties with Moscow that granted them increased political and economic autonomy. Bilateral treaties with other republics (and oblasts) followed, because Yeltsin found them to be a useful means of ensuring Russia's federal integrity.[15]

Historical-Institutional Arguments

A series of early, important analyses of nationalist mobilization in the Soviet republics can be labeled historical-institutionalist arguments. This work, by Ronald Suny, Philip Roeder, and Rogers Brubaker, demonstrates how the Soviet Union's nationality policies and federal structure created ethnic republican elites and furnished them with institutional resources, territories, and identities that they would later use to forge autonomy campaigns during glasnost.[16] Roeder used the term "ethnofederalism" to describe the Soviet policies and institutions developed with regard to ethnic minorities. Roeder, Suny, and Brubaker analyze how Soviet ethnofederalism influenced ethnic politics in the union republics, but their arguments are equally relevant to politics in the autonomous republics of Russia. These studies have informed almost all subsequent work on ethnic and republican politics in the Soviet Union and Russia, and have stimulated theorizing in ways that go beyond the authors' original insights.[17] Though there are differences among the authors—Roeder shows how economic and political changes at the Soviet center inspired republican leaders and counter-elites to mobilize their populations, Brubaker focuses on ethnicity and territory, and Suny discusses each of these as well as the content of nationalist programs—the discussion here emphasizes the commonalities in their arguments, rather than differences.

According to these scholars, a key aspect of Soviet ethnofederalism that would eventually create the conditions for nationalist mobilization in the union republics was Lenin's decision to endow minority populations with territorial rather than cultural autonomy. The privileging of territory over culture granted certain populations nominal "homelands" in the form of republics or autonomous regions, and it provided them with rights within those homelands. The ethnic territories at the top of the Soviet Union's administrative hierarchy—the union republics—were given extensive administrative, cultural, and political rights, including the right to secede (at least on paper), as well as the right to establish republican ("national") communist parties, writers' and composers' unions, academies of science, and other formal institutions. The second highest group of ethnic territories—autonomous republics—did not receive as many rights and resources as union republics, but they were relatively privileged compared with Russia's nonethnic oblasts and krais. Finally, autonomous oblasts (regions) and autonomous okrugs (areas), administratively situated below the autonomous republics, were also supplied with special rights and privileges, albeit highly circumscribed ones.[18]

Other key aspects of Soviet nationalities policy that served to nurture and institutionalize ethnicity at individual and group levels within the republic included the policies of *korenizatsiia* (indigenization) and the system of internal passports. *Korenizatsiia* policies granted preferences to titular nationalities within their own republics in higher education, enterprise management, job training, the Communist Party, and government administration. These privileges were designed to advance the position of titular populations vis-à-vis other nationalities, including Russians, and sometimes produced discrimination against nontitular nationalities, depending on the context and the historical period.[19] In addition, the Soviet regime established institutions for educated titulars, including ethnic research institutes, writers' and artists' unions, and publishing houses, as well as an enormous bureaucracy.

By the late Soviet era, titulars in many republics had made significant gains in education and professional achievement. They served in varied capacities from the Communist Party, universities, trade unions, the Council of Ministers, writers' unions, local government administration, security organs, and the Academy of Sciences. Titular peasants became "proletarianized," moving into newly industrialized Soviet cities.[20] State-defined incentives and quotas succeeded in moving titulars from farm to factory, from primary school to university, and into the highest reaches of management and government administration. Thus, *korenizatsiia* created an educated middle class and a local political leadership out of the titular population, and it simultaneously neutralized their separatist aspirations by assimilating them to a Russified, Soviet social order.[21]

With the introduction of the internal passport system, citizens had to record their nationality as one of the officially recognized nationalities of the Soviet state. Generally, citizens inherited a nationality from their parents; it was completely unrelated to place of birth or place of residence. Only children of "mixed" parentage could choose their nationality at the age of sixteen years. Nationality became an official marker of identity as individuals had to report their nationality in all official encounters with the state, including, for example, entrance into higher education, obtaining employment or a promotion, and admission to the Communist Party.

The system of ethnoterritorial federalism and internal passports functioned moderately well during the Soviet era in terms of administrative control and stability. Though several instances of interethnic conflict occurred as well as the occasional appeal for change from the national regions,[22] for the most part Soviet central rule constrained the possibilities and limits of public expression of nationalist sentiment. And though nationalist intellectuals emerged in the 1960s as part of the dissident and human rights movement in republics such as Ukraine, Georgia, and Armenia, expressions of unofficial nationalism were generally muted or suppressed, inspiring Soviet leaders to doggedly maintain that "the national question has been solved once and for all."

However, the appearance of nationalist movements in the union republics at the end of the 1980s gave the lie to these claims.[23] Ethnofederalist policies of indigenization and passport identity within the context of industrializing, pseudostate republican territories ended up providing, according to Ronald Suny, "a social and cultural base" for republican counterelites to establish broad-based nationalist movements. In Suny's words: "A state that had set out to overcome nationalism . . . had in fact created a set of institutions and initiated processes that fostered the development of conscious, secular, politically mobilizable nationalities."[24]

Significant differences existed among union republics in the degree to which they mobilized along nationalist lines. Moldova, Georgia, Armenia, the Baltics, and Ukraine backed nationalist programs and made stronger demands on Moscow than the republics of Central Asia. Roeder offers an institutionalist explanation for this variation by identifying how the consequences of Soviet central policy affected the Soviet Union's most advantaged titular ethnic groups. Titulars in Georgia, Armenia, and the Baltics, he argues, were so successful at building an indigenous cadre and intelligentsia inside their republics that Moscow redirected resources away from them and toward the underdeveloped Central Asian republics. Then, when the Soviet economy contracted at the end of the 1980s, titular elites in the advanced republics found their own social mobility and opportunities frustrated, inspiring them to seek national autonomy from Moscow.[25]

Historical-institutional explanations offer a rich and provocative analysis of the effects of central state policy on elites and institutions in the republics. They carefully show how Soviet policies created ethnic elites and endowed them with resources and territories. However, these accounts are relatively quiet on the question of why ethnic populations followed elites. Were the existence of ethnic identity and a growing sense of group consciousness among titular populations sufficient to motivate people to support nationalist leaders, asking them to assume the enormous individual risks that nationalist mobilization entailed in the late Soviet era? By focusing on elites, most historical-institutional explanations leave an open space for further analysis of nationalism at the mass level, and in particular, the relationship between nationalist elites and ethnic populations.

Another, more recent institutionalist argument by Dmitry Gorenburg examining nationalism in Russia's republics does not assume that ethnic masses automatically follow nationalist elites. Gorenburg demonstrates that variation in popular nationalist support among republics is correlated with "the density and number of ethnic institutions in each region."[26] The extent to which ethnic institutions such as native language education, academic institutes studying local culture, cultural institutions, and ethnic preferences in government employment had penetrated a republic determines the degree to which nationalist movements could successfully mobilize the masses. The existence of these institutions strengthened ethnic identities and established dense social networks among titulars in high-mobilization republics such as Tatarstan and Bashkortostan, thereby facilitating mass mobilization. In republics where institutional penetration did not reach as far (e.g., Chuvashia and Khakassia), popular support for nationalism was correspondingly lower.

With the exception of Gorenburg's, most historical-institutional arguments explain the outcome of successful nationalist separatism that transformed the union republics into independent states. By focusing on how institutions motivated the behavior of ethnic elites, they assume that ethnic masses automatically heeded elite appeals. Thus, though institutionalist explanations go a long way toward explaining elite behavior in separatist republics, we are still in need of an explanation for why similar institutions failed to produce nationalist separatism in other republics, such as those in Central Asia. Historical-institutionalist explanations shed little light on why, in places where nationalist elites appealed to the masses, titular ethnic groups failed to mobilize.

Economic-Structural Arguments

Another important and influential approach to understanding ethnonationalist mobilization in Russia's republics focuses on economic and other structural conditions in the republics. The most straightforward of the economic hypotheses maintains that high levels of separatist activity among certain of Russia's republics during the early 1990s can be attributed to the fact that they possessed greater economic wealth than other republics. Kathryn Stoner-Weiss, for example, writes that political intransigence and tax revolts in the republics of Tatarstan, Bashkortostan, and Sakha "were part of a broader strategy to widen the economic control rights of these wealthy republics over the proceeds from the extraction and sale of oil, gas and diamonds located on their territories."[27] Similarly, James Hughes notes that "the single most important common factor among the four most 'secessionist' . . . republics (Chechnya, Tatarstan, Bashkortostan, and Sakha) is that they all have significant economic resource endowments."[28]

Other comparative macroeconomic analyses also consider how various forms of economic development engender republican separatism. Three studies by Kisangani Emizet and Vicki Hesli, Daniel Treisman, and Henry Hale systematically compare republics, categorizing them into groups based on their degree of separatist behavior toward Moscow. The authors then statistically test several hypotheses to observe which factors correlate with high degrees of separatism.[29] All report a similar finding that a high level of republican economic development is correlated with greater republican separatism, although each measures economic development in a different way.

Emizet and Hesli, who looked only at the union republics, consider a republic to be socioeconomically developed if it had a low family size, a large urban population, many women workers, a high rate of consumer goods production, and a high growth rate in its food industry as of 1991. For Treisman, who examined all of Russia's autonomous regions, economically advanced republics were those with wealth and resources, as indicated by high levels of industrial output and export, high levels of raw materials production, and large populations. Hale, who examined both union republics and Russia's autonomous republics, also found that relatively wealthy republics—as indicated by retail commodity turnover per capita—were most likely to engage in nationalist activity.

The authors account for their findings using slightly different explanations. Emizet and Hesli as well as Hale maintain that Moscow's status as a rapidly transforming, potentially hostile center inspired economically advanced republics to seek secession to protect the privileges already attained in the late Soviet era. In other words, leaders in relatively rich republics had more to lose than leaders in poor republics if new elites hostile to regional autonomy were to win power in Moscow and recentralize the state. Poor regions, according to this logic, chose to remain part of the union or the Russian Federation because they depended on it for the "goods of modernity."[30]

Treisman argues that the economically advanced republics were more separatist than others because their leaders understood that wealth, a large population, and bountiful resources increased their economic potential as an independent state and therefore strengthened their bargaining position in negotiations with the center.[31] Conversely, republics with weaker economies barely pressed Moscow for autonomy because leaders there weighed the cost of seceding against the benefit of continuing to receive subsidies and transfers from the center.[32]

Economic-structural explanations build on a general logic developed by theorists examining national separatism in other parts of the world, such as Gellner, Gourevitch, Hechter, Horowitz, and Nairn.[33] This logic, greatly simplified, is that economic conditions produced by modernization and industrialization (i.e., economic development) influence people to support nationalist secession when they expect to personally profit from it. Economic-structuralist explanations of Emizet and Hesli, Treisman, and Hale have usefully shown how the wealth and social development of the population might influence elite strategies. Yet they have less to say about where and how the masses fit into republican separatism. These accounts assume that republican leaders acted autonomously within their republics, crafting policies toward the center.[34] Though we observe that some republican leaders strategically took advantage of mobilization to strengthen their negotiating position with the center, there is no direct evidence that republican populations reflexively followed the commands of local leaders.

Characterizing ethnic populations as passive tools of politicians overestimates the power of ethnicity as a basis for political behavior. It assumes that ethnic populations are naturally or automatically nationalist, or will become nationalist once they are told to do so by politicians. This view suggests that republican leaders act strategically while ethnic populations act out of a sincere commitment to ethnonationalism. Such a distinction between crafty leaders and credulous masses rings false and is also empirically inaccurate insofar as local populations and nationalist movements did not allow republican leaders to direct their political behavior. This view of Russia's ethnic populations essentializes them as dependent, and it echoes the totalitarian school's view of an inert, hegemonized Soviet citizenry. Thus, while economic-structural hypotheses clearly delineate economic and structural influences on elite strategies, they make the invalid assumption that the ethnic masses are either perpetually nationalist or easily become so at the command of nationalist leaders.

A more accurate explanation for nationalist separatism in Russia, I argue, must consider the contest for political control among subrepublican actors that resulted from the Soviet state's collapse and Moscow's weakness during the first few years of Russian statehood.[35] The contest for local power took place among former communist leaders and emergent ethnonationalist opposition movements in several of Russia's most secessionist republics. Republican nomenklatura leaders, concerned above all with maintaining power, suddenly found themselves detached from the protection of central Communist Party authorities and answerable to emerging local constituencies. These constituencies—in particular, opposition nationalist movements—began to mobilize popular support behind a program of increased rights for titular nationalities and greater republican sovereignty.

In republics such as Tatarstan and Yakutia where nationalists were gaining popular support, the very visible fact of growing crowds at rallies and the rising status of opposition political figures in both local parliaments and on the street represented a clear threat to incumbents. In these places, Communist leaders were pressured into addressing nationalist programs and forced into petitioning Moscow for greater autonomy. In other republics, such as Chechnya and Tuva, nationalists replaced key Communist leaders and pressed nationalist claims on Moscow directly. In yet other re-publics, weak nationalist movements with little popular support meant that Communist leaders could ignore their appeals with impunity. Thus, analyt-ical attention should be directed toward the variable of popular support for nationalist movements because it can explain variations in republican secessionism. The republics in which opposition nationalist movements mobilized ethnic populations to vote and participate in street rallies were the ones making the strongest autonomy demands on Moscow. Conversely, republics with weak nationalist movements did not mount a serious chal-lenge to central state authority. The next section considers two approaches that address the role of mass populations in republican separatism.

Demographic Arguments

Another kind of explanation that takes a structural approach to explaining nationalist separatism emphasizes the demographic composition of the pop-ulation living in a substate region. This explanation, which I call the "eth-nic demography hypothesis," maintains that separatism is more likely if an ethnic group forms a majority of the region's total population and less likely if an ethnic group is a minority. Donald Horowitz makes this claim (among many others) in his seminal work *Ethnic Groups in Conflict,* writing, "The strength of a secessionist movement and the heterogeneity of its region are inversely related."[36]

The fact that large numbers of ethnic Russians live alongside titular eth-nic groups in most of Russia's republics is frequently invoked as an expla-nation for why the republics did not secede and why ethnonationalism was weaker there than in the union republics. Lapidus and Walker, for example, write that sizable Russian populations in the republics "make Russia less vulnerable to fragmentation along ethnic lines than the former USSR, Yugo-slavia, and Czechoslovakia."[37] As of 1991, they report, Russians formed an absolute majority in nine republics and a plurality in another three. Hughes notes that titulars constitute a simple plurality in only three of Russia's re-publics (Tatarstan, 48 percent; Kalmykia, 45 percent; Kabardino-Balkaria, Kabardins, 48 percent and Balkars, 9 percent), and an absolute majority in only four (Tuva, 64 percent; North Ossetia, 53 percent; Chechnya, 58 per-cent; and Chuvashia, 68 percent). He concludes that the "spatial dispersion of Russians in strength throughout the bulk of the territory of the federa-tion" impedes separatism.[38]

These analysts do not necessarily believe that demography alone accounts for why nationalist separatism occurred or failed to occur, but they
see relative ethnic percentages as an important background condition, or as
one of several critical factors. This argument seems so commonsensical
that analysts often provide no explanation as to why demography should
matter to nationalist separatism. Yet the empirical evidence in support of
the demographic hypothesis is weak.[39]

Although none of Russia's republics seceded (with the possible exception of Chechnya), they displayed varying levels of nationalist separatism,
allowing us to observe whether the relative size of ethnic groups is correlated with separatist behavior. For some of the most nationalist and separatist republics, the ethnodemographic hypothesis is supported: Chechnya
and Tuva contained titular majorities (58 and 64 percent, respectively),
while Tatarstan had a titular plurality (48.5 percent), according to the 1989
census (see figure 1.1). Yet according to the demography argument, we also
expect that the two other republics with titular majorities—Chuvashia (68.7
percent) and North Ossetia (53 percent) would experience high levels of nationalist separatism. Chuvashia, in fact, experienced moderate to low levels of nationalist separatism,[40] while North Ossetia witnessed interethnic
violence between Ossets and Ingush but little Ossetian mobilization for independent statehood.[41]

In addition, two other republics in which titulars formed a plurality (besides Tatarstan) also demonstrated moderate to low and very low nationalist separatism, respectively: Kabardino-Balkaria and Kalmykia.[42] Moreover, the republics of Yakutia and Bashkortostan challenge the demography
argument because both have small titular ethnic groups but mounted strong
separatist campaigns against Moscow. Yakuts form 33.4 percent of Yakutia's population, and Bashkirs make up 22 percent of Bashkortostan's population. Another highly separatist republic with a very small titular population is Abkhazia, where the ethnic Abkhaz (17 percent) challenged the
Georgian central state.

If an ethnic group's demographic domination leads directly to political
mobilization, why are there so many republics in which small minorities
mobilize for separatism? Because the behavior of Russia's republics both
supports and contradicts the ethnic demography hypothesis, analysts should
more carefully specify the logic by which relative group size either stimu-
lates or hinders nationalist separatism. Many accounts that rely on the demography explanations make two main assumptions, both of which tend to
overpredict ethnic mobilization. The first assumption is that members of an

Figure 1.1. The Ethnic Composition of Russia's Autonomous Republics, 1989

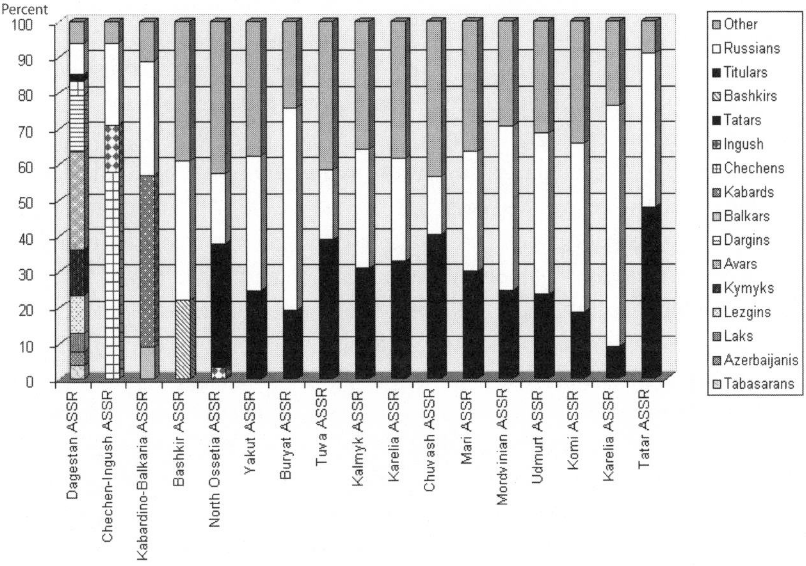

Note: ASSR = Autonomous Soviet Socialist Republic.
Source: Data compiled from the 1989 USSR All-Union Census.

ethnic group, by virtue of claiming an ethnic identity, will naturally support nationalist goals. The second assumption is that different ethnic groups within a region automatically hold opposing preferences. With regard to Russia, these assumptions mean that titular groups in the republics are automatic nationalists, while members of other ethnic groups (usually Russians) are not.

The issue of whether a particular ethnic group backs a particular political program, such as nationalism, is an empirical question. If analysts instead assume that ethnic groups at all times want to establish their own nation-state, they are committing the same fallacy as primordialists, who see ethnic groups as bounded, coherent nations waiting for the right moment to achieve statehood. Moreover, such assumptions reproduce Leninist and Stalinist understandings of the nation that see ethnic groups as natural national communities.

Also, the assumption that different ethnic groups in the republics held opposing political attitudes can be questioned by the fact that a significant minority of Russians in several republics (including Estonia, Latvia, and

Tatarstan) supported referenda on republican state sovereignty. In the 1991 vote for Ukrainian independence, in which 90 percent of the population participated, many Russians voted for Ukrainian national independence.

The surprising fact that, at a certain point in time, many (though not all) Russians shared an "enthusiasm for secession" with Ukrainians suggests the limits of the demography hypothesis's explanatory power.[43] The demography hypothesis makes the critical assumption that the political preferences of ethnic groups will not coincide. Yet we know that republican separatism in the Soviet Union and Russia arose in an extremely unstable and rapidly changing environment. We also know that many Russians accepted the principle—established by Soviet state policy—that the republics "belonged" to the titular ethnic group. As the central state imploded, individuals, ethnic populations, and other actors were very unsure of what the future held. It is precisely these fluid and ambiguous conditions that permit the formation of new social identities (e.g., Soviet citizens one day, ethnic Russian Ukrainian citizens the next) as well as the evolution of varied political preferences, which may separate people into distinct and opposing ethnic groups but also may integrate them into a cohesive society.

Furthermore, even if an ethnic minority in a region mobilizes for nationalist secession and even if an ethnic majority in that region opposes separatism, these divergent preferences will not necessarily affect political outcomes because groups do not always mobilize in direct proportion to their population size. In many republics, ethnicity was more salient an identity to titulars than to Russians, and nationalist grievances spoke more to the interests of titular groups than to Russians. Thus, the level of Russians' participation in mass-level ethnic politics was lower than that of titular ethnic groups. Russians formed fewer organizations and staged a smaller number of counterdemonstrations than titulars. They did not always actively oppose titulars' campaigns for nationalist separatism. In short, Russians generally did not display the same *intensity* of preferences as titular groups.

Many Russians, of course, felt deep concern about, and even fear of, republican separatism and mobilized against it. This set of Russians, however, was not necessarily equal to the proportion of Russians in the total republican population. If the intensity of Russians' preferences could not match the intensity of titulars' political commitments, it is less likely that a Russian population—even when it constituted a numerical majority in a republic—would influence political outcomes. The simple observation that Russians did not mobilize in the same way and to as large a degree as titulars calls into question arguments that rely on demography to explain political outcomes. In general, demographic hypotheses conceive of ethnic groups in Russia's republics as bounded blocs of political interests—a conception that both overpredicts republican separatism and explains little of its variance.

Cultural Arguments

Cultural arguments maintain that the key motivator of nationalist mobilization is group members' sense of a shared culture—a culture different from that of the ethnic group that controls the central state. According to this argument, a sense of cultural difference, based on a unique language, religion, customs, history, and sense of shared fate, engenders among group members a need for public recognition, greater rights and resources, and independent statehood. An important distinction should be made between cultural arguments that consider cultural identity to be a sufficient condition for producing nationalist mobilization and cultural arguments that consider identity to be a background condition, or one of a number of factors contributing to mobilization.

Analysts with a primordialist understanding of identity generally believe cultural difference alone can account for nationalist mobilization. Primordialists view ethnic identity as the most fundamental identity a person can have and therefore the one by which they condition their political behavior. As Clifford Geertz, who articulated a primordialist argument without necessarily accepting its veracity, writes, "Congruities of blood, speech, custom, and so on" connect individuals in intensely felt bonds—bonds that are expressed when people organize themselves into a political community.[44]

In the post-Soviet literature, a primordialist point of view is expressed in the work of Helene Carrere d'Encausse, whose book, *The End of the Soviet Empire: The Triumph of the Nations,* sees Soviet nationalities as permanent nations seeking their own state from time immemorial.[45] This primordialist perspective gives rise to the so-called ancient hatreds argument according to which ethnic groups' long-held desire to establish a nation-state have been thwarted by the nationality currently controlling "their" territory. According to this story (unfortunately still so popular among journalists), the source of political oppression—whether a central state or dominant ethnic group—is the natural target of the separatist group's "ancient" hatred. Constructivist approaches, conversely, disagree that ethnic groups move through history as organized, mobilized political communities, constantly in quest of a state. Instead, these approaches show how ethnic and cultural identities are intentionally constructed through the actions of historians, journalists, politicians, and others with specific political agendas.

Nevertheless, many constructivist analysts believe, along with primordialists, that once cultural identities become socially established they invariably motivate people to mobilize politically along ethnic lines. Because individuals feel an emotional attachment to their ethnicity and a sense of community with other group members, analysts conclude that individuals will make political decisions based on how they affect the group. This kind of ethnic solidarity is often referred to as a "national consciousness." Thus, many observers who recognize the constructed and fluid origins of ethnic identity nonetheless consider ethnic identity and the political behavior of ethnic group members as predetermined and unchanging. In this understanding, once a person feels herself to be a member of an ethnic group, she will automatically support a nationalist program or she will oppose any policy that might benefit another ethnic group.[46]

One kind of culturalist hypothesis argues that ethnic groups whose cultures are most distant from the culture of the central state are highly likely to mobilize for national secession. According to this model, it is the attributes of an identity that guide individual political behavior. Thus, the Central Asian republics—with their Muslim, clan-based, "traditionalist" culture—should have been more nationalist than Ukraine, Moldova, and Georgia—rather than the other way around.[47] In fact, "cultural distance" hypotheses are predicated on two ideas: first, that cultural attributes themselves generate group consciousness and solidarity; and second, that certain attributes such as religion (identified as socially relevant by the analyst rather than the actors themselves) produce political conflict between groups. Again, this is an essentialist way of conceptualizing the link between cultural identity and political action.

In the Soviet context, national consciousness was not simply present or absent among titular ethnic groups in the republics. It is incorrect to assume that most titular nationalities supported independent nationhood *before* the campaigns for sovereignty that began in the late glasnost period. Certain ethnic populations, such as those in the Baltic republics, and certain elites may have supported nationalist programs, but this does not mean that all nationalities in all the republics did. Whether an ethnic population comes to support nationalism does not depend on the content of its cultural attributes or on the depth of emotional attachment to its identity.

Another culturalist hypothesis maintains that historical grievances—such as the past colonization, oppression, or coercion of a minority ethnic group—

give rise to political demands for independent nationhood. Such grievances usually blame the central state or an ethnic "other" for obstructing the destiny of the nation by preventing them from establishing an independent state. The case of Chechnya, whose Chechen and Ingush populations were deported by Stalin in 1944, suggests that a recent historical grievance may have inspired ethnic populations to mobilize in support of nationalism.

Yet the Balkars in Kabardino-Balkaria and the Karachai in Karachaevo-Cherkessia, who were also deported, did not exhibit any significant level of nationalist mobilization. It is not a question of a lack of ethnic entrepreneurs willing and able to construct and "sell" grievances to ethnic populations. Balkar and Karachai ethnic entrepreneurs organized ethnonational movements, yet popular support for these movements remained limited. Thus, we observe that mass populations do not always respond to ethnic entrepreneurs who promote historical grievances. Moreover, republics with less dramatic histories of Soviet oppression, such as Tuva, managed to develop ethnonationalist movements that garnered considerable popular support among the titular population.[48]

So whereas in some cases ethnic individuals may assume the significant risks and costs associated with nationalist mobilization in order to right a historical injustice, evidence from Russia suggests that the presence or absence of historical grievance cannot account for all variation across republics.

In general, ethnic minorities in the Soviet Union had a number of legitimate grievances against the Soviet center and against Russians. They also had reasons to be appreciative of the Soviet system because they benefited from central policies in ways that modern Soviet citizens recognized as valuable. Titular groups became increasingly educated, urbanized, bilingual, and even ethnically self-aware due to affirmative action programs and ethnofederalism. Why and when do attitudes of blame for past oppression trump attitudes of gratitude toward and identity with the Soviet state? The assumption that historical grievances are sufficient to mobilize ethnic populations does not adequately recognize the possibility of the latter alternative.

Proponents of culturalist arguments that emphasize historical grievances assume that ethnic groups are predisposed to accept a narrative of blame regardless of how it relates to their other experiences and interests. They maintain that historical grievances have more power to mobilize people than other kinds of grievances. My own research finds that a different kind of grievance motivated ethnic groups to mobilize—a grievance that concerned their own and their children's life chances.

Interethnic Job Competition and Ethnic Representation

Popular support for nationalism developed in certain of Russia's republics —Tatarstan, Chechnya, Tuva, Bashkortostan, and Yakutia—because increasing competition for higher education and jobs allowed nationalists' issue framings to resonate with titular populations experiencing fear concerning their life chances. Nationalist leaders articulated issues about blocked job opportunities. But instead of bemoaning rising job competition, they described an ethnic division of labor in which titulars were underrepresented in urban and white-collar professions compared with Russians.[49] Paradoxically, the ethnic division of labor issue framing *contradicted* the actual situation of rising titular professionalization and achievement.

At the beginning of the Soviet era, Russia's autonomous republics were characterized by an ethnic division of labor, in which titular ethnic groups lived and worked in the countryside in low-skilled agricultural jobs while Russians lived and worked in the cities. Though many Russians were also rural dwellers, they were much more likely than titulars to occupy highly skilled jobs in urban areas. The Soviet state, however, resolved to advance the position of minority nationalities through the policies of industrialization, urbanization, public education, Russification, and *korenizatsiia,* or indigenization. Following World War II and accelerating in the 1960s, titular ethnic groups moved from farm to factory and assumed jobs alongside Russians.

Education had perhaps the greatest effect on the lives of titulars. *Korenizatsiia* policies encouraged secondary, specialized secondary, and higher education (*vysshii obrazovanie, srednii spetsial'nii obrazovanie*) for titulars in order to develop qualified "indigenous cadres" to administer republican government and work in republican industries. Especially during the last few decades of Soviet rule, titulars made important gains. From 1979 to 1989, a higher percentage of titulars were receiving high school and higher education than in previous decades. And in certain republics including Tatarstan and Yakutia, titulars' *rate* of higher education outpaced Russians'. Therefore, although Russians with higher or secondary specialized education still outnumbered comparably trained titulars by 1989, the dramatic rise in titular higher education led to an increase in their demand for white-collar jobs.

By the time national revival began in the late 1980s, titular ethnic groups had undergone astounding professional mobility. They were working in white-collar jobs in numbers almost proportional to their share of the total workforce in each republic. As might be expected, they occupied a majority of white-collar jobs in republican rural areas. But they were also very strongly represented in the coveted highest echelons of urban economies, and they worked as directors of enterprises in numbers *equal to or greater than* their share of the total population in almost all republics.[50] They had also obtained significant representation in the Communist Party and in government administration, as well as in academia.

Meanwhile, ethnic Russians living in the republics were also moving to the cities as part of the Soviet Union's broader trends of urbanization and industrialization.[51] Like titulars, Russians worked in white-collar jobs in more or less equal proportion to their share of the total workforce in each republic as of 1989. The high degree of both Russian and titular professional mobility is shown in figure 1.2, which presents a ratio of titular to Russian representation in the white-collar workforce compared with each group's percentage of the total workforce.[52] A ratio of 1 indicates that both titulars and Russians are equally represented in white-collar jobs in proportion to their percentage of the total workforce. A ratio greater than 1 means that titulars occupy white-collar jobs in numbers greater than their percentage of the workforce compared with Russians. A ratio less than 1 indicates that as a proportion of each group's overall representation in the workforce, titulars are underrepresented compared with Russians. The average for all republics is 0.814 (see the dotted line in the figure 1.2), which indicates that in a majority of republics, ethnic Russians are only slightly more proportionately represented in white-collar jobs than titulars.

The degree of titular advancement varied across the republics. By 1989, some republics had relatively equal ethnic representation in the economy, while others still had titular-dominated agricultural sectors. Yet even in the republics with the largest proportion of rural and uneducated populations—such as Tuva, Chechnya, and Dagestan—titulars had been making significant professional strides. For example, titulars' rate of higher education exceeded that of Russians between 1979 and 1989 in Chechnya and Yakutia,[53] while in Tuva, equal numbers of Tuvans and Russians graduated with higher educational degrees in 1989.[54] Moreover, titular ethnic groups in some republics were overrepresented in certain occupations compared with Russians. Yakuts worked in the humanitarian intelligentsia (as doctors, teachers, and scientists) and in the creative arts, academia, and industry (as engineers, economists, agronomists) in numbers greater—by a factor of two to four times in the cities—than their overall percentage of the republic's workforce.

All of this means that demand for white-collar jobs was rising at the same time that the Soviet economy had stopped growing. By the end of the Soviet

Figure 1.2. Ratio of Titular/Russian Representation in the White-Collar Workforce

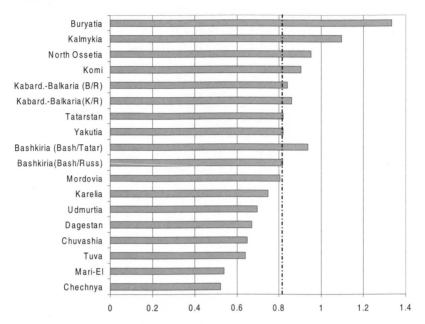

Source: USSR All-Union Census, Goskomstat.

era, the country was in the midst of a deepening macroeconomic decline that had begun during Brezhnev's "era of stagnation." State employment, although still artificially high, was starting to drop. Soviet citizens expected that their lives and those of their children would progress along familiar, state-established trajectories: secondary school followed by higher education or technical training, followed by secure jobs and advancement up the career ladder. But with the macroeconomic crisis and general uncertainty of 1989 and 1990, the state could no longer guarantee its citizens educational and job opportunities.

Growing labor competition caused people to experience material dissatisfaction, frustration, and fear of job loss. Because this affected all people, why would only titulars respond by mobilizing in support of nationalism?[55] Soviet enterprises did not formally organize job applications or work collectives along ethnic lines. And Soviet citizens held class, regional, professional, and generational identities, in addition to ethnic ones. Why would they think of themselves as competing along ethnic lines? How, in other words, did ethnic group boundaries become politically salient?

Nationalist leaders in certain republics constructed grievances about a supposed ethnic division of labor, or unequal representation of titulars and Russians in white- and blue-collar positions, in higher education, and in political administration. Titular ethnic groups worked in agrarian jobs in the countryside, nationalists claimed, while Russians occupied prestigious jobs in the city. The best jobs requiring the best educations were "given" to Russians, condemning titulars to a subordinate social status. It is critical to note that the nationalists' framing of the issue of blocked job opportunity not only failed to reflect the fact that the Soviet state promoted titular mobility; it also painted titulars as victims of the Soviet—and ethnically Russian—state. Once nationalists established that titulars had been getting the short end of the stick within their "own" republics, they could blame the current state and make a compelling case that a sovereign state should be established in which titular rule would bring greater ethnic group rights.

A comparison of the issues mentioned in the founding programs of nationalist organizations in the republics, as well as a comparative discourse analysis of newspaper articles from each of these republics, indicates that this framing was only present in the highly nationalist republics of Tatarstan, Tuva, Chechnya, Bashkortostan, and Yakutia. In republics where nationalist leaders articulated issues other than an ethnic division of labor, such as Mordovia and Mari-El, ethnic minorities failed to support the nationalist movements.[56]

Although nationalists articulated various kinds of issues, ranging from language education, to demographic decline, to assisting the ethnic "diaspora," I argue that the issue that resonated most strongly with ethnic groups was that which addressed job attainment and professional advancement. In Tatarstan, for example, the nationalist Tatar Public Center, in its founding program, began by outlining Tatars' socially disadvantaged position vis-à-vis Russians and ended by tying this fact to the endangered future of the Tatar nation. Since the beginning of the Soviet era and lasting to the present day, the platform argued, Tatars outnumbered Russians in rural areas, exhibiting a slower rate of urbanization, "lower qualifications," and a subordinate social status in general. Thus, in order for the "full-fledged development of the Tatar nation (*natsii*)," rural Tatars must secure employment in the urban economies of Tatarstan's cities. The platform advocated specific solutions to rectify this injustice: Tatars, it said, should be provided with preferences and set-aside positions in the republican economy and free job placement in "any economic sphere."[57] It also recommended regulating the "national composition of higher educational institutes."

Similarly, in Yakutia, the founding charters of the moderate nationalist group, Sakha Omuk, and the radical nationalist group, Sakha Keskile, included issues related to equalizing Yakut representation in the republican economy. Sakha Omuk focused on the upper echelon of the economy, stating that Yakuts should have greater representation in enterprise management as well as in government. Sakha Keskile targeted a different audience by advocating a cadre policy (i.e., quotas) for Yakut youth in republican industry.[58] Conversely, in Mordovia and Mari-El, nationalist movements did not articulate issues concerning equal representation of ethnic groups in the labor market; consequently, these republics remained politically quiescent.[59]

The nationalists' issue framing about ethnic underrepresentation persuaded people to understand their experience of labor competition as bound up with the fate of their ethnic group. Titulars learned to place blame on Russians, rather than on co-ethnics or other ethnic minorities with whom they were also competing for jobs. For example, many Yakuts believed that Russian workers were better paid and given better housing and privileges.[60] In Tuva, a Tuvan woman expressed similar complaints in a 1990 *Komsomol'skaia Pravda* article: "The Russians have got the best places. . . . They get enormous wages and multi-room apartments before everyone else. While I, the owner of this land, have to play second fiddle."[61] Nationalist leaders, therefore, attracted popular support not by simply picking up on preexisting attitudes, but by actively creating grievances that interpreted economic information in ethnic terms. The ethnic division of labor issue resonated because it plausibly made sense of titulars' experience of rising competition for increasingly scarce educational and professional positions.

In conclusion, structural socioeconomic inequalities among ethnic groups by themselves did not produce nationalist mobilization in Russia's republics. People there were interested in improving their worsening educational and professional opportunities. But because the boundaries of ethnic groups are not necessarily fixed nor politically meaningful before the moment of political mobilization, it took specific issue frames put forward by nationalist leaders for people to interpret their economic interests in ethnic terms. In the high-mobilization republics of Tatarstan, Chechnya, Tuva, Bashkortostan, and Yakutia, titular populations came to understand their experience of growing competition for education and jobs as part of a general, state-led hindering of their ethnic group's economic opportunities. The nationalist program of equalizing the representation of ethnic groups and acquiring state sovereignty resonated with people as the proper solution to this injustice. As a result, mass support for nationalism in these republics grew in the late Soviet and early post-Soviet periods. In Mordovia and Mari-El, however, where nationalists did not articulate issues concerning equal ethnic representation, mass nationalist mobilization was significantly lower.

Conclusion

This discussion has attempted to suggest that for individuals who identify with an ethnic group, the journey from ethnic group member to nationalist supporter is longer and less direct than is generally believed. Though the various arguments considered here have emphasized how a variety of variables influence ethnic group members to support nationalism, they fail to appreciate individual agency among ethnic group members. Variables such as ethnic group size and demography, group position as a cultural minority within a central state, economic resources, and strategic elites, in and of themselves, do not motivate nationalist action.

Recent work by Mark Beissinger also critiques the idea that nationalist mobilization is the relatively unproblematic outcome of structural factors. He conceives of nationalism as mass behavior—a unique approach that stresses particular events and contentious activity over individual or group attitudes. His understanding agrees with Rogers Brubaker, who views nationhood as "something that suddenly crystallizes rather than gradually develops; as a contingent, conjuncturally fluctuating and precarious frame of vision."[62]

This chapter has argued that many studies of separatism by substate regions conceptualize nationalism as an *idea* that is either automatically present among ethnic communities or is easily transmitted from elite to mass. I maintain that nationalism should not be thought of as an idea or set of attitudes that is present or absent, but as a fundamentally *political* phenomenon that develops out of a dynamic interaction between ethnic identity, individual experience, and elites' issue framings. Viewing nationalism as a political phenomenon suggests that nationalist mobilization and popular support for nationalism should be viewed as a highly provisional and rather rare outcome. Nationalism can be much shorter-lived than most existing accounts perceive—it can come and go within a given population, while ethnic affiliations remain. It is possible for individuals to genuinely and intensely identify with their ethnic group yet to neither automatically support a nationalist program nor respond to nationalist elites' appeals for statehood or the subjugation of the ethnic "other." The variation in nationalism among Russia's ethnic communities living in the republics suggests the transience and contingency of nationalism. Ethnic groups respond to nationalist appeals less frequently than is generally assumed. The republics also demonstrate that as a political phenomenon, nationalist mobilization, once begun, may be more readily curtailed or "demobilized" than is generally recognized.

Notes

1. These actors were nationalists according to Ernest Gellner's definition of the term. For Gellner, nationalism is "a political principle which holds that the political and national unit be congruent"; *Nations and Nationalism* (Ithaca, N.Y.: Cornell University Press, 1983), 1.

2. Though the various authors' arguments considered here may not fit tidily into these four categories, and though significant differences among the arguments exist, these categories help shed analytical clarity on the phenomenon of nationalist mobilization. Also, certain other arguments do not fit into these categories at all and thus are not discussed here. E.g., Stephen Hanson's original explanation for the lack of popular support for separatism among Russia's republics emphasizes how a change in central state ideology, from Marxism-Leninism to Russian statehood (associated with democracy), made it difficult for republican populations (especially ethnic Russians) to oppose Moscow and support a nationalist call for sovereign statehood. See Stephen E. Hanson, "Ideology, Interests, and Identity: Comparing the Soviet and Russian Secession Crises," in *Center–Periphery Conflict in Post-Soviet Russia,* ed. Mikhail A. Alexseev (New York: St. Martin's Press, 1999), 15–46.

3. Gail Lapidus and Edward W. Walker, "Nationalism, Regionalism, and Federalism: Center-Periphery Relations in Post-Communist Russia," in *The New Russia: Troubled Transformation,* ed. Gail Lapidus (Boulder, Colo.: Westview Press, 1995), 79–113.

4. This argument is developed in my manuscript, "Why Secession Fails: The Rise and Fall of Ethnic Nationalism in Russia."

5. The sixteen autonomous republics located inside the Russian Soviet Federated Socialist Republic sat just below the union republics in the Soviet administrative-territorial hierarchy. In the current Russian Federation, there are twenty-one republics (including Chechnya), as well as ten autonomous okrugs and one autonomous oblast.

6. Yet most autonomous republics declared sovereignty one after another during a three-month period: June 1990: North Ossetia; August: Karelia, Komi, Tatarstan; September: Udmurtia, Yakutia; October: Buryatia, Bashkiria, Kalmykia, Mari, Chuvashia; November: Checheno-Ingushetia; December: Mordovia, Tuva; January 1991: Kabardino-Balkaria; May: Dagestan. See M. N. Guboglo, *Bashkortostan i Tatarstan: Paralleli etnopoliticheskogo razvitiia* [Bashkortostan and Tatarstan: Parallels in ethnopolitical development], no. 77 (Moscow: Institute of Ethnography and Anthropology, Russian Academy of Sciences, 1994).

7. For more on sovereignty declarations in Russia, see Jeff Kahn, "The Parade of

Sovereignties: Establishing the Vocabulary of the New Russian Federalism," *Post-Soviet Affairs* 16 (2000): 58–89.

8. E. Chernobrovkina, "Reshat' vam samim" [Decide for yourselves], *Vechernaia kazan,* August 10, 1990, 1.

9. By the spring of 1991, most republics supported the new USSR Union Treaty that Gorbachev and Yeltsin had negotiated and that allowed them the right to sign as members of both the USSR and Russia.

10. See Elizabeth Teague, "Center–Periphery Relations in the Russian Federation," in *National Identity and Ethnicity in Russia and the New States of Eurasia,* ed. Roman Szporluk (Armonk, N.Y.: M. E. Sharpe, 1994), 42; and also Darrel Slider, "Federalism, Discord, and Accommodation: Intergovernmental Relations in Post-Soviet Russia," in *Local Power and Post-Soviet Politics,* ed. Theodore Friedgut and Jeffrey Hahn (Armonk, N.Y.: M. E. Sharpe, 1994), 249.

11. Nine of the sixteen former autonomous republics voted for Yeltsin. Chechnya boycotted the referendum; Tatarstan discouraged voting, making its 22.6 percent turnout too low to count; a majority in Tuva endorsed Yeltsin in questions one and two, but voted to hold early presidential elections—a rejection of Yeltsin. Of the assertive republics, Sakha alone voted for Yeltsin on all four questions. Ralph Clem and Peter Craumer, "The Geography of the April 25 (1993) Russian Referendum," *Post-Soviet Geography* 34 (October 1993): 481–96; also see Lapidus and Walker, "Nationalism," 97.

12. Elizabeth Teague, "North-South Divide: Yeltsin and Russia's Provincial Leaders," *RFE/RL Research Report* 2, November 26, 1993, 7–23.

13. Mordova, Dagestan, Adygei, Karachai-Cherkessia, and Chuvashia also rejected the constitution. Lapidus and Walker, "Nationalism," 100–1.

14. Leading American and Russian observers of post-Soviet ethnic politics, including Gail Lapidus, Valery Tishkov, and Leokadia Drobizheva, agree with this coding.

15. See Daniel Treisman, *After the Deluge: Regional Crises and Political Consolidation in Russia* (Ann Arbor: University of Michigan Press, 1999).

16. Philip Roeder, "Soviet Federalism and Ethnic Mobilization," *World Politics* 43, no. 2 (January 1991): 196–233; Ronald Suny, *The Revenge of the Past: Nationalism, Revolution and the Collapse of the Soviet Union,* (Stanford, Calif.: Stanford University Press, 1993); Rogers Brubaker, *Nationalism Reframed: Nationhood and the National Question in the New Europe* (New York: Cambridge University Press, 1996).

17. My own research is indebted to these works, especially that of Suny and Roeder.

18. Also, there were eighty-nine officially recognized nationalities without control of a territorial unit. John Slocum, *Disintegration and Consolidation: National Separatism and the Evolution of Center–Periphery Relations in the Russian Federation,* Occasional Paper 19 (Ithaca, N.Y.: Cornell University Peace Studies Program, 1995).

19. E.g., the state used nationality to repress or force the migration of certain ethnic groups, especially during collectivization in the early 1930s and World War II in the 1940s.

20. Yuri Slezkine, "The USSR as Communal Apartment, or How a Socialist State Promoted Ethnic Particularism," *Slavic Review* 53 (Summer 1994): 413–52.

21. Victor Zaslavsky. "Nationalism and Democratic Transition in Postcommunist Societies," *Daedalus* 121, (Spring 1992): 102. For more on passports, see Victor Zaslavsky and Yuri Luryi, "The Passport System in the USSR and Changes in Soviet Society," *Soviet Union 6, Part 2* (1979): 147ff; and Rasma Karklins, *Ethnic Relations in*

the USSR: The Perspective from Below (Boston: Allen & Unwin, 1986), 23, 31–32, 42–43.

22. E.g., the Tatar Autonomous Soviet Socialist Republic appealed to Moscow for an upgrade to Union status in the 1930s and 1970s.

23. Also giving the lie to these claims were the interethnic violence that broke out between Russians and Kazakhs at Kazakhstan State University in 1986 and Uzbek beatings and riots against Kirghiz squatters in Osh, Uzbekistan, in 1990.

24. Suny, *Revenge of the Past,* 126.

25. Roeder, "Soviet Federalism," 216–19.

26. Dmitry Gorenburg, *Minority Ethnic Mobilization in the Russian Federation* (New York: Cambridge University Press, 2003), 24.

27. Kathryn Stoner-Weiss, "Federalism and Regionalism," in *Developments in Russian Politics 4,* ed. Stephen White, Alex Pravda, and Zvi Gitelman (Durham, N.C.: Duke University Press, 1997), 239.

28. James Hughes, "From Federalism to Recentralization," *Developments in Russian Politics 5,* ed. Stephen White, Alex Pravda, and Zvi Gitelman (Durham, N.C.: Duke University Press, 1998), 134.

29. Kisangani Emizet and Vicki Hesli, "The Disposition to Secede: An Analysis of the Soviet Case," *Comparative Political Studies* 27 (January 1995): 493–536; Daniel Treisman, "Russia's 'Ethnic Revival': The Separatist Activism of Regional Leaders in a Postcommunist Order," *World Politics* 49 (January 1997): 212–49; Henry Hale, "The Parade of Sovereignties: Testing Theories of Secession in the Soviet Setting," *British Journal of Political Science* 30 (2000): 31–56. These studies are also notable for the hypotheses tested that were *not* confirmed by the evidence, including the interesting (and robust) finding that the size of the Russian populations in the republics did not influence secessionism.

30. This logic, in which ethnic group leaders attempt to ward off threats to their group's privileged position, was delineated by Robert Bates in "Modernization, Ethnic Competition, and the Rationality of Politics in Contemporary Africa," in *State Versus Ethnic Claims: African Policy Dilemmas,* ed. Donald Rothchild and Victor Olorunsola (Boulder, Colo.: Westview Press, 1983), 159.

31. Treisman, "Russia's 'Ethnic Revival,' " 239. He also finds that high administrative status (republic vs. oblast or okrug) is highly correlated with activism, because republics could use their greater institutional resources, access, and experience to successfully bargain with the center.

32. Treisman finds other factors besides wealth that strengthened the bargaining position of republican leaders, including strong ethnic movements; institutionalized federal borders, and the experience of leaders. See Treisman, "Russia's 'Ethnic Revival,' "; and Treisman, *after the Deluge: Regional Crises and Political Consolidation in Russia* (Ann Arbor: University of Michigan Press, 1999). In his book, Treisman makes the argument that republican economic wealth caused Moscow to respond: central leaders granted aggressive republics special bilateral agreements, including tax breaks, credits, subsidies, and political autonomy. In general, Moscow gave the ethnic republics greater privileges than the oblasts and other nonethnic regions, institutionalizing a system of asymmetric federalism.

33. E.g., Ernst Gellner linked macroeconomic change with ethnonational mobilization, arguing that nation-states were originally created by the effect of modernization and industrialization on economically marginalized groups exhibiting distinct genetic-so-

matic, linguistic, or religious traits from the economically dominant or state-bearing population. Scholars concerned with twentieth-century nationalist movements extended Gellner's approach. E.g., Donald Horowitz's work on Africa and Southeast Asia and Michael Hechter's research on Great Britain sees the relative economic backwardness of ethnic groups as provoking those groups' desire to increase their economic prospects through greater autonomy or independent statehood. Other work focusing on separatism in Western Europe has argued the opposite. Tom Nairn and Peter Gourevitch claim that economically *advanced* elites in politically peripheral regions of Western Europe advocated national secession in order to build on their region's economic potential. See Ernst Gellner, *Thought and Change* (Chicago: University of Chicago Press, 1964), 147–78; Gellner, *Nations and Nationalism;* Donald Horowitz, "Patterns of Ethnic Separatism," *Comparative Studies in Society and History* 23 (1981): 165–95; Horowitz, *Ethnic Groups in Conflict* (Berkeley: University of California Press, 1985); Michael Hechter, *Internal Colonialism: The Celtic Fringe in British National Development 1536–1966* (Berkeley: University of California Press, 1975); Hechter, "Group Formation and the Cultural Division of Labor," *American Journal of Sociology* 84 (1978): 293–318; Peter Gourevitch, *Paris and the Provinces* (Berkeley: University of California Press, 1980); and Tom Nairn, *The Break-up of Britain: Crisis and Neo-Nationalism* (London: NLB, 1977).

34. Henry Hale's account is a partial exception insofar as he recognizes that support for nationalism may differ among republican leaders and other subrepublican actors. He believes, however, that the same macroeconomic factors will motivate all republican actors.

35. Elise Giuliano, "Secessionism from the Bottom Up: Democratization, Nationalism, and Local Accountability in the Russian Transition," forthcoming, *World Politics.*

36. Horowitz, *Ethnic Groups,* 267.

37. Lapidus and Walker, "Nationalism." Also see Monica Duffy Toft, *The Geography of Ethnic Violence: Identity, Interests and the Indivisibility of Territory* (Princeton, N.J.: Princeton University Press, 2003).

38. Hughes, "From Federalism to Recentralization," 131, 134.

39. Similarly, Treisman and Hale's analyses both find that the size of the Russian and titular populations in the republics are not statistically related to republican activism. Treisman, "Russia's 'Ethnic Revival,' " 232; Hale, "Parade of Sovereignties," 50.

40. Gorenburg, *Minority Ethnic Mobilization.*

41. See Valery Tishkov, *Ethnicity, Nationalism and Conflict in and after the Soviet Union* (London: Sage Publications, 1997).

42. Timur Muzaev, *Etnicheskii Separatizm v Rossii* [Ethnic Separatism in Russia] (Moscow: Panorama Publishers, 1999); *RFE-RL,* 1988–92; *Current Digest of the Soviet Press,* 1988–94.

43. This is Horowitz's phrase; *Ethnic Groups,* 268.

44. Clifford Geertz, *Old Societies and New States: The Quest for Modernity in Asia and Africa* (New York: Free Press, 1963); Quoted in Treisman, "Russia's 'Ethnic Revival.' " Also see Geertz, *The Interpretation of Cultures* (New York: Basic Books, 1973).

45. Helene Carrere d'Encausse, *The End of the Soviet Empire: The Triumph of the Nations* (New York: Basic Books, 1993).

46. Many international relations theorists conceptualize ethnic identity in this way. See, e.g., Barry Posen, "The Security Dilemma and Ethnic Conflict," in *Ethnic Conflict and International Security,* ed. Michael Brown (Princeton, N.J.: Princeton University Press, 1993), 103–24.

47. Emizet and Hesli, "Disposition to Secede," reject the idea that degree of difference in cultural identity (language difference, phenotype differences) can account for either conflict between groups or national separatism. Identity alone, they say, does not trigger the consciousness necessary for a group to mobilize. Rather, political or economic or cultural grievances must be present. Treisman, "Russia's 'Ethnic Revival,' " also rejects the idea and testing for it, finds no relationship.

48. A. Kuzhuget and M. Tatarintseva, *Etnopoliticheskaia situatsiia v Respublike Tyva* [The ethnopolitical situation in the Republic of Tuva], no. 74 (Moscow: Institute of Anthropology and Ethnography, Russian Academy of Sciences, 1994); Leokadia Drobizheva, *Natsional'noe Samosoznanie i natsionalizm v rossiiskoi federatsii nachala 1990-x godov* [National consciousness and nationalism in the Russian Federation at the beginning of the 1990s] (Moscow: IEA-RAN, 1994); and Zoia Anaibin, "Ethnic Relations in Tuva," in *Culture Incarnate,* ed. Marjorie Balzer (Armonk, N.Y.: M. E. Sharpe, 1995), 102–12.

49. I adapt Michael Hechter's concept of a cultural division of labor. See "Group Formation and the Cultural Division of Labor," *American Journal of Sociology* 84 (1978), 293–318.

50. Mari El and Tuva are exceptions, although Tuvans still comprised a large number (40 percent) of enterprise directors in Tuva. *Narodnoe Khoziaistvo Rossiiskoi Federatsii* [The economy of the Russian Federation] (Moscow: Goskomstat, 1990).

51. Moshe Lewin describes how these processes transformed the entire Soviet population in *The Gorbachev Phenomenon* (Berkeley: University of California Press, 1988).

52. These ratios were compiled by the author based on raw data collected by Goskomstat in 1989. These data are unpublished and were kindly provided by Dmitri Gorenburg, "Professional'no-otraslevoi sostav intelligentsia naseleniia titul'noi i russkoi natsional'nostei Absolytnie znacheniia" [Titular and Russian ethnic group composition of white-collar economic sectors].

53. G. S. Denisova, *Etnicheskii Faktor v Politicheskoi Zhizni Rossii 90-x godov* [The ethnic factor in Russia's political life during the 1990s] (Rostov-on-the-Don: Rostov State Pedagogical University, 1996), 86–88.

54. The educational level of Yakuts and Chechens grew by more than 100 percent in the 1970s and 1980s. Leokadia Drobizheva, "Processes of Disintegration," in *The New Russian Diaspora: Russian Minorities in the Former Soviet Republics,* ed. Vladimir Shlapentokh, Munir Sendich, and Emil Payin (Armonk, N.Y.: M. E. Sharpe, 1994), 47.

55. According to the ethnic competition framework associated with Frederik Barth and Susan Olzak, rising job competition may spur mobilization as groups begin competing for scarce resources in the same economic niche, especially following sudden macroeconomic change. See Frederik Barth, ed., *Ethnic Groups and Boundaries* (Boston: Little, Brown, 1969); and Susan Olzak, *The Dynamics of Ethnic Competition and Conflict* (Stanford, Calif.: Stanford University Press, 1992).

56. I collected approximately 40 to 100 newspaper articles published in each of Russia's sixteen republics that address some aspect of ethnic politics by culling through several years of local newspapers in two Moscow libraries. The articles were published during the period 1989–93 and include standard news reports, official statements by political leaders, editorials, letters to the editors, and statements by nationalist organizations. See "Why Secession Fails."

57. Damir Iskhakov, *Sovremennie natsional'nie protsessi v respublike Tatarstan*

[Current ethnic processes in the Republic of Tatarstan] (Kazan: Russian Academy of Sciences, 1992.)

58. A. M. Ivanov, *Etnopoliticheskaia situatsiia v Respublike Sakha (Yakutiia)* [Ethnopolitical situation in the Republic of Sakha (Yakutia)], no. 61 (Moscow: Institute of Ethnography and Anthropology, Russian Academy of Sciences, 1994); Drobizheva, "Processes of Disintegration"; Muzaev, *Etnicheskii Separatizm,* 206–10.

59. Ustav, MOO "Marii ushem"; V. D. Sharov, *Etnopoliticheskaia situatsiia v Respublike Marii El* [The ethnopolitical situation in the Republic of Mari El] no. 63 (Moscow: Institute of Ethnography and Anthropology, Russian Academy of Sciences, 1994), 5; and Ustav, *Erziansko-mokshanskogo obshchestvennogo dvizheniia Mastorava,* g. Saransk, 1989.

60. Marjorie Mandelstam Balzer, "A State within a State: The Sakha Republic (Yakutia)," in *Rediscovering Russia in Asia,* ed. Stephen Kotkin and David Wolff (Armonk, N.Y.: M. E. Sharpe, 1995), 143.

61. *Komsomol'skaia Pravda,* August 3, 1990; quoted in Ann Sheehy, "Russians the Target of Interethnic Violence in Tuva," *RFE-RL Research Report,* vol. 2 (September 14, 1990): 13–17.

62. Rogers Brubaker, cited in Mark Beissinger, *Nationalist Mobilization and the Collapse of the Soviet State* (New York: Cambridge University Press, 2002), 11.

2

Institutional Legacies and Language Revival in Ukraine

Alexandra Hrycak

Scholars of nationalism agree that there is no easy or predictable relationship among ethnicity, language, and national mobilization. Neither raw numbers nor economic conditions can explain when identities based on the dimensions of ethnicity and language become politically salient. The issue of what drives shifts in the political salience of language and other attributes is squarely on the agenda not only of this volume but also of analyses

Work on this chapter was facilitated by a Reed College Paid Leave Award, by financial support provided by the Reed College Levine Fund, and by the Kennan Institute of the Woodrow Wilson International Center for Scholars, which organized the Multiculturalism Workshop before which previous versions of this project were presented. The author is extremely grateful for helpful comments provided by many colleagues, including Dominique Arel, Laada Bilaniuk, Erin Hofmann, Nancy Popson, Blair Ruble, and the participants in the Multiculturalism Workshop. She also thanks Michael Flier and other participants for their comments on a version of the chapter presented at a 2004 session of the Annual Convention of the Association for the Study of Nationalities. Finally, she thanks Erin Hofmann and David Mandell for their patience and guidance during the final stages of revisions.

of identity politics throughout the world. In the introduction above, Arel, following Laitin, asks us to return to the question of how people came to conceive of themselves in relation to others in order to understand how current identities took shape in Ukraine and Russia.[1] In response, many of the scholars contributing to this volume examine how identities were fought over in the past by state agents and ethnonational entrepreneurs, and some also explore how the outcomes of these identity battles have influenced post-Soviet life in both public and private domains.

This chapter explores the impact of the institutional legacies of the past on the identities that are emerging in Ukraine. It focuses in particular on how these legacies have shaped the implementation and public reception of policies to revive the Ukrainian language. The revival of Ukrainian has been a matter of great political salience for more than fifteen years. During the final years of Soviet rule, intellectuals raised concerns over the disappearance of Ukrainian from schooling and many other realms of life. With the help of the independence movement, policies were introduced to encourage the reintroduction of Ukrainian. Since this time, the relative status of Russian and Ukrainian has been a recurring focus of political debate in this country.

Many accounts of Soviet and post-Soviet national mobilization lead us to expect that efforts to revive Ukrainian should have provoked protest among Russian speakers. This is because today Ukraine is home to the largest population of Russian speakers outside Russia. The use of Russian remains extensive in many elite domains, particularly in higher education, science, business, and the media. Young people still speak Russian almost universally in informal settings in many Ukrainian cities. Only among Western Ukrainians—who were never ruled by the Russian Empire—is Russian not widely used. Observers predicted that conflict between advocates of the Ukrainian national revival and defenders of the linguistic status quo should have escalated after independence and resulted in ever-deepening divisions in society. But many Russian speakers have accepted moderate forms of the Ukrainian language revival. Their acceptance of this revival has created an important source of stability and has decreased the salience of ethnolinguistic issues in everyday life. This outcome makes Ukraine an important case for understanding how potentially polarizing debates can be resolved without escalation.

In this chapter, I use schooling as a site for understanding why norms regarding ethnicity and language intersect in complicated ways that have created openings for moderate forms of language revival and may have foreclosed options for more polarizing forms of ethnolinguistic mobilization.

My focus will be on explaining why Ukrainians have accepted educators' efforts to promote the revival of Ukrainian in schools. In Ukraine, school language policy is based loosely on a 1989 law. This law mandated that schooling should be conducted in a child's native language, but it also guaranteed parents the right to choose their child's medium of instruction. However, after Ukraine became independent, educators made a gradual shift away from parental choice. They began instead to insist that schooling be conducted in a child's native language. As a result, today, at school entry, most schoolchildren are assigned to schools on the basis of their ancestry. This means that millions of children from Russian-speaking families are now being educated in Ukrainian. One might expect that this shift away from parental choice would provoke protest among Russian speakers. After all, elections in Ukraine are frequently dominated by politicians who consider the revival of Ukrainian to threaten the rights of Russian speakers in Ukraine. Yet no significant movement of parents or educators has formed to try to alter how educators have implemented this policy. In short, no effort has been made to defend parental choice against educators' expectations that children should be educated in the language of their ancestors.

To solve the puzzle of why this potentially contentious school policy has met with public acceptance, I argue that it is necessary to look beyond contemporary political debates and election rhetoric to examine the primary institutional legacies that shape educators' and parents' norms regarding language, identity, and schooling. The following analysis does so by exploring three of these institutional legacies. The first institutional legacy is of pre-Soviet origin: the emergence and acceptance of the norm that children should be educated in their native language. I will demonstrate that this "native language principle" was the accepted blueprint among educational elites for well over a century.

I will next examine two interrelated institutional legacies of Soviet origin that affect the legitimacy of alternatives to native language schooling: "parental choice" and blurred "Sovietized" identities. I will argue that many Ukrainian educators and scholars understood the policy of parental choice in a child's medium of instruction to be the Soviet state's alternative to the native language principle. They assumed that, through policies of parental choice, the Soviet state in reality promoted the Russian language rather than providing parents with genuine choices for their child's education.

Third, I demonstrate that Sovietization, or the imposition of Soviet identities, blurred boundaries between Russians and Ukrainians. As ethnic Ukrainians became "Soviet," they switched to Russian as their language of convenience. But this shift to Russian did not mean that they more strongly identified with "Russians" or "Russian speakers" as a group than they did with "Ukrainians" or "Ukrainian speakers." Instead, Sovietization required a renegotiation of identities. While for the most part Russian and Ukrainian nationality continued to be defined by ancestry, Russian and Ukrainian as languages came to have complicated and context-specific meanings and functions. As a result of the legacy of blurred Soviet identities, in post-Soviet Ukraine, many parents who speak Russian as a language of convenience do not have a strong preference for Russian rather than Ukrainian as their child's medium of instruction. Their preferences regarding Russian and Ukrainian in various social domains are not determined as simply as contemporary political rhetoric about "Russian speakers" and "Ukrainian speakers" suggests.

Understanding the influence of these three institutional legacies on policy preferences and identity formation after the Soviet Union's collapse is a vital first step for understanding the broader puzzle of why some identities and not others become polarized. My analysis of these institutional legacies has three main parts. First, I review recent literature on language politics in post-Soviet Ukraine. I lay out the logic of arguments that predicted conflict escalation after the Soviet state collapsed. Then I explain the general theoretical concerns that guide my exploration of the institutional legacies that have shaped norms regarding schooling and moderated how parents who speak Russian respond to the Ukrainian national revival. Second, I examine the processes of institutionalization that shaped schooling and language policy in Ukraine and made native language a defining attribute of how educators and others viewed nationality. Third, I explore how these institutional legacies moderated this country's divisions and created favorable conditions for the acceptance among parents of a moderate form of linguistic revival defined by the native language principle.

Two Explanations of Policy Formation during Legitimacy Crises

This section explores two contrasting explanations of how policy is made in the context of deep political divisions regarding identity issues. The first explanation I examine follows the logic of conventional social scientific arguments that assume that deep political divisions regarding identity create openings for state capture by extremist groups that escalate ethnic conflicts.[2] The second explanation I present is based on historical institutionalism and assumes that politics is based on battles for legitimacy that are often won by state bureaucrats who embrace preexisting conventions and norms. I argue that this second explanation is useful for understanding how the collapse of the Soviet Union led to the revival of the Ukrainian language. For the sake of convenience, I refer to the first explanation as the political escalation thesis and the second as historical institutionalism.

Many accounts of Soviet and post-Soviet national mobilization assume that deep political divisions regarding identity are likely to lead to the escalation of conflict. These approaches provide a useful starting point for understanding the shape of the new polities, political interest groups, and political institutions that emerged from the remnants of the Soviet Union. But such approaches overestimate the likelihood of state capture by the extreme political proposals that dominated electoral campaigns and parliamentary debates after the Soviet Union's collapse.[3] Were these approaches accurate, we would have expected Ukraine today to be much more polarized along ethnolinguistic lines than is the case.

In the 1990s, Ukraine seemed to be a prime candidate for ethnolinguistic schism. It inherited complex and potentially deeply divisive language problems from the Soviet Union. The Catholic and Ukrainian-speaking west seemed deeply opposed to the Orthodox east, with its high proportion of Russians and Russian speakers, on a broad range of issues. These regional divisions provoked great skepticism and concern regarding Ukraine's future once the Soviet Union had collapsed. Wilson, for example, dubbed Ukrainian nationalism a "minority faith" and deemed Ukraine the "unexpected nation" because of its high levels of ethnic, linguistic, and regional diversity and low level of national consciousness.[4] Some observers concluded that dangerous, militant forms of nationalism had emerged in Ukraine and were likely to escalate conflicts over identity. Others indicated that Ukraine was teetering on the brink of ethnic strife.[5] And indeed, among elected officials in Ukraine, the status of Russian has continued to be a matter of great salience. Proposals to make Russian a second official language have repeatedly surfaced in parliamentary debates and election campaigns. Pro-Russian-language political constituencies remain vocal and mobilize voters during elections. Conflicts over the Russian language's status have dominated parliamentary discussions of issues having to do with Ukraine's identity, and a pro-Russian-language platform has proven to be a useful tool in presidential elections.

Ukraine's politicians and its electorate remain divided along regional and linguistic lines.[6] Yet Ukraine has failed to adopt policies that are in line with the pro-Russian-language platform that powerful politicians and parties have tended to advance during elections and other times of political opportunity. Furthermore, the election of politicians who advocate pro-Russian-language policies has not led to changes in the basic logic of schooling policy adopted in 1989. Nor has the government's political elite pursued policies that have received the support of the various ethnolinguistic protest groups and political entrepreneurs that have sought to protect the interests of Russian speakers in Crimea and Eastern Ukraine. Instead, in the politically sensitive domain of schooling, language policy continues to be driven by a native language revival program that in important respects has been championed mainly by state bureaucrats and educators.

The weakness of support for Ukraine's state-mandated policies of linguistic revival among influential political actors presents a puzzle not only for the political escalation thesis but more broadly for approaches that assume that states construct and propagate policies that reflect the preferences of the actors who dominate, define, and win elections. Such discussions predict that ethnolinguistic divisions in politics almost inevitably escalate and lead to broader polarization. Elections and other periods of high political opportunity in Ukraine have indeed stirred up local expressions of ethnolinguistic assertiveness in many regions. But ethnolinguistic protest in this country has tended to die down immediately after elections. The politicization of language has not produced sustained, nationwide mass mobilization among Russian speakers or triggered a cascading tide of separatism. Extremists who argued for radical solutions have remained marginal and failed to spread beyond their initial power base (Western Ukraine in the case of Ukrainian hypernationalists, Donetsk and Crimea in the case of advocates of pro-Russian positions). Neither variety of extremism has gained the upper hand.[7]

A focus on elections overpredicts escalation. Studies that treat the present-day electoral process, ethnolinguistic entrepreneurs, and overall demographics as the main sources of pressure regarding what new rules should govern national identity after the demise of the Soviet state are not able to explain why states like Ukraine that faced conflicting ethnolinguistic demands did not adopt the extreme positions that actors who dominated elections seemed to favor. The development and public acceptance of the Ukrainian revival becomes less puzzling if we realize that lawmakers and pressure groups do not determine state policy on their own. State bureaucrats and administrators of state institutions also influence policy—particularly at times of deep political division. As Skocpol has long argued, state bureaucrats develop their own autonomous policy interests and their own conceptions of the public good. Their policy agendas are relatively autonomous from those that lawmakers and pressure groups propose. Normally, their ability to act in pursuit of these policy goals is limited. But it expands at times of deep political division among elected officials, politicians, political parties, and other powerful political actors. State bureaucrats can exploit such political divisions to pursue their own policy interests in defiance of the preferences of these other political actors.[8] To be effective at such times, however, state bureaucracies must pursue alliances with receptive politicians and groups that share their ideas.

Historical institutionalism is useful for understanding which ideas are deemed legitimate. This body of theory also helps explain why the ethnic and linguistic cleavages that dominated elections in Ukraine have not carried over into all social domains since the Soviet state's collapse. By taking into account a larger set of actors within the political system, historical institutionalists offer an alternative to arguments that assume that state breakdown creates opportunities primarily for extremism or state capture by groups that monopolize money, votes, or conventional political resources. Indeed, they have found that state breakdown, by contrast, creates legitimacy crises. Such legitimacy crises, in turn, also create favorable opportunities for states to adopt alternative policies that conform to models or blueprints for national development that state elites consider legitimate.[9]

Historical institutionalism argues that it is necessary to focus research on the development of normative arrangements—both formal and informal— that provide order and orientation to society and politics and that help to shape and moderate the outcomes of the activities of elected officials during legitimacy crises. Historical institutionalism thus offers a useful starting point for understanding how normative arrangements and organizational environments within which political systems are located shape and moderate identity claims.

Two broad hypotheses emerge from the above discussion. The first one argues that state breakdown and ethnolinguistic divisions create openings for policymakers to embrace the rhetoric of ethnic entrepreneurs who are prone to escalating ethnolinguistic tensions. My own approach suggests otherwise. Following the historical institutionalist model, I argue that state breakdown leads to legitimacy crises. Such crises create openings not only for ethnic entrepreneurship but also for institutional gatekeepers within the state to make their own autonomous policy proposals. These two groups operate with different interests and may espouse different templates or blueprints for policy. In short, at times of deep political division, there are potentially two broad sets of policy alternatives: proposals from ethnic entrepreneurs, and proposals from within state administrative institutions. I argue that the policies that win such legitimacy contests are often those that best fit institutional gatekeepers' conceptions of the public good. These conceptions cannot be determined a priori or by examining contemporary political rhetoric. They require an analysis of the development, articulation, and institutionalization of blueprints or models of national development. This is the subject of the following sections.

The Institutionalization of the
Native Language Principle

This section examines the process by which leading educators forged ideological commitments to native language schooling. My examination will demonstrate two points: that long before Soviet rule, leading intellectuals and educators in Ukraine came to view native language to be a defining attribute of nationality; and that they have long assumed education in a child's native language (rather than parental choice) to be the most legitimate basis for schooling policy. I also show that from the mid–nineteenth century on, Ukrainian educators responded to political devolution and liberalization with efforts to introduce Ukrainian as a medium of instruction.

Ukrainian educators' commitment to Ukrainian as both native language and medium of instruction in schools dates back to the second half of the nineteenth century. At this time, the Russian Empire ruled Eastern Ukraine and the Austrian Empire ruled Western Ukraine.[10] National mobilization among Ukrainians in both regions was initiated in response both to changing social, economic, and political realities that eroded the legitimacy of serfdom and dynastic rule, as well as to the local impact of two main models of nationalism and nationhood that emerged in Central and Eastern Europe at that time.[11] Polish, Hungarian, and other local national movements developed a model of "popular" nationalism. Advocates of this type of nationalism sought to break free of dynastic states and establish nation-states, each of which was to be defined as the homeland of a unique nationality that spoke a distinct native language. The Romanov Empire and other dynastic states responded to these irredentist challenges with an alternative model of nationhood, "official" nationalism. Through this second type of nationalism, dynastic states reconfigured themselves into nation-states by promoting an official state language and elevating the symbolic and political status of those who spoke it.

In emulation of the "popular nationalism" that Poles and neighboring nationalities developed, early advocates of the Ukrainian language soon began to question not only dynastic rule but also the model of official nationhood dynastic states promulgated. These "Ukrainophiles," as early supporters of the Ukrainian language were called, faced challenging conditions. Polish, Hungarian, Romanian, and other national movements as well as advocates of official nationalism all claimed local Ukrainians for their own nation-building projects. Even local Ukrainian clergy and church authorities—who were still in charge of the only schooling available in most local villages—at first opposed efforts to develop Ukrainian into a full-fledged standard language and introduce it into the school system.[12] But by the 1860s, leading educators and educational reformers began to believe that Ukrainian was not only a distinct native language but also more suitable than any other language as a medium of instruction for Ukrainian children.

Despite their emerging convergence on the native language principle, educators who wished to introduce Ukrainian into schools faced very different political conditions in the Austrian and Russian empires. Their belief that Ukrainian should be introduced into the school system was easier to act on in Western than in Eastern Ukraine. Long before Soviet rule, Ukrainian was introduced to the school system in Galicia. To attract public support to their cause, in the 1860s Western Ukrainian educators and intellectuals who supported education based on the native language principle formed the Prosvita (Enlightenment) Society, a federation of civic organizations.[13] Legal reforms brought about mainly by the pressure of Poles and other more mobilized nationalities created favorable conditions for these early advocates of Ukrainian schooling in the Province of Galicia. In 1873, the Galician provincial school board passed an act supporting the establishment of a free system of locally funded elementary schools in which instruction would be conducted in the pupil's native language. Ukrainian educators in close alliance with branches of the Prosvita Society and other like-minded civic organizations began to develop a rudimentary school system of teachers' seminaries and Ukrainian-language primary and secondary schools, as well as a network of rural reading rooms and schools for adults.[14]

By 1912, Ukrainian was the medium of instruction in more than 2,000 elementary schools and 10 secondary schools in Galicia. There were also several university chairs in Ukrainian studies. An estimated 20 percent of the adult population of Galicia belonged to the Prosvita Society, which ran nearly 3,000 libraries and reading rooms. Over time, this system of native language education had not only promoted strong national consciousness among Western Ukrainians but also attracted young aspiring intellectuals to careers of civic engagement and employment in the growing educational system.[15]

In the 1860s, educational reformers in the Russian Empire also began to introduce Ukrainian as a medium of instruction in Eastern Ukraine. Around the time of emancipation from serfdom, populists established dozens of private Ukrainian Sunday schools to raise literacy in the countryside. State officials concerned about "Little Russian separatism" soon closed these schools and issued directives that prevented the establishment of Ukrainian schools. They also put a stop to various other activities that were intended to introduce the Ukrainian language into schools. Eastern Ukrainian intellectuals continued to devote great energy to raising public support for native language schooling. Prominent scholars and intellectuals of Ukrainian descent argued that illiteracy remained widespread in rural areas because schoolchildren were taught in Russian, a language they understood poorly. But official decrees and state repression blocked these early efforts to introduce Ukrainian into schools.[16]

Throughout the second half of the nineteenth century and the early twentieth century, the Russian state denied Ukrainian the status of an independent language and prohibited its use in schools as well as more generally, in most public domains. In 1863, the Russian Ministry of Education prohibited all Ukrainian-language publications intended for a broad popular audience. It was argued that grammar textbooks and other publications aimed at spreading literacy in Ukrainian might lead the broader population to view itself as a distinct nationality and spur separatism. In 1876, the Russian state issued a second and even more repressive edict. The Ems Ukaz banned use of Ukrainian in all arenas of public life. It prohibited the importation of Ukrainian books from abroad, banned organizations that were associated with cultivating loyalty to the Ukrainian language, and led to the dismissal of leading advocates of the Ukrainian language who held positions at Kyiv University. It was only after 1905 that Russian state officials loosened earlier restrictions on the Ukrainian language. A few city-based Prosvita Society branches and a handful of private schools that requested permission to provide instruction in Ukrainian were formed.

The collapse of the Russian state in 1917 and a brief, unsuccessful attempt to establish an independent Ukrainian state permitted Eastern and

Western Ukrainian educators to expand the reach of the Prosvita Society system. Public response was positive. By 1921, the Prosvita Society's total membership had grown to 400,000 and branches had arisen in many rural localities in Eastern Ukraine. Prosvita's efforts to introduce vernacular schooling continued after 1920, when Eastern Ukraine became the basis for a Soviet Ukrainian republic under Bolshevik rule, while Western Ukraine was divided among Poland and neighboring countries until it was annexed by the Soviet Union during World War II.

Despite Bolshevik resistance to such activities, Prosvita and similar societies founded hundreds of rural primary schools in Eastern Ukraine and spread support for the institutionalization of native language education among the rural intelligentsia in Eastern Ukraine. Prosvita was dissolved by the Soviet state in 1922. But by then it had helped to pave the way for Soviet Ukrainian educators to adopt the native language principle. This became the blueprint for a moderate form of nationalism that encouraged public schools and other state educational organizations intended for Ukrainians to adopt the Ukrainian language, while allowing other nationalities to develop schooling in their respective native languages.

Soviet Schooling Policy: From the Native Language Principle to the Principle of Parental Choice

Soviet Ukrainian educators and their supporters in the Ukrainian Communist Party who sought to introduce the native language policy into schooling and other domains faced considerable resistance to their efforts.[17] They found that early Bolshevik leaders were reluctant to allow them to continue the reorganization of the school system they began after the collapse of the Russian Empire. The Bolshevik leadership tolerated the use of Ukrainian in villages but opposed broader state promotion—particularly in cities, which they considered important sites for socialist modernization that should remain Russian linguistic and cultural zones.

At first, Bolsheviks accused Ukrainian intellectuals and party leaders who advocated the broader use of Ukrainian in schools and other institutions of playing into the hands of the "reactionary powers" and the "bourgeois nationalists." However, in 1923 the Soviet central leadership responded to signs of growing popular unrest by deciding to make good on earlier promises to end Russification and raise the status of Ukrainian. Party leaders noted at this time that the intelligentsia and the countryside gave considerable support to raising the status of Ukrainian. To co-opt these groups, reluctant party leaders conceded to demands for Ukrainian to be introduced into schools, state institutions, and other realms.

During the period of "nativization" or "Ukrainianization," state policies introduced the native language principle throughout the republic. Soviet Ukrainian Party leaders publicly denounced the vestigial Russian imperialism implied by earlier Bolshevik promotion of the Russian language and culture. They commanded party members and government officials to learn to speak Ukrainian, show respect for the Ukrainian language and culture, and recruit Ukrainians into the party. Russified party officials and civil servants in cities resented official decrees that forced them to use Ukrainian in their work. However, many educators welcomed nativization. With the assistance of thousands of newly trained rural teachers and instructors, Ukrainian was introduced into a growing school system and many universities, until a majority of ethnic Ukrainian pupils and students attended Ukrainian-language institutions.[18]

In 1933, the Soviet state began to attack many aspects of Ukrainianization. Supporters of Ukrainianization were purged from the Commissariat of Education, scholarly institutes, and pedagogical institutes. The Soviet central state imposed a top-down reorganization of the educational administration. Thousands of Ukrainian schools and most universities were forced to move away from the native language principle and return to Russian as their medium of instruction.[19] Most urban primary and secondary schools adopted Russian as their primary medium of instruction.[20] Ukraine's educational institutions were reorganized and subordinated administratively to the Moscow-based All-Union Commissariat of Education. A 1938 decree made the Russian language a mandatory subject in all Soviet schools, greatly increased the number of hours of Russian instruction, and increased central state support for a territorially differentiated bilingual education system within which ethnic Ukrainians in cities were expected to study in Russian. Russian also began to be reintroduced as the language of instruction in post-secondary education. A 1958 law introduced a policy of "parental choice" in both the language of instruction and the study of other languages. Only in the countryside and in newly annexed Western Ukraine did most ethnic Ukrainians continue to attend Ukrainian-language schools. In cities elsewhere in Ukraine, the policy of "parental choice" compelled most children to attend either Russian schools or a new type of bilingual school in which Russian was in fact the primary language of instruction and Ukrainian was studied as a separate subject.[21]

By the time glasnost began, there were few schools with instruction in

Ukrainian in Eastern Ukraine's cities. Overall, more than half of all school-children in Ukraine were taught in Russian.[22] Ukrainian was rarely used as a medium of instruction in higher education except in the west, and even there, instructors were pressured to teach scientific and technical subjects in Russian. The almost universal use of Russian in universities and in positions of authority in most workplaces encouraged many parents to send their children to Russian or bilingual Ukrainian-Russian schools. Ukrainian was restricted more and more to rural or Western Ukrainian schools. Policy changes had made schools in which instruction was officially conducted in Ukrainian more reliant on Russian-language textbooks and other materials. Scientific and technical professional publications that had once been published in Ukrainian were increasingly issued only in Russian.

Schooling Reforms: Intellectuals and the Return to the Native Language Principle

The promotion of the Russian language in Ukraine caused considerable resentment. Russification was implemented in a way that alienated one stratum of Soviet Ukrainian society more than any other: educational administrators, educators, and writers. Leading educators and scholars continued to believe fervently in the native language principle.[23] They considered the policy of parental choice to mark a return to the Imperial Russian model of "official nationalism." But they found their ability to promote the Ukrainian language in education much diminished after the prominent party figures, scholars, and administrators who supported Ukrainianization were purged.[24] Many educators and writers remained committed to the native language principle. They resented Soviet efforts to displace Ukrainian from education and culture. But they were compelled by career pressure to write or teach in Russian.[25] For decades, they lacked a way to recoup their lost cultural and organizational autonomy.

Glasnost presented Ukrainian intellectuals with a political opportunity, a watershed moment in history that allowed them to develop the leverage to delegitimate promoters of the Russian language and initiate a return to the native language principle. Once glasnost was introduced, prominent Ukrainian intellectuals were quick to mobilize all resources at their disposal to demand a national revival. They used their access to unions, the media, the party, educational organizations, and other state-based organizations within which educators worked as bases for establishing independent organizations. These new organizations placed pressure on the republic's government to reintroduce Ukrainian literature and language as obligatory subjects in all the republic's schools. Reformers further demanded that the number of schools with Ukrainian as their principal medium of instruction be brought into correspondence with the ethnic composition of the republic. In their effort to reintroduce the native language principle to schooling, they were victorious.

The movement to revive the Ukrainian language initially took root among writers, scholars, and students in Western Ukraine and Kyiv. There, advocates of Ukrainian revival staged cultural events through which they raised funds and recruited members for the first civic organizations that were independent of the party and the state. They helped found several prominent cultural organizations in Western Ukraine that later spread to Kyiv. One of the most politically significant was the Taras Shevchenko Ukrainian Language Society (ULS). The ULS grew out of the Native Language Society (Tovarystvo Ridnoi Movy), which was established in L'viv in early 1988 and modeled on the earlier Prosvita Society.[26] Aided by networks of Western Ukrainian intellectuals and students, this moderate group helped overcome the Soviet Ukrainian government's campaign to portray the growing national revival movement as dangerous and militant. Through dozens of cultural and artistic events, the group encouraged support for a native language revival among Eastern Ukrainian intellectuals, in particular university students and members of the cultural and scholarly elite.

By the beginning of 1989, when the ULS held its first official inaugural congress in Kyiv, it had received the blessing of crucial allies in the party and the official cultural establishment. Its leader was a well-known poet who was a member of both the Writers' Union and the Communist Party, Dmytro Pavlychko. It received strong support from the Institutes of Philology and Literature of the Ukrainian Academy of Sciences. The ULS grew to become the largest civic group not under direct state and party control. By mid-1989, its size had increased from an initial membership of 10,000 to an estimated 70,000. By September 1989, the ULS had formed a coalition with other opposition groups, the People's Movement in Support of Perestroika, or Rukh. Rukh, which itself represented a total membership of a mere 300,000 at its height, would use its autonomy from the state and party to lead the political fight against the Ukrainian Communist Party leadership. In particular, students, writers, and educators who supported the native language principle and were affiliated with Rukh's moderate leadership were central in organizing the student hunger strikes and demonstrations that finally led the party leadership to step down and persuaded the Ukrainian parliament to support native language revival and later independence.[27]

In October 1989, Rukh—together with university students and influential scholars—organized mass protests in Kyiv. In response, Ukraine's Rada passed a constitutional amendment making Ukrainian the official state language (*"derzhavna mova"*) and adopted a law increasing the use of the Ukrainian language in public life. To alleviate concerns raised by groups representing non-Ukrainians and to increase public support for Ukraine's independence from the Soviet Union, the parliament also passed measures to reassure Russian speakers. These included promises of parental choice in a child's medium of instruction and a Special Declaration of the Rights of Minorities promising all citizens full rights to speak the Russian language and extending ethnocultural rights and the full use of minority languages wherever any ethnic group lived compactly.[28] These concessions helped the moderate nationalism of Pavlychko and his wing of Rukh to win the eventual support of influential allies in the party elite as well as the broader public. Ukrainian independence received overwhelming public support in a referendum following the Soviet Union's collapse.

Public Response to Schooling Policy in Postindependence Ukraine

Since Ukraine's independence, educational reformers at the helm of the Ministry of Education have initiated a return to native language education and moved away from the policy of parental choice.[29] The ministry's guidelines state that the proportion of schoolchildren attending Ukrainian-language schools must be brought into conformity with the demographic composition of the local population. The ministry's interpretation of school language policy has clear appeal to Ukrainian speakers. It affords them expanded opportunities to educate their children. However, it is less clear why Russian speakers would accept it. After all, by law, parental choice in education is an inalienable right.

Why has the return to the native language principle in schooling not led to more resistance among Russians or, more broadly, Russian speakers? If we follow the logic of the escalation hypothesis, the primary explanation of the effects of ethnocultural schism on politics, we might expect the highly uncertain social and economic conditions of the transition from Soviet rule to fuel language-based conflicts. Native language schooling policy also goes largely against the preferences of powerful political elites. When running for office, numerous politicians who represent Eastern and Southern Ukraine, including Leonid Kuchma and Victor Yanukovych, repeatedly expressed their dissatisfaction with pro-Ukrainian policies. A significant share of the public has voted for such politicians. Yet many voters who support these politicians seem to endorse or at least accept the native language policy as it applies to schooling. Indeed, many Ukrainians who speak Russian in daily life accept schooling reforms that require their children to learn a language they themselves do not speak at home.

Historical institutionism offers an explanation for why Ukrainians have accepted native language revival and why the gradual shift to Ukrainian at school entry remains an issue of low political salience in Ukraine.[30] After discussing public preferences for Ukrainian- as opposed to Russian-language schooling, I will build on the discussion of institutional legacies above to provide several chief reasons why Ukrainians who speak Russian have accepted the native language revival. These reasons result from all three main institutional legacies examined above: the native language principle, the policy of promoting Russian as if this were identical to parental choice, and blurred or hybrid "Soviet" identities.

First, it is important to note that the majority in Ukraine supports native language education (see table 2.1).[31] Other forms of native language revival have proved to be politically controversial. But among ethnic Ukrainians as well as ethnic Russians, native language schooling still receives more support than any other alternative. In 1999, the Kyiv International Institute of Sociology conducted a nationwide poll in which respondents were asked whether they would choose Russian, Ukrainian, or some other language as their child's medium of instruction in school. Most ethnic Ukrainians who were polled indicated a preference for Ukrainian-language schools, and most ethnic Russians indicated a preference for Russian-language schools. In other words, this poll suggests that the "native language principle" satisfies a clear majority of the population. More than half of ethnic Ukrainians indicated a preference for Ukrainian. Only a fifth preferred Russian. The remaining quarter indicated that they had no opinion (see table 2.1). Two-thirds of ethnic Russians indicated a preference for Russian as their child's medium of instruction. A tenth of ethnic Russians prefer Ukrainian and not Russian as a medium of schooling. This poll suggests that among both ethnic groups, the majority prefers native language schooling. The political constituency for "parental choice" is far smaller than the overall share of the population that speaks Russian as a language of convenience.

The private approval and acceptance of policies at least some ethnic Ukrainians vote against at election time may at first seem puzzling. But an explanation can be found if we consider the way Soviet legacies shaped the norms and expectations of the broader society and eased the popular acceptance of native language revival. Ukrainian state builders have adopted a model of nationhood that grounds national identity in an ancestral language and homeland. Nationality thus defined was already solidified or legitimated during the Soviet era. It was reinforced among all Soviet Ukrainian citizens both at the individual level, through passport nationality and the "native language" census category, as well as at the macroinstitutional level, through their residence in a territory that was identified as the homeland of Ukrainians.[32] Since Ukraine's independence, ancestral language and homeland continue today to be treated as enduring aspects of one's national identity, just as in the past.

What is more, in contrast to a century ago, very few people in positions of authority are willing to question publicly that Ukrainians and Russians are distinct nationalities or that Ukrainian and Russian are distinct languages. Even if many Ukrainians are aware that Soviet rule complicated or eroded the salience of their ancestral language and nationality, efforts to revive Ukrainian among future generations accord legitimacy among many in Ukraine. In short, many Russian-speaking Ukrainians do not resist the Ukrainian language revival more vigorously because they feel unambiguously that Ukrainian (and not Russian) is their native language. Somewhat similarly, they may feel that Russian is a language of convenience that they used under Soviet rule and will continue to use when necessary.[33] As the survey examined above suggests, only a minority of ethnic Ukrainians seem to feel unambiguously that they prefer Russian rather than Ukrainian as their child's medium of instruction.

Historical institutionalism argues that legitimacy crises create openings for models of national development that are deemed legitimate. Ukrainians who came of age during the Soviet era were socialized in a way that blurred or complicated the everyday salience of the national identity and native language they inherited from their parents and grandparents. But they became "Soviet" rather than Russian.[34] Few in post-Soviet Ukraine identify strongly with Russia.[35] The increased use of Russian among Ukrainians in the Soviet era was a response to the social and political incentives the Soviet state and

Table 2.1. The Preferred Medium of Instruction for My Child's School (percent)

Preferred Medium	Ukrainians	Russians
Ukrainian	56	11
Russian	19	65
Hard to say	10	10
No answer	15	13

Source: Kyiv International Institute of Sociology Omnibus Survey, February 1999.

its policies created. It was not the outcome of a dramatic personal choice or a deep political conviction that they should reject their nationality. It was a response to advancement opportunities in higher education, the military, the state bureaucracy, and many workplaces, which created powerful incentives to switch to Russian as the language of convenience. Ukrainians who feared that their children's advancement might be blocked because of a lack of fluency in Russian often felt their children should attend Russian-language or bilingual schools (and in many eastern cities, they had no alternative but to do this, as there were so few Ukrainian-language schools). Learning Russian was advantageous in the Soviet system.

In past decades, Ukrainian disappeared from public life and various state institutions shifted increasingly to Russian. The public use of Ukrainian became restricted in large urban centers to farmers' markets where local dialects predominated. As the number of contexts within which they heard and used standard Ukrainian diminished, the remaining speakers of Ukrainian began to lose fluency in the literary standard, relying increasingly on local dialects as well as Russian phonetic features, syntax, and vocabulary.[36] Some upwardly mobile Ukrainians in urban areas stopped speaking Ukrainian altogether because they lost fluency in the literary standard and did not want to be associated with peasants and uneducated people who spoke a dialect. As the result of both class anxiety and their waning knowledge of standard Ukrainian, such individuals who considered themselves Ukrainian by nationality were consequently embarrassed to speak Ukrainian and more likely to speak Russian. This group of Russian speakers may not find it convenient or natural to relearn Ukrainian, but many of its members are willing to support a Ukrainian revival among future generations.[37]

Today, incentives and opportunities have changed. Ukraine's independence makes competence in standard Ukrainian an increasingly important skill in the future. As proficiency in standard Ukrainian becomes necessary, parents' attitudes toward Ukrainian as a medium of instruction are slowly and gradually becoming more favorable. In other words, Russian speakers who do not speak Ukrainian may welcome the opportunity for their children to learn it, particularly now that independence has created advancement opportunities for Ukrainian speakers.

Shifts in opportunities make it imperative for at least some Ukrainians to brush up on their Ukrainian. Yet the Russian language's dominance in the broader society has made it difficult and perhaps even unnecessary for all Ukrainians to alter their current language practices or preferences in response to the Ukrainian language revival. Indeed one further reason why the public has accepted native language education is that reforms in highly Russified localities have proceeded primarily at school entry. Rather than forcing older pupils who were educated in Russian to switch to Ukrainian-only programs, educators have added more hours of instruction in Ukrainian and have established new elite college preparatory schools in which the medium of instruction is Ukrainian. Moreover, Ukrainian-language schooling has been introduced very slowly in regions that are hostile to the Ukrainian language revival.

The reintroduction of Ukrainian has had its intended effect in Western Ukraine and in many rural and small town schools, where most Ukrainian schoolchildren are now taught in Ukrainian. But in oblasts with a Ukrainian population of less than 60 percent, reforms have proceeded at a slow pace. In the period 1990–91, only 48 percent of schoolchildren nationwide were receiving education in the Ukrainian language. In 2002–3, the percentage was 73.5. The number of schools in which instruction is conducted in Ukrainian has increased considerably in past years; in 2002–3, 1,622 more schools offered instruction in Ukrainian.

However, the number of schools still has not been brought into concordance with the ethnic composition of the regions of Ukraine. In 2002, Ukrainian was the language of instruction in 220 out of 1,193 general education schools in Donetsk. According to the 2002 census, 56.9 percent of the population of Donetsk is Ukrainian. Similarly in Luhansk, Ukrainian is the language of instruction in 214 of 794 schools, while 58 percent of the population is Ukrainian. The proportion of children in Ukrainian-language schools in Crimea remains well below the target set by education policymakers.[38] In Crimea, 4 out of 575 education institutions conduct instruction in Ukrainian, while 24 percent of the population is Ukrainian. In Sevastopol, Ukrainian is the language of instruction in only 1 of 67 general educational institutions. According to the census, 22 percent of the city's population is

Ukrainian. Although such localities lag far behind state targets, Ukraine's state builders have done little to punish school systems that have not implemented the 1989 language law, thus avoiding further deepening divisions.

Accepting such local differences in implementation was a wise choice. It may explain why advocates of more extreme nationalism who reject the current policy have failed to generate a substantial public following among Russian-speaking Ukrainians. Despite their efforts to escalate tensions, groups that seek to challenge Ukraine's current language policies have failed to attract widespread popular participation or allegiance and are unlikely to grow stronger as a movement, in part because they seem reluctant to cooperate with one another. Various groups and leaders in Crimea and Eastern Ukraine have focused attention on language issues, but each has somewhat different goals from the others and most have a highly localized power base. There does not seem to exist a single set of leaders or groups able to attract the allegiance of a broad following or capable of forging a national coalition of groups that focus on language issues. Indeed, polls find a high degree of alienation from politicians and party politics as well as from civic groups that might seek to challenge state policies on language or ethnonational issues.[39]

Another crucial reason why Russian-speaking Ukrainians have accepted native language revival through schooling is that most political parties and blocs that support the revival of the Ukrainian language have avoided framing Ukrainian speakers and Russian speakers as two hostile camps. The activities of this moderate group may have helped to legitimate the native language principle that is now being institutionalized through schooling reforms. Moderates within the national independence movement and, later, those who helped form the Our Ukraine bloc, have taken great pains to make clear that they view both Russians and Russian speakers as important potential beneficiaries of genuine Ukrainian revival, because both groups would benefit from a prosperous Ukraine. Although the current model of nationhood these moderates adopt focuses attention on an aspect of identity that at least potentially divides the population along ethnic lines, their avoidance of inflammatory rhetoric has prevented advocates of more extreme measures from splitting Ukrainians along ethnic lines in daily life, and this undoubtedly helps to decrease the potential political friction caused by schooling reforms.

Finally, schoolchildren themselves have responded positively toward the particular form that the native language revival has taken. Children's attitudes toward Ukraine are being shaped by new cultural and literary works and by the popularity of Ukrainian-language hip hop ensembles and pop stars. During the past decade, Ukraine's cultural establishment has produced an impressive wave of films, memoirs, and books sympathetically depicting early writers and scholars who advocated Ukrainianization and documenting the extreme brutality with which Soviet authorities treated this group, which came to be called the "martyred renaissance" (*rostriliane vidrodzhennia*). Ukrainianization and its martyrs have swiftly reentered the school curriculum and seem to command legitimacy among a new generation of Ukrainians in both Western and Eastern Ukraine.

For all these reasons, the public and educators have accepted a policy of nation building modeled on a historic policy of Ukrainianization that enjoyed legitimacy among leading intellectuals, rather than adopting policies that corresponded more closely to the preferences of the competing political factions in postindependence Ukraine that failed to come to a consensus on Ukraine's identity as a state.

Conclusion

This chapter has asked why Ukraine accepted a policy mandating that schooling be conducted in a child's native language, rather than demanding that parents choose their child's medium of instruction. I argue that the language of schooling has not acted as a fulcrum for nationwide popular protest in Ukraine because educators have chosen to remain on a course of moderate nation building that encourages a slow and decentralized process of reviving the Ukrainian language that begins at school entry. I further argue that Russian-speaking parents have accepted a moderate native language revival because of the push and pull of the institutional legacies of the past, as well as because they see utility in their children learning Ukrainian.

Ukraine inherited complex and potentially deeply divisive language problems from the Soviet Union. It has quietly accepted—and legitimated —a school policy that closely resembles the model of national development adopted by Ukrainian intellectuals during the nineteenth century. The "native language" principle was only briefly and incompletely institutionalized during the first decade of Soviet Ukrainian rule. But it retained legitimacy. When perestroika and glasnost relaxed restrictions, a coalition of government bureaucrats and intellectuals took advantage of this political opportunity to recapture control over the organizational resources and personnel they needed to pursue the language revival. But educators have implemented this policy in a decentralized way. It has proceeded quickly in areas where Ukrainian was already spoken widely. But it is proceeding very slowly in Russified areas that feared, and continue to fear, draconian nationalist measures.

The above examination of Ukraine's first decade of independence has examined factors that worked to legitimate a moderate approach to linguistic revival and allowed the school system to handle Soviet legacies regarding language and identity in a way that did not escalate tensions regarding language. In the politically sensitive domain of schooling, Ukraine's educators have implemented the Ukrainian language revival in a gradual manner that may have displaced potential macrolinguistic cleavages to the local level, thus preventing ethnic Russians and ethnic Ukrainians from unifying around the language they both speak.[40]

Indeed, language behavior remains surprisingly unchanged at the interpersonal level in most large Ukrainian cities. By not provoking anxieties, state builders have initiated schooling policies that will be likely to broaden the use of Ukrainian in daily life in the future in Eastern Ukraine and, perhaps some day, in Crimea. Judging from its first decade and a half of linguistic revival, Ukraine will continue for some time to be a linguistically heterogeneous nation. But it is likely to exhibit surprising stability along a course of moderate national revival and not extremist or militant nationalism.

Furthermore, in the distant future, it is likely that if all things remain the same, current schooling policies and broader state efforts to improve the status of Ukrainian will slowly, quietly, and imperceptibly encourage Ukrainians to speak more Ukrainian. Because of the legacies of Soviet rule, the language revival is likely to be gradual and decentralized. Urban areas where Russian dominated for much of the twentieth century are likely to remain largely bilingual, although Ukrainian language proficiency will increase.

Notes

1. See, in particular, Kanchan Chandra and David Laitin, "A Constructivist Framework for Thinking about Identity Change," paper prepared for the conference "Modeling Constructivist Approaches to Ethnic Identity and Incorporating Them into New Research Agendas," Laboratory in Comparative Ethnic Processes 5, Stanford University, Stanford, Calif., May 11, 2002.

2. One leading example is Donald L. Horowitz. See his "Democracy in Divided

Societies," *Journal of Democracy* 4 (1993), no. 4: 18–38, and his *Ethnic Groups in Conflict* (Berkeley: University of California Press, 1985).

3. For a review of the main approaches as they apply to the case of Russia, see chapter 1 of the present volume by Elise Giuliano.

4. See Andrew Wilson, *Ukrainian Nationalism in the Nineties: A Minority Faith* (Cambridge: Cambridge University Press, 1997); and Wilson, *The Ukrainians: Unexpected Nation* (New Haven, Conn.: Yale University Press, 2000).

5. There are numerous examples of dire predictions for ethnic relations in post-Soviet Ukraine. Recall President George H. Bush's 1991 "Chicken Kiev" speech, in which he warned the Ukrainian parliament of the dangers of "suicidal nationalism." Similarly, the political scientist Benjamin Barber, in his best-selling *Jihad versus McWorld*, identified Ukraine as a prime example of a modern day "jihad." Barber contended that Ukraine's leaders, like Serbians, have rejected modern liberalism and fallen under the spell of what he calls "neo-tribal nationalism"; see Barber, *Jihad versus McWorld* (New York: Ballantine Books, 1996). David Laitin also predicted escalation in *Identity in Formation: The Russian-Speaking Populations in the Near Abroad* (Ithaca, N.Y.: Cornell University Press, 1998), 178–80, 185–87, 341–43. The sociologist of nationalism Rogers Brubaker, somewhat similarly, viewed Ukraine as a nationalizing state that was striving to adopt a definition of national membership that is closer to an "Eastern," ethnically exclusive ideal type than it is to the "Western" ethnically inclusive style. See Rogers Brubaker, *Nationalism Reframed: Nationhood and the National Question in the New Europe* (New York: Cambridge University Press, 1996).

6. Examinations have found that Ukraine's political system is more sharply divided along regional and linguistic lines than by ethnicity. See Ian Bremmer, "The Politics of Ethnicity: Russians in the New Ukraine," *Europe-Asia Studies* 46 (1994): 261–83; Dominique Arel and Valeriy Khmelko, "The Russian Factor and Territorial Polarization in Ukraine," *Harriman Review* 9 (1996): 81–91; and Stephen Shulman, "Cultures in Competition: Ukrainian Foreign Policy and the 'Cultural Threat' from Abroad," *Europe-Asia Studies* 50 (1998): 287–303.

7. See Anna Fournier, "Mapping Identities: Russian Resistance to Linguistic Ukrainisation in Central and Eastern Ukraine," *Europe-Asia Studies* 54 (2002): 415–33; Paul S. Pirie, "National Identity and Politics in Southern and Eastern Ukraine," *Europe-Asia Studies* 48 (1996): 1079–1104; Arel and Khmelko, "Russian Factor"; and Andrew Wilson and Sarah Birch, "Voting Stability, Political Gridlock: Ukraine's 1998 Parliamentary Elections," *Europe-Asia Studies* 51 (1999): 1039–68.

8. See Edwin Amenta and Yvonne Zylan, "It Happened Here: Political Opportunity, the New Institutionalism, and the Townsend Movement," *American Sociological Review* 56 (1991): 250–65.

9. See Theda Skocpol, "Bringing the State Back In: Strategies of Analysis in Current Research," in *Bringing the State Back In*, ed. Peter Evans, Dietrich Rueschemeyer, and Theda Skocpol (Cambridge: Cambridge University Press, 1985), 3–37; and Skocpol, *Protecting Soldiers and Mothers: The Political Origins of Social Policy in the United States* (Cambridge, Mass.: Belknap Press of Harvard University Press, 1992).

10. The idea that the population living on the borders of the Russian and Austrian empires could be divided into distinct nationalities defined by a common language and homeland can be attributed to the activities of various local writers and scholars operating with a new model of nationhood that they intended to utilize to emulate the examples of then dominant core states. See Wilson, *Ukrainians*.

11. On the emergence of these two contrasting modes of nationalism, see Benedict Anderson, *Imagined Communities* (New York: Verso, 1983); Eric Hobsbawm, *Nations and Nationalism since 1780* (Cambridge: Cambridge University Press, 1990); and Ernest Gellner, *Nations and Nationalism* (Ithaca, N.Y.: Cornell University Press, 1983).

12. On attitudes toward vernacular Ukrainian in Galicia, see Paul Magocsi, "The Language Question as a Factor in the National Movement," in *Nation-Building and the Politics of Nationalism: Essays on Austrian Galicia*, ed. Andrei Markovits and Frank Sysyn (Cambridge: Harvard University Research Institute, distributed by Harvard University Press, 1982), 220–38.

13. On the establishment and activities of Prosvita, see John-Paul Himka, *Galician Villagers and the Ukrainian National Movement in the Nineteenth Century* (New York: St. Martin's Press, 1988).

14. See Jozef Miaso, "Educational Policy and Educational Development in the Polish Territories under Austrian, Russian and German Rule, 1850–1918," in *Schooling, Educational Policy and Ethnic Identity,* ed. Janusz Tomiak (New York: New York University Press, 1991), 163–84; and Janusz Tomiak, "Education of the Non-Dominant Ethnic Groups in the Polish Republic, 1918–1939," in *Schooling,* ed. Tomiak, 185–208.

15. As Austrian civil servants, those who taught in the Western Ukrainian educational system benefited from favorable work conditions that made education an attractive occupational choice for Galician national activists, many of whom were children of impoverished peasants or village deacons or priests. See Himka, *Galician Villagers.*

16. See Bohdan Krawchenko, *Social Change and National Consciousness in Twentieth-Century Ukraine* (New York: St. Martin's Press, 1985), 25. For a concise discussion of the Russian state's role in schooling and its impact on the Ukrainian language in the Russian Empire, see Krawchenko, *Social Change,* 24–29.

17. Stalin, aware that such a policy seemed to contradict earlier Soviet campaigns against nationalism, maintained that nativization programs would later be phased out, and that "we who are in favor of the fusion of national cultures in the future into one common culture (both in form and content), with a single common language, are at the same time in favor of the blossoming of national culture at the present time." See Walker Connor, "Nation-Building or Nation-Destroying?" *World Politics* 24 (1972): 319–55. See also Steven L. Guthier, "The Popular Base of Ukrainian Nationalism in 1917," *Slavic Review* 38 (1979): 30–47.

18. See George Liber, *Soviet Nationality Policy, Urban Growth, and Identity Change in the Ukrainian SSR, 1923–1934* (Cambridge: Cambridge University Press, 1992).

19. See Krawchenko, *Social Change,* 135–38.

20. For overviews of Soviet education policy changes and how they affected the status of Ukrainian and other non-Russian languages, see Dominique Arel, "Language and the Politics of Ethnicity: The Case of Ukraine," Ph.D. dissertation, University of Illinois at Urbana-Champaign, 1993; Yaroslav Bilinsky, "The Soviet Education Laws of 1958–59 and Soviet Nationality Policy," *Soviet Studies* 14 (1962): 138–57; Brian Silver, "Social Mobilization and the Russification of Soviet Nationalities," *American Political Science Review* 68 (1974): 45–66, and Silver, "The Status of National Minority Languages in Soviet Education: An Assessment of Recent Changes," *Soviet Studies* 26 (1974): 28–40. For a discussion of bilingualism as the new norm in Soviet urban schools, see Barbara A. Anderson and Brian Silver, "Equality, Efficiency, and Politics in Soviet Bilingual Education Policy: 1934–1980," *American Political Science Review* 78 (1984): 1019–39.

21. In the late 1970s, central state campaigns and migration further reinforced the trend toward Russian language use in schools. Increased migration from Russia and other republics to Eastern Ukraine's industrial cities also laid the foundation for more extensive use of Russian in Ukraine's cities. Children of migrants attended schools within which Russian was the language of instruction, and thus acted as a further Russifying force in Ukraine's industrial cities. The number of bilingual and Russian schools and the overall hours of Russian instruction increased steadily throughout the republic. Russian became the preferred language of instruction, play and extracurricular activities even in Ukrainian-language kindergartens and in primary grades in schools. See Yaroslav Bilinsky, "The Soviet Education Laws of 1958–59 and Soviet Nationality Policy," *Soviet Studies* 14 (1962): 321–23. In Ukrainian-language city schools as well as in bilingual city schools, the number of subjects that were taught in Ukrainian decreased sharply. Many Ukrainian-language schools in cities were closed or reclassified as bilingual Ukrainian-Russian. Universities, polytechnics, and vocational schools also decreased the number of subjects taught in Ukrainian, with most universities becoming de facto Russian-language institutions.

22. See Volodymyr Kulyk, "Revisiting A Success Story: Implementation of the Recommendations of the OSCE High Commissioner on National Minorities to Ukraine, 1994–2001" (Hamburg: Centre for OSCE Research, Institute for Peace Research and Security Policy at the University of Hamburg, 2002), 11; and Roman Solchanyk, "Russians in Ukraine: Problems and Prospects," in *Cultures and Nations of Central and Eastern Europe: Essays in Honor of Roman Szporluk*, ed. Zvi Gitelman (Cambridge, Mass.: Harvard University Press for Ukrainian Research Institute, Harvard University, 2000), 544.

23. Ivan Dzyuba most eloquently made this point in his classic *Internationalism or Russification* (New York: Monad Press, 1970). But even supporters of Russian nationalism who associated closely with dissidents and critics of the Soviet state were aware that this policy was introduced in a way that smacked of "Russification." For a broader discussion of this point, see Anatol Lieven, *Ukraine and Russia: A Fraternal Rivalry* (Washington, D.C.: U.S. Institute of Peace, 1999).

24. There is no definitive estimate of how widespread or strong support for Ukrainian-language promotion continued to be among educators and scholars in Ukraine during the decades following the end of Ukrainianization. My own interviews with state cultural administrators, theater studies scholars, theater institute instructors, and managers and personnel in city theaters in L'viv, Kyiv, and Kharkiv suggested that overt state promotion of the Russian language through edicts and administrative measures was usually conducted in a clumsy, heavy-handed way that resulted in resentment and often bolstered commitment to the Ukrainian language among those who had been mentored by survivors of the 1930s purges. Among the hated measures most frequently mentioned to me in the course of my interviews were unwritten rules that compelled all employees of artistic and cultural institutions in Soviet Ukraine to praise Russian works and feature them prominently in their work. Usually, this was achieved by always pairing any Ukrainian work with a corresponding Russian work on a similar topic. Yekelchyk reports a similar finding of resentment against clumsy administrative measures promoting Russian culture in his study of Soviet Ukrainian opera. See Serhy Yekelchyk, "Diktat and Dialogue in Stalinist Culture: Staging Patriotic Historical Opera in Soviet Ukraine, 1936–1954," *Slavic Review* 59 (2000): 597–624.

25. Benedict Anderson's theory of Creole nationalism in Latin America and Bohdan

Krawchenko's argument about national mobilization in Soviet Ukraine both rest on similar assumptions and claims that blocked mobility has a powerful reinforcing effect on peripheral national mobilization.

26. See Wilson, *Ukrainian Nationalism,* 230 ff.

27. Students and intellectuals placed great importance on raising the prestige of the Ukrainian language. For an analysis of the model of nationhood they developed, see Alexandra Hrycak, "The Coming of 'Chrysler Imperial': Ukrainian Youth and Rituals of Resistance," *Harvard Ukrainian Studies* 21 (1997): 63–91.

28. Kulyk, "Revisiting a Success Story," 14.

29. On post-Soviet schooling policy, see Jan Germen Janmaat, *Nation-Building in Post-Soviet Ukraine: Educational Policy and the Response of the Russian-Speaking Population* (Utrecht: Netherlands Geographical Studies, 2000).

30. As noted above in my review of two contrasting explanations of policy formation in societies that are politically divided, prominent theories argue that rapid social change, in particular increasing economic uncertainty and deteriorating living standards, are conditions that intensify ethnolinguistic conflict.

31. It is difficult to gauge the strength of support for schooling in Ukrainian among ethnic Ukrainians from just one poll. However, other polls conducted at other times further support my finding that most ethnic Ukrainians prefer Ukrainian as a medium of instruction. A September 1992 survey of public opinion in L'viv, Kyiv, and Sevastopol suggests that schooling in Ukrainian received very strong support in Western and Central Ukraine, but very little in Southern Ukraine. An overwhelming majority of ethnic Ukrainians polled in L'viv and Kyiv supported sending their children to schools in which Ukrainian was the medium of instruction. However, only 37 percent of ethnic Ukrainians in Sevastopol preferred to send their children to a school in which Ukrainian was the medium of instruction. See Bremmer, "Politics of Ethnicity," 277.

32. See Brubaker, *Nationalism Reframed.*

33. According to the most recent Ukrainian census of 2001, 85 percent of ethnic Ukrainians consider their native language to be Ukrainian and 14 percent consider it to be Russian, while 96 percent of ethnic Russians chose Russian and only 4 percent chose Ukrainian. See Derzhavnyi komitet statystyky Ukrainy, *Richna statystychna informatsia. Naselennia* (Kyiv: Derzhavnyi komitet statystyky Ukrainy, 2001).

34. Catherine Wanner, *Burden of Dreams: History and Identity in Post-Soviet Ukraine* (University Park: Pennsylvania State University Press, 1998).

35. Lieven cites a 1994 Democratic Initiatives poll in which people were asked who they "generally identified with." Only 3 percent indicated "the people of Russia," while 34 percent said "the people of the former Soviet Union" and 34 percent said "the people of Ukraine." See Lieven, *Ukraine and Russia,* 45.

36. See Laada Bilaniuk, "Speaking of Surzhyk: Ideologies and Mixed Languages," *Harvard Ukrainian Studies* 21 (1997): 93–118.

37. Indeed, according to one empirical study, most Kyiv university students more often speak Russian with their friends than the general public in this city. However, they are far more likely to endorse stronger state support for the revival of the Ukrainian language. See Hanna Zalizniak and Larysa Masenko, *Movna sytuatsiia Kyieva: Den' siododnishnyi ta pryideshnii* (Kyiv: Kyiv Mohyla Academy, 2001).

38. See V. K. Symonenko et al., *Pro rezul'taty analizu stanu vykonannia kompleksnykh zakhodiv iz vsebichnoho rozvytku ukrains'koi movy, planuvannia ta vykorystan-*

nia koshtiv Derzhavnoho biudzhetu Ukrainy ta ikh vprovadzhennia (Kyiv: Rakhunkova palata Ukrainy, 2003). Available at http://www.ac-rada.gov.ua/Ua/44/2003.

39. On the public's alienation from politics and civic life, see José Casanova, "Ethno-Linguistic and Religious Pluralism and Democratic Construction in Ukraine," in *Post-Soviet Political Order,* ed. Barnett Rubin and Jack Snyder (New York: Routledge, 1998), 85; and Mykola Riabchouk, "Civil Society and Nation-Building in Ukraine," in *Contemporary Ukraine: Dynamics of Post-Soviet Transformation,* ed. Taras Kuzio (Armonk, N.Y.: M. E. Sharpe, 1998), 90–91.

40. See Wilson, *Ukrainians.*

3

"Russian Islam" and the Politics of Religious Multiculturalism in Russia

Katherine Graney

Due to its particular pattern of historical development, Russia has for most of its existence been faced with the challenge of managing an ethnically diverse and geographically dispersed population. However, in the post-Soviet period, the Russian state confronts its multiethnic and multiconfessional population for the first time as a self-described democratic state. Having claimed the status of a democracy, Russia now faces the challenge of constructing new ways to effectively represent the political, cultural, and religious needs of the roughly one in five Russian citizens who are not ethnic Russians. At the very heart of this task is the issue of how to most effectively engage the country's largest religious minority, the estimated 15 to 20 million Muslims who live within the borders of the Russian Federation.[1] The questions of religious minority rights in general and Muslim minority rights in particular are important aspects of the larger debate about democratic citizenship theory,[2] and they currently feature prominently on the political agenda in states such as France, Germany, and the United Kingdom.[3]

This chapter examines the challenges and the opportunities that face the

Russian state as it seeks to "remake the traditional compromises" that have guided relations between the state and its Muslim minority.[4] Much changed and quite challenging international and domestic political circumstances, the difficult legacy of a brutal atheist regime, and the rapid growth and proliferation of Islamic communities and institutions in Russia all complicate the state's efforts to create new regimes of religious multiculturalism. Furthermore, though there is substantial agreement among political and religious actors at both the federal and regional levels in Russia that as part of any attempt to accommodate religious rights and needs in the new democratic context the Russian state is justified is, indeed, obliged to patronize, protect, and promote some Islamic actors and forms of Islamic practice while simultaneously delegitimizing others, there is less consensus about what such a state-sanctioned realm of "Russian" Islam should look like.

Two major different proposed versions of what a truly "Russian" form of Islam is and how to best develop it currently exist in Russia. The first is a regionally based, bottom-up strategy promoted primarily by political and religious elites from the Republic of Tatarstan and based on the early-twentieth-century Muslim modernist movement that emerged from that region. The second, formulated by researchers affiliated with the Volga Federal District head Sergei Kirienko in Nizhnii Novgorod, is a much more top-down, centralizing vision, one that seems equally as concerned with consolidating the Moscow's social and political control over Russia's Muslims as with developing functional religious institutions for them.

The choices that the Vladimir Putin administration makes in constructing a realm of official, state-sanctioned "Russian" Islam will have important consequences for the future of Russia as a democratic and federal state. The challenge of crafting a legitimate and meaningful regime of religious governance for Muslims in Russia—one that does not allow corporate and individual rights to religious liberty to be swept aside in the face of state security concerns—is a daunting one. As Dominique Arel notes in the introduction to this volume, federal elites in Moscow must be cognizant of the danger that they might inadvertently harden religious cleavages in Russia during this process. In this respect, it is useful to examine the experience of two other states that have taken different approaches in their "official" relationships with Islam in their states: Turkey, which embodies a maximalist approach of attempting to control all aspects of Islamic life; and France, which represents a more minimalist approach to state administration of Islam.

Democracy and Religion in Russia

Although it is necessary to recognize that a "perfectly secular state" never exists, the militantly atheist Soviet regime came close to that ideal, first dismantling and then subjecting to close and hostile state scrutiny and control the meager remnants of the Orthodox, Muslim, Buddhist, Jewish, and other religious institutions in Russia.[5] Thus, one of the most important tasks facing the new Russian state upon the demise of the USSR was to create a more democratic and productive relationship between different religious confessions and the state. Concerns about how to negotiate the "leading role" historically reserved for the Russian Orthodox Church in Russian society weighed heavily in decisions regarding the formation of religious policy.

Equally as problematic is the issue of what role Islam and the Muslim minority will play in the process of defining new national and state identities for Russia in the post-Soviet period. For several reasons, including the rise in the global "clash of civilizations," the sovereignty-seeking activities of Russia's Muslim republics, and the partial "Islamization" of the conflict in Chechnya, debates over Islam and Russia's Muslim minority have become intensely politicized in the past decade. Indeed, the question of how the Muslim minority "fits" in the new Russia has perhaps replaced even Russia's eternal and destructive history of anti-Semitism as the most contentious and potentially violence-provoking religious problem facing the country.[6]

How multiethnic and multiconfessional states can create regimes of religious governance that will simultaneously allow different confessional groups to exercise their rights to religious profession and practice while also fostering common civic identities and loyalties to the state is a question of great interest to contemporary democratic theorists.[7] Among the insights that are most relevant for the Russian case are the following: First, if there exists a majority or traditionally favored confessional group that has a "special" relationship to the state, minority confessions will require their own particular types of recognition by and relations to the state.[8] And second, absolute secularism is an illusion, and as such, fostering a greater public voice for all religious voices, both majority and minority, within the framework of a democratic political system, is a crucial aspect of a mature, functional multiculturalism, and one of the markers of a truly diverse public sphere in a democratic society.[9] Also persuasive is the argument that creating more effective and representative institutions that mediate between the

state and its religious, and in particular its Muslim communities, will promote integration and political participation in society on the part of these
groups.[10]

Russia's Post-Soviet Regime of Religious Governance

Although the 1993 Russian Constitution and the 1997 Law on the Freedom
of Conscience and Religious Association in Russia have done an admirable
job of laying the legal basis for a functional set of church–state relationships
in Russia, with regard to the Muslim minority in particular, this system remains largely unrealized and its implementation delayed by both a lack of
political will on the part of the Russian state and by developments both inside and outside Russia. The principles of both multiculturalism and religious tolerance are enshrined in the 1993 Russian Constitution. Article 3
states that the "multinational" people of Russia are the source of the state's
sovereignty, and whereas article 14 establishes Russia as a secular state
where "no religion may be instituted as state-sponsored or mandatory," and
all religions are "separated from the state," it also establishes the equality
of all religions before the law. Article 28, meanwhile, guarantees to all citizens the "freedom of religious worship, including the right to profess, individually or jointly with others, any religion, or to profess no religion."
    In practice, these legal principles have been embodied in the creation of
a type of "official pluralism" that provides some measure of religious diversity and tolerance in Russia, but a measure that is "limited, regulated and
controlled by the state, and [that does not] challenge the supremacy of the
Orthodox Church."[11] Specifically, religious confessions in Russia have
been divided into two categories. Creeds considered "traditional" to Russia, including Orthodoxy, Islam, Judaism, and Buddhism, are afforded some
degree of state sanction and legal protection. All other creeds thus deemed
"not traditional" to Russia are considered morally and legally suspect in the
country. Specifically, the controversial Russian Federation Law on Freedom
of Conscience and Religious Association, adopted on October 1, 1997, recognizes the "special role of Orthodoxy in the history of Russia and in the
establishment and development of its spirituality and culture," while simultaneously "respecting Christianity, Islam, Buddhism, Judaism and other
religions which constitute an integral part of the historical heritage of the
peoples of Russia."[12] Some found the reservation of a "special role" for the
Russian Orthodox Church in public life in Russia troubling.[13] However, in

practice, the church has not turned this declarative recognition of its special role into formal political influence, instead "eschewing active campaigning, forbidding clerics to run for office, and refusing to endorse specific candidates or parties."[14] Rather, in exchange for official recognition of its role as "guardian of national morals and identity," the Russian Orthodox Church hierarchy has "implicitly blessed the democratic process," requiring only that the state continue to "defend a sense of Russian identity that is based in part on Orthodox values."[15]

In accordance with their special designation of Islam, Judaism, and Buddhism as "traditional" faiths in Russia, both the Russian Orthodox Church and the Russian government have fostered ties with officially recognized representatives of these confessions, ties that are guided by what appear to be a simple set of rules. In exchange for their total loyalty to the Russian state and their acceptance of the special role of Orthodoxy in Russian society, state-sanctioned representatives of these other confessions will be spared the type of harassment and persecution other "nontraditional" groups face and will even be given a limited symbolic presence and consultative role in Russian politics and public life.[16]

To facilitate this relationship, Putin has established both an Interreligious Council and a Presidential Council on Cooperation with Religious Organizations. The Interreligious Council has been a key player in the debate over religious education in Russia, successfully lobbying the Ministry of Education in the spring of 2003 to replace the controversial proposed "Fundamentals of Orthodoxy" course with the more multicultural "Fundamentals of Religious Doctrines" curriculum.[17] Yet, despite giving some degree of state recognition, legal standing, and state support to the three other "traditional confessions" in Russia, and thus establishing at least the rudiments of a regime of religious pluralism, the influence of these structures remains quite limited and their efficacy doubtful, especially with regard to the Russian state's relations with its Muslim minority and the Muslim religious leadership in the country.

Islam and Politics in Post-Soviet Russia

Like Muslim minorities in other Western democracies, Russia's Muslim population is marked by great ethnic, linguistic, and sectarian diversity. Yet Russia's Muslim minority is significantly larger than that of any other Western democracy—France's Muslim population is estimated to be from 3.5 to

5 million,[18] Germany's is about 3.3 million,[19] while the United Kingdom's is home to more than 1.5 million Muslims.[20] Though like its European neighbors, Russia has many Muslim residents who do not hold citizenship (mainly refugees from Central Asian and the Caucasus),[21] in general, for Russia the cultural and social divides that separate Muslims from the rest of the country are much smaller and present less of a challenge in terms of finding solutions to both multicultural and security dilemmas than for other Western democracies. Yet Russia also faces its own unique challenges in attempting to create new and effective regimes of religious pluralism regarding its Muslim population.

Because space does not permit a full discussion of the history of relations between the Russian state and its Muslim minorities throughout the Tsarist and Soviet periods, it will have to suffice to observe that it is a history that ranges from the outright persecution and forced conversion of Muslims in Russia to a grudging accommodation of Muslim demands for the provision of their civil rights and religious needs as supposedly equal citizens of the Russian polity. During the Tsarist era, one Muslim Spiritual Board, established in 1789 in Ufa, served as the state's main mechanism for co-opting and controlling Muslim clergy and Muslim populations, while during the Soviet era this system was expanded somewhat to manage the affairs of the Muslims of the USSR.[22]

The degree to which these spiritual boards functioned as agents of Soviet power and control is reflected in their charters, each of which contained exhortations for all Muslim believers to engage in patriotic activity and to fulfill their obligations to the Soviet state.[23] In exchange for their political quiescence, Islamic elites who worked within the four Soviet Spiritual Boards were afforded contacts with the wider Islamic world, albeit heavily supervised and extremely limited ties. However, all the Spiritual Boards remained woefully underfunded, were lacking in educational and administrative resources, and were also subject to constant supervision and infiltration by the Soviet state. Thus they were in no way "able to cope with the assignments they were expected to perform," and the number of well-trained Muslim clergy available to serve the USSR's large (and growing) Muslim population dwindled drastically throughout the years of Soviet rule.[24] These inadequate provisions for the administration and practice of Islam, coupled with the Soviet state's extensive antireligious and pro-atheist campaigning, radically weakened the salience that the category "Muslim" held as a marker of self-description for Soviet Muslims (see Arel's introduction).

It has become commonplace to refer to a great "revival" occurring among Russia's Muslim communities since the collapse of communism, giving the impression that the category "Muslim" enjoys new power as both a means of self-identification and as a social and political category in Russia. And indeed, it is clear that the term is appropriate—given the proliferation of the number of officially registered and unregistered Muslim communities in Russia (as of January 2003, there were 3,700 communities officially registered, with estimates of up to 3,000 more nonregistered Muslim communities existing in Russia),[25] the number of reopened and newly built mosques in the country (5,500 in 1998, as opposed to fewer than 200 in 1989),[26] the increase in the number of Islamic educational institutions in Russia (more than 106 Islamic religious schools in 1998, including 5 "Islamic universities" in Moscow, Dagestan, and Kazan, and more than 100 madrassas throughout Russia),[27] the number of Islamic centers providing cultural and educational services to Muslim populations (more than 50 as of January 2003),[28] the number of Muslims from Russia making the hajj annually (more than 10,000 a year from Dagestan alone),[29] and the increased availability of Islamic literature in Russia.

Yet it is important not to overestimate the impact or misconstrue the forms of the Islamic revival in Russia. In particular, it is necessary to stress that this process has occurred mainly at an elite level, in a top-down manner, and that it is intimately connected with the struggle for power within Russia's regions and between the regions and the center in Moscow. This is evidenced by the proliferation of "independent," regional-level Muslim Spiritual Boards, sixty-seven of which were registered with the Ministry of Justice as of January 1, 2003. The establishment of these regional institutions is closely associated with the process of sovereignty seeking among Russia's Muslim regions in the early 1990s, when having one's own independent Muslim Spiritual Board was considered both an important trapping of statehood and an integral part of the internal process of ethnonational revival in the Muslim republics such as Tatarstan and Bashkortostan.

A second factor influencing the appearance of so many regional institutions of "official" Islam were the rich streams of resources coming into Russia in early 1990s from around the Islamic world, and the desire of both political and religious elites in Russia's Muslim regions to capitalize on those resources and the opportunities they presented. Galina Yemelianova has referred to these actors as "New Muftis," because many of them appeared to be, like their secular "New Russian" counterparts, "self-obsessed, over-materialistic, corrupt and theologically incompetent, more interested in their own power than in truly representing and administering to the Muslim population in Russia."[30]

Several federal-level umbrella organizations seeking to play a unifying role or at least a dominant role at the all-Russia level of Islamic politics have also emerged in Russia in the post-Soviet period. The Soviet-era Spiritual Board of Muslims of European Russia and Siberia, located in Ufa, Bashkortostan, was renamed the Central Spiritual Board of the Muslims of the Russian Federation, and its Soviet-era head, Mufti Talgat Tadzhuddin, then became the self-proclaimed "grand mufti" of all Russia. Three lower-level Muslim administrative boards, one serving the Muslims of the European part of Russia, one serving the Muslims of the North Caucasus region of Russia, and one designated for the Muslims of Asiatic Russia, were also created in the early 1990s and were, theoretically, subservient to Tadzhuddin's Central Spiritual Board in Ufa.

A serious challenger to the inherited authority of Tadzhuddin's Ufa-based organization emerged on the scene in Moscow in 1996, namely, the Council of Muslims of Russia (CMR). The CMR was founded by Mufti Ravil Gainutdin, who still serves as its chairman. Ironically, Gainutdin is also the head of the Spiritual Board of Muslims of European Russia, and thus is theoretically subservient to Tadzhuddin in the "official" hierarchy of Islam in Russia. However, Gainutdin's Moscow-centered organization has quickly become a powerful rival to Tadzhuddin's board, and relations between the two muftis and the two organizations are openly hostile. The two muftis refuse to appear together at public functions, and each routinely accuses the other of corruption and incompetence. Tadzhuddin portrays Gainutdin and the CMR as "radicals" and "Wahhabists" who promote Islamic extremism and terrorism in Russia, while Gainutdin and his allies criticize Tadzhuddin for his self-promoting and slavish attempts to please the Russian state and Russian Orthodox Church officials, such as renaming his organization the "Central Spiritual Board of the Muslims of Holy Rus,'" which he did in early 2003.[31] These two organizations compete strenuously for the loyalty of local and regional Muslim communities, and yet it is difficult to determine the exact numbers pledging loyalty to each—there appear to be significant numbers that do not belong to either Tadzhuddin or Gainutdin's organizations, instead choosing to give their loyalty to regional bodies such as the Coordinating Center for the Muslims of the North Caucasus, which was founded in 1998 and claims 2,000 member organizations.[32]

Wahhabism and "Alien" Forms of Islam in Russia

In most discussions of the Islamic revival in Russia, the element that one hears about more than any other is of course Wahhabism. There are, in fact, some true or at least "self-proclaimed" Wahhabist communities in Russia, although it is necessary to stress that this often-misused label is actually employed in Russia to cover a diverse and multifaceted array of groups, many of which prefer the label "*salafi.*"[33] Indeed, federal elites have chosen to employ almost indiscriminately the terms "extremist," "alien," and "Wahhabist" to any Muslim community or institution that does not have an "official" tie with a federally recognized Islamic administrative body or that has links to foreign nationals.[34] The accusation of such affiliations often has served as enough legal pretense to close various mosques and Muslim educational institutions, while little effort is expended on close investigation of actors and institutions that have been placed in the various unacceptable categories.[35]

One intriguing (and potentially disturbing) aspect of efforts to define and neutralize "unacceptable" forms of Islam in post-Soviet Russia by the imprecise use of the terms "Wahhabism" and "extremism" is the support that both political elites and religious leaders from all Russia's Muslim regions (including the Middle Volga and the North Caucasus) have given to it. There appears to be substantial agreement that "extremist," "alien," and "Wahhabist" elements are universally recognizable and universally deplored in Russia, which represents a rare coincidence of center–periphery interests. Consequently, regional governments have moved to shut down so-called Wahhabist institutions on their territory. For example, in 2000 Tatarstan adopted a stringent set of standards governing Islamic educational institutions in the republic, which resulted in the closing of all but eight madrassas, while in conjunction with federal authorities Bashkortostani leaders have closed down several Bashkir-Turkish lyceums and expelled virtually all foreign-born Islamic personnel from the republic.[36] Likewise, after some self-proclaimed Wahhabist communities participated in the armed raids on Dagestan in September 1999, the republic outlawed Wahhabism and invited federal authorities to help with the eradication of "extremism" on its territory.[37]

Remaking Relations between Islam and the State: A Tale of Two Islams

If there is a consensus among federal and regional political and religious elites about the danger of "Islamic extremism," there is less agreement about how best to create a new apparatus of "official" Islam in Russia that will foster the development of an indigenous, "authentically Russian" form of Islam in the country in the post-Soviet context. Indeed, the center's efforts in this realm are complicated by the fact that various federal and regional actors are competing to gain the available spoils of this process for themselves—spoils that include prestige, protection, and funding, as well as international and domestic patronage opportunities.

The following section explores two different ways that the process of reconstructing an official Islamic sphere could occur, each of which harbors a different vision of what a new form of "Russian" Islam would look like and how it would be administered. The first is a decidedly federalist, regionally driven, bottom-up vision led by the Republic of Tatarstan, which would base a new form of state-supported Russian Islam on a neo-jadidist form of what it calls "Euro Islam," a vision that would accommodate and celebrate the ethnic and regional diversity of Russia's Muslim communities. The second path is decidedly more centrist, based on Sergei Gradirovskii's controversial program entitled "Russian Islam," which grew out of Sergei Kirienko's Volga Federal District Center for Strategic Research in Nizhnii Novgorod. These two proposed models for the construction of a state-sanctioned Islamic sphere in Russia are radically different paths for the future of relations between the Russian state and its Muslim communities and between the center and the regions in Russia.

Tatarstan and the Idea of "Euro-Islam"

As was mentioned above, the Tatarstani government has attempted to prove itself a loyal ally to Moscow in the battle against unacceptable and illegitimate forms of Islam in the country, repeatedly assuring central authorities that "no religious extremism or Wahhabism of any type" exists in the republic.[38] Yet, motivated in part by the effort to shore up the gains in political and economic sovereignty that it gained during the Yeltsin era, and in part by a genuine desire to reconnect with the Islamic world and to continue the revival of Tatar language, history, and culture that it began in the 1990s, Kazan has also been extremely proactive in asserting itself as the potential home for any new administrative structures of "official Islam" in Russia *and* as the potential center for the development and propagation of new forms of indigenous Russian Islam. Both religious and political elites in Kazan possess a vision wherein while Kazan would serve as the administrative hub and center of Islamic scholarship and education in Russia, other Muslim regions would have autonomy to nurture their own versions of Russian Islam in their own languages and according to their own idioms, as long as they stayed within the limits delineated by the Tatarstan model of a highly ecumenical, tolerant, "Euro" form of Islam.

The role of the center in such a paradigm would be to provide the resources necessary to allow a regionally inspired, bottom-up, coordinated system of administrative and educational institutions to emerge among Russia's Muslims, and to give these institutions official state sanction. In short, such a vision is based on and would reinforce the principles of federalism introduced during the Yeltsin era and enshrined in the Russian Constitution and the treaties signed in the mid-1990s. In exchange for allowing and even helping the regions to construct a new system of official Islam in Russia (as with other aspects of Russian federalism in the post-Soviet era, the regions have tempered their calls for autonomy with requests for Moscow's financial and institutional support in this venture), the center would receive guarantees that the regions would continue to monitor and police the development of the greatly feared unofficial, extremist, "non-Russian" types of Islam in their midst.

In pretending to the role of leader of the process of redefining official Islam in Russia, the Shaimiyev regime in Tatarstan has consistently portrayed the republic as the home of what it has variously called Tatar Islam, Euro Islam, or Russian Islam, a religious worldview that draws heavily on the Muslim modernist movement called jadidism, which emerged in the late nineteenth and early twentieth centuries. Jadidism was an indigenous Russian variant of the broader movement among Muslims worldwide to engage modernity and to respond to the challenge of Western imperialism. Though the movement was centered in Kazan and largely founded by Volga Tatars, who were the most well educated and literate of all Russia's Muslims at the time, it quickly spread throughout the empire, from the Crimea to Central Asia.[39]

The modernist, moderate, and reformist discourse of jadidism was propagated by "a diverse group," yet jadidists across the Russian Empire were united by the fact that "to a person, they agreed that the cultural community with which they identified most, the Islamic, was faced with economic, social, intellectual and political challenges necessitating an urgent response."[40] The entity presenting those challenges was of course modern Western civilization, embodied locally in the Russian imperial state. Jadidists largely accepted that Muslim communities in the Russian Empire were in fact guilty of the stagnation, ignorance, backwardness, and fanaticism that European and Russian critics charged them with, while Europe and Russia functioned for jadidists as models of civilization and progress to be emulated by the Muslim world.[41] Jadidists argued that all aspects of Islamic society, but particularly the traditional Muslim educational system, needed radical reform if Russia's Muslims ever hoped for "full participation in the world being built by modern science and capital," or to achieve a more just, tolerant, and ultimately prosperous way of life.[42] Rather than withdrawing from modern European society out of fear and hostility, jadidists argued, Muslims in Russia should reform, adapt, and modernize, and thus "join the stream of global civilization."[43]

During the past decade, the Shaimiyev administration in Tatarstan has actively promoted the revival of jadidist ideas, offering the jadidist legacy as evidence that, because of its "unique historical and ethno-confessional history," Islamic civilization in Tatarstan developed in a way which fostered the most "universalist," "tolerant," and "integrationist" aspects of the Islamic faith.[44] The Tatarstani developmental path is openly contrasted with the evolution of Islam in the "Muslim East," which is criticized for its "emphasis on high theology."[45] The Shaimiyev regime also claims that while jadidist-type, modernist Islam may have been born in the Middle Volga region, in fact it is "indigenous" to all Muslims in Russia, not just Tatars.[46] Thus the "Russian" or "Euro" form of Islam that Tatarstan promotes is a type of neojadidism, where jadidist ideas have been conveniently updated to fit the exigencies of the newest manifestation of Westernization and modernization: globalization.

In June 2001, the Republic of Tatarstan and the Organization of the Islamic Conference (OIC) jointly sponsored a conference in Kazan celebrating over a millennium of Islamic civilization in the Volga-Ural Region, at which it was announced that negotiations were under way for Tatarstan to be given observer status at the OIC.[47] In his keynote speech to the conference, Tatarstani president Mintimir Shaimiyev praised jadidism as a unique contribution to the history of world Islam, and he cited jadidism's continuing relevance to the Islamic world. According to Shaimiyev, jadidist ideas were crucially important for the current age because jadidism sought to "open people's minds to the connections between East and West," because it "emphasized democracy and market economics," and because jadidists understood the importance of "technology and interconnectedness." Shaimiyev went on to say that Tatars and all Russian Muslims had a duty to fight "negative images" of Islam and to create a "new and positive" image of the faith that would "tell people the truth about the heart of Islam," namely, that Islam was a religion of "tolerance and modernity."

In his speech at the conference, the head of the Spiritual Administration of the Muslims of the Republic of Tatarstan (known as DUMRT), Mufti Gusman Ishaki, echoed Shaimiyev's words. He proudly told a story about an American journalist who came to Kazan to do a story on Islamic extremism in Russia and who, after "seeing what we had here in Tatarstan," left Kazan vowing that he would, "tell everyone he met that Islam in Kazan is how Islam should be." Ishaki ended his remarks by charging Tatars with the mission of "showing the sincere, true face of Islam to the world," namely, the face of "kindness and peace, not of terrorists in green headbands with machine guns yelling 'Allahu-a-Akbar.' " Tatarstani presidential adviser Rafael Khakimov's speech at the conference most clearly explicated the tenants of Kazan's version of Russian or Euro Islam. According to Khakimov, the future of Islamic development in Tatarstan and Russia as a whole entailed "absorbing and utilizing the values of the West" to better benefit from its economic and educational prowess. Khakimov also suggested that Tatarstan, due to its "unique historical and geographical conditions," had a special role to play in facilitating and easing the interaction between Muslims and Europeans in the twenty-first century.

The Tatarstani conception of Russian or Euro Islam is an explicit repudiation of the more traditionalist, legalistic forms of Islam that are found in much of the Middle East, such as Wahhabism, and it is consciously designed to align both Tatarstan and Russia with the more modernist and moderate versions of the faith found in Turkey and Southeast Asia. Tatarstan's leadership openly admits that it seeks to emulate Turkey's model of a successful, modern, and democratic state that honors and respects but is not ruled by its Islamic heritage—the Tatarstani parliament's 1999 decision to Latinize the Tatar alphabet (a decision that the Russian Duma has formally protested and apparently rendered illegal by passing a Cyrillic-only law in November 2002) was based on the desire to consciously align Tatarstan with Turkey and its progressive Islamic image.[48]

Significantly, other Muslim elites from around Russia have also argued that indigenous "Russian" Islam as practiced in their regions is also modernist and moderate. For example, the head of the Spiritual Board of Dagestani Muslims, Mufti Ahmad-Haji Abdullaev, has claimed that the "extremism" of Wahhabism is "totally incompatible" with Islam as it is "traditionally practiced" in Dagestan, and he has decried the fact that Dagestan, "where the first mosque on the European continent was built," and which used to be known as "the sea of knowledge of Islam," was now identified with the "atrocity of Wahhabism."[49]

In their efforts to position their republic as the potential administrative and educational center for a revived system of Russian Islam, Tatarstani religious elites also have cultivated strong contacts with Ravil Gainutdin's Moscow-based CMR. Tatarstan's Mufti Ishaki is listed as a cofounder, along with Gainutdin on the organization's Web site, and many of the main personages in the organization are ethnic Tatars who hail from, reside in, or were educated in Tatarstan. This is also true of the Moscow-based Union of Muslim Journalists, which was founded in May 2003 and is an open supporter of the CMR and Kazan's theological vision for "Russian Islam."[50] Thus Tatarstan, more so than other Muslim regions, has positioned itself strongly to wield influence over the process of restructuring an official Islamic sphere in post-Soviet Russia. The other important regional Muslim body, the Coordinating Center of the Muslims of the North Caucasus, has been weakened by interregional rivalries and power plays, and it has also tried to play both Gainutdin and Tadzhuddin's federal-level organizations against one another, a strategy that has backfired to some extent by leaving it somewhat isolated at the federal level.[51]

Tatarstan has strong incentives to continue to push forward in its quest to build a "bottom-up," region-led "official," Russian Islamic realm. Playing the "Euro" or "Russian" Islamic card is in fact one of the strongest strategies that Kazan can employ as it seeks to maintain or expand the political and economic privileges it received during the Yeltsin era. Reestablishing ties with the Islamic world is one of the best ways that Tatarstan can foster patronage and protection in the international community, resources that it can use to protect the more controversial aspects of its sovereignty-seeking project (the revival of Tatar language, history, and culture; and the Latinization of the Tatar alphabet) from the recentralizing imperatives of the Putin administration.

More problematic for the future success of this strategy is the question of how receptive other Muslim regions in Russia will be to the idea of Kazan becoming the center of a renewed "Russian Islam"—particularly Bashkortostan, whose capital Ufa has traditionally been the center of "official" Islam in Russia; and the North Caucasus, whose regional histories and Islamic theology and practices differ significantly from those of the Middle Volga region. Though historically Kazan has been home to the most intellectually and economically vibrant Muslim community in Russia, religious and political elites in other regions are somewhat resentful of the Volga Tatars' self-proclaimed "leading role" in reconstructing Russian Islam, and thus any hegemonic predominance by Kazan in this process might well be met with significant opposition.

More so than a lack of political will in Kazan or potential objections from other Muslim regions (which would almost certainly be given wide latitude to develop regional programs in local languages and idioms in any bottom-up, region-based program of revitalizing Russian Islam, even if Tatarstani political and economic elites continued to lead the process from Kazan), it is the Russian government's traditional impulse toward centralization and unitary government, which was only briefly abandoned under duress during the chaos of the Yeltsin era, that sheds doubt on the possibility that such a Tatarstan-directed program of recreating an official Russian Islamic sphere in the country will come to any sort of fruition. Though Putin has endorsed some of the Tatarstani initiatives regarding Islam, no large-scale programs or plans have yet emerged that would take Kazan's ideas and institutions and use them as a blueprint for a federation-wide renewal of Islamic education and administration.

In fact, Moscow has probably given support to Tatarstan's initiatives more because of a lack of a federal-level alternative than because of a genuine conviction that such a program is the best way to reconstruct the "official" realm of Islam in Russia. Furthermore, given the moves that the Putin administration has made in other policy realms that are aimed at recentralizing governance in Russia and depriving the regions of sovereignty (including the movement in the Duma to mandate Cyrillic script for all non-Russian languages in Russia), it seems highly unlikely that in the realm of Islam, the center would give unreserved, systematic, or sustained support to a bottom-up, region-led program of Islamic revival in Russia.

Gradirovskii's Program of "Russian Islam"

There are signs that at least some members of the federal government are decidedly uncomfortable with the idea of an official Islamic realm that would be developed from the bottom up in Russia. Specifically, a Nizhnii Novgorod think tank called the Center for Strategic Research, supported by the head of the Volga Federal District, Sergei Kirienko, has recently developed a program titled Russian Islam that would reconstruct an official Islamic sphere in Russia through a much more top-down, center-led process than the one initiated and envisioned by Tatarstan and the other Muslim regions.

The Nizhnii Novgorod program, authored by Sergei Gradirovskii, has been criticized by some Muslim (and non-Muslim) intellectuals in Russia as "insulting," and as representing a neo-imperial "onslaught" against Muslims in Russia, one that seeks ultimately to destroy them by reasserting strict state control over their religious and political lives.[52] Some of this skepticism regarding the Gradirovskii program is indeed warranted; however, there are other aspects of Gradirovskii's vision that may potentially be helpful as a guide for the future development of a coherent vision of a revived realm of official Islam and a specifically "Russian" form of Islam for the country.[53]

According to Gradirovskii, his program is based on observations and research about the trends governing the development of Islam in Russia in the post-Soviet period. Thus, he asserts that the conclusions presented in 'Russian Islam" are not ideological in nature, but rather are based on reasoned judgments derived from reflection upon empirical processes. The first and most important characteristic of what he calls the renaissance of Islam in Russia is that it is a *specifically Russian-speaking phenomenon;* according to him, because of the great ethnic diversity among Muslim communities that gather in Russia's urban centers (many of whose members are immigrants or refugees from the Central Asian states or from the North Caucasus), Russian has emerged as the lingua franca among Muslims, used for preaching and association in mosques and in publications and other mass media directed at Muslim populations in Russia.

For Gradirovskii, the evolution of Russian-language use among Muslims in Russia represents more than just a pragmatic response to a communications challenge; instead, it represents the beginning of the development of an entirely new "community of identity," the "Russian-speaking umma," which he envisions blossoming into a locus of scholarship and education for the rest of the Muslim world and a prospective source of "geo-cultural cooperation on a global scale." He argues that a revived Russian school of Islamic theology and law could have a "progressive" influence on Islam worldwide, and he imagines a time when thousands of students a year will come from the Islamic world to study "Russian Islam" (he compares this with the phenomena of students from developing countries coming to the "communist Mecca" of the USSR to study during the Soviet era).

The creative and sometimes inspiring vision of what a revitalized Russian-speaking umma (or what Gradirovskii calls "Russia's own umma") could be is the most useful part of the Nizhnii Novgorod proposal. Gradirovskii's attempt to think about how such a revived Islamic intellectual and faith community could contribute to both the overall development of progressive Islamic trends among the umma and to the development of a genuine multiculturalism in Russia—one where the adjective "Russian" celebrates diversity and signifies "entire cultural-civilizational phenomena and not just a shrunken, mono-ethnic, mono-confessional core," thus embracing Islamic as well as Orthodox elements—is a gripping and important one that should be a part of any serious discussion about the future of Islam in Russia.

That said, however, it must be emphasized that other elements of Gradirovskii's program do not seem informed by the same professed quest to create a future where Russia is "not afraid to strengthen the power of its internal diversity" and where Russia is pushed to understand itself as a "truly multi-ethnic and multi-confessional society." For example, his analysis includes the dubious assertion that "Russia's national republics are slowly but steadily becoming homogenized in favor of the titular populations" and that this process presages the "enclavization" and even potential "Balkanization" of Russia. Further threatening state security and social stability in Russia, according to him, is the fact that the number of Muslims coming into European Russia from "Southern origin points" (i.e., the North Caucasus and Central Asia) will "undeniably keep increasing" in the future, necessitating a comprehensive response from the central state in Moscow.

The policy directives given by Gradirovskii in his "Russian Islam" program also suggest that a more centralizing impulse informs his entire project. He argues that the federal government must take control of the process of Islamic education in Russia, establishing a set of state standards and curriculum for departments of Islamic theology at Russian universities, and that tuition at these institutions must be conducted only in Russian. The ultimate goal, he states, is to create a "unified educational space for Muslims" in Russia, encompassing standards, methods, subjects, and textbooks. Though the scope of state involvement necessary to achieve this unified educational space might give pause to those fearful of the historically heavy hand of the Russian and Soviet governments in such matters, Gradirovskii does suggest that Tatarstani scholars and scholars from other Muslim regions should be consulted by federal officials in shaping these standards.

Gradirovskii recommends that the federal government should also create a nationwide, Russian-language "Islamic mass media complex" in the country. As part of this project, the federal government would also put resources toward the development of a "competent, honest and objective" corpus of religious (Islamic) journalists and would delineate a clear policy governing the publication of Islamic materials in Russia. Finally, Gradirovskii calls for a radical revision of policy regarding "charitable" resources that come into Russia from other Muslim countries—what he calls "all financing that enters Russia from the South." In his view, all such funds must now be regarded by the federal government as being "a priori hostile," and if not outright banned, must be subjected to "a clear and strict set of regulations about use."[54]

Several aspects of Gradirovskii's program, from its title to its conclusions, have been criticized by Muslim and non-Muslim observers alike. For example, Ali Vyacheslav Polosin, the head of the Union of Muslim journalists of Russia, complained that the very title of Gradirovskii's program betrayed his ignorance and imperious attitude, because "Islam was given to all people and cannot be given a 'national characteristic.'"[55] Polosin also argued that the program was insulting to "ethnic" Muslims in Russia by implying that Russifying them was better than allowing them to develop "within their centuries-old national-cultural traditions." Similarly, I. V. Ponkin, director of the Institute of State-Religious Relations and Law in Moscow, called Gradirovskii's program a "provocative" gesture, whose calls for state control of the Islamic educational system were nothing but a thinly veiled attempt to assert centralized political control over Russia's Muslims.[56] Ponkin instead asserts that only Russia's Muslims themselves can direct the development of Islamic theology, education, and practice in Russia, arguing that any Islamic institutions, publications, or personnel associated with the central government in Moscow would immediately carry negative connotations for Muslims, and thus drive more and more of them to embrace the types of "extremist and radical" Islam that both the center and regions want to avoid.

An understanding of how (and how successfully) other countries have dealt with the problem of creating "official" Islamic regimes can shed additional light on the choice currently facing Russia—the choice between more or less centralized, top-down approaches. Thus, the following section examines the experience of two democracies whose approaches to religious multiculturalism in the Islamic sphere contrast quite sharply—Turkey and France.

Islam–State Relations in Turkey and France

In its approach to Islam, the modern Turkish state has privileged its security needs, including the imperative to preserve the principle of secularism, over the democratic imperative of allowing various Islamic voices to develop and be heard freely in Turkish society. To this end, the 1937 Kemalist Constitution created an extensive and well-funded Directorate of Religious Affairs that has since served as the "interpreter and executor" of an established, bureaucratized, "enlightened," and highly secularized form of "official" Islam, which does not challenge either the primacy of secularism republicanism in the lives of individual Turkish citizens or the leading role of the army and state in Turkish society.[57] The Directorate of Religious Affairs funds and administers all 80,000 mosques in Turkey, and all Imams in Turkey attend state-run educational institutions and are treated as civil servants.

Although some criticized the level of state control over Islam in Turkey as overbearing and undemocratic,[58] even this "maximal" level of attempted state control over Islam has not been entirely successful. Despite the lavish funding and the maintenance of an extensive network of state-sponsored mosques, "alternative" Islams still emerged in Turkey in 1970s and 1980s as vehicles for protest against the perceived economic, political, and cultural failures of the Kemalist project. However, the state's earlier efforts to sanction and privilege certain forms of Islam over others have largely succeeded, a fact to which the almost total absence of Islamic-inspired terrorist violence in Turkey attests.

The French government shares Turkey's deeply entrenched commitment to secularism. However, in marked contrast to Turkey, the French government has only recently abandoned its almost entirely "laissez-faire" approach to its Muslim minority. Though France's Muslims for the most part locate their geographic roots in the French colonies of Algeria and Morocco, this group is itself characterized by great ethnic diversity and by economic disadvantage—most French Muslims are poor, urban, and concentrated in ghettos.[59] Due both to the state's lack of an "official" relationship with its Muslim minority and to the fact that many French Muslim communities retain close ties to their states of origin, virtually all mosques in France are funded by foreign sources (e.g., the main Paris Mosque is almost entirely funded by Algeria), whereas few Imams in France speak French, and fewer still hold French citizenship.[60]

After the Islamic-inspired terrorist bombings in the Paris subway in the summer of 1995, the state began to seek ways to improve relations with and increase government oversight over its Muslim minorities. And though the security imperative has guided many of the policy changes that the French government has introduced during the past few years (French officials openly admit that they now have infiltrated and maintain surveillance over all the country's mosques),[61] the government has also made efforts to make the French democracy more responsive to the needs of its Muslim minorities. More ambitiously, the government has recently voiced its intention to help foster a form of "French Islam," or an "Islam of France," that is, in the words of the interior minister, Nicolas Sarkozy, "progressive, modern and liberal," and that will fight and replace the type of "foreign-inspired" Islam that currently exists in France, which Sarkozy characterized as the "Islam of the cellars and garages, the clandestine Islam that feeds and funds extremism."[62]

To this end, in February 2003 France established a democratically elected central governing body, the French Council for the Muslim Religion (there are also democratically elected regional affiliates of this organization), which is charged to work with the government to increase the number of French-trained, French-speaking imams in France; to decrease the influence of foreigners in French Muslim communities; and to make it easier for Muslims to have their religious needs (e.g., education and dietary concerns) attended to in France.

The voluntary and democratic approach of this venture into religious multiculturalism in France is commendable, yet the hazards of a less intrusive state approach to relations with its Muslim minority are evident in the French example as well. The new French body is already showing signs of internal strain and potential paralysis, with moderate delegates claiming that more extremist elements have "hijacked" the council and that the French government thus faces two equally bad choices—to continue to work with the extremist elements in the hope of co-opting them, or to mitigate the extremist influence by appointing more "mainstream" representatives and risk alienating the radicals even more.[63]

Conclusions: Which Russian Islam?

The heated reaction of Russian Muslims to Gradirovskii's program of Russian Islam (not to mention the historical record from both the Tsarist and Soviet eras) suggests that any Putin-administration efforts to create an official realm of "Russian Islam" that are too closely associated with federal officials, or that are suspected of carrying an overt centralizing political agenda, will be met with cynicism, apathy, and even outright opposition by Muslims in Russia. However, the same historical record suggests that

Moscow will most likely pursue just such a centralizing course, thus resembling the Turkish model for managing Islam in a democratic context more than the French version (Putin's usurpation of Tatarstan's role as the Russian liaison to the OIC is evidence of this trend). Indeed, the Turkish experience suggests that it is possible to accommodate a greater state role in the administration of religious life within a democratic framework.

Furthermore, both central and regional Islamic elites in Russia themselves have at various times called on the federal government to help the country's Muslims create a new and authoritative set of institutions to handle questions of mosque construction, the Hajj, dietary and other ritual concerns, contacts with the wider Islamic world, and, most important, the question of Muslim education at all levels in Russia.[64] In Turkey, the state provides generously for all these institutional needs. In Russia, none of the Muslim regions, even Tatarstan, which seeks to become the center of Islamic administration and education in Russia, possesses the material or bureaucratic resources necessary to create such a revitalized network by itself—only the Russian federal state does. However, Russia could improve significantly on the Turkish model by drawing on the French example and cultivating a genuine partnership between the federal government and the Muslim regions in the process of constructing an "official" Islamic sphere in Russia.

The issue of curricular and personnel policy in madrassas and Islamic universities in Russia is a sensitive one, wherein religious liberty and intellectual freedom must be honored in more than token ways, and where the state's professed concerns about security and Islamic "extremism" are not allowed undue influence. For Russia, the relevant question is: "Should all Muslim institutions in Russia have a uniform, state-approved curriculum based on the modernist, neojadidist interpretation of what is defined as 'Russian' Islam, like that found at the Russian Islamic University in Kazan (as Gradirovskii proposes and as is the case in Turkey)?"

The idea of centralized state control of religious curriculum may seem reminiscent of Soviet-era controls on religion, and thus may seem to carry the same risk of both failing to meet the true religious needs of Muslims in Russia and alienating them from the official state religious apparatus. However, if such a national set of Islamic curricular guidelines was developed by Russian Muslim elites themselves, in conjunction with both Russian and foreign Islamic scholars, it might serve not only as a counterweight to the spread of more "foreign," politically extremist forms of Islam in Russia but also provide the basis to resurrect, preserve, and share with the wider Islamic (and non-Islamic) world the unique Russian forms of Islamic history, philosophy, and theology that developed there in the centuries before communism (as Gradirovskii envisions in his program). Conversely, in addition to violating international and Russian constitutional norms about religious liberty, a heavy-handed, overly politicized and clumsy attempt to enact such curricular standards from above could have an effect exactly opposite that intended by the promotion of an official "Russian" form of Islam, driving Russian Muslims to seek sources of religious interpretation and instruction outside the state's official Islamic realm.

The very idea that the creation of an official, national Islamic (or any other confessional) realm by a modern state is necessary, desirable, morally permissible, or even possible is highly debatable. And yet, in the particular case of Russia, the consequences of not giving the political, religious, and educational needs of Russia's Muslim minorities the serious attention they demand could be quite serious (namely, that this void will continue to be filled by "foreign" and "extremist" forms of Islam and that Muslim alienation from the Russian polity may thus increase). Therefore, confronting the normative and practical challenges that will certainly arise in creating new institutions of "Russian Islam" nevertheless seems preferable to the alternative of standing by idly while neither the democratic commitments nor the security needs of the Russian state are moved forward.

Notes

1. The question of how many Muslims actually live in Russia is a disputed one. Before the October 2002 census, federal officials, including Putin himself, had been quoted as saying the number could be as high as 20 million. Though the census did not ask about religious affiliation, estimates derived from inferences about ethnicity and religion judged the number of Muslims in Russia to be at about 14.5 million. This revelation was met with anger by Muslim leaders in Russssia, who argued that the census failed to account for the "potentially millions" of Muslims from Central Asian countries that are in Russia illegally. On this question, see Liz Fuller, "Russia's Ethnic Groups By the Numbers," *Rfe/RL Russian Political Weekly* 3, no. 46, November 19, 2003; Il'ya Maksakov, "Musul'manskiye Milliony," *Izvestiya,* November 12, 2003; "Skol'ko Muslulman v Rossii?" *Tatarskii Mir* (Moscow), December 11, 2003.

2. See, e.g., Will Kymlicka and Wayne Norman, eds., *Citizenship in Diverse Societies* (Oxford: Oxford University Press, 2000); Will Kymlicka, *Multicultural Citizenship* (Oxford: Oxford University Press, 1995); and Jacob T. Levy, *The Multiculturalism of Fear* (Oxford : Oxford University Press, 2000).

3. See Nezar Al Sayyad and Manuel Castells, eds., *Muslim Europe or Euro Islam: Politics, Culture and Citizenship in the Age of Globalization* (Lanham, Md.: Lexington

Books, 2002); and Shireen T. Hunter, ed., *Islam: Europe's Second Religion; The New Social, Cultural and Political Landscape* (Westport, Conn.: Praeger, 2002). Also see the speech by the president of the EU Commission, Romano Prodi, to the Fondazione Don Tonino at Lecce, Italy, June 13, 2003, "The European Project in the World," in which, while affirming the Christian heritage of Europe, he stresses the necessity of increased dialogue "with Islam." Catalogued on-line at http://europa.eu.int/rapid/start/cgi/.

4. This, according to Tariq Modood, is the same dilemma currently faced by the United Kingdom regarding its own Muslim minority. See Tariq Modood, "Anti-Essentialism, Multiculturalism, and the 'Recognition' of Religious Groups," in *Citizenship,* ed. Kymlicka and Norman, 175–98, 195.

5. See Ralph Buultjens, "India: Religion, Political Legitimacy and the Secular State," in *Religion and the State: The Struggle for Legitimacy and Power,* ed. Robert J. Meyers, vol. 483 of *Annals of the American Academy of Political and Social Sciences,* January 1986, 93–109, 109. Also see the Summer 2003 issue of *Daedalus,* which is devoted to a reexamination of the principle of secularism.

6. Leokadia Drobizheva, director of the Sociological Institute of the Russian Academy of Sciences, reported in April 2002 that her latest survey data suggests that though anti-Semitic attitudes have decreased in Russia during the past decade, anti-Muslim and anti-Caucasian feeling has increased dramatically. See *Rfe/Rl Tatar-Bashkir Weekly Report,* April 12, 2002.

7. See n. 2 above.

8. Modood, "Anti-Essentialism," 185, 191.

9. Talal Asad, "Muslims and European Identity: Can Europe Represent Islam?" in *The Idea of Europe: From Antiquity to the European Union,* ed. Anthony Pagden (New York and Washington: Woodrow Wilson Center Press and Cambridge University Press, 2002), 209–27; Jeff Spinner-Halev, "Extending Diversity: Religion in Public and Private Education," in *Citizenship,* ed. Kymlicka and Norman, 68–95.

10. Modood, "Anti-Essentialism," 185–86. The authors of the individual country studies in Hunter, *Islam,* also note that the leaders of Europe's minority Muslim communities also have called on their respective states to establish some type of institutionalized relationship with them, mostly in vain.

11. Alexander Agadjanian, "Public Religion and the Quest for National Ideology: Russian Media Discourse," *Journal for the Scientific Study of Religion* 40, no. 3 (2001): 351–65; the quotation here is on 356–57.

12. The text of the 1997 Law on Freedom of Conscience and Religious Association is catalogued at the Stetson University Russian Religion News Web site at http://www .stetson.edu/~psteeves/relnews/freedomofconscienceeng.html.

13. Indeed, the inclusion of the clause recognizing the "special place" of the Russian Orthodox Church in the Russian polity seems to reflect directly the church's own view of its proper role in post-Soviet Russia, which is illustrated nicely by a 1997 quote from Patriarch Alexsei II himself, who noted that "Russia came to exist as a state on the basis of the Orthodox religion, so it is only on the basis of the Orthodox religion that the Fatherland can regain its magnificence." See Nikolas K. Gvosdev, "The New Party Card? Orthodoxy and the Search for Post-Soviet Russian Identity," *Problems of Post-Communism* 47, no. 6 (November/December 2000): 29–38; the quotation here is on 32.

14. Gvosdev, "New Party Card?" 32.

15. Gvosdev, "New Party Card?" 32.

16. For a discussion the types of challenges and harassment that "nontraditional"

confessions in Russia face, see the 2003 U.S. Department of State International Religious Freedom Report on Russia, available at http://www.state.gov/g/drl/rls/irf/2003/ 24430.htm.

17. Nadezhda Kevorkova, "Schoolchildren Will Study Fundamentals of Religious Doctrines," *Gazeta,* April 10, 2003. Catalogued at the Stetson University Russian Religion News Web site at http://www.stetson.edu/~psteeves/relnews/0304a.html#09a.

18. Remy Levean and Shireen T. Hunter, "Islam in France," in Hunter, *Islam,* 3.

19. Andreas Goldberg, "Islam in Germany," in Hunter, *Islam,* 33.

20. 2001 U.K. National Census, "Ethnicity and Religion" Results, available at http:// www.statistics.gov.uk/census2001/profiles/64.asp#ethnic.

21. Some estimates put the number of "illegal" Muslim residents from Central Asia and the Caucasus living in Russia at as many as 4 million. See n. 1 above.

22. The four Muslim Boards were to administer to the needs of the Muslims of Central Asia (located in Tashkent in Uzbekistan), European Russia and Siberia (located in Ufa in Bashkortostan), the Northern Caucasus (located in Buinaksk in Daghestan), and Transcaucasia (located in Baku in Azerbaijan). The Soviet system of ethnofederalism was also designed to create ways other than religion, namely, Marxist-Leninist ideology, of binding non-Russian (and especially Muslim) populations to the centralized state. On the history of Islam in the Soviet Union, see Yaacov Roi, *Islam in the Soviet Union: From the Second World War to Gorbachev* (New York : Columbia University Press, 2000).

23. Roi, *Islam,* 112.

24. Between 1945 and 1970, only eighty-five students graduated from the two Soviet-sanctioned medresehs in Bukhara and Tashkent—this to serve a population of Soviet Muslims that by 1989 had grown to more than 50 million. See Roi, *Islam,* 57, 114, 162.

25. See the Ministry of Justice document, *Svedeniya o religioznikh organizatsiyakh, zaregistirovannikh v RF na 1 Yanvarya 2003g* [Data about religious organizations registered in the Russian Federation as of January 1, 2003], catalogued at http://www .religare.ru/article3849.htm. Also see *Mir Religii,* April 9, 2003, catalogued at the Stetson University Russian Religion News Web site at http://www.stetson.edu/~psteeves/ relnews/0304a.html#09a.

26. Galina Yemelianova, "Islam in Russia: An Historical Perspective," in *Islam in Post-Soviet Russia: Public and Private Faces,* ed. Hilary Pilkington and Galina Yemelianova (London: RoutledgeCurzon, 2003), 15–60; the citation here is on 54.

27. Yemelianova, "Islam in Russia," 54.

28. See n. 25 above.

29. Yemelianova, "Islam in Russia," 54.

30. See Galina Yemelianova, "New Muftis, New Russians?" *Jamestown Foundation Prism* 5, no. 16 (August 27, 1999), catalogued at http://www.jamestown.org/pubs/view/ pri_005_016_005.htm.

31. See Artem Pukhov, "Talgat Tadzhuddin in a Nursery School," *Nezavisimaya Gazeta,* May 21, 2003, catalogued at the Stetson University Russian Religion News Web site at http://www.stetson.edu/~psteeves/relnews/0305e.html.

32. Events surrounding the U.S. invasion of Iraq in the spring of 2003 have changed the balance of power between Tadzhuddin and Gainutdin's organizations significantly and perhaps permanently. Despite the fact that in the past he had accused his rival Gainutdin of "extremism," in April 2003, Tadzhuddin himself used the forum of an antiwar

demonstration in Ufa to declare a "jihad" against the United States for its aggression against Iraq (from whence he had just returned on a failed peacemaking mission). This drew angry reactions from both the secular authorities in Moscow, including the Ministry of Justice and the Prosecutor General's Office, which immediately put Tadzhuddin and his Ufa organization under investigation. In response, Gainutdin called an extraordinary meeting of the main Islamic organizations in Russia, which later issued a fatwa essentially excommunicating Tadzhuddin. Since these events, Tadzhuddin essentially has become persona non grata in Russia, rarely leaving his residence in Ufa. The fatwa is available in Russian at http://islaminfo.ru and is also catalogued in English at the Stetson University Russian Religion Web site at http://www.stetson.edu/~psteeves/relnews/0304a.html#09a.

33. This is because their beliefs are not based solely on the writings of the Saudi Abd al-Wahhab but instead refer to a range of "purist" interpretations of Islam—e.g., Hasan al-Turabi from Sudan and Said Qutb from Egypt. Scholars estimate that 7 to 9 percent of the Muslims in Dagestan could be considered Wahhabi or Salafis, with much smaller numbers throughout the rest of the North Caucasus and other parts of Russia. See Galina M. Yemelianova, *Russia and Islam: A Historical Survey* (Houndsmills, U.K.: Palgrave, 2002), 186–87; and Amri Shikhsaidov, "Islam in Dagestan," in *Political Islam and Conflicts in Russia and Central Asia,* ed. Lena Jonson and Murad Esenov, Conference Papers Volume 24 (Stockholm: Swedish Institute of International Affairs, 1999), catalogued at http://www.ca-c.org/dataeng/06.shikhs.shtml.

34. For a nuanced analysis of this discursive strategy, see "A Clear and Present Danger: 'Wahhabism as Rhetorical Foil,'" Alexander Knysh, Saudi-American Forum, November 14, 2003, http://www.saudi-american-forum.org/Newsletters/SAF_Essay_24.htm.

35. The draft report of a task force led by the Federal Nationalities minister, Vladimir Zorin, charged with investigating religious extremism—excerpts of which were leaked in late 2002—unfortunately exemplifies the worst aspects of these tendencies, calling for nearly unlimited state prerogative in persecuting and neutralizing "extremist" organizations of any kind. Stung by the controversy surrounding the leaked report, Moscow has denied that it has any official standing. See Agence France-Press, January 24, 2003, and *Moscow Times,* January 24, 2003.

36. Rafik Mukhametshin, *Islam v obshchestvenno-politicheskoi zhizni Tatarstana v kontsye XX veka* [Islam in the social and political life of Tatarstan at the end of the 20th century] (Kazan: Izdatel'tsvo Iman, 2000), 48; *Russian Regional Report* 9, no. 6 (April 7, 2004).

37. Yemelianova, *Russia and Islam,* 186–87; Shikhsaidov, "Islam in Dagestan."

38. *Rfe/Rl Tatar-Bashkir Service,* September 24, 1999; September 27, 1999; October 6, 1999; October 8, 1999.

39. The jadidist movement was so named because of the "new method" (*usul-u-jadid*) of learning Arabic, which it promoted for use in *mektebs* in Russia. A very selective representation of the literature on Jadidism includes Mark Batunsky, "Russian Clerical Islamic Studies in the Late 19th and Early 20th Centuries," *Central Asian Survey* 13, no. 2 (1994): 213–35; Adeeb Khalid, *The Politics of Muslim Cultural Reform: Jadidism in Tsarist Central Asia* (Berkeley: University of California Press, 1997); Edward J. Lazzerini, "Beyond Renewal: The Jadid Response to Pressure for Change in the Modern Age," in *Muslims in Central Asia: Expressions of Identity and Change,* ed. Jo-Ann Gross (Durham, N.C.: Duke University Press, 1992); and Ayse-Azade Rorlich,

The Volga Tatars: A Profile in National Resilience (Stanford, Calif.: Hoover Institution Press, 1986).

40. Lazzerini, "Beyond Renewal," 151, 160.

41. Khalid, *Politics of Muslim Cultural Reform,* 191.

42. Khalid, *Politics of Muslim Cultural Reform,* passim; Lazzerini, "Beyond Renewal," 162.

43. Batunsky, "Russian Clerical Islamic Studies," 219.

44. Mukhametshin, *Islam v obshchestvenno-politicheskoi zhizni Tatarstana,* 3.

45. Mukhametshin, *Islam v obshchestvenno-politicheskoi zhizni Tatarstana,* 3.

46. F. M. Sultanov, *Islam I Tatarskoye natsional'noye dvizheniye v Rossiskom I mirovom Musal'manskom Kontekstye: Istoriya I Sovremennost'* [Islam and the Tatar National Movement in the Russian and world Islamic context: Past and Present] (Kazan: Shkola, 1999), 183.

47. All quotations from speeches are from the author's notes from the conference, which was held at the Tatarstan National Cultural Center "Kazan" in Kazan, June 8–11, 2001.

48. According to the November 2002 Duma Cyrillic-only bill, which Putin signed in December 2002, Tatarstan has one year to "reconsider" its own law on Latinization. Tatarstani leaders have vociferously condemned the Duma's actions, with Shaimiyev referring to the bill as "an invasion of human rights." In response to Tatarstan's staunch defense of its right to use the Latin alphabet (which the republic says is guaranteed both by its own constitution, the republic's 1994 treaty with Moscow and Article 68 of Russia's own constitution), Putin has called for "further dialogue" with Tatarstan on the issue. See *Rfe/Rl Newsline* November 28 and 29, 2002, and December 10 and 12, 2002.

49. See the interview with Mufti of Dagestan Ahmad-Hadjii Abdullaev, November 27, 2001, catalogued on the Web site http://islam.ru at http://eng.islam.ru/pressclub/inter/Mufti/.

50. Presentation of Radik Amirov, head of the Press Service of the Russian Council of Religious Affairs and executive secretary of the Union of Muslim Journalists, to the conference "Islam in Russia: History, Politics and Culture," at the Kennan Institute of the Woodrow Wilson International Center for Scholars, Washington, November 6, 2003.

51. Ali Bagarov, "Tret'ya kavkazskaya voina" ["Third Caucasian war"), *Russkii Zhurnal* [Russian Journal], July 9, 2002, available at http://religion.russ.ru/expert/20020709.html.

52. See Ali Polosin and Iman Porokhovoi, "Zayavleniye russkikh musul'man po povodu proyekta 'Russkii islam,'" April 24, 2003; available at http://religion.sova-center.ru/discussions/18BAA14/194EB28/18F876A?print=on ; and I. V. Ponkin, "Zaklyucheniye po proyektu 'Russkii Islam," *Gosudarstvo I Religii v Rossii,* March 15, 2003; available at http://religion.sova-center.ru/discussions/18BAA14/194EB28?15EBCC5?print-on.

53. All references to Gradirovskii's program are taken from his explanation of the project titled "Kyl'turnoye pogranich'ye: russkii islam" [Cultural frontier: Russian Islam], June 2003, catalogued on the Web site of the Center for Strategic Research of the Volga Region at http://antropotok.archipelag.ru/text/a258.htm.

54. The Russian Federal Ministry of Foreign Affairs has already intensified its efforts at regulating contacts with foreign Islamic organizations—when the Russian Islamic University in Kazan sought Qatar's help in renovating its dormitory in early 2003, R. T. Mufti Ishakov stressed that the venture "would have to undergo a thorough review

and legalization procedure" in Moscow first. See the *Rfe/Rl Tatar-Bashkir Report,* January 9, 2003.

55. Polosin and Porokhovoi, "Zayavleniye russkikh musul'man."

56. Polosin and Porokhovoi, "Zayavleniye russkikh musul'man."

57. See Gokhan Cetinsaya, "Rethinking Nationalism and Islam: Some Preliminary Notes on the Roots of the Turkish-Islamic Synthesis in Modern Turkish Political Thought," *Muslim World,* July–October1999, 350–76; Umit Cizre Sakallioglu, "Parameters and Strategies of Islam-State Interaction in Republican Turkey," *International Journal of Middle East Studies* 28, no. 2 (May 1996): 231–51 (the citation here is on 235–36); M. Hakan Yavuz, "Cleansing Islam from the Public Sphere," *Journal of International Affairs* 54, no. 1 (Fall 2000): 21–42 (the citation here is on 29); and M. Hakan Yavuz, *Islamic Political Identity in Turkey* (Oxford: Oxford University Press, 2003).

58. See Mustafa Erdogan, "Islam in Turkish Politics: Turkey's Quest for Democracy Without Islam," *Critique* 15 (1999): 25–50.

59. Levean and Hunter, "Islam in France"; Michael Wieriorka, "Race, Culture and Society: The French Experience with Muslims," in *Muslim Europe or Euro Islam: Politics, Culture and Citizenship in the Age of Globalization,* ed. Nezar Al Sayyad and Manuel Castells (Lanham, Md.: Lexington Books, 2002), 131–45.

60. Levean and Hunter, "Islam in France."

61. Elaine Sciolino, "France Creates Muslim Council to Handle Diverse Minority," *International Herald Tribune,* January 15, 2003.

62. Sciolino, "France Creates Muslim Council."

63. Hugh Schofield, "France Sets April Election Dates for Muslim Council," Agence France-Presse, February 24, 2003; Elaine Sciolino, "Can New Panel's Head Serve France and Muslims Too?" *International Herald Tribune,* April 22, 2003.

64. See, e.g., Rafael Mirgazizov's interview with the First Deputy Mufti of Tatarstan in *Respublika Tatarstan,* May 2001, 6–7, which is titled "Vakhkhabizmu-nyet, dzhadidizmu-da?" [Wahhabism—no, jadidism—yes?] and the interview with Mufti of Dagestan Ahmad-Hadjii Abdullaev, November 27, 2001, catalogued on the Web site http://islam.ru at http://eng.islam.ru/pressclub/inter/Mufti/.

4

Migration, Hostility, and Ethnopolitical Mobilization: Russia's Anti-Chinese Legacies in Formation

Mikhail A. Alexseev

Public responses to migration—especially in cases of new migration in post-Soviet Russia—present invaluable material for studying social origins and the perceptual logic of interethnic hostility and ethnopolitical mobilization. This chapter closely examines one such case—responses to migration of Chinese nationals in the Russian Far East (RFE) after the demise of the Soviet Union and across borders that stayed closed for more than half a century. The focus is on Primorskii Krai—the RFE's most populous territory with demographic, economic, and political trends largely representative of Russia's regions bordering on China. The central question is how perceptions of Chinese migration among local residents about a decade after the Soviet collapse came to relate to support for parties, politicians, and paramilitary groups that mobilized against "ethnic other" newcomers—such as Russia's far-right Liberal Democratic Party, led by Vladimir Zhirinovsky, and paramilitary Cossack detachments in counties along the Russia-China border. To what extent has Chinese migration been generating a legacy of hostility and ethnopolitical mobilization in the RFE during the first decade after the Soviet collapse?

To pose this question is to confront a puzzle. At first glance, developments in the RFE seem to be consistent with the intuitive logic directly linking migration, interethnic hostility, and political mobilization. Indeed, since the Sino-Russian border opened for travel by individuals in 1988, the migration of thousands of Chinese nationals in and out of the RFE has been generating alarmist sentiments from Vladivostok to Moscow about China's imminent takeover of Russia's Far Eastern territories.[1] A poll by the Russian Public Opinion Foundation in December 2002 suggested that proximity to the Chinese border was related significantly to dislike of China among the Russians. Whereas only 12 percent of the survey respondents across Russia viewed China negatively, 17 percent of respondents in Siberia and 29 percent in the RFE said they disliked China.[2] Opinion polls in Primorskii Krai from 1991 to 1998 registered not only a distinct rise in anti-Chinese sentiments but also a twofold rise in support for one of the most brutal forms of ethnic exclusionism—the wholesale deportation of ethnic minorities such as the Chechens and the Koreans from their historic homelands in Stalin's USSR.[3]

In 1995 and 1999—both election years to Russia's lower house of parliament, the State Duma—Vladimir Zhirinovsky vigorously appealed to these alarmist sentiments to mobilize public support for his expressly xenophobic and grossly misnamed Liberal Democratic Party (LDPR). Speaking in March 1995, he famously claimed that a predominantly economic Chinese migration in the RFE was, in fact, a "crawling, peaceful penetration" paving the way for China's military invasion. In the same statement, he claimed that China had already built "underground cross-border passages that could take up to a million people."[4] At a rally of about 600 people in Vladivostok in August 1999, he warned that Yeltsin's pro-Western policies would "oust the Russians from the Far East and give the land to the Chinese." Illustrating the linkage between hostility and ethnopolitical mobilization, the LDPR's leader proclaimed: "This cannot be allowed. It is time to turn from a meek sheep into a wolf in order to cheat and drive them away." Following up on this, another LDPR speaker called for building nuclear power plants along Russia's border with China "to burn Chinese like gnats."[5] The 1999 Duma election results also suggested that anti-Chinese hostility resonated well with voters in the RFE. In all the territories bordering China, Zhirinovsky's party did nearly twice as well at the polls as it did on average across Russia, winning 12.6 percent of the vote in Chita Oblast, 11.3 percent in Amur Oblast, 10.1 percent in Primorskii Krai, and 9.1 percent in Khabarovskii Krai.[6] Among local politicians in the RFE, the former Primorskii governor, Yevgenii Nazdratenko, became one of the most vocal catastrophizers about the impending "yellow peril," winning elections and remaining in office despite Yeltsin's attempts to remove him.

And yet, a more nuanced look at patterns of Chinese migration, public hostility, and support for xenophobic parties and politicians in the RFE suggests that the migration-hostility-mobilization logic is hardly as straightforward as it may appear. First, it is striking how little violence and organized collective action directed against Chinese migrants have taken place in Primorskii Krai regardless of widespread interethnic hostility, incendiary political rhetoric, and media alarmism. In my data set based on regional and Russian press reports and numbering nearly 3,250 events that involved Russian-Chinese interactions in Primorskii Krai from 1993 to 2000, fewer than a dozen were organized actions by the LDPR.[7] Only one of these—a petition in November 1995 to require all Chinese nationals to have entry visas when traveling to Russia—represented a specific act of antimigrant public mobilization. The absence of more vigorous exclusionist activities by the LDPR that would have lived up to Zhirinovsky's rhetoric—such as campaigning to close the border or to deport Chinese traders—has been conspicuous. Nor did the LDPR form or encourage the formation of volunteer groups in support of Operation Foreigner—a series of high-profile police sweeps and street identity checks launched in 1994 across Primorskii Krai with a view to identifying and deporting undocumented migrants. Overall, no acts of organized anti-Chinese group violence were reported in Primorskii from 1993 through 2000, even though, according to my data set, Russian-Chinese interactions in Primorskii did result in fifty-two murders and forty-four beatings (mostly targeting Chinese migrants and perpetrated by local individuals or small gangs).

Second, voting patterns in the 1999 Duma elections show that whereas Zhirinovsky sought to mobilize interethnic, antimigrant hostility, the latter was not necessarily something that accounted for his higher-than-average vote in regions bordering China. Significantly stronger-than-average support for the LDPR was recorded in three other Far Eastern regions— Sakhalin (10.6 percent), Kamchatka (11 percent), and Magadan (13 percent)—with significantly lower exposure to Chinese migration. Moreover, in the same election, the LDPR enjoyed less than the average level of support in some regions of Russia that experienced non-Russian in-migration in the 1990s on a larger scale than the Far Eastern border regions—most notably, in Krasnodar (4.8 percent) and Stavropol (5.1 percent), where the influx of Meskhetian Turks, Chechens, and other ethnic groups of the Caucasus became an explosive political issue in the 1990s.[8] Even the proximity of these regions to violent conflict in Chechnya apparently failed to galvanize the Russian nationalist vote represented by Zhirinovsky. In other words, the hostility-to-mobilization linkage can hardly be taken for granted either.

Third, hostility toward ethnic others may or may not be related to perceived exposure to migration, even though the latter may engender negative feelings toward migrant-sending states, as suggested by the 2002 Public Opinion Foundation poll. An analysis of my own survey of 1,010 Primorskii Krai residents conducted in September 2000 by the Public Opinion Research Center at the Vladivostok Institute of History, Archeology, and Ethnography showed that anti-Chinese hostility had little relationship to perceptions of the scale of Chinese migration.[9] Moreover, the same study revealed that fear of and hostility toward Chinese migrants was not significantly higher in cities, towns, and counties with a low population density—that is, in those areas where one would expect residents to feel more vulnerable to the influx of migrants. It was also established—comparing interdepartmental data from the Russian government agencies in Primorskii with survey data—that anti-Chinese hostility in Primorskii Krai from 1994 to 2000 persisted despite a dramatic reduction in the proportion of migrants who remained illegally in the area and who were deported by the Russian immigration and law enforcement agencies.[10]

In summary, the story of Chinese migration in the RFE after the Soviet collapse highlights important theoretical questions about ethnic hostility and mobilization. Why does more migration not necessarily translate into greater antimigrant hostility at the individual level? And why does interethnic hostility, in turn, not necessarily translate into readiness for ethnopolitical mobilization—understood here as support for political parties and paramilitary groups with distinct antimigrant, exclusionist agendas? To address these puzzles, this chapter asks more specifically: Once people become concerned about the influx of ethnic others (e.g., Chinese migrants in Russia), who among host populations is more likely to support ethnonationalist parties and antimigrant groups? How do perceptions of the nature of migration and its effects shape a proclivity for hostile responding and ethnopolitical mobilization?

This chapter presents a theoretically informed plausibility probe of these questions in the context of Chinese migration in Primorskii Krai since the Soviet collapse. I discuss five principal hypotheses that would explain variation in individual proclivities for ethnopolitical mobilization in a generalizable fashion: (1) the social background of individual respondents, (2) intergroup bias (a sense of ethnic group distinctiveness), (3) a threat to group position, (4) labor market competition, and (5) the interethnic security dilemma. The first four hypotheses are derived straightforwardly from social and psychological research on ethnic relations that reported significant empirical findings in other contexts. The fifth hypothesis represents my application of the interethnic security dilemma theory to research on immigration attitudes and antimigrant hostility. I discuss the applicability of these insights in the RFE context and use opinion data from my 2000 Primorskii survey to explore what role antimigrant sentiments have been likely to play in public support for Zhirinovsky's LDPR, local paramilitary Cossack groups, and politicians who articulated expressly anti-Chinese, anti-immigrant policies.

Indicators of Anti-Chinese Hostility and Mobilization in Primorskii Krai

The 2000 Primorskii survey showed that fear of Chinese migration and anti-Chinese hostility were widespread among local residents, comprising a large reservoir of social support for the likes of Zhirinovsky and Nazdratenko. Most respondents favored hostile political and military responses to Chinese migration—in conjunction with continued economic exchanges. About 65 percent of respondents said they supported a ban on travel by individuals across the Russia-China border, and 25 percent backed total border closure. In contrast, fewer than 1 percent of respondents wanted the border to be completely open.[11] Deportation of illegal Chinese migrants—that is, the overwhelming majority of Chinese migrant traders and workers in Primorskii—had the support of 89 percent of respondents. Nearly 80 percent of those polled also supported a ban on Russian residency rights (*vid na zhitel'stvo*) for Chinese nationals, and 60 percent of respondents wanted to ban Chinese migrant labor. A substantial proportion of respondents opposed Chinese migrants integrating into Russian society; 48 percent wanted to ban Chinese language media, 42 percent wanted to ban Russian-Chinese intermarriages, and 76 percent wanted to ban Chinatowns in Primorskii Krai—even though no Chinese newspapers circulated in Primorkii, only a handful of marriages was registered in the 1990s, and no Chinatowns similar to those in New York or San Francisco emerged after a decade of large-scale cross-border migration.[12]

These questions, however, measured support for government policies that did not necessarily require public mobilization. In contrast, three questions in the survey specifically reflected respondents' support for organized public action against the Chinese presence—perhaps the closest proxy indicators of individual proclivity for ethnonationalist mobilization in the Primorskii 2000 context. The first indicator was support for the Cossacks or other voluntary paramilitary groups helping to protect borders and stop the inflow of Chinese migrants. About 57 percent of respondents were supportive of such groups, with about 21 percent among them strongly supportive—a level of public support that the Arizona Minutemen on the United States–Mexico border could only hope to get in their wildest dreams. The second indicator was support for all or any of the "politicians and political parties campaigning against Chinese presence in Primorskii Krai"—the sentiment shared by 50 percent of respondents.[13] However, when it came to the third indicator, trust in Zhirinovsky's LDPR—a party that most vociferously called for repelling China's "crawling, peaceful penetration" into Primorskii Krai—the overwhelming majority of respondents did not seem to have anything to do with it. Only about 6 percent of those polled said that the LDPR was a political party they would trust the most—about the Russian average rate of support at the time and less than the percentage of the vote cast for the LDPR in Primorskii in December 1999. The most antimigrant and xenophobic of Russia's parliamentary parties had problems with public trust in a social context brimming with antimigrant hostility and xenophobia. Nevertheless, these survey data give us an opportunity to examine whether general support for antimigrant parties and groups, as well as support for a specific antimigrant party in Primorskii in 2000, had similar or divergent social bases and followed similar or divergent perceptual logic.

Social Bases of Anti-Chinese Mobilization

Whereas sociologists routinely test for the effects of age, gender, religious background, and place of residence on interethnic attitudes, findings in various contexts have been rather ambiguous—showing considerable sensitivity to political, historical, and socioeconomic contexts. Higher educational levels, however, have been rather consistently associated with greater

Table 4.1. Support for Anti-Chinese Mobilization by Social Group (percent)

Question	Age (years)				Gender		Education			Religion	
	30	31–45	46–59	60	Women	Men	S	SS	College	Rus Orthodox	Other
Which party or movement do you trust the most—LDPR (N = 978) (N = 984) (N = 969) (N = 979)	5.8	5.6	5.9	2.8	3.3	7.5**	7.2	4.4	3.5*	4.5	5.7
In response to Chinese migration in Primorskii Krai, give support to armed detachments of Cossacks or other such groups set up to maintain public order (N = 983) (N = 9 89) (N = 973) (N = 985)	60.8	54	62.8	56	58.1	58.3	58.7	62.1	52.8*	63.3	56.1**
In response to Chinese migration in Primorskii Krai, give support to politicians and political parties campaigning against Chinese presence (N = 967) (N = 973) (N = 958) (N = 969)	48.8	51.1	50.2	56.7*	50.4	52.2	54.7	51.5	45.1	55.3	49.7*

Note: Education categories are: S = secondary; SS = secondary specialized; College = college or university; and Rus = Russian. *N* is the number of respondents who answered both the row and column questions, out of the total of 1,010 respondents in the survey. The table shows what percentage of respondents in each column expressed support for the Liberal Democratic Party (LDPR), the Cossacks, and anti-Chinese parties/politicians. Statistically significant differences across columns within each category (e.g., between the percentage of men and women expressing support for the LDPR in the survey) are marked with asterisks: $* p < .05$ (less than 5 percent likelihood that the difference is due to chance or error); $** p < .01$ (less than 1 percent likelihood that the difference is due to chance or error); $*** p < .001$ (less than 0.1 percent likelihood that the difference is due to chance or error).
Source: 2000 Primorskii survey.

ethnic tolerance.[14] As the 2000 Primorskii survey reveals (see table 4.1), the age, gender, education, or religion of respondents in the probability sample of local adult population did not consistently explain the variation in all three indicators of ethnonationalist mobilization—support for the LDPR, the Cossacks and similar paramilitary groups, and "politicians and parties campaigning against Chinese presence."[15]

Table 4.1 shows substantial fragmentation of the social bases of support for anti-Chinese collective action in Primorskii Krai. Local males with complete or incomplete secondary education, regardless of age or religious background, were the most consistent social group likely to lend support to the LDPR. However, these "lowbrow males" were not the social group that consistently expressed support for the Cossacks, whose primary constituency appeared to be Orthodox believers without a college education irrespective of age and gender. But then, Orthodox believers over sixty years of age of both sexes and all educational levels came out as consistent supporters of anti-Chinese parties and politicians in general.

The data also reveal that the urban–rural divide had little relationship to a proclivity for anti-Chinese mobilization. No city or rural county in the survey sample exhibited systematic support or opposition for all three measures of mobilization. None of the mobilization measures, in turn, enjoyed consistent support in all cities and counties where the survey was held. Comparing the two largest Primorskii Krai cities in the sample, for instance, one finds that support for the Cossacks was consistently greater than chance in Vladivostok, but opposition to the Cossacks was consistently greater than chance in Ussuriisk.[16] (Ironically, the largest Cossack organization in Primorskii and the RFE is the Ussuri Cossack Army.) Overall, education (at lower levels) and religion (Russian Orthodox background) appeared to be the most significant social indicators of ethnonationalist mobilization in response to Chinese migration.

The general ambiguity of social indicators, on the one hand, and the significance of education and religious background, on the other, prompt one to look more closely at the perceptual, symbolic logic of anti-Chinese mobilization.

The Perceptual Logic of Anti-Chinese Mobilization

This section explores several issues related to the perceptual logic of anti-Chinese mobilization. These include intergroup bias (sense of group distinctiveness), labor market (socioeconomic niche) competition, threat to group position (majority–minority status reversal), and the interethnic security dilemma.

Intergroup Bias (Sense of Group Distinctiveness)

Donald Horowitz summarized studies in social psychology and psychoanalysis tracing interethnic hostility to "dichotomization as a result of juxtaposition and comparison."[17] He referred to well-established findings that a perception of intergroup differences accounts for persistent intergroup bias. Individuals consistently perceive out-groups as more homogenous than in-groups regardless of actual group homogeneity levels.[18] As a consequence, "ingroup–outgroup divisiveness elicits competitive tendencies: not merely through the need for positive distinctiveness, but more basically because social categorization directly influences individuals' perceptions of their goals."[19] The greater the perceived difference between typical characteristics of one's ethnic group in contrast to another group, the more entrenched the ethnic markers, the greater the hostility potential.[20] Hence, it is plausible that the sense of group distinctiveness would also account for a mobilization proclivity among individuals.

The image of Chinese migrants as a distinct and distant ethnic group was widespread among the Primorskii public in the 2000 poll. Contrasting the Chinese and the Russians, twice as many respondents saw the Chinese as more hardworking, entrepreneurial, and greedy; three times as many respondents saw the Chinese as more cunning; and twenty times as many respondents saw the Chinese as less generous. Moreover, 56 percent of Primorskii residents in the survey disapproved of their relatives marrying Chinese citizens (only 4 percent approved of such marriages). Close to 50 percent of those polled said that Chinese migrants in Primorskii Krai would not assimilate into Russian society. One sees in these numbers widespread fears that if Chinese migrants settled down in Primorskii, they would not internalize Russia's social norms but would promulgate Chinese norms and culture. With their strong and distinct "groupness," Chinese migrants would be more likely over time to seek autonomy within Russia and protection from across the border.[21] In everyday life, these sentiments mirrored the dire warning I heard numerous times in the RFE ever since my first taxi ride in Vladivostok: "One day we shall wake up and find that half the population here is slit-eyed."

A statistical analysis of the 2000 Primorskii poll shows that the sense of group distinctiveness does not uniformly affect the proclivity for mobilization. On the one hand, perceived social differences between the Russians and the Chinese considerably raised the proclivity for partisan anti-Chinese mobilization. Respondents who felt more strongly than others that the Russians and the Chinese differed on such dimensions of social behavior as selfishness, tidiness, politeness, honesty, and responsibility were also likely to support anti-Chinese parties and the LDPR.[22] On the other hand, as table 4.2 shows, most respondents who supported the LDPR, the Cossacks, or anti-Chinese parties and politicians in general had a neutral attitude toward Russian-Chinese marriages. Whether opposing or supporting Russian-Chinese marriages, an average Russian in Primorskii Krai was about equally likely to back anti-Chinese parties or paramilitary groups. This finding rules out the possibility that hostility toward the Chinese was significantly driven by the threat of competition in the marriage market.

Indeed, whereas the majority of local Russians opposed marriages of their relatives with the Chinese, few local Russians conceived of Chinese migrants—either male or female—as desirable marriage partners. Deepseated aversion to Chinese males on the part of local Russian females—on the grounds of intimacy and cultural differences—was systematically revealed in the majority of readers' letters in the dating and marriage sections of the Vladivostok newspapers. Having a Chinese husband or wife was a popular line in jokes representing the typical "not-so-ideal world" that I heard during my six visits to the region from 1999 to 2001. It is therefore understandable that, as table 4.2 shows, the Russians' opposition to marriages with the Chinese did not translate into stronger support for xenophobic parties and groups. Counterintuitively, however, trust in the capacity of Chinese nationals to assimilate culturally in Russia (become "Russified") was significantly associated with stronger support for anti-Chinese parties. This finding runs against the intergroup bias hypothesis.

Labor Market (Socioeconomic Niche) Competition

Few would dispute that economic motivations affect interethnic relations and political mobilization. Susan Olzak's research in particular showed that competition for labor markets or socioeconomic niches between incumbent and immigrant populations had been one of the major drivers of interethnic violence throughout American history.[23] Drawing on the analysis of hundreds of cases, Olzak linked ethnic violence in the United States to "racial job queues," business failure, and subsequent labor union mobilization—in response to racial desegregation and/or large-scale migration across ethnic lines.

Table 4.2. Support for Anti-Chinese Mobilization and Sense of Group Distinctiveness (percent)

Question	Russian–Chinese Marriages			Chinese Capacity to Assimilate	
	Support	Neutral	Oppose	High	Low
Which party or movement do you trust the most—LDPR	4.5	6.5 (N = 910)	5.2	11.3 (N = 831)	4.2*
In response to Chinese migration in Primorskii Krai, give support to armed detachments of Cossacks or other such groups set up to maintain public order	54.6	63.5 (N = 917)	54.2	61.6 (N = 837)	58.5
In response to Chinese migration in Primorskii Krai, give support to politicians and political parties campaigning against Chinese presence	32.6	58.5 (N = 904)	43.3	64.6 (N = 828)	50.6***

Note: N is the number of respondents who answered both the row and column questions, out of the total of 1,010 respondents in the survey. The table shows what percentage of respondents in each column expressed support for the Liberal Democratic Party (LDPR), the Cossacks, and anti-Chinese parties/politicians. Statistically significant differences across columns within each category are marked with asterisks: * $p < .05$ (less than 5 percent likelihood that the difference is due to chance or error); ** $p < .01$ (less than 1 percent likelihood that the difference is due to chance or error); *** $p < .001$ (less than 0.1 percent likelihood that the difference is due to chance or error).

Source: 2000 Primorskii survey.

The scale of Chinese economic migration in the RFE since the early 1990s—despite the political visibility of the issue—has been too small to engender racial job queues or to force Russian companies out of business in significant numbers. The number of Chinese guest workers in Primorskii Krai from the mid-1990s to 2001 fluctuated somewhere between 7,000 and 10,000—not a significant proportion, given Primorskii's population of more than 2 million. (Even counting tourists, the average number of all Chinese nationals in Primorskii on any given day around 2000 was no more than about 1.5 percent of the krai's population.)[24] Moreover, Chinese cross-border trade not only provided local Russians with a wider variety of goods at affordable prices (shopping at Chinese markets became standard consumer behavior in the RFE), but it also gave RFE residents new opportunities to make money. As Larin documented, in the mid-1990s, the number of Russian "shuttle" traders going into China exceeded the number of Chinese shuttle traders in the RFE by about 10 times.[25] Moreover, most Chinese migrants in Primorskii Krai and elsewhere throughout the RFE have been operating in distinct and largely separate socioeconomic niches, such as street markets and farms, complementing local economies and posing little direct threat to most local jobs. Russian construction companies hired the Chinese not necessarily because the latter commanded lower wages, but because these companies had trouble finding local Russians willing and able to do physically demanding, mediocre-paying construction jobs.

In the 2000 Primorskii survey, respondents who said they were urban blue-collar workers (*gorodskie rabochie*) and the unemployed—two of the economic groups most likely to be threatened by the influx of Chinese labor—were no more likely than other respondents to support the LDPR, the Cossacks, or antimigrant politicians and parties in general (see table 4.3).

At first glance, these findings appear to uphold the labor market competition theory. After all, with migrants not competing en masse for local jobs, the blue-collar workers and the unemployed would have little reason to feel threatened and to mobilize against Chinese migrants. The problem with this explanation is that in the same survey, a substantial number (55 percent) of respondents expressed a belief that Chinese migration reduced job opportunities for local Russians. If blue-collar urban workers and the unemployed had no more inclination to support the LDPR and the Cossacks than did members of occupational groups that were less likely to compete with Chinese guest workers, then the threat of labor market competition was unlikely to be a major factor in anti-Chinese mobilization in Primorskii in 2000.

The survey also found that agricultural workers in Primorskii were sig-

Table 4.3. Support for Anti-Chinese Mobilization by Type of Employment (percent)

Question	Urban Blue-Collar Workers	vs. Others	Agricultural Workers	vs. Others	Unemployed	vs. Others
Which party or movement do you trust the most—LDPR ($N = 972$)	3.0	5.9	20.0	4.6***	4.3	5.4
In response to Chinese migration in Primorskii Krai, give support to armed detachments of Cossacks or other such groups set up to maintain public order ($N = 977$)	55.3	59.0	66.0	57.9	57.1	58.4
In response to Chinese migration in Primorskii Krai, give support to politicians and political parties campaigning against Chinese presence ($N = 961$)	44.0	52.8	68.1	50.5**	59.1	50.8

Note: "+" shows that respondents placed themselves in that occupational category; "·" shows they placed themselves in other categories. N is the number of respondents who answered both the row and column questions, out of the total of 1,010 respondents in the survey. The table shows what percentage of respondents in each column expressed support for the Liberal Democratic Party (LDPR), the Cossacks, and anti-Chinese parties/politicians. Statistically significant differences across columns within each category are marked with asterisks: * $p < .05$ (less than 5 percent likelihood that the difference is due to chance or error); ** $p < .01$ (less than 1 percent likelihood that the difference is due to chance or error); *** $p < .001$ (less than 0.1 percent likelihood that the difference is due to chance or error).
Source: 2000 Primorskii survey.

nificantly more likely than others to support the LDPR and anti-Chinese parties or politicians—even though a considerably smaller proportion of Chinese migrants engaged in agriculture than in trade or construction.[26] From the labor market competition standpoint, this relationship may plausibly be related to widespread perceptions among local Russians that the Chinese have nearly superhuman excellence when it comes to farming. As the former chief of Primorskii Krai's branch of the federal migration service told me in an interview in Vladivostok, "The Soviet and Russian agriculture ministries designated Primorskii as an area of inhospitable farming [*zona trudnodostupnogo zemledeliia*], but the Chinese have never seen it as one bit inhospitable."

And yet, this explanation is hardly complete or decisive. A more direct and empirically grounded explanation has to do with the strong societal opposition in Primorskii—and in Russia in general for that matter—to privatization of agricultural land and to allowing foreigners to buy and sell land in Russia. In the 2000 Primorskii survey, 95 percent of respondents said they opposed allowing Chinese nationals to buy and sell land in Primorskii Krai. This straightforwardly and unambiguously indicates that support for anti-Chinese parties and politicians by agricultural workers most likely stemmed from their proximity to land and sensitivity to land privatization, rather than from actual competition for jobs with Chinese farm workers. This would also explain why the unemployed and the blue-collar workers—who were more exposed to Chinese migrant labor competition than local farmers—did not exhibit a similarly strong proclivity for anti-Chinese mobilization.

Finally, the 2000 Primorskii poll respondents predominantly believed that Chinese shuttle traders, businesses, and local governments gained more from cross-border interactions than Russian shuttle traders, businesses, and local governments did. However, respondents who felt more intensely than others that the Chinese gained relative to the Russians were no more likely to support anti-Chinese parties, politicians, and paramilitary groups than respondents who felt the Russians gained the same or more than the Chinese. If anything, labor market competition in its own right fails to provide a comprehensive and convincing rationale for anti-Chinese hostility and mobilization potential in the RFE.

Threat to Group Position (Majority-Minority Status Reversal)

One of the most distinguished sociological theories is that of racial prejudice as a threat to group position.[27] The plausibility that any ethnic majority group might become a minority—and migration is one of the principal drivers of such status reversal—unleashes a fear of losing important, if not vital, group privileges. This fear would propel members of the incumbent majority to mobilize against the influx of outsiders.

Indeed, the 2000 Primorskii survey shows that the more local residents felt that Chinese migration threatened Russian sovereignty over the area— the bedrock of their majority privilege—the more they were likely to mobilize behind anti-Chinese parties, politicians, and paramilitary groups. As shown in table 4.4, respondents who felt that Russia would no longer be able to claim sovereignty over Primorskii if the proportion of Chinese immigrants there reached 10 percent were twice as likely to support anti-Chinese parties and paramilitary groups than respondents who felt that Russian sovereignty would only be challenged if the proportion of Chinese migrants exceeded 75 percent of the local population. In other words, the perceived threat to majority group position turned out to be among the most significant predictors of anti-Chinese hostility and mobilization. The poll also revealed that despite Zhirinovskii's vehement rhetoric and local anti-immigrant initiatives, the LDPR was not seen as the type of party worth mobilizing for in response to the threat of status reversal. This suggests that a proclivity for ethnic mobilization is not necessarily going to translate into mobilization behind specific nationalist parties. In the LDPR case, this analysis indicates that despite its disproportionately high electoral support in the RFE, local residents still did not see it as capable to implement changes that would reduce the threat to Russian majority status in the borderlands. After all, only about 6 percent of the 2000 Primorskii survey respondents said they had trust in the LDPR.

However, the threat-to-group-position theory does not specify under what conditions majority group members may become more or less threatened by a phenomenon such as migration. What would explain sensitivity to status reversal in migrant-receiving societies? It is on this count that a threat to group position faces confounding evidence in the case of Chinese migration in the RFE.

It has been well documented that even though the number of Chinese nationals visiting Primorskii Krai increased threefold between 1995 and 2002, the number of visitors who failed to return to China during this same time period dropped by more than 25 times.[28] Increasingly better regulated tourism and trade accounted both for the increase in the overall number of Chinese visitors and for a sharp drop in the number of the Chinese overstaying their visas. It is precisely migrants in that latter category that one

Table 4.4. *Support for Anti-Chinese Mobilization and Threat to Russian Majority Position in the Russian Far East* (percent)

Question	Proportion of Chinese Population That Would Threaten Russian Possession of Primorskii Krai (Respondents' Perceptions)					Sig.
	10%	20%	30%	50%	>75%	
Which party or movement do you trust the most—LDPR (N = 743)	0	6.5	5.5	5.8	4.7	
In response to Chinese migration in Primorskii Krai, give support to armed detachments of Cossacks or other such groups set up to maintain public order (N = 747)	42.9	35.5	23.8	20.8	20.4	**
In response to Chinese migration in Primorskii Krai, give support to politicians and political parties campaigning against Chinese presence (N = 732)	28.6	22.2	21.7	12.1	14.9	***

Note: N is the number of respondents who answered both the row and column questions, out of the total of 1,010 respondents in the survey. The table shows what percentage of respondents in each column expressed support for the Liberal Democratic Party (LDPR), the Cossacks, and anti-Chinese parties/politicians. Statistically significant differences across columns within each category are marked with asterisks: * *p* < .05 (less than 5 percent likelihood that the difference is due to chance or error); ** *p* < .01 (less than 1 percent likelihood that the difference is due to chance or error); *** *p* < .001 (less than 0.1 percent likelihood that the difference is due to chance or error).
Source: 2000 Primorskii survey.

would expect to turn into illegal settlers who would bring in families and friends and—according to the "crawling penetration" theory—would gradually outnumber the local Russian population. Given a sharp decline in illegal Chinese migrants—the ostensible "crawling infiltrators"—one would expect Primorskii residents to become less threatened by and less prejudicial toward the Chinese from the early 1990s to the early 2000s.

And yet, Primorskii polling data show that during the same time period, perceptions of the Chinese threat and anti-Chinese prejudice actually hardened. Between 1994 and 1998, according to the Sotsium Vladivostoka surveys by the Institute of History, Archeology, and Ethnography of the Peoples of the Far East of the Russian Academy of Science (IHAE), the gap between local residents who saw Chinese "peaceful penetration" as threatening Russia's sovereignty and those who did not widened by 5 percentage points—from 45-to-26 to 47-to-23.[29] The share of respondents who felt threatened by Chinese expansion into the RFE increased from 45 percent in the 1994 IHAE poll to more than 56 percent in the 2000 Primorskii poll. Between 1994 and 1998 the gap between those respondents polled by IHAE who approved and those who disapproved of the presence of Chinese nationals in Primorskii widened by 6 percentage points, from 5-to-33 to 4-to-38. The proportion of Primorskii residents who disapproved of Russian-Chinese marriages increased from 33 percent in the 1994 poll to 48 percent in the 1998 poll. Moreover, the share of respondents in the same polls who said Russian-Chinese marriages were a private matter dropped from 58 to 36 percent. In the 2000 Primorskii survey, 56 percent of those polled disapproved of Russian-Chinese marriages and 36 percent expressed a belief that it was a private matter. Finally, looking at anti-Chinese prejudices expressed in ethnic stereotypes, only 5 percent in the IHAE 1992 poll saw the Chinese as inherently "aggressive" as an ethnic group. This share rose to 20 percent in the 1997 poll, to 27 percent in the 1998 poll, and to more than 40 percent in the 2000 Primorskii poll.

The Interethnic Security Dilemma

Going back to the original definition by John Hertz: "Whenever . . . anarchic society has existed—and it has existed in most periods of known history on some level—there has arisen what may be called the 'security dilemma' of men, or groups, or their leaders. Groups or individuals living in such a constellation must be, and usually are, concerned about their security from being attacked, subjected, dominated, or annihilated by other groups and individuals."[30] At the heart of the security dilemma is concern for relative power derived from a desire for self-preservation, strongly associated with the absence or weakness of government authority.[31] Regarding ethnic relations, the security dilemma refers to obsession with relative power "when proximate groups of people suddenly find themselves newly responsible for their own security."[32] Interethnic migration, especially in remote borderlands amid territorial disputes, is precisely a process that would make formerly separate groups proximate and potentially insecure.

The resulting migration security dilemma has the same underlying logic as does the security dilemma in international relations, but the similarity is not straightforward. In international relations, the security dilemma may be seen as a situation where challenging a hypothetical adversary could lead to war with the same probability as not challenging the hypothetical adversary. In the first instance, the war would result from the adversary's retaliation to one's attack. In the second instance, the war would result from the adversary taking advantage of one's perceived weakness. With respect to migration, the security dilemma has to do with fewer direct threats. These threats, nonetheless, are related to interethnic violence and third-party intervention in one's state—and as such are serious security threats. The immigration security dilemma is a situation where challenging incoming migrants with tough exclusionist policies may provoke violent backlashes by migrants against the native population, whereas allowing migrants to come and stay in the country may provoke no less violent backlashes by the natives against the migrant populations.

I observed a telling illustration of both parts of the dilemma in the town of Pogranichnyi on the Russian-Chinese border in the fall of 2000. The potential for migrant backlash was in full view when the attempted detention of a Chinese woman by the Russian railroad patrol resulted in a dozen or so Chinese tourists surrounding the Russian officers and pushing them away from the woman. In the same town on the same day, the potential for the native backlash revealed itself when a local Russian man, yelling obscenities, threw a track suit in the face of a Chinese trader who was selling it at the railroad station market. To this, I may add persistent themes in interviews with local residents and government officials to the effect that an increasing Chinese presence in Primorskii Krai without a tough response by the Russian government would one day invite China's military intervention not only to protect the Chinese diaspora but also to annex parts of the RFE.

Given the remoteness of Primorskii Krai from Russia's political center, its sparse population, and its location on a long and disputed border with

China, one would expect the security dilemma to engender hostility toward the Chinese regardless of actual migration scale. In this sense, the preemptive overrating of the security threat in the region would also resonate with the arguments of the Copenhagen School scholars who showed how "societal security" can be endangered by escalating retaliatory clashes between majority and minority nationalisms in European states when identity issues are interpreted as survival issues in public discourse.[33] The security dilemma logic also accounts for Roger Petersen's finding that emotions of "resentment" explained most ethnic violence in Central and Eastern Europe during the twentieth century. This is because Petersen defined "resentment" as an emotional response to the hypothetical threat that under anarchy—weakening central authority—social hierarchies may shift in favor of others. Resentment, in this sense, is not merely about "the belief that one's group is in an unjust position" and that the situation can be improved through violence against the presumably most vulnerable group highest up in the "ethnic status hierarchy."[34] It is also about the urge to hedge one's group against the destabilizing and status-threatening effects of the vanishing rules of the game.

Besides accounting for this logic of emotional response to uncertainty, the security dilemma theory has an additional explanatory value. It suggests that native populations may target not only the most vulnerable groups highest in the ethnic status hierarchy but also even those marginal migrant groups associated with speculative threats to security and group privilege. In other words, the added value of the immigration security dilemma in relation to prior research is that it would explain the urge for disproportionate preemptive retaliation—and, hence, exaggerated and paradoxical hostility—against marginally small ethnic minorities that do not engage in any hostile behavior against the natives. It thus explains why a few thousand poor and disorganized Chinese traders in the RFE would be viewed as armies of "creeping infiltrators" and give rise to local public discourse about the utility of Russia's nuclear deterrent.

The application of the security dilemma logic to my study of anti-migrant hostility[35] suggests that interethnic mobilization would arise in response to (1) perceptions of "emergent anarchy" (speculative assessments of government strength, sense of isolation from central authority); and (2) the indistinguishability of a "defensive" (legal visits, trade) intent versus an "offensive" (illegal settlement, territorial claims) intent of migrants and migrant-sending states. In addition, this approach suggests that a general sense of uncertainty about the security implications of migration would enhance public readiness to mobilize—even when actual conditions and the scale of migration itself warrant no alarmist sentiments. This uncertainty would also enhance intergroup bias, raise concern about hypothetical economic competition, and heighten a sense of threat to majority position—even though none of these perceptions may seem to be warranted by the scale and nature of migration.

In the 2000 Primorskii survey, the "security dilemma complex"—a sense of isolation from central Russia, suspicions about China's intent, economic vulnerability, and concern about security implications—turned out to be the most significant and strongest predictor of a proclivity for anti-Chinese mobilization (see table 4.5). In particular, respondents who viewed Chinese migration as a security threat to Primorskii Krai were more than twice as likely to support anti-Chinese parties and politicians than respondents who did not view Chinese migration as a threat. In fact, uncertainty about the security implications of Chinese migration was the only indicator in the 2000 Primorskii survey analyzed here (cf. tables 4.1–4.5) that significantly affected all three indicators of mobilization, including support for the LDPR. Insecure respondents were three times more likely to support the LDPR than secure respondents. In addition, respondents who felt that migration would benefit only a minority (under 25 percent) of Primorskii residents were three times more likely to give support to anti-Chinese parties and politicians than respondents who believed migration would benefit a vast majority (over 75 percent) of Primorskii residents.

This analysis, however, points out that Primorskii residents hardly trusted the LDPR to reduce Primorskii Krai's isolation from central Russia, to protect the RFE against China's territorial claims, and to help local Russians benefit from cross-border exchanges with China.

The security dilemma logic offers insights into the key puzzles that confounded theories of intergroup bias, labor market competition, and threat to group position in this study of Chinese migration in Primorskii Krai. First, it explains why Russians in the 2000 Primorskii survey were more likely to mobilize behind xenophobic parties and groups if they thought that ethnic Chinese migrants could easily become culturally assimilated ("Russified"). This fear of assimilating minorities is particularly counterintuitive given persistent public demands from San Diego to Paris that immigrants should strive to assimilate as quickly as possible into receiving societies. Though running contrary to the idea that group distance engenders intergroup hostility, this finding makes perfect sense if one considers that assimilation would only be an issue in Primorskii if Chinese migrants had already been settling there in large numbers. And this is precisely what local residents

Table 4.5. Support for Anti-Chinese Mobilization and the Logic of the Security Dilemma (percent)

	Perceptions of:							
	"Anarchy"		Intent		Economic Opportunity		Security Implication	
	Primorskii krai isolated from central Russia		China claims Russian Far East territory		Percentage of Primorskii residents to benefit from cross-border exchanges by 2005–10		Chinese migration is a security threat to Primorskii krai	
Question	Yes	No	Yes	No	<25%	>75%	Yes	No
Which party or movement do you trust the most: LDPR (N = 684) (N = 758) (N = 581) (N = 921)	3.6	5.0	6.6	3.6	7.8	5.7	7.5	2.5*
In response to Chinese migration in Primorskii Krai, give support to armed detachments of Cossacks or other such groups set up to maintain public order (N = 692) (N = 764) (N = 591) (N = 930)	72.2	47.7***	63.6	48.6***	69.7	50.0**	65.0	40.6***
In response to Chinese migration in Primorskii Krai, give support to politicians and political parties campaigning against Chinese presence (N = 687) (N = 757) (N = 586) (N = 915)	59.2	42.8***	57.5	44.3***	56.0	18.0***	63.8	29.5***

Note: N is the number of respondents who answered both the row and column questions, out of the total of 1,010 respondents in the survey. The table shows what percentage of respondents in each column expressed support for the Liberal Democratic Party (LDPR), the Cossacks, and anti-Chinese parties/politicians. Statistically significant differences across columns within each category are marked with asterisks: $*p < .05$ (less than 5 percent likelihood that the difference is due to chance or error); $**p < .01$ (less than 1 percent likelihood that the difference is due to chance or error); $***p < .001$ (less than 0.1 percent likelihood that the difference is due to chance or error).
Source: 2000 Primorskii survey.

feared, especially given overblown estimates of the scale of Chinese migration. It is most likely, therefore, that asking about Chinese assimilation activated respondents' concerns that Chinese migration could translate into Chinese settlement or "penetration"—a perception that, in turn, induced a stronger proclivity for anti-Chinese mobilization. In short, the logic of group distinctiveness was itself shaped by the logic of insecurity.

Second, the intergroup security dilemma would explain why a fear of labor market competition is likely to emerge even when the scale of economic migration is not large enough to engender ethnic job queues or native business failure. In the 2000 Primorskii survey, a proclivity for mobilization was related not so much to respondents' employment or job status as to uncertainty about migration's effect on economic opportunities for receiving communities as a whole. The crucial point is that insecurity galvanized a prospective or speculative threat of labor market competition. And this was the type of threat that affected respondents regardless of whether their own job situation made them more vulnerable to competition with Chinese migrants. In other words, the threat of labor market competition may be more acute than it seems when migration, however insignificant in size, raises a general sense of uncertainty and insecurity.

Third, the security dilemma perspective enables one to understand why prejudice and hostility toward Chinese migrants in Primorskii Krai increased from the early 1990s to the early 2000s even though the pool of prospective illegal Chinese settlers decreased by more than 25 times, ostensibly weakening the threat to the Russian majority position. This is because, through the lenses of the security dilemma, a threat to group position would be related not only to the actual migration scale or to migration trends but also to population balances between migrant-sending and migrant-receiving states. Not surprisingly, given China's almost tenfold advantage over Russia in population size, Russian scholars frequently refer to "China's demographic overhang" (*demograficheskoe navisanie*) over the RFE. One scholar in Primorskii Krai quantified the concept of China's "demographic pressure" (*demograficheskoe davlenie*) on the southern part of the RFE (Primoskii and Khabarovskii krays, Amur Region, and Jewish Autonomous District). By his estimate, this pressure amounted to 63,000 Chinese nationals per one Russian, per 1 kilometer of the Russian-Chinese border in the RFE and, more ominously, to 380,000 Chinese per one Russian in the 1-kilometer-wide strip of borderland.[36]

Against this background, the Primorskii public was exposed to reports of persistent and substantial population decline in the krai. The realization that since the early 1990s deaths had consistently outstripped births in Primorskii became a major concern, aggravating the sense of "demographic overhang" from across increasingly more populous China. Adding to the sense of isolation from central Russia were recurrent clashes between former governor Nazdratenko and the Kremlin, during which Nazdratenko skillfully manipulated the specter of Far Eastern secessionism to secure both greater decisionmaking autonomy and subsidies from Moscow.[37] At the same time, Nazdratenko presented himself as a strongman who could effectively prevent Chinese migration from turning the RFE into an "Asian Balkans"—hardly a public discourse that would make local residents feel more safe and secure.[38] And in taking a visible public stand against implementation of the 1991 Russia-China border demarcation agreement, Nazdratenko made Chinese territorial claims a major public and political issue in Primorskii. The visibility of this issue raised the specter of Sino-Russian territorial disputes, including violent border clashes of the late 1960s, activating suspicions about the intent of Chinese migrants and their government. In this context, it is understandable why the sense of threat to Russian majority position in Primorskii increased in the 1990s despite a sharp drop in illegal Chinese migration.

The Migration-Hostility-Mobilization Puzzle Revisited

One major finding of this study, borne out most strongly and unambiguously by empirical evidence, is that antimigrant hostility arises predominantly in response to symbolic threat perception associated with uncertainty about migration's consequences—rather than in response to the actual migration scale. The case of Chinese migration in Primorskii Krai shows that low migration rates and a sharp decline in illegal migration may still accompany substantial support for anti-immigrant parties and groups in a climate of political and economic uncertainty and insecurity. In the 2000 Primorskii opinion survey, the perceptual "security dilemma complex"—embedded in uncertainties about the security and economic consequences of migration—came out as the most powerful correlate of interethnic hostility. In political discourses about Chinese migration in Primorskii Krai, this security dilemma complex was most vividly manifested in the images such as the "Asian Balkans" and "crawling penetration" used by parties and politicians to mobilize public support.[39] Significantly, this logic is palpable even in the absence of "the spiral dynamic"—that is, before receiving societies and migrants may engage in hostile preemptive measures to improve their own security that would in turn make both sides feel less secure and thus lead to escalation of hostility. However, the analysis suggests that in conditions similar to Primorskii Krai, the risk of sudden spiraling of interethnic hostility through mutual retaliation is high.

The hostility-to-mobilization part of the puzzle is more complex, although this study is at least suggestive in some important respects. One major point that comes through consistently in tables 4.1 through 4.5 is that the overall proclivity for mobilization was related more strongly and significantly to the attitudes than the social attributes of respondents. The perceptual logic of insecurity turned out to be a particularly prominent driver of support for anti-Chinese parties and groups. This finding suggests that negative intergroup sentiments may spread across various social groups with relative ease, even though social bases of support for mobilization would still remain weak and fragmented. The divergence among social groups supporting the LDPR and the Cossacks—despite a significant overlap in the anti-Chinese objectives and rhetoric of both organizations—would explain the absence of coordinated mass public actions against Chinese migration in Primorskii Krai in the 1990s and early 2000s, even in areas such as Khasan County, where both the LPDR and the Cossacks have had a large support base.

The fragmentation of social support for anti-Chinese mobilization in Primorskii actually had a more complex underlying logic. To provide a partial insight into this complexity, I ran statistical tests with the 2000 Primorskii data with all fifteen predictors of hostility listed in tables 4.1 through 4.5. The tests enabled me to find out how each of these fifteen predictors—such as age, gender, or perception of threat to majority status—was related to mobilization when all the remaining predictors were held constant. To give a partial example, I was able to ascertain whether support for the LDPR was significantly different among males versus females who had the same age, occupation, religious background, views about Russian-Chinese marriages, sense of group distinctiveness between Russians and the Chinese, and all other explanatory factors.[40] The same applied to the analysis of support for the Cossacks and anti-Chinese parties and politicians in general.

These tests established that only one category of respondents in the 2000 Primorskii survey—agricultural workers—consistently supported the LDPR.[41] Support for the Cossacks and similar paramilitary groups was also consistent among only one group of respondents—Primorskii residents who felt that China harbored territorial claims on the RFE. This analysis would explain why the LDPR and the Cossacks had such limited mobilization support base. First of all, only about 5 percent of the 2000 Primorskii sample—representative of the krai population—classified themselves as agricultural workers. Even though more than 70 percent of them also believed China had territorial designs on the RFE and more than 60 percent backed the Cossacks, these findings actually indicate that social support for the LDPR and the Cossacks converged within a marginal and at the same time widely dispersed social group—making anti-Chinese mobilization a costly endeavor with limited impact.

Moreover, this study indicates that even these narrow social bases of support for both the LDPR and the Cossacks were fragmented. General support for the LDPR was strongest among males with lower levels of education, but only 7 percent of respondents who were males and 8 percent of respondents who had a secondary education or less were also agricultural workers. The overlap between the two social groups who identified with the Cossacks' anti-Chinese agenda—respondents with pre-college education and Russian Orthodox Christians—was less than 30 percent. Religious background as Russian Orthodox could have bridged the LDPR and Cossack constituencies, but though more than 60 percent of Russian Orthodox respondents supported the Cossacks, fewer than a third of agricultural workers said they were Russian Orthodox believers.

It is also important to note that agricultural workers hardly represent a shining social role model in Primorskii or in Russia in general. Hence, they are hardly a group that would find it easy to attract followers in the rest of the society—even if other social groups shared concerns of rural workers about migration. Parties and groups associated with this "country bumpkin" image would thus have to fight an uphill battle to mobilize nonrural groups for action.

In more sophisticated multiple regression tests that simultaneously assessed the impact of all fifteen predictors on general support for anti-Chinese parties and politicians, three were statistically significant: a perception of Russian-Chinese group differences, the estimated scale of economic benefits from migration for local residents, and concern about the security of Primorskii Krai. These tests are reported in my forthcoming publications elsewhere.[42] In other words, politicians who made the case that the Chinese were different, that migration restricted economic benefits for the local population, and that the security of Primorskii Krai was threatened stood a good chance of mobilizing public support. Yet, these perceptions were not significantly related to support for the LDPR and the Cossacks—specific organizations that could plausibly mobilize the public not only to support anti-Chinese measures in policies but also to organize protesters and confront Chinese migrants at the grassroots level. This dichotomy explains why—despite overblown anti-Chinese alarmism and hostility, strong electoral support for Nazdratenko, and a higher-than-average vote for LDPR—so few organized anti-immigrant protests and no organized anti-Chinese violence occurred in Primorskii Krai. Despite brimming with the rhetoric of Balkanization, Primorskii Krai thus did not turn into the "Asian Balkans."

It is also worth considering—perhaps as a question for further research—to what extent elite political discourses themselves shaped exaggerated anti-Chinese sentiments. The prevalence of attitudes versus attributes in support for anti-Chinese mobilization suggests that this is indeed a plausible proposition. In this case, it would come to light that the key elite players in Primorskii Krai who could mobilize anti-Chinese public action had divergent goals and interests. But actual anti-Chinese collective action by local residents—for example, demonstrations, protests, border sit-ins, attacks on migrant traders—was not one of these goals. Nazdratenko needed the anti-Chinese vote to win gubernatorial elections and to survive pressure from the Kremlin to resign. The LDPR needed the anti-Chinese vote to clear the 5 percent threshold for the Russian State Duma. And the Ussuri Cossacks—according to my interview with their chieftain in Vladivostok (May 31, 1999)—were hoping that the federal and Primorskii governments would reward their tough stand on Chinese migration and border enforcement by transferring into their property large plots of arable land along the Russia-China border and by allowing the Cossacks to bear firearms.

The 1990s left Primorskii Krai with a new legacy of anti-Chinese hostility, but it is a legacy predominantly rooted in symbolic, perceptual logic. As long as the social bases of anti-Chinese mobilization remain fragmented and marginal, and as long as political elites pursue divergent goals, the spillover of hostility into collective action is unlikely. However, with the scale of Chinese migration and concomitant threats persistently exaggerated from the Kremlin to Vladivostok from the early 1990s to the time of writing in late 2003, the symbolic anti-Chinese legacy will remain alive, with generally negative consequences not only for ethnic relations but also for the socioeconomic development of Pacific Russia.

Conclusion: Could Anti-Chinese Hostility
Morph into Ethnic Violence in the RFE?

This study contains some important clues to the provocative question of whether anti-Chinese hostility could morph into ethnic violence in the RFE. First of all, organized, large-scale anti-Chinese violence in Primorskii and elsewhere in the RFE is unlikely unless Chinese migrants start coming in larger numbers and establish visible permanent settlements. At present, the Chinese concentrate in small areas on the margins of major cities, and most migrants are highly mobile. They do not have sizable stakes in local real estate or other assets that would tie them down in the RFE. In other words, the Chinese are a moving target. Most Chinese are ready to move back across the border at the first sign of confrontation with the Russian public or government authorities. According to Tamara Troyakova, a research fellow at the Vladivostok Institute of History, Archeology, and Ethnography of the Peoples of the Far East, most Chinese migrant traders went back to China for the duration of the census taking in October 2002 for fear of being registered and harassed by Russian government officials. In Petropavlovsk-Kamchatski in 2002, public demonstrations against the allegedly encroaching Chinese presence dissipated after sweeping raids produced barely a dozen Chinese nationals staying illegally in Kamchatka's capital.

But this study also indicates that even if Chinese migration becomes more sizable and leads to permanent settlement in the RFE, organized anti-Chinese violence would still be unlikely absent a confluence of other conditions and conflict "triggers." The first major condition would be increasing sense of isolation from central Russia among local Russians—arising, for example, from the breakdown of transportation systems (disruptions on the Trans-Siberian Railroad), rising prices for airline and railway tickets (especially if local incomes stagnate or decrease), the worsening energy crisis (which would be related to the Kremlin's inability to connect the RFE to Russia's high-voltage LEP 500 grid), and nonpayment of salaries of federal employees who include border guards, customs officials, the military, and the Interior Ministry personnel (police). Generally speaking, deteriorating public services, persistent crime, and endemic corruption are all factors that local residents would interpret as Russian government weakness, which, in turn, would enhance the sense of abandonment, isolation and, consequently, alienation among the RFE residents. Because most of these developments have plagued the RFE since the early 1990s, however, they are not likely to induce anti-Chinese mass violence on their own.

The second condition—and the most likely proximate trigger of anti-Chinese public action in the RFE—would be advancement by China of territorial claims against Russia. These claims would have to be more substantial and symbolic than border demarcation disputes of the 1990s, which failed to trigger violent backlashes against Chinese migrants in Primorskii. For example, one can think of China's abrogation of the 1991 border demarcation treaty; China's wide-scale dredging of the Amur River or construction of damns on the Amur and its tributaries that could potentially flood territories currently under Russian control; demands on the Russian government to return Chinese names to cities such as Ussuriisk or Dal'nerechensk; or the establishment of large new military bases by China along the Russian border in violation of the treaty prohibiting major troop deployments within 100 kilometers of the border.

The third major factor has to do with the economic effects of Chinese migration. If increasing Chinese migration fails to generate tangible economic benefits for the majority of Primorskii residents, an important constraint on anti-Chinese animosity would be absent. As an illustration, suppose that the number of Chinese traders and markets increase, but the quality of consumer goods they sell remains shoddy and illicit trade in the RFE's natural resources increases. These developments would also exacerbate the sense that Chinese migrants thrive on local corruption and are likely to turn the murky economic environment of Russia's "Wild East" to their unilateral advantage—stripping Russia of important strategic assets as a result.

Finally, even if all these ingredients are in place, one would still need to see the rise of agitators, politicians, and ethnic entrepreneurs who could organize street protests against the Chinese and campaign for office using not only anti-Chinese messages but also promoting specific policies to "cleanse the Russian lands of the 'yellow peril.'" Symbolic political action by such groups and individuals would furnish focusing events and triggers that could unleash anti-Chinese violence. For example, one can envision the xenophobic far-right Zhirinovsky Bloc and the new xenophobic centrist party, Rodina (Motherland) building up their networks in Primorskii Krai and the RFE. One can also envision the rise of these parties—evident in the 2003 Duma election—changing the tone in regional governments and leading to a relaxation of local bans on extreme racist and "Slavic fascist" groups such as Russian National Unity and Limonovtsy (supporters of the firebrand Russian fascist ideologue, Eduard Limonov). The temptation by mainstream politicians to manipulate these groups for short-term gains such as winning elections or distracting public attention from acute socioeconomic problems would also increase the likelihood of anti-Chinese violence.

By allowing one to identify these signposts of putative Russian-Chinese communal violence, this study also suggests, however, that at the time of writing in January 2004, a massive and deadly concatenation of such circumstances in the short term—within the next two years or so—is unlikely, if not outright unthinkable.

Notes

1. Viktor Larin, director of the Vladivostok Institute of the History, Archeology, and Ethnography of the Peoples of the Far East, counted more than 150 articles in the Primorskii and Russian press from 1993 to 1995 that voiced these threats while providing no specific data on Chinese migration to substantiate them. E.g., the Russian national daily *Izvestiia* asked "The Chinese in the Far East: Guests or Masters?" Another Russian daily, *Komsomol'skaia Pravda,* wondered, "Will Vladivostok Become a Suburb of Kharbin?" A Vladivostok mass-market tabloid, *Novosti,* warned: "The Chinese Are Unarmed, but Very Dangerous." See Viktor Larin, *Kitai I Dal'nii Vostok Rossii v pervoi polovine 90-kh: problemy regional'nogo vzaimodeistviia* (Vladivostok: Dal'nauka, 1998), 72. For a detailed analysis of public perceptions see Mikhail A. Alexseev, "Socioeconomic and Security Implications of Chinese Migration in the Russian Far East," *Post-Soviet Geography and Economics* 42, no. 2 (2001): 95–114; and Mikhail A. Alexseev, "Economic Valuations and Interethnic Fears: Perceptions of Chinese Migration in the Russian Far East," *Journal of Peace Research* 40, no. 1 (January 2003): 89–106.

2. Georgy Ilyichev, *Izvestiia,* December 2, 2002, 3.

3. Mikhail A. Alexseev, "Chinese Migration in the Russian Far East: Security Threats and Incentives for Cooperation in Primorskii Krai," in *Russia's Far East: A Region at Risk?* ed. Judith Thornton and Charles Ziegler (Seattle: University of Washington Press, 2002), 319–48.

4. Agence France-Press, March 10, 1995. This was a clever, if totally erroneous, statement. On the one hand, millions of people in the Soviet Union, including this author, watched television documentaries showing thousands and thousands of Chinese citizens armed with pickaxes and shovels digging the tunnels to protect them from a feared Soviet nuclear attack in the 1960s. But these tunnels were not dug under the Sino-Soviet border. On the other hand, a reference to hostile "penetration" via tunnels conjures up the description of the alleged global Jewish conspiracy against Russia in the infamous Protocols of the Elders of Zion—which became an anti-Semitic manifesto in Russia at the turn of the twentieth century. In this way, Zhirinovsky's message was likely to appeal to his core anti-Semitic constituency across Russia.

5. Leonid Vinogradov, "Zhirinovsky Curses Communists, Yabloko, Upholds LDPR," ITAR-TASS, August 11, 1999.

6. Michael McFaul, Nikolai Petrov, and Andrei Riabov, eds., *Biuleten' nomer 4: Itogi Vyborov, Tablitsa P3,* Moscow: Moscow Carnegie Center, http://pubs.carnegie.ru/

elections/Bulletins/default.asp?n=bulletin0400.asp. Across Russia as a whole, the LDPR won just 6 percent of the 1999 Duma vote.

7. Mikhail A. Alexseev, "Chinese Migration and Nationalist Activism in the Russian Far East, 1993–2000," an event database of 3,250 event summaries on developments affecting Chinese migrants in Primorskii krai, Russia; the summaries are coded to standard specifications developed as part of the Global Event Data Systems and Conflict and Peace Database projects; http://www.rohan.sdsu.edu/~alexseev (San Diego: San Diego State University, 2002).

8. Mikhail A. Alexseev, "Globalization at the Edges of Insecurity: Migration, Interethnic Relations, Market Incentives and International Economic Interactions in Post-Soviet Russia's Border Regions," Working Paper, Center for Security Studies and Conflict Research, Zurich, 2001.

9. Alexseev, "Economic Valuations and Interethnic Fears," table 2. The Primorskii 2000 survey was based on a probability sample of respondents, following a multistage random sampling procedure from six locations within Primorskii krai. The sample was stratified by location (border vs. nonborder), population change, and population density, rural/urban population split, and economic indicators (average wage purchasing power and trade with China). The areas include the cities of Vladivostok and Artem and the counties of Ussuriisk (including the city of Ussuriisk), Dalnerechensk, Khasan, and Lazo. Voting districts served as primary sampling units (*psus*). In cities, the *psus* were selected randomly (by drawing lots), and in rural areas where voting districts vary significantly in size, by random selection proportionate to estimated population size (a method that ensures random representation of small and large size *psus* without skewing the sample toward either one or the other unit type). The number of dwellings in each *psu* was then counted and classified by type and proportions of residents in each *psu* by dwelling type were estimated. Interviewers then selected the dwellings and the respondents randomly by drawing lots.

10. Baseline data are avalaible in Alexseev, "Socioeconomic and Security Implications of Chinese Migration," table 1. For the most recent data on some of the same migration categories, see I. Yegorchev, "Nemnogo Istorii," *Sovetskii Sakhalin,* October 21, 2000, at http://dlib.eastview.com; and Dmitrii Chernov, "Kitatiskaia bolezn' Dal'nego Vostoka: Diaspora zhivet po svoim zakonam" [The Chinese disease of the Russian Far East: The diaspora lives according to its own laws], *Vremia novostei,* February 19, 2003, 6, at http://dlib.eastview.com.

11. In Russia or in Primorskii, no influential newspaper replicated persistent calls by the *Wall Street Journal* to abolish borders.

12. At the same time, regulated cultural exchanges with China had the approval of most Primor'e residents in the survey (71 percent). About 56 percent of respondents supported the idea of setting up Chinese cultural centers in the area, and 62 percent of respondents favored increasing Chinese language instruction in the local schools. Here and thereafter, the source for Primorskii 2000 survey data are Mikhail A. Alexseev, "Economic Valuations and Interethnic Fears: Perceptions of Chinese Migration in the Russian Far East," Opinion Survey Conducted in Primorskii krai, September 2000, $N = 1,010$, Stratified Random Sampling Proportionate to Estimated Population Size." Deposited at the Library Archive at the Vladivostok Institute of History, Ethnography, and Archeology of the Russian Academy of Sciences, Vladivostok 690000, Pushkinskaia Street, 89. Reference numbers are, as transliterated from Russian: fond 1, opis'2, delo 435; posted on "Russia in Asia" Web site, http://www.rohan.sdsu.edu/~alexseev.

13. Moreover, about 40 percent of those polled said they were ready to physically assist police in identifying and catching illegal Chinese immigrants.

14. E.g., regarding gender and immigration attitudes, Peter Burns and James G. Gimpel, "Economic Insecurity, Prejudicial Stereotypes, and Public Opinion on Immigration Policy," *Political Science Quarterly* 115 (Summer 2000), found that in 1992 women in the United States held more positive views of blacks than men, but both sexes had the same likelihood to hold negative stereotypes of Hispanics. In the same study, urban dwellers expressed more negative views of blacks and Hispanics than rural residents in 1992. In 1996, by contrast, urban dwellers had more positive views of Blacks and Hispanics than rural residents. With respect to age, E. M. J. Smith, "Ethnic Minorities: Life, Stress, Social Support, and Mental Health Issues," *The Counseling Psychologist* 13 (1985): 537–79, found that in the United States socialization in the post–civil rights era engendered more favorable interracial attitudes—but this should not necessarily be the case in societies that were not affected by the civil rights movements in the same way as the United States.

15. The latter question in the context of the survey reflected on support for the former governor Yevgenii Nazdratenko and his alarmist warnings of impending Sinification of Primorskii krai.

16. For Cossacks and Vladivostok Pearson's R was .079, $p < .01$; for Cossacks and Ussuriisk, Pearson's R was $-.092$, $p < .01$.

17. Donald L. Horowitz, *Ethnic Groups in Conflict* (Berkeley: University of California Press, 1985), 182; the literature summary is on 141–86.

18. John C. Turner, "The Experimental Social Psychology of Intergroup Behaviour," in *Intergroup Behavior,* ed. John C. Turner and H. Giles (Chicago: University of Chicago Press, 1981).

19. Turner, "Experimental Social Psychology," 97–98.

20. J. F. Dovidio and S. L. Gaetner, "Intergroup Bias: Status, Differentiation, and a Common In-Group Identity," *Journal of Personality and Social Psychology* 75, no. 1 (1998): 109–20; J. L. Gibson and Amanda Gouws, "Social Identities and Political Intolerance: Linkages within the South African Mass Public," *American Journal of Political Science* 44, no. 2 (2000): 278–92.

21. Sergei Pushkarev, then head of the Russian Federal Migration Service for Primorskii krai, interview with the author, Vladivostok, August 15, 2000.

22. Correlation between general party/politicians support and sense of social differences was especially strong and significant, given the large number of cases in the survey (Pearson's $R = .217$, $p < .001$). (For the LDPR, Pearson's R was .132, $p < .01$.)

23. Susan Olzak, "Labor Unrest, Immigration and Ethnic Conflict in Urban America, 1880–1914," *American Journal of Sociology* 94 (May 1989): 1303–33; Olzak, *The Dynamics of Ethnic Competition and Conflict* (Stanford, Calif.: Stanford University Press, 1992).

24. Alexseev, "Socioeconomic and Security Implications of Chinese Migration."

25. Larin, *Kitai I Dal'nii Vostok Rossii.*

26. Approximately four times as many Chinese guest workers were engaged in trade than in agriculture, according to Primorskii Goskomstat.

27. Herbert Blumer, "Race Prejudice as a Sense of Group Position," *Pacific Sociological Review* 1 (1958): 3–7.

28. Alexseev, "Socioeconomic and Security Implications of Chinese Migration."

29. Alexseev, "Chinese Migration in the Russian Far East: Security Threats and In-

centives for Cooperation;" Institute of History, Archeology, and Ethnography of the Peoples of the Far East, Russian Academy of Sciences, *Sotsium Vladivostoka* [Vladivostok opinion survey results: autumn, 1991, 1992, 1994, 1997, 1998], Interim Report, 1998.

30. John Hertz, "Idealist Internationalism and the Security Dilemma," *World Politics* 2 (1950): 157.

31. Robert Jervis, "Cooperation under the Security Dilemma," *World Politics* 30, no. 2 (1978): 167–214. In one textbook definition, the security dilemma is "the chronic distrust that actors living under anarchy feel because, without sanctions or regulatory rules, rivals do anything, including using aggression, to get ahead, with the result that all lose security in a climate of mistrust." See Charles W. Kegley Jr. and Eugene R. Wittkopf, *World Politics: Trend and Transformation,* 7th ed. (New York: St. Martin's Press, 1999), 428.

32. Barry Posen, "The Security Dilemma and Ethnic Conflict," in *Ethnic Conflict in International Politics,* ed. Michael E. Brown (Princeton, N.J.: Princeton University Press, 1993), 103.

33. Ole Waever, Barry Buzan, Morten Kelstrup, and Pierre Lemaitre, *Identity, Migration and the New Security Agenda in Europe* (London: Pinter, 1993).

34. Roger D. Petersen, *Understanding Ethnic Violence: Fear, Hatred, and Resentment in Twentieth-Century Eastern Europe* (New York: Cambridge University Press, 2002), 56.

35. In particular, see Alexseev, "Socioeconomic and Security Implications of Chinese Migration"; Alexseev, "Globalization at the Edges of Insecurity"; Alexseev, "Ugrozhaet li Rossii kitaiskaia migratsiia? Territorial'naia bezopasnost', ekonomicheskoe razvitie I mezhetnicheskie otnosheniia v Primorskom krae" [Is Chinese migration a threat to Russia? Territorial security, economic development, and interethnic relations in Primorskii krai], *Mirovaia ekonomika I mezhdunarodnye otnosheniia* [World economy and international relations, IMEMO journal], nos. 11–12 (November–December 2000); Alexseev, "Chinese Migration in the Russian Far East: Security Threats and Incentives for Cooperation;" and, in a comparative setting, Alexseev, "Peaceful Infiltrations: The Security Dilemma and Anti-Migrant Hostility in the Russian Far East and the European Union," paper presented at the CEEISA/ISA International Convention, Budapest, June 26–28, 2003.

36. P. Ya. Baklanov, Geograficheskie, sotsial'no-ekonomicheskie i geopoliticheskie faktory migratsii kitaiiskogo naseleniia v raiony rossiiskogo Dal'nego vostoka [Geographic, socioeconomic and geopolitical factors of Chinese migration in the regions of the Russian Far East], paper presented at the Roundtable, "Prospects for the Far East Region: The Chinese Factor," Institute of History, Archeology, and Ethnography of the Far Eastern Branch, Russian Academy of Sciences, Vladivostok, June 28, 1999.

37. Mikhail A. Alexseev and Tamara Troyakova, "A Mirage of the 'Amur California': Regional Identity and Economic Incentives for Political Separatism in Primorskiy Kray," in *Center-Periphery Conflict in Post-Soviet Russia: A Federation Imperiled,* ed. Mikhail A. Alexseev (New York: St. Martin's Press, 1999).

38. Yevgenii Nazdratenko, *I vsia Rossiia za spinoi . . .* [And all of Russia Behind Our Back . . .] (Vladivostok: Ussuri, 1999).

39. The case of Mexican migration into California would be an opposite example. Despite the fact that Latinos came to outnumber the non-Hispanic whites in the state in the early 2000s, the gubernatorial election campaigns of 2002 and the recall campaign

of 2003 did not see the main candidates use mobilizing images such as "Californian Balkans" or "crawling penetration." The security dilemma logic would predict, however, that such rhetoric would have been much more prominent if, e.g., Mexico's population exceeded that of the United States by a factor of ten and if California politicians used secessionist rhetoric to resolve disputes with the federal government.

40. The actual statistical method I used enabling this type of analysis is called multiple regression. This is a widely used basic statistical procedure suitable for the kind of question raised in this study.

41. Consistently here means there was less than 5 percent probability that agricultural workers would support the LDPR by chance alone. For all of the remaining fourteen correlates of mobilization, the probability of association only by chance with support for the LDPR was unacceptably high (above 5 percent in a one-tailed significance test).

42. See Mikhail A. Alexseev, *Immigration Phobia and the Security Dilemma: Russia, Europe, and the United States* (New York: Cambridge University Press, 2005).

Part II

The Struggle to Define a Category

5

Beauplan's Prism: Represented Contact Zones and Nineteenth-Century Mapping Practices in Ukraine

Steven J. Seegel

How was the territory of present-day Ukraine represented in maps during the nineteenth century, how did these discursive practices overlap, and what were the roles of official state actors and unofficial nonstate elites in this process? Ukraine as a case study is a conceptual dynamic of superimposed national movements and Imperial efforts at demographic measurement, categorization, and control. For nineteenth-century cartography, while the encompassing empires' surveyors and "scientists" rationalized the exact location of borders and physical landscapes, local ethnographers and national activists developed varying strategies of subversion or resistance. Representing a modern Ukraine in base units proved to be nearly impossible for those involved in nation-, state-, and empire-building projects, because markers such as language and confession could be designed to stand in for a plurality of identities and geopolitical bodies at a time when these were scarcely viable options. State actors and nonstate elites alike developed interdependent cartographic policies in Ukraine within each of the bordering contact zones. Together they constructed the attributes, categories, and dimensions of Ukrainians in such a strict model-building manner that the markers of modernity often bore little resemblance to everyday mixed psychological realities on the ground.[1]

Issues of Policy and Identity:
Modern Cartography and Its Paper Quarrels

Because an open public sphere for resolving categorical issues and territorial disputes was generally lacking in Ukraine, historical and demographic claims were mediated in the symbolic battlefield of maps, a quasi-public paper arena for competing Imperial policies and for the achievement of national collective recognition. Particularly after 1863, Ukrainian national activists sought publicly to negotiate an independent visual space in maps, farther removed from the legacies of the early modern Polish-Lithuanian Commonwealth (Rzeczpospolita Obójga Narodów, Polskiego i Litewskiego) and Cossack Hetmanate, and carved out in between the partitioning Russian and Austrian (later, Austro-Hungarian) powers. Though not being specific about actual borders, Ukrainian cartographers argued for their own cultural, linguistic, historical, and eventual political distinctiveness by drawing from four remotely interactive vantage points: Romanov, Hapsburg, Polish-Lithuanian, and Little Russian. The possible bases for a modern Ukraine in maps involved a process whereby "Ukrainians" were variously centered and conceptually represented, suggesting an ambiguous polycentricity, and occasional confusion, of political and cultural identities.

By bracketing the metageographical notions of East/West for the nineteenth century, or the presupposed Europe/Asia fault line, with all its geopolitical baggage, and conscientiously avoiding the organizing Cold War paradigm of Russia and Eastern Europe, I introduce the more local notion of a "contact zone."[2] A contact zone may be defined as a representational site for multiple regional identities at a time when being multiple was an unlikely, if not impossible, goal to achieve politically. What began as a Great Power impetus in Western, Central, and Eastern Europe to measure every inch of claimed territory in accordance with objective "scientific" accuracy led to the need to define the meaning of "nationality" and its constitutive categories, above all in censuses, museums, and maps.[3] These modes of totalistic measurement and representation involved a process whereby the agendas of Imperial cartographers stood on a collision course with the perceptions of national and ethnolinguistic activists within borders under more direct challenge in 1914 and afterward. In its very fragility as a region during the long nineteenth century, the territorial identities of Ukraine and Ukrainians may be examined comparatively as a prism of separate yet overlapping contact zones.

Taxonomy and Toponymy: Categorizations in Nineteenth-Century Maps of Ukraine

Given such outstanding problems of naming and classifying, what were the processes by which nineteenth-century cartographers constructed, deconstructed, and reconstructed political and cultural identities within the territory of Ukraine? Persistent historical references to the early modern Polish-Lithuanian Commonwealth among elites were badly suited to compete with the later "scientific" discourse of pigeonholing entire communities of people within territorial borders and according to presumptions of race, ethnicity, and spoken language. From the final partition of the Commonwealth until the start of the European Great War, cartographers played a prominent role in the visual representation of modern nations and states, appearing not only at postwar treaty agreements but also beforehand at academic conferences or policymaking sessions. Naming places was often a dual act of attempting to replace one hegemonic place name with another. For both the Romanov and Hapsburg empires, maps were primarily a top-down geopolitical cement for state officials to rationally control their administrative domains and to represent their power within an increasingly militarized, expansionist, and rivalrous European state system. For the old Commonwealth's political nationalists, adhering until at least 1863 to the theoretically inclusive idea of a prepartitioned Poland, Lithuania, or Poland-Lithuania, or for Polish civic and later ethnonationalists who sought to build an exclusivist "Poland," maps were used selectively as a historical device to recover a Eurocentric homeland from Romanov and Hapsburg control. For Ukrainian national activists, maps were the future-oriented means to develop an autonomous if not independent cultural and ethnolinguistic space removed from Russian, Polish, and Austrian (later, Austro-Hungarian) dominion. We turn now to the interrelations between official state and unofficial nonstate actors, to the discursive categories they utilized, and to the maps they themselves produced, consumed, and disseminated.

Contact Zone One: Saint Petersburg / Moscow
and Romanov State-Imperial Policies

Since at least the Petrine reforms, the foreign policy of the Romanov Empire had been consistently intertwined with cartographic bigness. Territorial expansion, settlement, and administration meant that the autocratic state needed to amass a centralized trove of descriptive resources for its terra incognita and all the inhabitants to be counted within it. Generally lacking traditions of private property and cadastral mapping for the resolution of local disputes, the principal characteristics of Russian cartography throughout the eighteenth and nineteenth centuries were unity, accuracy, and totality. Maps were protected by the state in secret archives, and they could not be produced for public consumption without the imposition of censorship and other bureaucratic restrictions. Alternative mapmakers in one or more of the annexed borderlands were simply unacceptable to the tsars. Printed maps, such as those in school history textbooks or even general wall maps, also had to be carefully monitored and edited. The Romanovs continuously held to the conviction that the empire had to be measured mathematically and mapped in its totality, and that this knowledge belonged only to the privileged ruling elite. Once the emplotted borders had been fixed, a historiographical narrative of "acquisition" or "reunion" had to be standardized for the rest of a mostly illiterate population. Ultimately, Russia as a Great Power spanning the ideologically constructed space of Europe and Asia (and North America, counting Alaska) was placed on iconographic display. For the sake of communal pedagogy, the exhibited map had to reflect the enlightened "European" reality of "Russia" in all its totality, and on its own terms.[4]

Vasilii Nikitich Tatishchev (1686–1750), the historian and *encyclopédiste,* set the precedent in 1737 when he proposed that geography and cartography ought to be used to represent the entire territory of Tsarist Russia.[5] The connection with the military nature of the empire was particularly evident. Tatishchev designed a 198-point questionnaire in order to complete the first general map of Russia, as ordered by Peter I and begun by the secretary of the Senate, Ivan Kirilovich Kirilov (1695–1737), who took charge of collecting, registering, and storing all maps and surveys in 1721, the key date after which Muscovy officially became an empire. An incredibly exhaustive effort, the general atlas was finally completed in 1745 after the deaths of Peter I and Kirilov himself. Despite the administrative efforts of Peter I, Catherine II, and Paul I, eighteenth-century geographical practices were largely uncoordinated. Russian geographers often lacked a necessary training in modes of geodesic measurement, which in early modern Europe presupposed territorial administration, agroindustrial modernization, and population settlement and control. Russian-language cartography during the early nineteenth century would come to be dominated by the War Ministry and the Military-Topographical Service and Depot. Paul I ordered the establishment of a special Imperial drafting office for maps, and the Military Topographical Depot was established in Saint Petersburg in 1797 to prepare and compile maps for both military and general use. It would also serve as the state archive for all collections and new labors. After 1800, the depot was the first step toward a systematic survey and assiduously updated surveillance of all Russian territories.

For those elites who did not accept the incorporation of the Polish-Lithuanian Commonwealth, Russian state-imperial practices were viewed as aggressive and illegal. The land surveys initiated by Catherine II in 1766 sought to be comprehensive in Ukraine, but they were done in a rather poorly coordinated manner. The etching of large-scale atlases was always a collaborative effort, prone to grave financial strains and delays. After 1795, Imperial officials monitored territorial calculations using charted astronomical points. As with later Soviet practices on enormous scales, it was *illegal* to publish any maps of plans of the Russian territory without prior *military* approval of the head of state. Romanov expansion and liquidation of the Cossack Hetmanate, acquisition of the Crimean Khanate, and administrative gerrymandering of provinces entailed a continuous need for surveying and surveillance, cooperation and co-optation of local elites.[6] Provincial officials were usually held accountable for the coordination of data to be collected, with the implicit assumption that such territories would be kept intact as part of the Russian state apparatus. Special attention was accorded to the renamed territories of "European Russia." An enormous amount of time and energy and resources was allocated via the military ministries for these geodesic surveys (*s"ëmki,* or early modern equivalents of aerial photography) in the liquidated administrative territories of Ukraine, even before the 1831 Uprising.

After the Napoleonic Wars and Congress of Vienna, detailed topographical maps of the Grand Duchy of Finland and the Kingdom of Poland were printed after extensive work by an Imperial corps of surveyors. From 1819 to 1844, a unified large-scale map of the "western borderlands of Russia as a possible theater of military events" was produced. At the request of Alexander I in 1822, Fyodor Fyodorovich Schubert (1789–1865) became the first director and chief administrator of a new military-topographical corps, responsible for the education of officers in mathematics, geodesics, and standardized Russian. The task at hand among the officers stationed in the partitioned territories, including Ukraine, was one of loyal profession-alization. Strict demands were made in repeated instructions. For instance, the maps carried by each officer had to be kept in alphabetical order; the officers had to provide a statistical description of each area; and it was an obligation, subject to imprisonment, to provide all correct names of rivers, cities, hills, and the like. A decree was passed in October 1819 with the detailed directive for particular coloration of the *gubernii* (provinces) as official political-administrative units, and in 1821 and 1822 two guidebooks codified an elaborate system of classification for different kinds of thematic maps. Cartography was incorporated into the social and gubernatorial structures of the army and subject to direct orders from Saint Petersburg. Imperial centralization therefore precluded ventures of private production and consumption.

In Ukrainian territories, some topographers of the former Commonwealth had joined Napoleon's forces, and as a result, were not trusted entirely to work for the Russian Empire. With some exceptions, there existed little enthusiasm among former Polish or Polish-Lithuanian officers for mapping out the entire expanse of "European Russia," and for transforming the territories of the old Commonwealth, including Ukraine, into *gubernii, oblasti, okrugi,* and *uezdy.* However, several works were indeed finished as joint projects, such as the *Topographical Map of the Kingdom of Poland (Topograficzna Karta Królestwa Polskiego)* from 1822 to 1843. When the remarkably comprehensive *Statistical Atlas of the Polish Kingdom* was eventually completed in 1840, it was a precocious work of Imperial mapping, relying heavily upon local labors. Secretly, Nicholas I ordered the publication of 300 exemplary maps of the Kingdom of Poland (namely for transportation and waterways), only to be published internally within the Military Topographical Depot. But at this early stage, social demography and its classification schemes were not a major priority.

The Imperial Russian Geographical Society (IRGO) was established in 1845 and modeled partly on the British Royal Geographical Society. As applied to Ukraine, the organization was particularly important because it represented a shift eastward away from military-topographical surveys (*s"ëmki*) of the Kingdom of Poland and "European" provinces toward a more Central Asian, Siberian, and Far Eastern orientation. From the outset, it had a more colonial and civil-institutional aim, incorporating the statistical, nautical, and ethnographical research of individual geographers, agronomists, urban planners, explorers, and cartographers who were sent out from Saint Petersburg and Moscow. The Napoleonic theater of war gave way to a more varied interest in expansion and settlement during the second half of the nineteenth century.[7] In terms of social structure, becoming a geographer or cartographer no longer necessarily meant joining the armed forces. After the 1848 revolutions and the debacle of the Crimean War, ethnography, anthropology, and demography—all means of "objectively" collecting and sorting empirical data into constructed categories—emerged in greater conjunction with Great Power expansion and enumerative administration. Meanwhile, the nineteenth-century romantic Imperial and state-centered schools of Russian historiography consistently sponsored publications and included reproductions of Russian-language maps, dividing the sprawling expanse of the Imperial state along the Ural Mountains "objectively" into European and Asiatic components.[8]

In 1859, Aleksandr Afinogenovich Il'in (1832–89), a former officer who associated himself closely with the headquarters of the IRGO in Saint Petersburg, founded the first major cartographic publishing firm in late Imperial Russia. Il'in's firm produced pedagogical wall maps for public consumption as well as scholarly works by geographers. The publicist use of lithography and engraving gave the many atlases, albums, textbooks, and educational wall maps a special aesthetic aura. The maps had the financial support of the Romanov tsars, but despite the liberal reforms of Alexander II, the Ministry of Internal Affairs and the Ministry of National Enlightenment closely censored them. "European Russia" became the most commonly used shorthand for the empire's western borderlands. The IRGO served as a professional organization for conservatively progressive gentlemen-scholars, a private passion and public hobby for expert explorers, civil servants, and statisticians like Pyotr Semyonov, who were sent to distant *gubernii*. For the Russocentric civil servant Semyonov, dedication to the study of geography became a patriotic endeavor from center to periphery, one that fell perfectly in line with the territorial integrity *and* territorial expansion of the Romanov state. He actively participated in the debates surrounding the Great Reforms, and in line with the natural determinism and civilizing missions of his age, believed that geography could be an ameliorative means because of, rather than in spite of, Russia's climate and sprawling vastness.

The establishment of regional branches for the IRGO was a crucial means of communication and of tremendous importance for Ukraine and the partitioned areas of the former Commonwealth. In 1851, two regional departments were founded in Tiflis (labeled "Kavkaz") and Irkutsk ("Siberia"); in 1867–68, Orenberg; in 1868, the "Northwestern" office in Wilno; in 1872, the "Southwestern" branch in Kyiv; in 1877, Omsk ("Western Siberia"); in 1894, Priamursk/Khabarovsk; in 1897, Tashkent ("Turkestan"); and in 1913, Iakutsk. The Kyiv and Wilno branches were closed down and liquidated in 1876, ostensibly because they were acting independent of the IRGO. Alexander II's final decision was made on the advice of the Ministry of Internal Affairs. Apparently the scholars at these outposts were to blame, especially in Kyiv, where they were conducting research according to "Little Russian" ethnographical specifications, thereby promoting de facto propaganda in the Ukrainian language.[9] The systematic collecting of flora and fauna and charting of rivers and canals fell within the parameters of policy, but failure to subscribe to a centrally located Great Russian Imperial identity, primus inter pares, could not be tolerated. Under the autocratic policy of the tsars, Ukrainians, Belarusians, and Russians were part of a unified historical category, which in principle presupposed enlightenment and civilization but in practice relied upon racial, ethnic, and ethnolinguistic Great Power categories of superior and inferior communal groups. These more modern typifications were alien to the decentralized political nation of the former Polish-Lithuanian Commonwealth, the memory of which seemed to have been erased, destroyed, forgotten, or ignored by 1863.

The cartographic firm of Il'in theoretically stated its openness, declaring that it "accepts orders for all kinds of lithographic work: engraving and printed geographical maps, color lithography, artistic publications, etc., and publishes geographical maps, school atlases, specialized maps, globes, geographical essays, and textbooks on geography." In practice, however, it served as a depot for publications of organizations closely dependent upon the centralizing and expanding Imperial state. These organs included the Military-Topographical Administration of the General Army Headquarters, Imperial Russian Geographical Society, Ministry of the Road of Information, Surveying Department, Mining and Mountaining Committee, Geological Committee, Central Statistical Committee, and Society for the Study of the Amur Region. Its Russian-language historical maps for textbooks and schoolroom walls included *The Expansion of Russia since Ivan IV, The Russian Empire since Ivan the Terrible, The Growth of the Roman Empire, Eastern Europe in the Ninth Century and Rus', The Rus' of Moscow and Lithuania,* and *The Russian Empire since Peter I.* As with British, French, and Prussian-German maps and atlases, many of which were simply translated into Russian, Eurocentric maps of the Great Powers and ancient civilizations (Greek and Roman) received special preference. The catalogue as a whole reads like Jorge Luis Borges's famous Chinese encyclopedia, with eclectic "civilizational" pages devoted to iconography, landscape painting, school atlases, lunar and planetary maps, historical novels, agrarian economy guidebooks, and natural science textbooks. It also had miscellaneous pages devoted, for example, to "tables according to physiognomy," comprised arbitrarily of types of primitive peoples (*tipy narodov*): Eskimos, Malaysians, Chinese, Negroes, Australian Aborigines, and Indians. In Russian Great Power Imperial maps following from the Enlightenment, civilization contrasted with barbarism along fictitious racial and ethnic lines.

Of all of the maps and atlases published by the firm of Il'in from its founding in 1859 until its expropriation by the Bolsheviks after World War I, not one stipulated an autonomous or independent Ukraine, and not one historical or topographical map acknowledged the Polish-Lithuanian Commonwealth or the Cossack Hetmanate as anything other than a teleological narrative of ultimate acquisition and incorporation.[10] Later examples included the *Educational Atlas of Russia* (1884, 1889) by I. Poddubnyi; the *Atlas for Russian Studies* (1889) by N. N. Tornau; the *Hypsometric Map of European Russia* (1889) and *Map of European Russia* (1896) by the geologist A. A. Tillo; the *Illustrated Map of the European Part of Russia* (1896) by N. Pavlov; and the *Wall Map of the European Part of Russia with Illustrations of the Ethnic Types, Occupations and Trade* (1900, 1901, 1903, 1905, 1908) and the *Pictorial Map of the Habitats of Game Animals in the European Part of Russia* (1905) by N. Shipov. During the IRGO's first fifty years, it had published 460 volumes and had collected hundreds of maps and atlases from elsewhere in Europe. For the territory of Ukraine and Ukrainian identities, Russian state cartography thereby served as a tool and exhibit of Imperial power in an actual and symbolic paper battlefield.

Contact Zone Two: Vienna/Galicia and Hapsburg Imperial Constructions in Maps

The production of maps, the construction of nationalities, and the preservation of empires went hand in hand with the policies of Russia, Austria, and Prussia, the three partitioning powers of Poland-Lithuania. In terms of nineteenth-century cartography, official state-imperial policies and the enumeration of essentialized identities with ascribed foundations, the Romanov and Hapsburg administrators had more similarities than differences, even though they ultimately differed on the forms of questions they asked, as in the censuses. From 1772 onward, Hapsburg Imperial cartographers undertook the project of administrating their newly annexed territories. Historical justification for the "Kingdom of Galicia and Lodomeria" (Königreich Galizien und Lodomerien) was made as a fait accompli, whereby the Hapsburgs revived medieval Hungary's twelfth-century claim to the land.

At the end of the eighteenth century and in conjunction with state-imperial practices, crude manuscript maps gave rise to more rigorous measurement. Lesser-known territories and their habitants therefore had to be named and sorted rationally into categories. Official Austrian elites colloquially designated the Ukrainians as Ruthenians (Ruthenen), and the territory in proxy shorthand as Galicia (Galizien). Though Galicia certainly functioned as an outpost for divergent Polish and Ukrainian nationalisms after 1863, it remains to be determined to what extent the parameters for these national movements were shaped by Hapsburg Imperial policies, and how tolerant these policies were. Compared with the lawless armed lootings and Tsarist repressions in the Russian partitioned zone of the Commonwealth, they were more than lenient.[11] Yet the Hapsburg monarchy was one cornerstone of the conservative geopolitical equilibrium established by the Congress of Vienna in 1815, which favored state-imperial security over nations and presupposed that states had to be centralized in more modern forms. Both the Austrians and Russians were sine qua non discursive practitioners in social-demographic constructions of the categories characteristic of European Great Power imperialism. Both sought to maintain border security among potentially disruptive "nationalities." In short, both were superb pigeonholers.

The imperial topographical surveys undertaken by the Romanovs and Hapsburgs significantly contributed to the emergence of maps as an elite, then popular, object of science during the long nineteenth century. Hapsburg cartography, like Polish-Lithuanian cartography, had a stronger mathematical tradition than Russian cartography. Josef Liesganig (1719–99), a mathematician who worked at the astronomical observatory in Vienna, fulfilled the initial task of arranging a uniform topographic map. In service to Empress Maria Theresa, he surveyed the territory of "Galizien." His results were printed posthumously in seventy-nine sheets from 1790 to 1824. Geographers and cartographers of the Hapsburg Empire repeatedly memorialized "The Kingdom of Galicia and Lodomeria" in large-scale maps and historical atlases.

Unlike the military-topographical corps of the Russian Imperial service, the Austrian variant was more civil in the sense of social openness and political alertness. Private publishing firms consistently functioned back in Vienna, where editors did not have to deal directly with preemptive censorship. Hapsburg cartography could be placed on par with British, French, Dutch, Portuguese, and Spanish statist initiatives, although the major difference in both was the absence of an overseas empire. In 1805, the *Atlas of the Austrian Empire* was published, and in 1839 a new institute for military topography and surveillance was founded in the seat of the monarchy. The use of color lithography commonly included iconographic representations of an enlightened ruler. New methods of urban planning extended into broader comparisons with other European cities, as in *Ferdinand the First's General Map of Europe,* printed from 1845 to 1847.

By the middle of the nineteenth century, administrative maps of Galicia and Lodomeria were being published with greater frequency. Detailed geological maps of Galicia and Bukovina were sponsored by the Hapsburgs in the 1870s. New modern and modernizing variants of maps were introduced, such as hydrographic and demographic. By the 1870s, the imperial concept of Mitteleuropa came into extensive currency, and this originally Germanocentric notion was employed to include the Austro-Hungarian territory of contemporary Ukraine.[12] Special attention was accorded to measuring and classifying ethnolinguistic in-groups for censuses, based on spoken language. With the rise of positivist sciences and the emerging interest in statistics, the first comprehensive demographic atlas of Galicia with specifically "ethnic" categories was published in 1874–75.

Essentialist categorizations were apparent in mid–nineteenth century Russian and Austrian "ethnographic" maps, which by definition ascribed civilizing missions to themselves and nonhistoricity or prehistoricity to select others based on imaginary racial distinctions or "tribal" in-group languages. The *Ethnographic Map of European Russia (Etnograficheskaia karta Evropeiskoi Rossii),* compiled by the ethnographer and statistician Pyotr Köppen (1793–1864) and published in 1851 in Saint Petersburg under the aegis of the Imperial Russian Geographic Society, made no distinction among the Great, White, and Little Russians. He placed greater taxonomic emphasis on the other in-groups. The Austrian statistician, ethnographer, cartographer, and census compiler Karl von Czoernig (1804–89) collectively categorized the "Ruthenians" in Galicia, Bukovina, and the Carpathian mountain region in his 1855–56 *Ethnographic Map of the Austrian*

Monarchy (*Ethnographische Karte der Österreichischen Monarchie*), published in Vienna.

From the 1850s to 1870s in Central and Eastern Europe, the discursive practice of mapping *Nationalitäten* had acquired what seemed to be a valid social-scientific foundation. Nationalities were based in a circular manner on unit categories of race and ethnicity, which in practice meant the newly established discourse of ethnolinguistics. In spite of the Great Reforms, the major Russian Imperial maps of the period followed the trends in Prussian and Austrian scholarship, creating a strict dichotomy between civilization and ahistoricity. But as for the official Hapsburg policy, the Ruthenians were one of many cultural rather than political minorities within the empire's territorial space for whom language was the single most important marker of identity. In the significant year of 1863, when Mykola Kostomarov (1817–85) wrote in the journal of the Imperial Russian Geographical Society that "the ethnographer ought to be a contemporary historian, a historian who expounds upon older ethnography in his work," he had already anticipated the political phase of categorical representation and mobilization.

Contact Zone Three: Poland-Lithuania
and Its Partial Cartographic Legacy for Ukraine

With reference to the territories of contemporary Ukraine, the nature and character of the Commonwealth's cartography changed dramatically after the last partition in 1795, when politically unaffiliated geographers, astronomers, and mathematicians could no longer enjoy the patronage of a state to secure employment and conduct their research. Because the dispossessed or displaced could only include the boundaries as the incorporative Great Powers had demarcated them, subversive maps and atlases became essential as alternative markers of identity emplotment. Unlike in Muscovy, mathematical mapmaking could be dated back to the Jagiellonian dynasty in the fourteenth century. After 1772, 1793, and 1795, the cartographers of Poland-Lithuania had to serve while confined within the *gubernii* established by the Romanov Empire. The other option was to emigrate and continue the project of collecting, producing, and disseminating maps independently.

From the Russian Imperial perspective, the Commonwealth was best treated as a matter of historical amnesia. Catherine II's army looted Warsaw in 1795 and purloined the map collections of the Załuski Library, the

Crown Register, and the personal collection of Stanisław Poniatowski II. On this basis, the tsarina established the collections of National Public Library and the Army Register in Saint Petersburg. Polish-Lithuanian cartography was given a new opportunity, however, during the Napoleonic wars. In 1809, the Topographical Bureau was established in the army of the Grand Duchy of Warsaw to collect and reproduce military surveillance maps for the French army. After the Treaty of Vienna, the cartographic activities of the Congress Kingdom were concentrated in the Quartermaster General Staff of the Polish Army and the Topographic Bureau of Engineering Corps, where research was coordinated and supervised by tsarist administrators. The Astronomical Observatory at the University of Wilno, which had been reformed under the last king, Poniatowski, and his National Committee on Education, was taken over by unprepared Russian administrators who transformed celestial observations into militarized territorial imperatives.

After the November Uprising of 1831, the Military-Topographical Service attempted once again to confiscate maps and atlases, but the insurrectionists apparently managed to bribe some of the Russian officers. General Józef Chłopicki's collection went to the libraries in Kraków (Biblioteka Czartoryskich and Biblioteka Jagiellońska); General Wincenty Krasinski's collection was moved to Poznań; and Jan Henryk Dąbrowski's collections were acquired by the Society of the Friends of Sciences in Warsaw, although later "transferred" to Saint Petersburg. The pre-1772 territories of the *kresy* (borderlands) were memorialized in poetry, prose, and landscape painting, and the more overtly messianic romantics framed the events melodramatically as dismemberment, the allegorical losing of one's body or soul (figure 5.1).[13]

The ennobling but half-mythic idea of an inclusive, nonimperial Commonwealth was carefully maintained among "Polish" map collectioneers, resulting in major points of contention between "Polish" and "Ukrainian" cartographers (in modern ethnolinguistic terms) in trying to sort through the diversity of the former early modern state. For patriotic émigrés of the territories of the old Commonwealth, including Ukraine, after the final partition they did not have maps, censuses, or museums that they could again call their own. Their archives became their virtualized national museums, and they quickly spread to the least censored area, the Hapsburg zone. Józef Maksymilian Ossoliński established the Ossolineum Library in L'viv (Lwów, Lemberg) in 1817.[14] Historical atlases were published in West European languages and intended for an international audience of sympathizers for renewed statehood. For example, the edited maps of Jan Potocki (1761–1815) were reprinted in Saint Petersburg in 1805 after the looting of the Załuski Library,

Figure 5.1. Johann Esaias Nilson, *Kołacz królewski* (*The royal cake*), Paris, 1773

and reclassified as the *Atlas archaeologique de la Russie européenne.* The atlas was reprinted in 1810 and 1812, and finally officially translated as a Russian edition by V. Anastashevich in 1823, with a dedication to the tsar. Internal and external émigré publications included those of Maria Regina Korzeni-owska (1793–1874), the aunt of Joseph Conrad, Joachim Lelewel (1786–1861), Stanisław Staszic (1755–?), Leonard Chodźko (1800–71), Jan Marcin Bansemer (1810–40), Piotr Zaleski (1809–83), Stanisław Plater (1794–1851), and the director of the Bibliothéque Polonaise in Paris, Feliks Wrotnowski (1803–71). Lelewel and the geographer Eugeniusz Romer (1871–1954), who had studied in Vienna and was later present at the signing of the Treaty of Versailles, together gathered more than 5,000 thematic maps and atlases of the lands making up the former Commonwealth.

After 1863, Hapsburg Galicia became an outpost for a narrower Polish national cartography that often excluded Jews, Ukrainians, Belarusians, and Lithuanians on ethnic, racial, or religious grounds, subscribing to theories of encirclement and thereby ignoring more complex early modern modes of belonging. Before its final destruction, the former Commonwealth was not quite an empire, but an early modern state having a decentralized political structure. The governing elite pooled and protected its properties, but they were without a strong military to rival the Great Powers. Before the 1863 uprising, cartographers were "Polish" in the sense that they viewed themselves as dispossessed political-cultural actors in the name of a "Poland-Lithuania," which they supposed to be permanently unified as "Poland." They printed maps in English, French, German, and Polish, an expression of their multiple linguistic identities in a Eurocentric high cultural framework. Their shared principal aim as semiprofessional geographers, lithographers, engravers, collectors, and editors was a historical point of contention: to memorialize the pre-1772 Rzeczpospolita and place it on the same plane as Western Europe, while excluding the narratives of the three partitioning empires. Defining the distinctive physical boundaries of "Ukraine" was therefore not an outstanding priority. More imperialistic "Poles" presupposed it to be included in a larger humanistic scheme, which paradoxically resisted Great Power imperialism and subscribed to a tolerant definition of civilization and culture. Lelewel's family was actually part German; Chodźko's was Polish-Ukrainian; Romer's was Austrian and Hungarian; and each was multilingual and multicultural in the broadest sense of the word. On balance, these activists and émigrés were more concerned with the idea of the old Commonwealth than with counting or measuring minorities within borders that no longer existed. Idealistically, they believed in the secular and democratic ideals of their former state, which did not classify Jews, Ukrainians, Lithuanians, or Belarusians as ethnographic material, nonhistoric groups, or more bluntly, tribes.[15]

As a result, the meaning of "nationality" did not enter "Polish" discourse until after 1863, when exclusivist nationalism emerged in its modern variants with official racial, ethnocentric, and ethnolinguistic constructions. After that point, politically active or academic Polish national cartographers tended to congregate in Hapsburg Galicia, or Little Poland (Małopolska), where they quickly became involved in census taking and other administrative projects. There, Wincenty Pol (1807–72) stood between romanticism and positivism, memorializing the Commonwealth as "Polish" rather than "Polish-Lithuanian." A poet turned scientist, Pol composed verses commemorating the lost landscapes, and he later became the first professor of geography at Jagiellonian University. Eugeniusz Romer became professor of geography at the universities in L'viv in 1911, and an eventual member of the Polish Academy of Sciences. Challenging Austrian statistics, he revised pro-Polish maps and atlases of Galicia in the late 1890s and early 1900s, and himself produced a larger geographical atlas in Vienna in 1908. His magnum opus, the *Geographical-Statistical Atlas of Poland* in 1916, spanned the gray area between history, science, and propaganda, molding together a demographic imperative for "proving" that Poland not only existed but actually consisted of nearly 30 million displaced people and could be defined by a unified historical language and culture.[16] In terms of modern tensions among imperial, state, and national territorialization, the discursive categorizations constitutive of the Ukrainian question, or for that matter, the Jewish, Lithuanian, and Belarusian questions, were largely ignored in actual terms until the very end of the long nineteenth century.

Contact Zone Four: "Little Russia"/"Ukraina": Beauplaniana and Historiography

Ukrainian cartographic practices were not disconnected from the practices of the other three contact zones. After 1795, and especially after 1863, modern territorial maps of empires, states, and nations promised a totalizing, systematic means for politically ordering lands and peoples, while making legible contested categories such as "nationality." Appropriately, the most famous early modern map of Ukraine, Guillaume de Vasseur de Beauplan's *Description d'Ukranie* (1652), was drawn by a military engineer who served four different monarchs in times of war.[17] Later borrowings of his work had numerous twists and turns. Polish Romantic references, such as those of Julian Niemcewicz (1758–1841), who reprinted the map in 1822, pointed idealistically to the political culture of the old Commonwealth. Beauplaniana also emerged in Hapsburg and Romanov Imperial historiographies. The Austrian historian Johann Christian von Engel (1770–1814) referred to Beauplan rather prosaically for descriptions of the Cossacks. The first known acknowledgment of the *Description* in Russian was made by Prince Nikolai Repnin (1778–1845), the Little Russian general governor and amateur historian. Nikolai Ustrialov (1805–70) and his brother Fyodor (1808–72) cited the map as a source for their integrative narratives of Russian Imperial history. Dmitrii Bantish-Kamenskii (1788–1850), an Imperial Russian historian and geographer, reproduced the general map in his *Istoriia Maloi Rossii,* where he treated it as unbiased. His loyalist version of Little Russian history, published in Russian in four volumes and four editions (1822, 1829–30, 1842, 1903) did much to popularize the maps of Beauplan until the very end of the nineteenth century (figure 5.2).

On the broader geopolitical scene, Beauplan's map was referred to by policymaking geographers in the mid–nineteenth century: Pyotr Köppen (1798–1864), the Russian-German statistician, ethnographer, and bibliographer; Count Karl von Czoernig, the Austrian census taker / statistician; and Pyotr Semyonov, author of the vast *Geographical-Statistical Dictionary of the Russian Empire,* published in Saint Petersburg in 1863. It was cited as a symbolic cartographical battleground for "Little Russia" between Poland and Russia by Mykola Markevych (1804–60), Mykola Kostomarov (1817–85), and Panteleimon Kulish (1819–97). In the territorial discourse of "objective" nations, states, and empires, Beauplan could be utilized to prove just about anything.

The 1860s and 1870s were a major caesura, leaving behind the romantic tropes of Cossackdom and the Commonwealth and moving toward a more positivistic interpretation of Little Russian history and geography. The discursive buzzwords were science, sources, and objectivity, but this tended to pose more questions than answers. The Ukrainian social activist Volodymyr Antonovych (1834–1908) called for a retranslation from the original French, and he ultimately concluded that Beauplan had oversimplified the tactical sea movements of the Cossacks. In practice, he meant that the map had underestimated the legacy of a distinctively Ukrainian Cossack statehood while relying too heavily on official Polish versions.

Vasil' Liaskorons'kyi (1860–1928), professor at the Nizhinskii lycée,

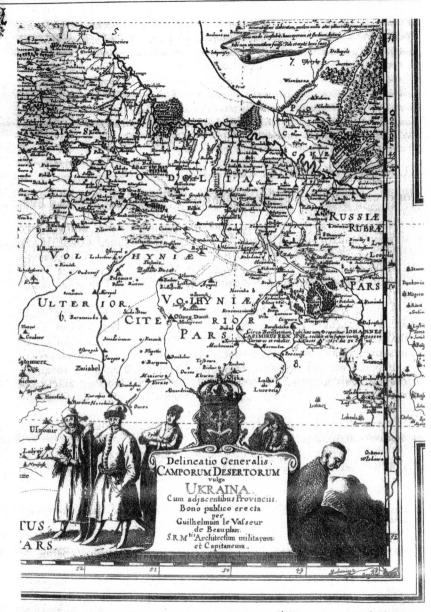

Рис. 22. Фрагмент Генеральної карти України Г. Боплана, що зберігається в Дрезденській бібліотеці. Зменшення в 1,6 раза

Figure 5.2. Fragment of Beauplan's 1652 *Description d'Ukranie,* reprinted, D. M. Bantysh-Kamenskii, 1829

was the first to attempt to place the *Description* comprehensively and attempt to place it in a broader historical perspective. Liaskorons'kyi was apparently more fearful of Polonocentric irredentism than of Russocentric imperialism. He challenged the historical narratives of Polish topographical and historical atlases at the turn of the century. In Kyiv, Liaskorons'kyi published his cartographical commentaries and critiques in Russian, as did his immediate contemporary and director of the library, Veniamin Kordt (1860–1934), whose *Materialy po russkoi kartografii* was printed in three editions (1899, 1906, 1910). Liaskorons'kyi devoted thirty years of research to as organizing the cartographical collections of the Kyiv University Library, using the resources from the libraries in Königsberg, Paris, Amsterdam, and London.

From the imperial vantage by the middle of the nineteenth century, Russians, Austrians, and Poles represented an ethnographic Ukraine in the maps as a mere borderland, with its regional inhabitants at an earlier stage of more primitive development. Ethnographic mapping by the Great Powers presumed civilizing missions and presupposed territorial indigenization. Circulating examples of this interpretation at the time included Heinrich Kiepert's *Ethnographic Map of the Russian Empire* (*Etnograficheskaia karta Rossiiskoi imperii*), published in Berlin in 1862; Rodrich d'Erkert's *Ethnographic Atlas of the West Russian Gubernii and Neighboring Oblasti* (*Etnograficheskii atlas zakhodno-rossiiskikh gubernii i sosednykh oblastei*), published in Saint Petersburg in 1863; Nestor Terebenev's *Map of Russia and Its Tribes* (*Karta Rossii i plemeni*), published in Moscow in 1866; and M. Mirkovich's *Ethnographic Map of the Slavic Peoples,* published in Saint Petersburg in 1867. In 1874, Mirkovich worked together with A. F. Rittich in Moscow and Saint Petersburg to produce the large-scale *Ethnographic Map of Slavic Nationalities* (*Etnograficheskaia karta slavianskikh narodnostei*). There, Ukrainians and Belarusians were perpetually united with their Russian Imperial brethren, and did not alone constitute an essential "nationality."

On an official state-administrative level, Ukrainian (or Ruthenian-Ukrainian) national activists lacked the basic training of their Russian, Austrian, and former Commonwealth neighbors in astronomy and mathematics. But they were not simply passive while other cartographic ascriptions of nationality and identity were being produced and disseminated, or while variegated notions of scientific accuracy were consistently invoked in state-imperial academic disciplines. In the 1860s, Mykhailo Kossak published a series of popular scientific ethnographic maps of the "Little Russian" people in the

L'vovianin journal, printed in the form of calendars by the Staropiganskii Institute. There, cartography, pedagogy and historical literacy went hand in hand. Early ethnographic work was concentrated in Galicia, more specially in L'viv. The maps were mostly Eurocentric or Russocentric reproductions. In L'viv, publications of maps and atlases after the Great Reforms included the 1861 Russian-language *Ethnographic Map of Little Russia* (*Karta etnohrafichna Malorusy*) (figure 5.3). Searching for a demographic imperative for national mobilization, but still on the level of cultural rather than political identity formation, Kossak sought to construct a distinctive Ukrainian cultural and political identity from among the Little Russians/Rusyny within the borders of the Hapsburg and Romanov empires.[18]

Cartographers in the Imperial Russian Geographical Society played a major role in replicating modern notions of mutually exclusive identities for Ukrainian territories. Statistical research after the Great Reforms and the Uprising of 1863 stimulated socioeconomic mapping and aggravated concerns about administrative territoriality and demographics. Pavel Chubinskii (1839–84), a Russian-Ukrainian ethnographer and geographer, was the director of its "southwestern" branch in Kyiv and editor of the seven-volume *Works of the Ethnographic-Statistical Expedition in the West Russian Regions* (*Trudy etnografichesko-Statisticheskoi ekspeditsii v zapadno-russkii krai: Iugo-zapadnyi otdel*, Saint Petersburg, 1872–77), which included Ukraine, Belarus, and Bessarabia. He himself authored two additional social-demographical maps in the collection, the *Map of the Jewish Population of the Southwestern Region* and the *Map of Catholics, and Enumeration of Poles in the Southwestern Regions*. The Russian-Ukrainian linguist and cartographer Kostiantyn Mikhail'chuk (1840–1914), edited the last volume, and he compiled his own *Maps of the South Russian Dialects and Languages* (*Karty iuzhno-russkikh narechii i govorov*, 1871).

One of the main journals for map commentaries was the *Chronicles of the Nestor Historical Association* (*Chtenia v istoricheskom obshchestve Nestora-Letopisa, 1879–1914*), an intermediary organization between the IRGO and the Shevchenko Society (NTSh), based at Kyiv University since 1874. Occasional IRGO, and then *Nestor,* contributors included historians, scholars, and activists who in the 1860s and 1870s gathered and synthesized heritage materials for the purpose of assembling a demographic collective of Little Russians / Ruthenians / Ukrainians. Some of these cartographic collectors and amateurish critics, rather than producers, included V. S. Ikonnikov (1841–1923), V. B. Antonovych (1834–1908), and M. F. Vladimirsky-Budanov (1838–1916). O. M. Lazarevsky (1834–1902), Ia. F. Holovatskii

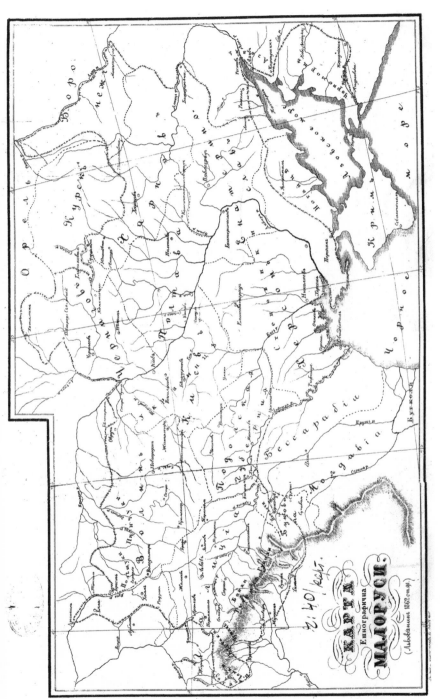

Figure 5.3. Mykhailo Kossak, *Karta Etnohrafychna Malorusy,* L'viv, *L'vovianin,* 1862

(1814–88), and K. M. Feofilaktov (1818–1901), the professor and rector of Kyiv University, who criticized Russian Imperial maps of *gubernii* using more detailed geological maps of Hapsburg maps of Galicia and Bukovina.

After the Kyiv branch of the IRGO was closed in 1876, the Prosvita publishing firm began to print in 1880, and the first department of geography was founded in 1882 at L'viv University. These three events significantly modernized the representations of Ukraine in maps. Comparatively, a nationally oriented geography and cartography elsewhere in Ukraine was weakly developed. In Odessa, for instance, many navigational charts and hydrographical maps of the Black Sea and Sea of Azov were printed and revised throughout the nineteenth century. A special admiralty college was based there, and the first private firm for cartography was founded independently in the city in 1839, lasting remarkably until 1922. However, although the Odessa Historical and Antiquarian Society (1844–1919) often published scholarly material on geography and cartography, the frequent contributors, like Apollon Skalkovskii (1808–98), a statistician and member of the Russian Academy of Sciences in Saint Petersburg, determinedly analyzed seventeenth- and eighteenth-century maps of Ukraine from the Imperial "urge to the sea" perspective.

Inland, however, the national movement gradually acquired (or ascribed to itself) a bolder geopolitical and geocultural imperative. Issues of identity, and in the Ukrainian case mutually exclusive identities, rose to the surface by midcentury. In Galicia, other leading Ukrainian national activists went one step further and envisioned the possible benefits of a completely independent cartographic foundation. In wanting to have a "scientific" basis for cartography and a political basis for a modern Ukraine, the encyclopedic Mykhailo Drahomaniv (1841–95) paid close attention to publishing firms in Paris and Geneva, especially the nineteen-volume *Nouvelle Géographie Universelle: La Terre et Les Hommes* of Elisée Reclus, printed from 1876 to 1884, which represented Ukraine in its eighth chapter.

The Ukrainian national publishing firm Prosvita actively sought to attain Western European standards for cartographical productions, but in practice this proved to be very difficult with respect to the choice of historical sources and mode of categorical representation. After completing his ethnographic research for the IRGO in 1876, Iakov Holovats'kyi (1814–88) produced the Russian-language *Ethnographic Map of the Russian Nationality Settlement in Galicia, Northwestern Hungary and Bukovina (Etnograficheskaia karta russkogo narodonaseleniia v Galichine, severovostochnoi Ugrii i Bukovine)*. The only map he produced for the "national" region was actually a duplicate of the 1856 map by the Hapsburg statistician and census expert Karl von Czoernig. Prosvita would reprint this map again in an uncolored version in 1887, under the authorship of O. Kostkevich and with the Ukrainian title *Map of Galicia, Bukovina and Hungarian Rus'* (*Karta Halychyny, Bukovyny i Uhors'koï Rusy*), and again by Stepan Tomashivs'kyi (1875–1930) in Saint Petersburg in 1910 as the *Ethnographic Map of Hungarian Rus'* (*Etnohrafichna karta Uhors'koï Rusi*). The 1892 Ukrainian-language ethnographic map *Ukraine-Rus' and White Russia* (*Rus'-Ukraina i Bila Rus': Karta etnohrafichna*) was created by two students and national activists at L'viv University, Myron Kymakovych and Liubomyr Rozhans'kyi (1878–1925), and published independently in L'viv by the Rus' Pedagogical Society. It divided the population of the territory into thirteen nationalities, compartmentally separating the Rusyns-Ukrainians, White Rusyns, Great Russians ("*moskali,*" ethnically considered), Poles, Romanians, Tatars, and others. By this point, it was standard practice in Ukraine to "scientifically" measure and sort in-groups into single, essentialized categories, and to attempt to order them territorially.

The semiprofessional career of Hryhorii Velychko (1863–1933), a history instructor in L'viv whom Stepan Rudnyts'kyi hagiographically called "the Nestor of Ukrainian Geography," may be taken as a case example for the dynamics of Ukraine's many contact zones. Born in Mykolaev, Velychko matriculated at L'viv University in 1883, where he studied theology, philosophy, and then geography. He pursued his studies abroad in Vienna, Paris, and Saint Petersburg, and he returned to Galicia in 1892–93. There he taught at gymnasiums in L'viv, Drohobycz, Peremysl', Stanislawów, and Tarnopil', while writing about geographical "science" in both Polish and Ukrainian.

Velychko aimed to gather as many international sources as possible in other to compile a Ukrainian ethnographic map that might be suitably historical. In his search for documentation, he encountered the problem of an a priori enumeration of nationalities. He cited early romantic nationalist as well as later racially and ethnically oriented works that dealt with Ukrainian territories. These examples included the works of two Slovak national activists, Jan Čaplovich (1780–1847) and Pavlo Šafařik (1795–1861). who published romantic nationalist maps in 1828 (Leipzig) and 1842 (Prague), respectively. Later sources were more specialized in terms of nationalities issues, as, for example, in the previously mentioned map of A. F. Rittich in 1874, where there were a grand total of forty-six European collective groups, and where Russians, Ukrainians, and Byelorussian's were all one

color, without definite territorial boundaries. As the editors of Prosvita, Drahomaniv and K. Pan'kivs'kyi spent three long years from 1889 to 1892 raising funds for the publication of a map that would accurately depict the
Ukrainians in their "natural" geographical homeland, dispersed between the
boundaries of the Visla, Bug, Dnipro, Donets basin, Azov Sea, Kuban, and
Caucuses regions. Velychko's work would therefore be on par with all the
measurements and representations by mapmakers and atlas makers in Western and Central Europe. The original plan was for him to consult not only
with national Galician Ukrainian scholars but also with professionals at the
Military Institute in Vienna, because Drahomaniv was so worried about the
appearance of the map.

Evidently, Velychko had finished with the lithography by 1893, when the
map was sent to the Prosvita editors. A correspondence followed between
Drahomaniv and Ivan Franko, both of whom fretted about being unquali-
fied critics of the map's quality and content. With reluctance, Drahomaniv
agreed to write the review privately. Seeking to maximize the demographic
presence of Ukrainians, he criticized Velychko for relying on Russian
("*moskali*") numbers and blindly respecting the Imperial nomenclature.

Ultimately, there was a two-year delay in the final production of the map
by Prosvita. The reasons were not entirely clear. Perhaps Velychko took
Drahomaniv's criticisms harshly, but it is more likely that the delay was editorial, and for political reasons. Or a more prosaic reason was the fact that
Velychko was between teaching jobs in Drohobycz and Peremysl'. In any
case, the lithography was done pseudonymously by "Rusyn" (Andrei An-
dreichyn) in L'viv, and the final Ukrainian version of the map—*Ethnographic Map of the Ukrainian-Rus' Nation* (*Narodopysna karta Ukraïn-
s'ko-rus'koho narodu*)—was printed by Prosvita in 1896 (figure 5.4). On
the map there are nineteen nationalities, with the "Ukrainians-Rusyns" followed by Romanians, Magyars, Slovaks, Poles, Belarusians, Rosiany,
Cherkesy, and Tatars; then by diasporic peoples: Bulgars, Germans, Virmeny,
Greeks, Jews; and then by Kalmyks, Nogaitsy, Kabardyntsi, Chechens, and
Kirghiz. Velychko's conception of Ukrainian territoriality was primordial-
ist, outlining the "ancient" lands settled and colonized under Polish and
Russian rule. In 1897, also in L'viv, Prosvita published 10,000 copies of a
reduced variant of the map and used it for its annual lithographed calendar.
In 1899, Velychko became an active member of the Shevchenko Scientific
Society, and in 1902 he published part of an unfinished work in L'viv:
Geography of Ukraine-Rus' (*Heohrafiia Ukraïny-Rusy*).

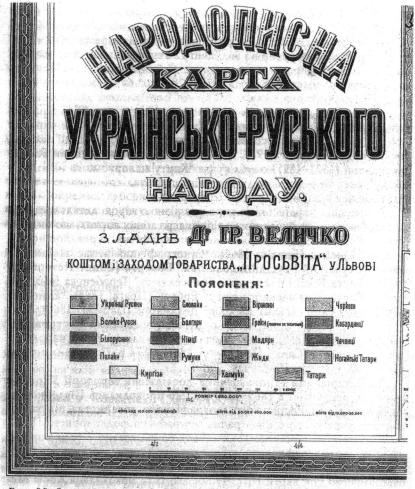

Рис. 99. Заголовок і легенда "Народописної карти українсько-руського народу" Г. Величка (Львів, 1896). Зменшення в 1,6 раза

Figure 5.4. Hryhorii Velychko, *Narodopysna karta ukraïns'ko-rus'koho narodu*, L'viv, 1896

Velychko's work played a major role in establishing L'viv, and in the broader sense Hapsburg Galicia, as the primary outpost for a modern Ukrainian national cartography. By the turn of the century, M. S. Hrushevs'kyi (1866–1934) used maps in a more popular manner in his *History of Ukraine-Rus'* (L'viv, 1898–1903), and *Illustrated History of Ukraine* (Kyiv and L'viv, 1913) to provide the basis for an independent Ukrainian historiography. Isidor Sharanevich (1829–1901), an archaeologist and professor at L'viv University, edited a number of historical maps transmitted from Vienna. Vasil' Il'nyts'kyi (1823–95) was a writer and pedagogue who used historical maps as illustrations for popular publications. Oleksander Barvinskii (1847–1927) was a Prosvita activist and editor of *Dilo* who authored a number of Ukrainian-language maps: *The Illustrated History of Rus'; A Map of Rus' under the Princes; and A Map of Rus' during the Grand Duchy of Lithuania and Cossackdom* (L'viv, 1904). Mykola Arkas (1852?– 1909), a composer and amateur historian, color-lithographed thematic maps: *Lands Where the Ukrainian People Live Now; Ukrainian Lands across Three Centuries after Christianity;* and *Eastern Europe in the Ninth Century after Christianity.*

From a different starting point, Stepan Tomashivs'kyi, a Ruthenian translator in the Hungarian military service who became a historian and a specialist on demographics, published articles and maps in the journals of the Shevchenko Society from 1900–16, dealing with the idea and territorial boundaries of Hungarian Rus'. In the Subcarpathian region, he criticized the overrepresentations of Magyars and of Ukrianian-Rusyns. In 1906, he published his own ethnographic maps of Hungarian Rus' in Saint Petersburg, after a bitter correspondence with official Hapsburg statistical committees. Finally, Stepan L'vovich Rudnyts'kyi (1877–1937) published in 1907 the first Ukrainian-language world maps, the *Map of the Western and Eastern Hemispheres* (*Karty pivkul' zakhidnoi i skhidnoi*). Paralleling the career of Eugeniusz Romer in Poland, Rudnyts'kyi published maps during and after World War I of all the ethnic/ethnographic territory of Ukraine and, in subsequent years, maps of Europe, Asia, South and North America, Australia and Oceania, and Africa. Before the Polish-Bolshevik War and the formal establishment of the Soviet Union, he produced the first historical-pedagogical atlas of Ukraine. In the overall context of late-nineteenth-century "objective" categorizations and terminological confusions, each of these activists envisioned a future map of Ukraine as a separate territorial modern nation or state. Though introduced in the nineteenth century, imperial and ethnographic mapping practices that framed categorical "identities" in the modern language of science would survive well beyond the European Great War and Bolshevik Revolution.

Conclusion: Ukrainian Cartographies and Identities in Contact

The notion of a contact zone serves as a reminder of Ukraine's historical and cartographic complexities. Commemorating the land of Ukraine territorially is never an easy ordeal; one must warn dually against strict constructivism and backward projections of identity essentialism. As Dominique Arel has shown in his introduction to this volume, identity as a variable may be subdivided into a number of socially constructed components (attributes, categories, and dimensions), each having a number of possible outcomes and potential choices that may be fought over as labels in different regions. Here, the four dynamic contact zones and their cartographic representations have distinctive legacies for an early modern, modern, and postmodern, as well as a centralized and decentralized Ukraine. Even in the nineteenth century, the historical choices for a Ukrainian modernity were often indeterminate in spite of all scientific efforts at defining and ordering, and not simply East versus West, or Asiatic Russia versus Europe.

From Peter I onward, and especially throughout the long nineteenth century, geography and cartography were Russian *Imperial* sciences. Though cartography did indeed serve the purpose of modernization, it was also a top-down policy of measurement, categorization, and control on the part of the Imperial state. This may also be said of the Hapsburg Empire, which was oriented conservatively toward the classification schemes of empire building and empire saving, although its cartographic practices—in Galicia, for example—had a more civil orientation than those of the Romanov Empire. Both official imperial policies shared the need for developing strategies of in- and out-group labels in their mapping practices and political modes of representation. The memorialized legacy of the early modern Polish-Lithuanian Commonwealth, either as a state or a sort of virtualized empire, persisted after the partitions and well into the 1860s.

One basic way of challenging or refuting a map is by undermining the veracity of its sources, claiming or disclaiming it as "evidence." But to say that something is constructed from sources is not the same as saying that the source, or the construction, is invalid or unreliable. In this sense, long before the notion of national self-determination was raised after World War I and the Bolshevik Revolution, the critique of available evidence within the limited discursive practices for Ukraine did not provide much of a forward direction. Similar to the phases of other national movements in Central and Eastern Europe, Ukrainian national activists faced the central paradox that the majority of their documentary "sources" for cartography and final territorial constructions were sketchy as long as being "Ukrainian" was merely ethnolinguistic according to Imperial categories of measurement and territorial placements. A free, literate, and active public sphere hardly existed for debate and discussion about these issues.

The European Great Powers and their antagonistic civilizing missions standardized political and cultural identities territorially based on language, ethnicity, and race. Ukraine and Ukrainians were caught between an early modern sense of localness and a modern sense of collective identification with nations, states, or empires. They did not then have access to postmodern notions of displacement, hybridity, and multiple citizenships. Altogether, official state policy actors and unofficial nonstate activists seeking recognition among territorially based empires and nations were incapable of moving beyond the confused discursive racial, ethnic, and ethnolinguistic categories in the maps they themselves created. In examining Ukraine as a fragmented series of contact zones and begging the question of what a Ukrainian identity *is,* one also needs to consider the nineteenth-century foundationalist framework underlying Imperial and ethnographic mapmakers' elaborate attempts to blueprint modernity by representation and categorization.

Notes

1. Multiple skepticisms toward the conventional historiographical teleologies of national, state, and imperial projects of centralization are a relatively new occurrence in Ukraine and its neighboring polities. See Timothy Snyder's important argument in *The Reconstruction of Nations: Poland, Ukraine, Lithuania, Belarus, 1569–1999* (New Haven, Conn.: Yale University Press, 2003), 1–12.

2. The notion of "contact zone" is discussed in a historiographical context by Nataliia Iakovenko, "Ukraïna mizh skhodom i zakhodom: Proektsiia odnieï idei," *Paralel'nyi svit: Doslidzhenniia z istoriï uiavlen' ta idei v Ukraïny XVI–XVII st* (Kyiv: Krytyka, 2002), 333–65. I develop this further in "Blueprinting Modernity: National Cartography and Scientific Ordering in Russia's European Empire and Former Poland-Lithuania, 1795–1917," Ph.D. dissertation, Brown University, 2005.

3. See David I. Kertzer and Dominique Arel, eds., *Census and Identity: The Politics of Race, Ethnicity, and Language in National Censuses* (Cambridge: Cambridge

University Press, 2002); and Thongchai Winichakul, *Siam Mapped: A History of the Geo-Body of a Nation* (Honolulu: University of Hawaii Press, 1994). Also see Benedict Anderson, "Census, Map, Museum," in *Imagined Communities: Reflections on the Origins and Spread of Nationalism* (London: Verso, 1991). The recent return of imperial Russian discursive constructions of race and ethnicity is examined in *Rasizm v iazyke sotsial'nykh nauk,* ed. Viktor Voronkov et al. (Sevastopol: Aleteiia, 2002).

4. On meliorism, territorial expansion and cartography, see Matthew H. Edney, *Mapping an Empire: The Geographical Construction of British India, 1765–1843* (Chicago: University of Chicago Press, 1997); and Edney, "Cartography without Progress: Reinterpreting the Nature and Historical Development of Mapmaking," *Cartographica* 30, nos. 2–3 (1993): 54–68.

5. For Tatishchev and Russian cartography, see Alexei V. Postnikov, "Outline of the History of Russian Cartography," in *Regions: A Prism to View the Slavic-Eurasian World—Towards a Discipline of "Regionology,"* ed. Kimitaka Matsuzato (Sapporo: Hokkaido University Press, 2000), 1–50.

6. For some of these administrative policy issues, see Zenon E. Kohut, *Russian Centralism and Ukrainian Autonomy: Imperial Absorption of the Hetmanate, 1760s–1830s* (Cambridge, Mass.: Harvard University Press, 1988); Theodore R. Weeks, *Nation and State in Late Imperial Russia: Nationalism and Russification on the Western Frontier, 1863–1914* (Dekalb: Northern Illinois University Press, 1996); David Saunders, "Russia's Ukrainian Policy, 1846–1905," *East European Quarterly* 25 (1995): 181–208); Jerzy Borzecki, "Issues of Language Identity in the Population Censuses of the Polish-Russian Borderlands: Reexaminations and Comments," *Polish Review* 44, no. 1 (1999): 29–46; Stephen Velychenko, "Identities, Loyalties and Service in Imperial Russia: Who Administered the Borderlands?" *Russian Review* 54 (April 1995): 188–208; and Terry Martin, "The Empire's New Frontiers: New Russia's Path from Frontier to *Okraina,* 1774–1920," *Russian History* 19, nos. 1–4 (1992): 181–201.

7. Alexei V. Postnikov, *Karty zemel' rossiiskikh* (Moscow: Nash Dom–L'Age d'Homme, 1996); and *Geograficheskie issledovaniia i kartografirovanie Pol'shi v protsesse soznaniia "Topograficheskoi karty tsarstva Pol'skogo" (1818–1843 gg.),* Deposited Scientific Work (Moscow: RAN, Institut estestvoznaniia i tekhniki im. S. I. Vavilova, 1995). Also see Nathaniel Knight, "Science, Empire, and Nationality: Ethnography in the Russian Imperial Geographical Society, 1845–1855," in *Imperial Russia: New Histories for the Empire,* ed. Jane Burbank and David L. Ransel (Bloomington: Indiana University Press, 1998). For the most recent official history of the RGO (IRGO), see A. G. Isachenko, *Russkoe geograficheskoe obshchestvo: 150 let* (Saint Petersburg: Progress, 1995).

8. See Mark Bassin, *Imperial Visions: Nationalist Imagination and Geographical Expansion in the Russian Far East, 1840–1865* (Cambridge: Cambridge University Press, 1999); and for the larger question of historiography and geography, see Thomas Sanders, *Historiography in Imperial Russia: The Profession and Writing of History in a Multinational State* (Armonk, N.Y.: M. E. Sharpe, 1999); Katarzyna Błachowska, *Narodziny Imperium: Rozwój terytorialny państwa carów w ujęciu historyków rosyjskich XVII I XIX wieku* (Warsaw: Wydawnictwo Neriton, 2001); and Andreas Kappeler, *Der schwierige Weg zur Nation: Beiträge zur neueren Geschichte der Ukraine* (Vienna: Bohlau, 2003).

9. Jarosław Hrytsak, *Historia Ukrainy, 1772–1999: Narodziny nowoczesnego narodu* (Lublin: Instytut Europy Środkowo-wschodniej, 2000), 84–89.

10. *Katalog kartograficheskogo zavedeniia Il'ina* (Sevastopol, 1909); L. K. Kil'du-

shevskaia, "Izdatel'skaia deiatel'nost' 'Kartograficheskogo zavedeniia A. Il'ina," *Knizhnoe delo v Rossii vo vtoroi polovine XIX—nachale XX veka,* ed. I. I. Frolova and O. N. Ansberg (Sevastopol: Rossiiskaia Natsional'naia Biblioteka, 1992), 97–111.

11. On the Habsburg policies and identities, see John-Paul Himka, "The Construction of Nationality in Galician Rus': Icarian Flights in Almost All Directions," in *Intellectuals and the Articulation of the Nation,* ed. Ronald Suny (Ann Arbor: University of Michigan Press, 1999), 109–64; and *Nationbuilding and the Politics of Nationalism: Essays on Austrian Galicia,* ed. Andrei S. Markovits and Frank E. Sysyn (Cambridge, Mass.: Harvard University Press, 1982). For maps themselves, see Alicja Puszka, *Nauczyciele historii i geografii państwowych szkół średnich w Galicji w okresie autonomii, 1868–1914* (Lublin: Towarzystwo Naukowe KUL, 1999).

12. Michael Heffernan, *The Meaning of Europe: Geography and Geopolitics* (London: Arnold, 1998); Martin W. Lewis and Karen E. Wigen, *The Myth of Continents: A Critique of Metageography* (Berkeley: University of California Press, 1997); Jeremy Black, *Maps and History: Constructing Images of the Past* (New Haven, Conn.: Yale University Press, 2000).

13. On geography, territoriality, and space, see Jacek Kolbuszewski, *Kresy* (Wrocław: Wydawnictwo Dolnosląskie, 1995); Stanisław Eile, *Literature and Nationalism in Partitioned Poland, 1795–1918* (London: Macmillan, 2000); and Jeremy Smith, ed., *Beyond the Limits: The Concept of Space in Russian History and Culture* (Helsinki: Studia Historica 62, 1999).

14. Jean Baudrillard, "The System of Collecting," in *The Cultures of Collecting,* ed. John Elsner and Roger Cardinal (Cambridge, Mass.: Harvard University Press, 1994), 7–24; Thomas Richards, *The Imperial Archive: Knowledge and the Fantasy of Empire* (London: Verso, 1993).

15. As Brian Porter has noted in his discussion of modern Polish nationalism, "Neither Dmowski nor Popławski believed that Poland should be shaped according to some specific historical geography, nor (paradoxically) did they think that Poland could exist if divided by diversity. One will find few references in National Democratic writing to the maps of 1772, 1648, or any other significant date in Poland's past. Their idea of history was not limited by any cartographic images." Porter, *When Nationalism Began to Hate: Imagining Modern Politics in Nineteenth-Century Poland* (New York: Oxford University Press, 2000), 204.

16. See Romer's Versailles diaries, *Pamiętnik paryski* (1918–19), ed. Andrzej Garlicki and Ryszard Świętek (Wrocław: Ossolineum, 1989); on Polish–German borders and identities, Guntram Henrik Herb, *Under the Map of Germany: Nationalism and Propaganda, 1918–1945* (London: Routledge, 1997), 19–23.

17. *Boplan i Ukraïna: Zbirnyk naukovych prats'* (L'viv, NAN, 1998); *Kartohrafiia ta istoriia Ukraïny: Zbirnyk naukovykh prats'* (L'viv: NAN, 2000); R. I. Sossa, *Istoriia kartohrafuvanniia terytorii Ukraïny: Vid naydavnishykh chasiv do 1920 r.: Korotkyi narys* (Kyiv: Naukova Dumka, 2000); A. B. Pernal and D. F. Essar, "The 1652 Beauplan Maps of the Ukraine," *Harvard Ukrainian Studies* 9 (1985): 61–78.

18. Other category-laden imperial and ethnographic maps in circulation at the time in L'viv included the 1863 Russian-language *Map of the Hutsul Population Dispersal* (*Karta rozselennia Hutsuly*); the 1868 Habsburg imperial *Ethnographic Map of Eastern Galicia* (*Ethnographische Karte von Ost-Galizien*), with categories of Slavs, Rusyns, Poles, Jews, and Germans; and the 1869 Russian-language *Map of the Little Russian Nation [Narod]* (*Karta maloruskogo naroda*).

6

Arbiters of the Free Conscience: Confessional Categorization and Religious Transfer in Russia, 1905–1917

Paul W. Werth

Among the fundamental characteristics of the Tsarist autocracy was its deep implication in the Russian Empire's religious affairs. Until its collapse in 1917, the regime remained committed to upholding not only the predominance of Orthodoxy over the so-called foreign confessions, and of Christianity over heterodoxy, but also of religion in general over irreligion and "nihilism." In this context, even the non-Orthodox religions enjoyed forms

Support for the research for this chapter was provided by the National Council for Eurasian and East European Research and by the International Research and Exchanges Board, with funds provided by the National Endowment for the Humanities, the United States Information Agency, and the U.S. Department of State, which administers the Russian, Eurasian, and East European Research Program (Title VIII). The author also thanks the Slavic Research Center of the University of Hokkaido, which provided a congenial atmosphere for the completion of the final version of the chapter. For critical assessments of earlier versions of the chapter, the author thanks in particular one anonymous reviewer, as well the participants of the workshop on "multicultural legacies" in Russia and Ukraine at the Kennan Institute in 2002–3.

of state patronage that were designed to ensure the authority of established religious elites within their respective communities.[1] And just as every imperial subject belonged to a social estate that bestowed certain obligations and privileges, he or she was also ascribed to one or another recognized confession. Partly for ideological reasons, and partly because of the state's administrative inadequacies, confession even lay at the foundation of the empire's record keeping, as religious clerics maintained the records of births, marriages, and deaths that were crucial for determining the age and legitimacy of children, ascertaining inheritance rights, determining eligibility for exemptions from military draft and for entering state service.[2]

If confessional belonging represented a universal attribute of all the tsar's subjects, then ascription to specific religions determined particularistic rights and limitations. Rules governing the conclusion of marriage varied according to subjects' confessional affiliation, and some interconfessional unions were prohibited altogether as a result of churches' canonical provisions.[3] Significant legal and administrative restrictions, especially as regards place of residence and access to education and certain occupations, were imposed on Jews, while "persons of Polish origin"—a phrase often understood simply to refer to Catholics—faced limitations on their rights to obtain land in the Western Provinces.[4] In essence, Russia had not constructed a civil order in which rights and obligations were universally shared by the entire citizenry, and religious confession represented one of the principal sources of the society's division into particularistic components.

This situation compelled the state to approach the question of religious conversion with circumspection. If the rights conferred by civil law differed according to religious confession, and if the very records that established civil status were confessional in nature, then the state obviously had a great interest in regulating confessional affiliation and clearly establishing the criteria whereby subjects could be said to belong definitively to one religion or another. This task was conditioned furthermore by the state's ideological commitments to Orthodoxy and to Christianity. The state had historically promoted conversion to Orthodoxy, if not always through direct support for missions, then at least by providing certain incentives for would-be converts.[5] Until 1905, conversion from Orthodoxy—or "apostasy," as it was defined even in formal law—was completely prohibited, as was conversion from Christianity (of any confession) to heterodoxy. Even conversion among non-Orthodox faiths usually required the permission of the state, which sought to prevent the interference of the representatives of one foreign confession in the affairs of another.[6] In short, to maintain the existing hierarchy of religious confessions and to ensure the foundations of an order dependent on confessional distinctions, the state arrogated for itself the right to act as the ultimate arbiter of religious identity in the Russian Empire.

By the late nineteenth century, however, the state found it more and more difficult to exercise this prerogative. To be sure, most imperial subjects remained within the confessions of their ancestors, even if their commitments to those religions sometimes weakened in the face of rapid social and economic change. But on the whole, Russia's confessional landscape became increasingly fluid and complex. Growing numbers of formally Orthodox subjects sought to return to the religions from which they or their ancestors had been converted earlier, while new religions and teachings began to draw ever more adherents from the ranks of the Orthodox. Compelled by the state's civil and criminal law to remain in Orthodoxy against their convictions, such believers became ever more frustrated with their position and ever more hopeful that full legal recognition of their religious beliefs would soon be granted. Many state officials themselves became increasingly uncomfortable with the idea of using secular law and police power to maintain religious discipline, arguing that this was both ineffective and incompatible with modern values. In response to these difficulties and in line with these growing doubts, in April 1905 the autocracy substantially liberalized laws regulating conversion and in October of that year explicitly granted "freedom of conscience" to the empire's population.

This chapter examines the repercussions of this dramatic reform for the processes through which confessional affiliation, or religious "identity," was defined in the last decade or so of Imperial Russia.[7] My concern is primarily with contests over categorization between state agents, eager to retain some degree of control over religious change in the new confessional order, and individual subjects, concerned above all with having their formal status reflect their self-understanding. Focusing principally on the legal and administrative adjudication of believers' requests for "confessional transfer" in the years after 1905,[8] I argue that if the state made important concessions to the religious aspirations of the empire's subjects, it nonetheless refused to relinquish its prerogatives as the ultimate arbiter of their confessional status and thus remained deeply implicated in their religious affairs. Even as some reformist officials promoted religious reform as part of a larger project of eroding particularism in favor of Russia's civic transformation and the establishment of a "national politics," the state's fundamentally confessional foundations placed profound limits on both the ability and the inclination of most officials to construe religious identity purely as a matter of individual choice.[9] Thus even as believers became more self-aware of their beliefs and conscious of their dignity as individuals, their religious identity remained at least partially conditioned by state imperatives.

From "Religious Toleration" to "Freedom of Conscience"

Although the religious reform of 1905 was clearly a product of the revolutionary crisis of that same year, there were crucial antecedents to the idea of freedom of conscience in the years and even decades leading up to 1905. Already by the 1880s, the refusal of many putative "converts" to Orthodoxy from earlier eras to make peace with their formal Orthodox status provided compelling proof that religious convictions were not reducible to bureaucratic ascription and that the law's blanket prohibition on "apostasy" from Orthodoxy required modification.[10] By the early twentieth century, issues of religious freedom became prominent in intellectual and scholarly circles. Legal scholars more openly condemned existing statutes as being outdated, motivated primarily by political expediency, and confused in their equation of nationality and confession.[11] Religion, ecumenism, and individual freedom became central issues for a vibrant segment of the Russian intelligentsia in the Silver Age, while the Orthodox Church's condemnation of Lev Tolstoy in 1901 raised the question of religious freedom to a broader public.[12] By the early twentieth century, then, issues of religious liberty and freedom of conscience, albeit in various forms, occupied a prominent place in public discourse.

Even the autocracy itself, engaged in modest reform efforts on the eve of 1905, began to make gestures toward modifications in confessional policy. Although retreating from an early draft that made direct reference to freedom of conscience, in a manifesto of February 1903 the emperor promised "to strengthen the steadfast observance by the authorities concerned with religious affairs of the guarantees of religious toleration contained in the fundamental laws of the Russian Empire."[13] By late 1904, another decree went considerably beyond this injunction for the autocracy merely to obey its own laws and instructed the government not only to eliminate immediately "all constraints on religious life not directly established by law" but also to review existing provisions on the rights of non-Orthodox groups.[14] The resulting review led to a decree of April 17, 1905, which substantially liberalized the empire's religious order. Transferring from one Christian faith to another was now fully legalized, some sects received at least implicit recognition, and Old Belief even gained something close to the status of a recognized non-Orthodox Christian faith.[15]

Yet the confessional order that emerged subsequently was neither complete nor entirely coherent, because the April decree provided for the definitive resolution of many issues only through further legislative deliberation. The October Manifesto, granted later in 1905 by an autocracy even deeper in crisis, made matters still more complex, by both explicitly granting Russian subjects "freedom of conscience" and providing for the establishment of a deliberative assembly (the Duma) that considerably complicated the legislative process. Because new draft laws designed to effectuate "freedom of conscience" became the object of intense legislative contestation and were ultimately never approved, it remained unclear throughout the period 1905–17 whether and how the October Manifesto's proclamation of a broad but poorly defined "freedom of conscience" actually superseded the more modest, but also more concrete, provisions of the April decree.[16]

Non-Orthodox believers were of course eager to invoke the October Manifesto, arguing that it eliminated all the ifs, ands, and buts contained in the April decree.[17] The government itself was less certain. The Department of Foreign Confessions noted in 1906 that the "freedom of conscience" identified in the manifesto "should undoubtedly be understood as a broadening of the confessional relief granted by the decree of April 17 and as the granting to each person of complete self-definition in matters of religion."[18] However, subsequent practice showed that this "self-definition" would in fact not be "complete" but would instead be conditioned primarily by the stipulations of the April decree. In essence, the state came to regard the Manifesto as a *promise* of "freedom of conscience" to be realized in new legislation, whereas the April decree and a series of supplementary administrative rulings would regulate affairs until that new legislation could be produced.

Even in theoretical terms, attempts to define "freedom of conscience" did not produce any real consensus. At one end were those contending that this concept implied the elimination of any and all limitations on religious life, the right to hold no religious beliefs at all, and—with a view toward concurrent developments in France—the full separation of church and state. The concern of such commentators was the establishment of a "rule-of-law state," as well as the recognition of faith as an affair of individual concern.

They tended to regard the April decree as a positive step in the expansion of religious freedom, but they emphasized its partial character, its many qualifications and limitations, and its failure to establish full freedom of conscience.[19] Perhaps the most influential of these commentators was Mikhail Reisner, whose work was analyzed in the Department of Foreign Confessions and served as a basis for its initial attempts to identify the practical implications of implementing freedom of conscience.[20] Other observers believed that freedom of conscience could be secured only by maintaining certain limitations on religious activity. These writers, many of them Orthodox clerics on the front lines of post-1905 interconfessional struggle, rejected the proposition that the freedom of personal, individual confession required unrestricted liberty in public confession, the formation of religious associations, and so on. For such commentators, freedom of conscience did not imply freedom of "propaganda" (i.e., proselytism) or the freedom to "seduce" (i.e., to convert others by assaulting the truth claims and sacred objects of their religions). In this view, the conscience of each person deserved *protection* from the encroachments of others, especially when those encroachments took extreme or "fanatical" forms.[21] In an important memorandum of 1906, the department itself offered a quite broad definition of "freedom of conscience" but immediately added that this freedom was subject "to limitations based on the requirements of state order."[22] In short, the meaning of "freedom of conscience" remained unclear and contested throughout the last decade of the old regime.

Regulating Confessional Transfer

If in some respects, the 1905 reform simplified the administration of Russia's confessional heterogeneity (e.g., by permitting the transfer of numerous "recalcitrants" to non-Orthodox faiths), then in other respects it created new problems in its wake or left old questions unresolved. In terms of the transfer of confessional status after 1905, four issues proved particularly complex: (1) the transfer of some former Uniates to Catholicism, (2) the problem of conversion from Christianity to non-Christian faiths, (3) the problem of Jewish conversion to other faiths, and (4) the matter of recognizing new faiths and sects. It is in considering contests over these particular cases of transfer that the remaining tensions between individual self-determination, on the one hand, and the imperatives of the state, on the other, become most readily manifest.

Returning to Catholicism

The largest number of transfers after 1905 was from Orthodoxy to Catholicism and included many former Uniates, who had been bureaucratically "reunited" with Orthodoxy in 1839 and 1875. The April decree had legalized conversions among Christian confessions, and such transfers should therefore have been fairly straightforward. But complications arose almost immediately, because this decree failed to stipulate even provisionally how precisely subjects were to go about changing their confessional status. Denied affiliation with Catholicism for decades, former Uniates scarcely felt compelled to wait for a well-defined procedure to appear. Instead they began transferring immediately, and Catholic hierarchs, lacking any guidance beyond the April decree itself, improvised a system for accepting these people into their church. By the time the Department of Foreign Confessions established basic rules for transferring as a supplement to the April decree in August (Circular 4628), tens if not hundreds of thousands of "recalcitrants" had been accepted into Catholicism. Nor were Catholic hierarchs informed of this circular in a timely fashion, so that in some cases they continued to employ their own system until 1908.[23] As a result, many people now belonged, in effect, to two confessions at once, because they had been accepted into Catholicism but had not yet been officially excluded from the ranks of the Orthodox.

Believing that they were Catholic, such transferees faced numerous complications when they discovered that the state did not share their assessment. Converts were prosecuted and even punished for having their children baptized with a Catholic rite or for burying their dead in Catholic graveyards. Students in schools and gymnasiums were suddenly barred from Catholic religious instruction and informed that they would be examined in Orthodoxy. Spouses were informed that their seemingly straightforward marriages were in fact "mixed" (i.e., interconfessional), that they had violated the law by having a Catholic ceremony, and that their children would have to be raised in Orthodoxy. Meanwhile, many Catholic priests found themselves under criminal prosecution for "knowingly administering Catholic rites to people of the Orthodox faith."[24]

The government had of course foreseen a mass exodus of formally Orthodox people to Catholicism after the April decree, and it therefore had not intended for the registration process to inhibit such transfers. But to the extent that confessional affiliation remained one of the central aspects of a person's sociolegal status, the government could not permit transfers to occur in a haphazard fashion without proper registration. For the most part, senior officials sought to accommodate the transferees while ensuring such registration. The interior minister, Peter Stolypin, and the Department of Foreign Confessions' director, A. Kharuzin, noted in 1909 that most of the transferees had acted in good faith and that the government's mode of action "should exhibit particular care and deliberation." The Warsaw governor general, Georgii Skalon, argued that the converts should without question be considered Catholic and that nowhere had the April decree indicated that confessional transfer depended on prior exclusion from Orthodox registers. The governor of Vil'na province added in 1909 that requiring the converts go through the formalities of transfer "could undoubtedly be interpreted as an attempt once again to force them to return to Orthodoxy and as an arbitrary measure."[25]

Despite these good intentions, however, nothing concrete was done, and with time—especially after Stolypin's assassination in 1911—the state became less accommodating. Most remarkably, in an appeals case in 1910, the Senate decided that any person who remained Orthodox according to official records should be considered "knowingly Orthodox" (*zavedomo pravoslavnym*) until those records had been changed. On this basis, in 1913 the Department of Foreign Confessions instructed the governor of Minsk Province that such people, until the transfer was official, "should be considered Orthodox even if they factually confessed the Roman Catholic faith." There were also reports that the governor had begun to assert that "permission" of the authorities was required for transfer, even though circulars made reference only to the *registration* of transfer.[26]

It was apparently only when three Catholic members of the State Council lodged a protest against the prevailing situation in January 1915 that a final resolution appeared. Appealing primarily to a basic sense of justice, the councilors also made reference to the Great War, noting that many people in question were now "defending the honor and dignity of their homeland with weapons in their hands and are risking their lives each and every hour." It was critical that they "may calmly regard the future of their families, being sure that nothing threatens either their conscience or their religious views."[27] The government finally decided that all those who left Orthodoxy before November 1, 1905, when Circular 4628 *should* have been known to everyone, were recognized as Catholic from the day of their acceptance by the Catholic hierarchs. All others would be regarded as Orthodox until they went through the procedure outlined in Circular 4628. Thus ten years after the initial reform of April 1905, the government finally created an order covering all eventualities. And yet this resolution notably appeared only in July 1915, when many of the transferees already found themselves under German occupation and thus beyond its purview.[28]

Transfers to Heterodoxy

If technical considerations occupied a prominent place in the experience of would-be Catholics, the issue of permitting the conversion of Christians to non-Christianity was by its very nature more controversial. The Committee of Ministers, in its deliberations leading to the April decree, had addressed this question with considerable circumspection, arguing that in general the state should neither recognize nor criminalize such conversion. Yet the committee had also recognized that there existed a certain category of people who "in reality" confessed a heterodox faith, despite their formal ascription to Orthodoxy, and who should therefore be permitted to return to the faith of their ancestors. Adopting a rather convoluted formulation that reflected this ambivalence, the April decree thus granted the right of exclusion from Orthodoxy to "those people who are registered as Orthodox, but who in reality confess that non-Christian faith to which they themselves or their ancestors belonged before their adherence to Orthodoxy."[29]

It bears emphasizing that the April decree did not actually recognize *conversion* to heterodoxy but rather the need to rectify the *inaccurate ascription* of certain subjects to Orthodoxy. The interested parties accordingly had to demonstrate first of all that they had actually practiced the non-Christian faith in question *before* April 1905—despite the fact that this would actually have represented a violation of the law at that time. By all indications, the vast majority of those who wished to abandon Orthodoxy in favor of Islam—above all some 50,000 baptized Tatar "apostates" in the Volga region—had few difficulties obtaining the state's recognition. Indeed, the law of April 1905 had been devised at least partly with precisely this group in mind. In contrast, numerous requests from Maris in Viatka Province, where a modestly sized movement for recognition as pagans developed, were rejected with the justification that the petitioners had fulfilled their "Christian obligations" before 1905 and therefore could not be regarded as having confessed paganism "in reality" before then.[30] The standard for pre-1905 "confession" of heterodoxy thus remained high, except for the baptized Tatar "apostates."

Petitioners also had to demonstrate a connection to "ancestors" who had confessed the religion to which they now sought to be ascribed. On the one hand, this stipulation made it possible for one to *return* exclusively to one's historic religion. Requests of those baptized from paganism or shamanism to convert to Islam or Buddhism were accordingly rejected.[31] On the other hand, the question arose: How far back in time could one claim to have had heterodox "ancestors" in order to receive satisfaction? In its 1907 bill to the Duma and in its own administrative dealings, the Interior Ministry ruled that "ancestors" should be construed to include only parents and grandparents— that is, those whom the petitioner "could have encountered while he was still alive and with whom it was possible to have had a more or less close moral connection and whose direct influence he could have felt."[32] Accordingly, in one of the very few cases in which Maris were permitted to return to paganism, the Interior Ministry acknowledged that the two petitioners' ancestors and relatives "were and remain pagans, and their father transferred to Orthodoxy only in 1865" with the goal of receiving material benefit. The context in which the petitioners lived and their recent family history suggested that their connection with paganism had never been broken.[33] In contrast, a few of the baptized Tatars who requested permission as Muslims had their petitions rejected when they claimed that their ancestors had been baptized shortly after the conquest of Kazan in 1552.[34] Here, the connection with Islam was simply too distant for the state to fulfill their request.

In general, these complications derived from the fact that the larger question of whether to recognize conversion to *any* faith—Christian or heterodox—remained open, especially after the appearance of the October Manifesto. Though the Ministry of Justice contended in 1906 that conversion to a non-Christian faith was still "unconditionally prohibited" for all citizens regardless of their initial confessional status, the Interior Ministry wrote that the refusal to recognize conversions to non-Christian faiths "would at the present time contradict the spirit of the Manifesto of October 17."[35] By the time it produced its draft law for the Duma on confessional transfer in March 1907, however, the Interior Ministry had retreated somewhat from that permissive position. The draft, while stopping short of criminalizing conversion to heterodoxy, still refused to recognize it, and when the Duma moved in 1909 to reinstate such recognition, Stolypin made it a point of defending the original draft in person.[36] This question—whether to recognize conversion from Christianity to heterodoxy—was a central factor in the draft's failure ever to make it past the State Council for legislative approval.[37]

Unsuccessful petitioners could not comprehend how these restrictions were compatible with "freedom of conscience." Indeed, they contended that the will of the sovereign was being openly violated by officials unwilling to register them in new faiths. As one group wrote to the Interior Ministry in 1910, with their exclusion from Orthodoxy, "we will [then] be satisfied in our conscience and convinced that the will of the Sovereign Emperor is being fulfilled unquestioningly for the benefit of the people who adore him." Another group wrote that they had been petitioning to be recognized as pagans for three years, "but artificial impediments have been erected." Having been referred back and forth between different government agencies, "we are unable to gain any explanation [for the rejection] and we cannot comprehend why we encounter such obstacles and red tape. . . . Thus instead of the desired peace, tranquility, and happiness heralded from the heights of the throne, smoldering irritation is growing and the gracious law is blatantly being violated." Yet another group of thirty-seven petitioners, complaining about the local clergy's efforts to block their recognition as members of the pagan sect "Kugu Sorta," asked rhetorically, "Should the clergy abolish the manifesto and the decrees of the Sovereign Emperor and prevent us from praying to God as our conscience dictates, as the Sovereign Emperor has allowed?"[38] A similar petitioner concluded that because of the rejection of his petition, "I am left without conscience, and such a situation is, I believe, desirable to neither the Sovereign Emperor nor the government."[39]

Yet even as they refused to recognize conversion to heterodoxy, state authorities did not actively persecute such petitioners. True, some pagans who had rejected Orthodoxy were fined for having buried their dead outside of Orthodox cemeteries and without Orthodox rites.[40] But the official position was that unauthorized transfer to non-Christianity should not result in criminal prosecution or "consequences that hamper [the apostate's] religious convictions." Thus when one Mari with Kugu-Sorta sympathies complained that he had been selected against his will as watchman for the local Orthodox church, the Department of Foreign Confessions upheld his complaint. The Mari in question could not be officially excluded from Orthodoxy and given Kugu-Sorta status, but at the same time he "cannot be persecuted for his belonging to it [Kugu Sorta], nor can he be compelled to fulfill any obligations with respect to the Orthodox Church."[41]

In general, Stolypin and his associates faced the unenviable task of reconciling two scarcely compatible imperatives: to be as deferential as possible to people's religious beliefs and aspirations (so long as they did not represent a political threat to the state) while not antagonizing the political right, which was crucial to the success of Stolypin's other reform projects and to his very political survival. Given the precariousness of Stolypin's position by 1909, it simply made little sense to violate the sensibilities of the believing Orthodox majority for the sake of a relatively small number of would-be pagans.[42] Still, Stolypin tried to ensure that even these pagans could at least practice their faith, even if that practice would not be given official sanction.

But it was clearly not enough for many of those who sought recognition as non-Christians that they merely eluded active persecution. Aside from the fact that their marriages lacked legal force without Orthodox sanction, these petitioners believed that state recognition conferred a certain legitimacy on their choice of religion. Thus one group admitted that they were able to practice their faith without interference, "but at the same time, it should be noted that our religious teaching, since it does not have governmental approval, is in effect private and not legal [*iavliaetsia kak by chastnym, nezakonnym*], and on that basis we cannot freely make use of all the religious rights that have been granted to us."[43] In short, freedom of conscience for many meant not only that the state would not inhibit its citizens' religious practice but also that it would respect their convictions enough to recognize their spiritual choices.

The Problem of Jewish Transfer

The transfer of Jews to other faiths raised a series of particular problems, in light of the fact that Jews were not understood to be a confessional group like most others. Indeed, the Department of Foreign Confessions was reluctant even to address the Jewish problem in the context of religious reform because "at the base of particularistic legislation about Jews is not merely a confessional marker; the law distinguishes Jews as a particular alien group [*inorodcheskaia gruppa*], which is placed in particular conditions in light of its national particularities."[44] Nonetheless, cases involving the desire of Jews to convert to other religions, or of converted Jews to return to Judaism, were bound to arise sooner or later, and this required the government to contemplate how the legitimate religious needs of Jews could be balanced against the supposed need to protect Russian society from Jewish exploitation and intrigue.

Most significant in this regard was determining when, and under what circumstances, religious conversion could liberate Jews from the general restrictions imposed on that population. Before 1905, Jewish converts to Christianity had been emancipated from legal restrictions, though an epidemic of seemingly insincere conversions by the late nineteenth century had raised doubts about this practice.[45] Some baptized Jews hoped to remain free from such restrictions after their return to Judaism on the basis of the April decree. However, in 1907 the Senate concluded that the April decree merely abolished criminal prosecution for the return to a non-Christian faith but did not terminate restrictions against those confessing non-Christian faiths. Thus Jews who had received the right to settle beyond the Pale based solely on their conversion to Orthodoxy "are subject [upon reconversion to Judaism] to exclusion from those communities to which they are ascribed and expulsion to the Pale of settlement."[46] Those wishing to confess Judaism would therefore be Jews in all senses of the term, legal restrictions included. Moreover, this principle was extended to Jews who converted to any other non-Christian faith (e.g., Islam).[47] It was only Christianity that could begin to erase a Jew's Jewishness.

Even here, the state refused to treat all forms of Christianity equally. If Jewish conversion to Catholicism, Lutheranism, and Orthodoxy terminated legal restrictions on the convert, then conversion to Christian sects, which became more frequent after 1905, ultimately did not. The Department of Foreign Confessions reported in 1909 that the Christian sectarian movement in the Russian south, and especially in Odessa, enjoyed "particular sympathy" among Jews.[48] Already regarding the Baptist faith as "a most dangerous [sect]," the government now fretted that "the interference of Jews in the sectarian movement, in light of their tendency to intrigue, may give sectarianism a completely undesirable political tint."[49]

Moreover, the government feared that these various Christian sects would merely be used as a front behind which Jews could continue their practice of Judaism after liberation from legal restrictions. The Interior Ministry accordingly began to argue for a more restrictive conception of Christianity, to prevent Jews from making use of the "extremely primitive organization of sectarian communities" to become Christians only nominally. An assistant interior minister, S. E. Kryzhanovskii, wrote to the Senate that the law permitting emancipation of converted Jews had been written when the term "Christian confessions" had referred to "entirely defined religions," whose dogmas and teachings were stable, generally known, and fully recognized by the state. In contrast, the sects in question lacked even recognized clergies, and "contemporary rationalistic sectarianism in all its innumerable branches does not represent anything definite and stable in either dogmatic or canonical respects." Conversion of a Jew to one of the given sects should therefore not be considered conversion to Christianity in the sense that the law implied, and Jewish converts to

Christian sects should accordingly not be liberated from legal restrictions applied to Jews.[50]

Although the Senate explicitly endorsed this opinion only in 1912, from at least 1910 the Interior Ministry was instructing its subordinates to remind Jews wishing to convert that their acceptance into Baptist, Evangelical, and even Russian-sectarian (e.g., Molokan) communities would *not* exempt them from legal restrictions imposed on Jews.[51] Still, the government did not prohibit such conversions outright and was even willing to recognize them, as long as the baptisms were conducted in accordance with the law. Thus Leon Rosenberg, the head of the "Evangelical-Christian Protestant Community of the Baptist Rite" in Odessa, received the Interior Ministry's approval to baptize a number of Jews once he had submitted certificates attesting to their successful examination in Christianity.

If Jews could at least convert to other heterodox faiths and to Christian sectarianism, albeit without being liberated from legal restrictions, they were not at all eligible for acceptance into the Karaite community, a small "sect" within Judaism whose members in Russia constituted a distinct confessional group subject to its own statutes. Decidedly privileged in comparison with rabbinical Jews, Karaites incurred few of the prejudices held against Jews generally.[52] They had obtained privileges in 1795 from Catherine II on the condition that they not accept any rabbinical Jews into their ranks. Petitions on the part of Jews wishing to join the Karaite community had accordingly been rejected in the past, for as the Karaite Spiritual Board itself declared in 1911, "the guiding motive [of such petitions] is the selfish and base goal to make use of the civil rights granted to Karaites or other privileges, or in order to satisfy a feeling of love" between a Jew and a Karaite. The Karaite faith, the board concluded, "is not in the least interested in filling its ranks with unbelieving adherents, who regard religion as a means of attaining their material aspirations and who, of course, will be bad Karaites."[53] In this case, the government's suspicions dovetailed with the Karaites' desire to maintain the insularity of their community. In any event, by 1907 the government established as a condition for any confessional transfer that the religious leadership of the target community actually agree to accept the prospective convert.[54]

New Religions and Sects

The very existence of sects (whether Christian or Jewish) brings us finally to the issue of new religions. Iurii Belov has recently asserted that legislation before 1905 was designed to ensure "the complete impossibility" of the formation of new sects within foreign faiths and to combat "schism" (*raskol*) among those confessions.[55] It certainly is true that all the recognized foreign confessions were state institutions and that therefore, as the Interior Ministry wrote in 1907, the "the protection of the inviolability of their rights and freedom constitutes, according to the law, a direct obligation of the [state] administration."[56] It was also the case that Russia's existing system of confessional administration did not make any concrete provisions for the appearance of new religious teachings. But the eventual recognition of Baptists as a religious community in the 1870s and the state's attempt to manage schism among Mennonites in the 1860s and among Lutherans in the Baltic region in the 1890s suggest that the state was open to legalizing new confessions under certain conditions, if only to prevent complete administrative chaos.[57] Thus the state had attempted—albeit slowly and with considerable confusion—to establish some kind of system for dealing with this problem before 1905. The Interior Ministry noted in 1906 that even without the proclamation of new freedoms, this was a lacuna that needed to be filled; the proclamation of "freedom of conscience" placed this question "at the top of the list."[58]

The existing system recognized several major confessions, and the law also made reference to a series of tolerated sects (e.g., Hernhutters, Baptists, and Scottish colonists). Most of these confessions or sects had some kind of statute or at least basic rules governing their religious affairs, and these statutes and rules had been combined into a single volume of the Law Code in 1857 (reissued in 1896).[59] Finally, in practice a few other confessions functioned by special arrangement, such as the Anglican Church, which was administered directly by the British Embassy.[60] All other religious groupings existed outside the law.

The dynamic religious situation in Russia by the end of the nineteenth century was scarcely compatible with this system. Primarily (but not only) among the Protestant faiths, various new religious teachings had begun to appear from around mid-century: Baptists, Evangelical Christians, the "Jerusalem Friends," the "Gyupfers," Seventh-Day Adventists, the "Catholic and Apostolic community," the New Brothers and Sisters, Malevantsy, the "Free Confession," the Busch Brothers, the Separatists, the Free Church of Christ, the Mariavites, and even a "Syrio-Nestorian Evangelical Church."[61] New teachings had also formed among non-Christian religions, such as Burkhanism in the Altai Region, Kugu Sorta (a reformed animism) in Viatka Province, and the so-called Vaisovtsy among Volga Muslims.[62] If anything, the proliferation of new movements was accelerating at the turn of the century, thus confirming the proposition that alienation from established churches and even crises of faith produced new forms of religiosity as often as secularism and atheism.[63] Many of these groups were of course very small, but others—most notably Baptists, Evangelical Christians, and Mariavites—could claim tens of thousands of adherents.[64]

Moreover, the significance of these groups did not depend so much on their size. Rather, their very existence raised basic theoretical questions concerning the relationship of state power to different confessions in the new order. The religious aspirations of these sectarians presumably warranted satisfaction if the principle of "freedom of conscience" was to be upheld, yet the inconstancy and indeterminacy of their dogmas and "clergy"—as we saw in the context of Jewish transfer—cast grave doubts on the advisability of allowing them to maintain their own parish records. Moreover, it was far from self-evident that the state, in the name of "freedom of conscience," should actively facilitate schism among confessions that had long been recognized and effectively integrated into the existing system of confessional administration.

By far the largest case of a potentially new religion after 1905 concerned the Mariavites—a movement inspired by the visions of a certain Feliksa Kozlowska. Arising in the 1890s, this movement eventually became a rebellion of dissident Catholic priests against the church hierarchy. Although Mariavites had not actually sought to break from the church and had even appealed directly to the pope in 1903, the Vatican dismissed Kozlowska's visions as hallucinations, and the Polish episcopate condemned the dissident priests in early 1906. In an encyclical that same year, the pope ordered the Mariavites to disband and to submit to the Polish hierarchy, and when they refused he excommunicated the group's leaders. Thus was born "the first schism in Polish Catholicism since the Reformation."[65]

The Interior Ministry had difficulty making sense of this crisis and was therefore initially reluctant to interfere. By the spring of 1906, however, conflicts between Mariavites and loyalist Catholics over church property had become so violent—eight persons were killed in one such a confrontation—that the imperial government could no longer stand aside. Notably, the Catholic hierarchy itself turned to the government for protection from the Mariavites, arguing that renegade priests could join other faiths if they wished but were not entitled to consider themselves Catholics while inciting the population against the episcopate. Because Catholic priests performed important functions of state service, the hierarchy argued, the government should aid in removing the Mariavites from their positions and ensuring the church's control of its property—that is, the parish churches and other buildings that were the objects of intense conflict.[66] In fact, the Catholic Church in Russia had been granted full control over the appointment and removal of its own parish clergy in December 1905, as part of the implementation of religious reform earlier that year. Some in the government were therefore reluctant to interfere in these matters now and perhaps even took pleasure in watching the Polish Catholic Church struggle with the consequences of its newly won freedoms.

Nonetheless, while seeking to secure the needs and to protect the interests of *both* the Mariavites and the members of the official church, the Interior Ministry made fairly clear in 1906 that its preference lay with the latter. "Not considering itself called upon to protect either the purity of the dogmas of the Roman Catholic church or its integrity, the Ministry, on the other hand, considered it incompatible with the dignity of the government to grant any kind of particular protection to a new religious movement with the goal of inflicting harm on Catholicism." The pope, siding unequivocally with what the Imperial authorities called "orthodox Catholics" (*pravovernye katoliki*), indicated that the Mariavites would have to be regarded as a sect, entirely separate from the Catholic Church. But the state could not be neutral in effectuating this divorce. If the proclamation of freedom of conscience entitled sects to "legal and independent existence," nonetheless such sects "may not, in the opinion of the Ministry, enjoy identical rights with religions existing in the state that have already been recognized by law, and whose protection is the duty of the government, on an equal basis with the defense of the legal rights of the Orthodox Church." "The church in question is a state institution," the Ministry continued, and therefore Catholic authorities "may obviously rely fully on the government's defense of their legal rights."[67] The ministry thus proposed a set of temporary rules for the Mariavites that declared them a recognized sect with the right of free confession and entrusted their parish records to civil officials (based on the Baptist model). The rights of the loyalist Catholic clergy and the church's property were to be protected.[68] In short, even in the case of Catholicism—surely the foreign confession that had shown itself to be the least reliable and the most politicized in the eyes of the government— the satisfaction of the religious rights of new sectarians could not be realized at the expense of a recognized and properly constituted confession.

This preference for the established Catholic Church turned out to be temporary, however. Having separated from the Catholic Church in 1906, the

Mariavite movement developed quickly thereafter, drawing adherents primarily from the peasantry and the working class. They eventually established seventy-four communities with some 160,000 adherents and thirty-
two priests. By approving a statute for this group in 1909, by recognizing it
as an "independent religious teaching" in 1912 with the right to keep parish
records, and by establishing a system for the appointment of Mariavite bish-
ops with imperial confirmation, the state created a full-fledged new confession in Russian Poland, entirely independent of its mother church in institutional terms. By 1913, recognizing that the 1906 rules left virtually all
church property (including parish churches) in the hands of the Catholic
Church, the government was even subsidizing the Mariavites and granting
their clergy free transport on Imperial railways.[69]

There were several reasons for this reorientation. First, in 1909 the Mariavites joined forces with the "Old Catholic" movement in Europe, which
had broken with the pope over the declaration of papal infallibility in 1870
and had established the so-called Utrecht Union of Churches based in the
Netherlands.[70] Presumably, the Mariavites' affiliation with an established
church institution facilitated their recognition as a distinct confession in
Russia. Second, the Mariavite clergy strictly refrained from engaging in
politics and condemned nationalism as being incompatible with universal
Christian love. A cause for hostility on the part of many politicized Poles,
socialist as well as nationalist, this circumstance obviously made the group
attractive to a government facing far more politics than it wished.[71] Finally,
by 1914 if not earlier, the government had recognized that the movement
represented a useful weapon against a troublesome Catholic clergy, who
"expend on this embittered battle with the 'internal enemy' the energy that
previously was enlisted for the purposes of opposing Russian interests and
the government in one form or another." Accordingly, the government
should cease protecting a hostile Catholicism from the Mariavites "for the
sake of abstract juridical principles."[72]

Conclusion

By almost any measure, believers in Russia enjoyed greater religious freedom after 1905 than they had before. Yet there nonetheless remained distinct limits to the regime's willingness to reform the existing religious order. For all but the most radical reformers, religion continued to represent
a fundamental source of morality and stability, and it therefore represented

something that the state could never afford to regard with indifference.[73] Nor did state officials at any point contemplate placing all confessions on equal footing, but they instead insisted that the Orthodox Church was and would remain "predominant and ruling," even if the precise forms and extent of that preeminence remained open for consideration. Pressured from the right by conservative elements unwilling to accept further encroachment on Orthodoxy, Stolypin's government also failed to invest the promise of freedom of conscience in the October Manifesto with proper legislative form. The religious reform of 1905 thus represented a significant, but undoubtedly partial, accommodation with a new, more dynamic religious reality in Russia in the early twentieth century. Though acknowledging the increasingly pluralistic character of Russian society, it tenaciously upheld certain prerogatives for the state in regulating confessional transfer. Perhaps as long as official religious status retained legal significance—as a category that conferred rights, imposed restrictions, and served as an expedient tool for the governance of the empire's population—the state could never afford to surrender entirely control over its regulation.

My concern in this chapter has been principally with contests in which the broader system of categorization itself was largely taken for granted by participants. Even the adherents of new religions and sects strove above all to establish an officially recognized place for themselves within the existing order, and not to contest the latter's legitimacy and relevance. But the processes I have described did have implications for the larger families of categories used to classify people and to frame individual and collective self-understandings.[74] Recent scholarship has documented the growing tendency of institutions and political elites in late Imperial Russia to deploy ethnicity as a mode of classification and has highlighted the important role of national politics in the Revolution of 1905 for the acceleration of this process.[75] Even as existing bureaucratic structures and legal statutes remained geared primarily toward regulating diversity in its confessional manifestations, the political salience of ethnicity was rapidly increasing. This reorientation was rooted in an emerging perception that categories based on religious confession failed to reveal a politically significant reality. The destabilization of religious identity—both reflected and accelerated by the reform of 1905—could only reinforce the proposition that religion was no longer capable of serving as the basis for stable political relations between subjects and the state. Although direct causality is difficult to establish, I propose that the complications arising from efforts to regulate confessional transfer after 1905 contributed to religion's eclipse as a mode of classification by nationality—a transformation clearly reflected in Tsarist wartime practices, though not fully institutionalized until the early years of Soviet rule.[76]

The Soviet system of classification of course rejected religion as the basis for documenting individual identity and thus firmly entrenched nationality as the defining element in the elaboration of categories of cultural identity. In this respect, Soviet practice served to codify a crucial shift that had begun in the later years of Tsarist Russia and that represented a fundamental break with older ways of conceptualizing diversity. The liberalization of the religious order in 1905, though no doubt reflecting the regime's willingness to ascribe greater significance to subjects' own self-identification, should also be understood in terms of this transition—when one institutionalized system of categorization was crumbling but had not yet been replaced by an alternative.

By the 1920s, however, such an alternative was essentially in place, and by the 1930s the Soviet system of categorization had become at least as rigid as the Tsarist system of categorization had been. Even before 1905, the Tsarist authorities had recognized that religious identity, if deeply rooted, was nonetheless mutable, and that as long as conversion did not encroach on the prerogatives of the privileged Orthodox Church, it should be recognized by the state through a revision of formal confessional status. In contrast, by the 1930s—despite original Bolshevik thinking on the matter—the Soviet state construed nationality as a primordial and essential attribute and both actively discouraged even voluntary assimilation and limited the freedom of Soviet citizens to determine their nationality. In different ways and for different reasons, then, nationality came to be ascribed in the Soviet Union as much as religion had been in Imperial Russia.[77]

Notes

1. Robert D. Crews, "Empire and the Confessional State: Islam and Religious Politics in Nineteenth-Century Russia, *American Historical Review* 108, no. 1 (2003): 50–83.

2. On these important records, see Charles Steinwedel, "Making Social Groups, One Person at a Time: The Identification of Individuals by Estate, Religious Confession, and Ethnicity in Late Imperial Russia," in *Documenting Individual Identity: The Development of State Practices Since the French Revolution,* ed. Jane Caplan and John Torpey (Princeton, N.J.: Princeton University Press, 2001), 67–82; Gene M. Avrutin, "The Power of Documentation: Vital Statistics and Jewish Accommodation in Tsarist Russia," *Ab Imperio* 4 (2003): 271–300; Paul W. Werth, "In the State's Embrace? Civil Acts

in an Imperial Order," *Kritika: Explorations in Russian and Eurasian History* 7 (2006), forthcoming.

3. On marriage and its religious foundations, see Gregory L. Freeze, "Bringing Order to the Russian Family: Marriage and Divorce in Imperial Russia, 1760–1860," *Journal of Modern History* 62, no. 4 (1990): 709–49; William Wagner, *Marriage, Property, and Law in Late Imperial Russia* (Oxford: Clarendon Press, 1994); Robert Crews, "Allies in God's Command: Muslim Communities and the State in Imperial Russia," Ph.D. dissertation, Princeton University, 1999; ChaeRan Freeze, *Jewish Marriage and Divorce in Imperial Russia* (Hanover, N.H.: Brandeis University Press, 2002); and V. Shein, "K istorii voprosa o smeshannykh brakakh," *Zhurnal Ministerstva Iustitsii* 3 (1907): 231–73.

4. A nuanced treatment of restrictions on Jews is provided by Benjamin Nathans, *Beyond the Pale: The Jewish Encounter with Late Imperial Russia* (Berkeley: University of California Press, 2002). On Poles/Catholics, see Witold Rodkiewicz, *Russian Nationality Policy in the Western Provinces of the Empire, 1863–1905* (Lublin: Scientific Society of Lublin, 1998), esp. 57–129; and L. E. Gorizontov, *Paradoksy imperskoi politiki: Poliaki v Rossii i russkie v Pol'she* (Moscow: Indrik, 1999).

5. On the promotion of Orthodoxy in the nineteenth century, see Paul W. Werth, *At the Margins of Orthodoxy: Mission, Governance, and Confessional Politics in Russia's Volga-Kama Region, 1827–1905* (Ithaca. N.Y.: Cornell University Press, 2002).

6. *Svod Zakonov Rossiiskoi Imperii* (Saint Petersburg: Tipografiia Vtorago Otdeleniia Sobstvennoi Ego Imperatorskago Velichestva Kantseliarii, 1857), vol. 11, part 1, arts. 4, 6, 8.

7. I share many of the concerns expressed by Rogers Brubaker and Frederick Cooper about excessively expansive and ambiguous meanings of the term "identity" in contemporary social science discourse. I accordingly use this category below sparingly and refer more frequently to "affiliation" and "status," because my concerns are principally with processes of categorization. See Brubaker and Cooper, "Beyond 'Identity,' " *Theory and Society* 29 (2000): 1–47.

8. Proposed legislation and administrative practice in these years tended to refer to "transfer" [*perekhod*] rather than "conversion" [*obrashchenie*], thereby acknowledging that the operation in question often involved a change in formal confessional status rather than a transformation in religious consciousness as such.

9. On the establishment of "national politics" (i.e., one extending across the entire country), see Charles Robert Steinwedel, "Invisible Threads of Empire: State, Religion, and Ethnicity in Tsarist Bashkiria, 1773–1917," Ph.D. dissertation, Columbia University, 1999, 267–313; and Francis William Wcislo, *Reforming Rural Russia: State, Local Society, and National Politics, 1855–1914* (Princeton, N.J.: Princeton University Press, 1990).

10. A. Iu. Polunov, *Pod vlast'iu Ober-Prokurora: Gosudarstvo i tserkov' v epohku Aleksandra III* (Moscow: AIRO-XX, 1996); and Paul W. Werth, "The Limits of Religious Ascription: Baptized Tatars and the Revision of 'Apostasy,' 1840s–1905," *Russian Review* 59, no. 4 (2000): 493–511. On the origins of these groups, see Theodore R. Weeks, "Between Rome and Tsargrad: The Uniate Church in Imperial Russia," in *Of Religion and Identity: Missions, Conversion, and Tolerance in the Russian Empire,* ed. Michael Khodarkovsky and Robert Geraci (Ithaca, N.Y.: Cornell University Press, 2001); A. V. Gavrilin, *Ocherki istorii Rizhskoi eparkhii XIX veka* (Riga: Filokaliia, 1999), 73–182; and Paul W. Werth, "Coercion and Conversion: Violence and the Mass

Baptism of the Volga Peoples, 1700–1764," *Kritika: Explorations in Russian and Eurasian History* 4, no. 3 (2003): 543–70.

11. For such a critique, see M. A. Reisner, *Gosudarstvo i veruiushchaia lichnost': Sbornik statei* (Saint Petersburg: Biblioteka "Obshchestvennaia pol'za," 1905). For a positive assessment, see M. Krasnozhen, *Inovertsy na Rusi: K voprosu o svobode very i o veroterpimosti, vol. 1: Polozhenie nepravoslavnykh khristian v Rossii,* 3rd ed. (Iur'ev: Tipografiia K. Mattisena, 1903).

12. Christopher Read, *Religion, Revolution and the Russian Intelligentsia, 1900–1912: The Vekhi Debate and Its Intellectual Background* (New York: Barnes & Noble, 1980), 13–39; Catherine Evtuhov, *The Cross and the Sickle: Sergei Bulgakov and the Fate of Russian Religious Philosophy* (Ithaca, N.Y.: Cornell University Press, 1997); Georgii Florovsky, *Puti russkago bogosloviia* (Paris: YMCA Press, 1983), 452–99; Pål Kolstø, "A Mass for a Heretic? The Controversy Over Lev Tolstoi's Burial," *Slavic Review* 60, no. 1 (2001): 81–85; Sergei Firsov, *Russkaia tserkov' nakanune peremen: konets 1890-kh–1918 gg.* (Saint Petersburg: Kul'turnyi tsentr "Dukhovnaia biblioteka," 2002), 99–125.

13. *Polnoe Sobranie Zakonov Rossiiskoi Imperii [PSZ],* 3rd series, vol. 23, no. 22581, February 26, 1903. On the earlier draft of the manifesto, see B. V. Anan'ich, ed., *Vlast' i reformy: Ot samoderzhavnoi k sovetskoi Rossii* (Saint Petersburg: Izdatel'stvo Dmitriia Bulanina, 1996), 445.

14. *PSZ,* 3rd series, vol. 24, no. 25495, December 12, 1904.

15. *PSZ,* 3rd series, vol. 25, no. 26126, April 17, 1905.

16. Informed treatments of the legislative process include Peter Waldron, "Religious Reform after 1905: Old Believers and the Orthodox Church," *Oxford Slavonic Papers* 20 (1987): 110–39; Aleksandra Andreevna Dorskaia, *Svoboda sovesti v Rossii: Sud'ba zakonoproektov nachala XX veka* (Saint Petersburg: Izdatel'stvo RGPU im. A. I. Gertsena, 2001); Diliara Usmanova, *Musul'manskaia fraktsiia i problemy "svobody sovesti" v Gosudarstvennoi Dume Rossii, 1906–1917* (Kazan: Matser Lain, 1999), 81–122; and Abraham Ascher, *P. A. Stolypin: The Search for Stability in Late-Imperial Russia* (Stanford, Calif.: Stanford University Press, 2001), 293–302.

17. See, e.g., Rossiiskii Gosudarstvennyi Istoricheskii Arkhiv [RGIA], f. 796, op. 442, d. 2110, ll. 26ob.-27; RGIA, f. 821, op. 133, d. 515, ll. 60ob.–61.

18. RGIA, f. 821, op. 10, d. 260, l. 121. The Department of the Religious Affairs of Foreign Confessions, in the Interior Ministry, had jurisdiction over all the empire's non-Orthodox religions and confessions.

19. See K. K. Arsen'ev, *Svoboda sovesti i veroterpimost': Sbornik statei* (Saint Petersburg: Biblioteka "Obshchestvennaia pol'za," 1905); Usmanova, *Musul'manskaia fraktsiia,* 81–86; V. K. Sokolov, "Svoboda sovesti i veroterpimost' (istoriko-kriticheskii ocherk)," *Vestnik prava* 5 (1905): 1–31; Iu. Skobel'tsyna, *Svoboda sovesti* (Saint Petersburg: Tipografiia S. M. Proppera, 1906) [politicheskaia biblioteka "Birzhevykh vedomostei," vyp. 30]. See also the positions of the Social Democrats and the Kadets: *Za svobodu sovesti* (Saint Petersburg: Izdatel'stvo "Rabochii Deputat," 1908); *Proekt zakona o svobode sovesti, sostavlennyi partiei narodnoi svobody dlia vneseniia v Gosudarstvennuiu Dumu* (Saint Petersburg: Tipografiia "Obshchestvennaia pol'za," 1907).

20. Reisner, *Gosudarstvo,* esp. 390–423; Dorskaia, *Svoboda sovesi v Rossii.* For a brief exegesis of Reisner in English, see Laura Engelstein, "The Dream of Civil Society in Tsarist Russia: Law, State, and Religion," in *Civil Society before Democracy:*

Lessons from Nineteenth-Century Europe, ed. Nancy Bermeo and Philip Nord (Lanham, Md.: Rowman & Littlefield, 2000), 34–36.

21. M. Krasnozhen, *K voprosu o svobode sovesti i o veroterpimosti* (Iur'ev: Tipografiia K. Mattisena, 1905); Krasnozhen, "Granitsy veroterpimosti," *Pribavleniia k Tserkovnym vedomostiiam* 34 (20 August 1905): 1429–32; "O bezuslovnoi svobode veroispovedaniia v Rossii," *Kholmsko-Varshavskii eparkhial'nyi vestnik* 18 (1905): 214–16; Nikon (Episkop Vologodskii i Totemskii), *Svoboda sovesti imeet svoi granitsy* (Saint Petersburg, n.d. [probably 1910]); Koren, "Svoboda sovesti, ili inkvizitsiia," *Kholmsko-Varshavskii eparkhial'nyi listok* 39 (September 25, 1905): 469–71.

22. The department defined freedom of conscience as "the right of each person with a sufficiently mature self-consciousness to recognize or declare his faith, or even the absence of such, with no limitations or any adverse legal consequences." See *Spravka o svobode sovesti* (Saint Petersburg: Tipografiia Ministerstva vnutrennikh del, 1906), 3. This memorandum can be found in draft in RGIA, f. 821, op. 10, d. 39, ll. 7–59ob. I cite here from a copy in the Russian National Library, Saint Petersburg.

23. Department circular 4628 (August 18, 1905), in RGIA, f. 821, op. 133, d. 540, ll. 3–4. On the improvisation by Catholic authorities: RGIA, f. 821, op. 10, d. 260 ll. 227–34; and Lietuvos Valstybės Istorijos Archyvas [LVIA], f. 378 (BS, 1905), b. 403.

24. RGIA, f. 821, op. 10, d. 260, ll. 218, 233ob., 231ob.; "Zapiksa chlenov Gosudarstvennago Soveta Meishtovicha, Skirmunta, i Lopatinskago" (January 15, 1915), in RGIA, pechatnye zapiski, folder 743, pp. 1–10 and appendices.

25. RGIA, f. 821, op. 10, d. 260, ll, 218ob.–219, 222, l. 225ob.

26. "Zapiska chlenov Gosudarstvennogo Soveta," 5, 7, 73.

27. "Zapiska chlenov Gosudarstvennogo Soveta," 10.

28. RGIA, f. 821, op. 10, d. 260, ll. 219, 238–40. I have addressed the issue of transfer to Catholicism after 1905 in greater detail in "Trudnyi put' k katolitsizmu: Sovest', veroispovednaia prinadlezhnost' i grazhdanskoe sostoianie posle 1905 g.," *Lietuvių Katalikų Mokslo Akademijos Metraštis* 26 (2005): 447-475.

29. *PSZ,* 3rd series, vol. 24, no. 26126 (April 17, 1905), section I, article 3. For the Committee's deliberations, see N. P. Solov'ev, ed., *Polnyi krug dukhovnykh zakonov* (Moscow, 1907), 8–14.

30. See, e.g., Gosudarstvennyi Arkhiv Kirovskoi Oblasti [GAKO], f. 582, op. 150, d. 118, l. 3.

31. RGIA, f. 821, op. 8, d. 796; RGIA, f. 821, op. 133, d. 284, ll. 1ob., 6; RGIA, f. 821, op. 133, d. 572; and RGIA, f. 821, op. 8, d. 798.

32. "Zakonoproekt Ministerstva vnutrennikh del: Ob izmenenii zakonopolozhenii, kasaiushchikhsia perekhoda iz odnogo ispovedaniia v drugoe" (no. 1473, February 20, 1907), in *Missionerskoe Obozrenie* (1908), 202.

33. GAKO, f. 582, op. 148, d. 91, ll. 16–16ob.

34. RGIA, f. 821, op. 8, d. 796, l. 88ob.

35. RGIA, f. 821, op. 10, d. 260, ll. 64, 121. In a 1906 memorandum, the Interior Ministry explicitly included "paganism" under the heading of non-Christian faiths.

36. RGIA, f. 821, op. 10, d. 39, ll. 283–88. For different perspectives on the Duma's deliberations of the draft, see P. V. Kamenskii, *Veroispovednye i tserkovnye voprosy v Gosudarstvennoi Dume tret'iago sozyva i otnoshenie k nim "Soiuza 17 Oktiabria"* (Moscow: Tipo-litografiia E. Kudinova, 1909), 64–106; and *Ne posiagaite na Pravoslavie!* (Vil'na: Elektro-tipografiia "Russkii Pochin," 1909).

37. Modified by the Duma, the draft was blocked by the State Council and languished in a committee formed to reconcile the differences. RGIA, f. 821, op. 10, d. 265, ll. 88–104ob.

38. RGIA, f. 821, op. 133, d. 430, ll. 5ob., 10–10ob., 18.

39. RGIA, f. 821, op. 133, d. 515, l. 60ob.

40. RGIA, f. 821, op. 133, d. 515, ll. 2–2ob. In this case, a 25-ruble fine was assessed on villagers. See also RGIA, f. 821, op. 133, d. 515, l. 143.

41. RGIA, f. 821, op. 133, d. 430, l. 39–39ob.

42. When the far-right Union of Russian People mobilized against the pending bill on confessional transfer in the Duma in 1909 and sent telegrams to Stolypin, they identified the recognition of conversion from Christianity to heterodoxy in the Duma's version of the bill as being among its most objectionable elements. RGIA, f. 821, op. 10, d. 39, ll. 216–60.

43. RGIA, f. 821, op. 133, d. 515, ll. 67ob.–68.

44. *Spravka o svobode sovesti*, 36. The Interior Ministry expressed similar concerns about limitations on "people of Polish origin" [*litsa pol'skago proiskhozhdeniia*], because they "have not a confessional, but a political foundation" (39–40). On the problem of defining Poles, see Gorizontov, *Paradoksy imperskoi politiki*, 100–18. On the largely unsuccessful attempts to address the Jewish problem separately after 1905, see Ascher, P. A. *Stolypin*, 164–17; and Hans Rogger, *Jewish Policies and Right-Wing Politics in Imperial Russia* (Berkeley: University of California Press, 1986), 83–106.

45. John D. Klier, "State Policies and the Conversion of Jews in Imperial Russia," in *Of Religion and Empire*, 93, 108.

46. RGIA, f. 1284, op. 224, d. 125, l. 12.

47. RGIA, f. 821, op. 133, d. 540, ll. 11–11ob. (Department circular 1213 of April 15, 1909).

48. RGIA, f. 821, op. 133, d. 283, l. 11, 14–15.

49. RGIA, f. 821, op. 133, d. 283, l. 11ob. Although Baptists had been among those benefiting from the more liberal religious order after 1905, the state remained convinced of their "harm." For details, see Heather Coleman, *Russian Baptists and Spiritual Revolution, 1905–1929* (Bloomington: Indiana University Press, 2005).

50. RGIA, f. 821, op. 10, d. 273, ll. 10–12.

51. RGIA, f. 821, op. 133, d. 283, ll. 7, 63ob., 83, 85.

52. See "Evrei-Karaimy," *Zhurnal Ministerstva vnutrennikh del*, chap. 1 (1843): 263–84. According to the 1897 census, there were merely 12,894 Karaites in the empire, most of them in Crimea. See P. Luppov, "Statisticheskiia dannyia o naselenii Rossiiskoi Imperii (po perepisi 1897 goda)," *Pribavleniia k Tserkovnym vedomostiam* 12 (March 19, 1905): 512.

53. RGIA, f. 821, op. 133, d. 802, ll. 3–6; and RGIA, f. 821, op. 10, d. 492. In 1910, the Interior Ministry also reminded its subordinates that Karaites enjoyed the protection of special laws in the empire and enjoyed all the rights of Russian subjects. Accordingly, "restrictive enactments regarding Jews should not be applied to Karaites." RGIA, f. 821, op. 133, d. 769, l. 9 (Department circular 3027, April 5, 1910).

54. RGIA, f. 821, op. 133, d. 515, l. 248; RGIA, f. 821, op. 10, d. 492, l. 43ob (Interior ministry circular 6428 of November 5, 1907).

55. Iurii Stanislavovich Belov, "Pravitel'stvennaia politika po otnosheniiu k nepravoslavnym veroispovedaniiam v Rossii v 1905–1917 gg.," cand. diss., RAN Institut Rossiskoi Istorii, Sank-Peterburgskii Filial, 1999, 53.

56. Zakonoproekt Ministerstva vnutrennikh del "Ob inoslavnykh i inovernykh religioznykh obshchestvakh," in *Katolicheskaia tserkov' nakanune revoliutsii 1917 goda: Sbornik dokumentov,* ed. Marian Radwan (Lublin: Towarzystwo Naukowe Katolickiego Uniwersytetu Lubelskiego, 2003), 235.

57. RGIA, f. 381, op. 8, d. 3707; RGIA, f. 821, op. 5, dd. 975, 980, 998, 1020. I have addressed the problem of sects within the foreign faiths in "Schism Once Removed: State, Sects, and the Meanings of Religious Toleration in Imperial Russia," in *Imperial Rule,* ed. Alexei Miller and Alfred J. Rieber (Budapest: Central European Press, 2004), 85–108.

58. *Spravka o svobode sovesti,* 19.

59. "Ustavy dukhovnykh del inostrannykh ispovedanii," vol. 11, part 1, of *Svod zakonov Rossiiskoi Imperii* (Saint Petersburg, 1857; reissued in 1896).

60. RGIA, f. 821, op. 5, d. 935.

61. On these groups, see "Liuteranskiia sekty v Estliandskoi gubernii" (Revel, 1893) (in RGIA, f. 821, op. 5, d. 1020, ll. 1–33ob.); I. Lindenberg, (Protoierei), "Protestanskiia sekty v Pribaltiiskom krae," *Rizhskiia eparkhial'nyia vedomosti* 10–15 (1891): 340–56, 376–82, 416–28, 455–57, 487–92, 507–12; and Iulii Osterblom, *Noveishiia religioznyia dvizheniia v Estliandii* (Saint Petersburg: Tipografiia F. Eleonskago, 1885); S. Smirnov, "Nemetskie sektanty za Kavkazom," *Russkii vestnik* 57 (1865): 230–57; S. D. Bondar', *Adventizm 7-go dnia* (Saint Petersburg: Tipografiia Ministerstva vnutrennikh del, 1911); Bondar', *Sovremennoe sostoianie russkogo baptizma* (Saint Petersburg: Tipografiia Ministerstva vnutrennikh del, 1911); *Iz istorii tserkvi adventistov sed'mogo dnia v Rossii* (Kaliningrad: IPP "Iantarnyi Skaz," 1993).

62. RGIA, f. 821, op. 133, d. 430, ll. 8–12ob.; Andrei Znamenski, *Shamanism and Christianity: Native Encounters with Russian Orthodox Missions in Siberia and Alaska, 1820–1917* (Westport, Conn.: Greenwood Press, 1999), 228–38; Paul W. Werth, "Big Candles and 'Internal Conversion': The Mari Pagan Reformation and Its Russian Appropriations," in *Of Religion and Identity,* ed. Khodarkovsky and Geraci, 144–72; the draft of the never-published book by S. G. Rybakov, "Novyia techeniia v russkom iazychestve: Sekty v iazychestve cheremis, votiakov i chuvash: vera "Kugu-Sorta" i drugiia" (1915), in RGIA, f. 821, op. 133, d. 643; E. V. Molostvova, "Vaisov Bozhii Polk," *Mir Islama* 1, no. 2 (1912): 143–52; M. Sagidullin, *K istorii Vaisvskogo dvizheniia* (Kazan: Tatarskii nauchno-issledovatel'skii ekonomicheskii institut, 1930); and Michael Kemper and Diliara Usmanova, "Vaisovskoe dvizhenie v zerkale sobstvennykh proshenii i poem," *Ekho vekov/Gasyrlar avazy* 3–4 (2001): 86–122.

63. New forms of veneration and religiosity were of course characteristic of Orthodox Russians in this period as well, and the teachings of the Baptists soon made their way from German to Russian and Ukrainian communities. See Coleman, *Russian Baptists;* Nadieszda Kizenko, *A Prodigal Saint: Father John of Kronstadt and the Russian People* (University Park: Pennsylvania State University Press, 2000); and J. Eugene Clay, "Orthodox Missionaries and 'Orthodox Heretics' in Russia, 1886–1917," in *Of Religion and Empire,* ed. Khodarkovsky and Geraci, 38–69.

64. *Statisticheskiia svedeniia o sektantakh (k 1 ianvaria 1912 g.)* (Saint Petersburg: Tipografiia Ministerstva vnutrennikh del, 1914), which counted a total of just under 400,000 sectarians of both Orthodox and other Christian origin. Mariavites are not included in this list, which apparently did not extend to the Kingdom of Poland.

65. Robert E. Blobaum, *Rewolucja: Russian Poland, 1904–1907* (Ithaca, N.Y.: Cornell University Press, 1995), 248. The short history provided here is based on Blobaum,

Rewolucja, 247–49; Nikolai Reinke, *Mariavity* (Saint Petersburg: Senatskaia tipografiia, 1910); Jerzy Peterkiewicz, *The Third Adam* (London: Oxford University Press, 1975), 7–34; and RGIA, f. 1276, op. 2, d. 601, ll. 1–2.

66. RGIA, f. 1276, op. 2, d. 601, ll. 2ob.–4ob. On confrontations, see also Gosu-darstvennyi Arkhiv Rossiiskoi Federatsii [GARF], f. 102 (O.O.), 1906, II otd., d. 12, ch. 2; Reinke, *Mariavity,* 15–16; and Peterkiewicz, *Third Adam,* 35.

67. The ministry cited an Imperial charter to the Kingdom of February 14, 1832 (ar-ticle 5), which stated that "the Roman-Catholic faith, as the faith confessed by the larger part of our subjects in the Kingdom of Poland, will always be an object of the govern-ment's particular care." RGIA, f. 1276, op. 2, d. 601, l. 20.

68. RGIA, f. 1276, op. 2, d. 601, ll. 9–18. The Council of Ministers approved the ministry's position with only a few minor revisions. Temporary rules for the Mariavites —intended to govern the new community until more comprehensive legislation on the formation of new religions and sects could be passed—went into effect in November of 1906.

69. RGIA, f. 1276, op. 2, d. 601, ll. 91–97; Ralph Tuchtenhagen, *Religion als min-derer Status: Die Reform der Gesetzgebung gegenuber religiösen Minderheiten in der verfassten Gesellschaft des Russishcen Reiches, 1905–1917* (Frankfurt: Peter Lang, 1995), 219–24.

70. Reinke, *Mariavity,* 24; Peterkiewicz, *Third Adam,* 39–43; "Starokatoliki i mari-avity," *Kolokol* no. 1051 (11 September 1909): 1. For the declaration on this issue by the Mariavite bishop Jan Kowalski, see "Mariavity," *Golos Moskvy* no. 10 (January 14, 1910).

71. On Mariavites' apolitical orientation, see "Pol'skaia natsional'naia tserkov'," *Vilenskii vestnik,* no. 2049 (April 16, 1910): 2; and "Mariavitizm v Tsarstve Pol'skom," *Vilenskii vestnik,* no. 2073 (May 15, 1910): 1–2.

72. RGIA, f. 1276, op. 2, d. 601, ll. 54ob.–56. Already in 1905, the Orthodox bishop of Kholm and Lublin had indicated that the growth of the Mariavite movement was dis-tracting the Catholic clergy from their struggle with the Orthodox. RGIA, f. 796, op. 442, l. 2128, l. 21.

73. See, e.g., the draft law of 1907, "Ob izmenenii zakonopolozhenii, kasaiu-shchikhsia perekhoda iz odnogo ispovedaniia v drugoe," in *Katolicheskaia tserkov',* ed. Radwan, 145–46; and RGIA, f. 821, op. 10, d. 265, ll. 90–104ob.

74. I.e., for "dimensions," to adopt the terminology of Kanchan Chandra and David Laitin, as presented in the introduction to the present volume. For the full elaboration, see their paper, "A Constructivist Framework for Thinking about Identity Change," pre-sented at the conference "Modeling Constructivist Approaches to Ethnic Identity and In-corporating Them into New Research Agenda," Massachusette Insitute of Technology, Cambridge, Mass., December 2002, esp. 3–5.

75. Charles Steinwedel, "To Make a Difference" the Category of Ethnicity in Late Imperial Russian Politics, 1861–1917," in *Russian Modernity: Politics, Knowledge, Practices,* ed. David Hoffmann and Yanni Kotsonis (New York: St. Martin's Press, 2000), 67–86; Peter Holquist, "To Count, to Extract, and to Exterminate: Population Sta-tistics and Population Politics in Late Imperial and Soviet Russia," in *A State of Nations Empire and Nation-Making in the Age of Lenin and Stalin,* ed. Terry Martin and Ronald Suny (Oxford: Oxford University Press, 2001), 111–144.

76. On the regime's wartime national politics and the institutionalization of nation-ality in the early Soviet period, see Eric Lohr, *Nationalizing the Russian Empire: The*

Campaign against Enemy Aliens during World War I (Cambridge, Mass.: Harvard University Press, 2003); Yuri Slezkine, "The USSR as a Communal Apartment, or How a Socialist State Promoted Ethnic Particularism," *Slavic Review* 53 (1994): 414–52; and Terry Martin, *The Affirmative Action Empire: Nations and Nationalism in the Soviet Union, 1923–1939* (Ithaca, N.Y.: Cornell University Press, 2001).

77. Martin, *Affirmative Action Empire;* Martin, "Modernization or Neo-Traditionalism? Ascribed Nationality and Soviet Primordialism," in *Russian Modernity,* ed. Hoffmann and Kotsonis, 161–82; Dominique Arel, "Fixing Ethnicity in Identity Documents: The Rise and Fall of Passport Nationality in Russia," *Canadian Review of Studies in Nationalism* 30, no. 1–2 (2003): 125–36.

7

Nation Building and Refugee Protection in the Post-Soviet Region

Oxana Shevel

The fall of communism opened the newly independent states of the former Soviet Union to global migration and refugee flows. By the end of the 1990s, the former Soviet states hosted 3.4 million refugees and other displaced persons—38 percent of Europe's and 15 percent of the world's total.[1] The challenge of refugee protection was daunting for the post-Soviet countries. The USSR was a refugee-producing, not a refugee-receiving, state, and the Soviet successor states had no legislative legacy or domestic expertise to deal with the refugee problem.[2] As the post-Soviet states began to create refugee policies and institutions, they all received similar cues from the international community. Since 1992, the Office of the United Nations High Commissioner for Refugees (UNHCR), a UN refugee agency mandated to supervise the application of the international refugee law and to promote a nondiscriminatory refugee policy, has been working on the ground in the post-Soviet region to affect emerging refugee regimes. Despite similar international pressures, however, a decade after they first encountered similar refugee problems, post-Soviet states exhibit varying receptivity to refugees. This chapter explores the causes of this variation through a comparison of Russia and Ukraine.

Russia and Ukraine are major refugee-receiving states in the post-Soviet region. By the end of the 1990s, they were hosting more displaced persons than any Western European country except Germany.[3] The two states are similar economically and in their democratic development, and, since 1991, they have faced refugee problems of a similar nature and magnitude. These similarities might lead one to expect similar refugee policies, but in fact these states have adopted rather different policies. Among interesting empirical puzzles is a receptive policy toward former Soviet citizens, in particular toward co-ethnics, in Russia but not in Ukraine, and a more generous policy toward refugees from the developing world in Ukraine than in Russia.

These puzzles raise more general questions. Why do some post-Soviet states accept refugees more readily than others? Why do some states privilege certain refugee groups (in particular co-ethnics of the titular nationality) while others do not? This chapter argues that to answer these questions, we have to understand how the politics of nation building and the strategies of international institutions act as the main sources of post-Soviet refugee policies and systematically lead to different policy outcomes.

The governing elites in new states such as the former Soviet republics have to answer the all-important question: Who belongs to the nation (and thus constitutes "us") and who does not (and thus constitutes the "other")? Contestation over this question is the politics of nation building. As Arel emphasized in the introductory chapter, the construction of categories of identity is a political, not a teleological, process and is it often highly contested. This chapter first compares the contestation over the definition of the nation in Russia and Ukraine, and it then focuses on the consequences of this contestation for policies toward different groups of refugees. As we will see, the politics of nation building in Russia and Ukraine did not simply amount to defining co-ethnics of the titular group as "us" and the rest as "other." Reflecting historical, cultural, and political legacies, different "images" of the nation were on the political menu, each resonating with different segments of the society and different elite groups. The nature and intensity of contestation over the national question mandated a more or less receptive policy toward different refugee groups. The politics of nation building thus determined which refugee groups were (or were not) to be assisted by the state. This reality presented a challenge to international refugee-assisting institutions that lobbied for a receptive and a nondiscriminatory refugee policy.

International refugee-assisting organizations such as the UNHCR initially approached the post-Soviet region exclusively through the prism of international refugee law, assisting only those refugees who fit the international legal definition of a refugee. The evidence from Russia and Ukraine is a testament to the potential of international actors to promote policies reflecting international human rights standards, but only when these actors are aware that in different domestic contexts the meaning of the same category (e.g., "refugee") can be different, and when they are prepared to adjust their strategies to take into account constraints and opportunities created by the domestic politics of refugee policy.

Similar Problem, Varying Response: The Refugee Problem and Refugee Policy in Russia and Ukraine

The 1951 Geneva Convention on the Status of Refugees and its 1967 Protocol define a refugee as someone who has crossed an international border; who is not a citizen of the state where he or she is seeking refuge; and who fled due to a "well-founded fear of being persecuted for reasons of race, religion, nationality, membership of a particular social group or political opinion."[4] A refugee, under international law (I will use the term "traditional refugee" throughout the chapter), is thus an international migrant who has fled political, religious, ethnic, racial, or social persecution; who has crossed an international border; and who is not a citizen of the host state. In Western states, virtually all refugees are traditional refugees: foreigners who have crossed an international border and are not citizens of the state where they are seeking asylum. The refugee problem in the West is thus amenable to, and can be analyzed within, the framework of international refugee law. In the post-Soviet context of state collapse and state formation, however, the refugee problem has turned out to be much more complex.

Although there is a sizable number of "traditional" refugees in both Russia and Ukraine, they are only a small part of the refugee problem in these states. Traditional refugees in Russia and Ukraine are asylum seekers from developing countries, most of them Afghans. Thus, in Russia from 1992 to 1998, the UNHCR reception center registered some 35,500 asylum seekers from 52 non–Commonwealth of Independent States (CIS) countries, 70 percent of them Afghans.[5] Between 1996 and the middle of 2000, asylum seekers from more than forty countries applied for refugee status in Ukraine,[6] with Afghans being the majority of applicants for refugee status each year.[7] Though most of the developing-world asylum seekers found themselves in Russia and Ukraine because they were not able to reach destinations further west, most Afghans have been in the USSR since the Soviet era, and as a result, a plurality of Afghans wants to remain in Russia and Ukraine rather than to move further west.[8]

Although traditional refugees are numerous, the refugee problem in the post-Soviet region in general, and in Russia and Ukraine in particular, is defined by the predominance of nontraditional refugees. Nontraditional refugees do not fit the refugee definition found in international law either because they did not cross an international border and/or because they are entitled to citizenship of the state where they seek refuge. However, they have usually fled for reasons similar to those of refugees—fearing ethnic, political, or religious persecution. In Russia and Ukraine, for example, as of 1999, 94 and 98 percent of the displaced persons, respectively, were nontraditional refugees.[9]

In the post-Soviet region, nontraditional refugees are a product of the "ethnic unmixing" that began on the territory of the former Soviet Union in the late 1980s.[10] When the Soviet Union fell apart, as many as 70 million people lived outside their "ethnic homelands."[11] The rise of nationalism in the Soviet republics, the ethnic conflicts of the late 1980s, and the disintegration of the Soviet Union in 1991 sent waves of former Soviet citizens, suddenly national minorities in the republics where they lived, to their "ethnic homelands."[12] Although "ethnic unmixing" has affected all nationalities of the former USSR, the outflow of Slavs (Russians, Ukrainians, and Belarusians) from the non-Slavic republics has been particularly significant. Russia and Ukraine, the two largest Slavic republics of the former USSR, have become the main destination countries for these migrants. As table 7.1 shows, among the former Soviet citizens who moved to Russia in the 1990s, approximately 60 percent were ethnic Russians; among migrants to Ukraine over the same period, 43 percent were ethnic Ukrainians.

The predominance of nontraditional refugees, many of them co-ethnics, raised a question that would be totally out of place in the Western context: Are refugees foreigners or members of the nation? In Russia and Ukraine, this is a highly ambiguous and a highly political question. Most nontraditional refugees in both states are either co-ethnics of the titular group and/or eligible for citizenship under the terms of the initial citizenship laws.[13]

Inclusive citizenship laws adopted in Russia and Ukraine in the early 1990s made most nontraditional refugees, including co-ethnics of the titular group, ineligible for an international legal definition of refugee.[14] This was an unforeseen and an unintended consequence. When initial citizenship

Table 7.1. Post-Soviet Migration to Russia and Ukraine, 1992–2002

	Russia Migrants				Ukraine Migrants			
Year	Population (thousands)	Total (thousands)	Percent of Population	"Ethnic Kin" as Percent of Migrants	Population (thousands)	Total (thousands)	Percent of Population	"Ethnic Kin" as Percent of Migrants
1992	148,704	925.7	0.6	66	52,100	504.6	1.0	46
1993	148,673	922.9	0.6	65	52,200	323.0	0.6	45
1994	148,366	1,146.4	0.8	63	52,100	178.0	0.3	42
1995	148,306	841.5	0.6	61	51,700	159.9	0.3	42
1996	147,976	631.2	0.4	58	51,300	123.8	0.2	43
1997	147,502	582.8	0.4	59	50,900	102.6	0.2	43
1998	147,105	494.8	0.3	59	50,500	66.8	0.1	42
1999	146,693	366.6	0.2	55	50,100	61.6	0.1	41
2000	145,925	350.3	0.2	54	48,900	49.7	0.1	43
2001	144,368	193.5	0.1	57	48,500	41.0	0.1	44
2002	145,182	184.6	0.1	53	48,000	36.3	0.1	42

Sources: For population data for Russia: 1992–2000, Goskomstat Rossii, *Rossiiskii statisticheskii iezhegodnik. Statisticheskii sbornik* (Moscow: Goskomstat Rossii, 2000), 53; for 2001, Goskomstat Rossii, *Chislennost i migratsiia naseleniia Rossiiskoi Federatsii v 2001 godu* (Moscow: Goskomstat Rossii, 2002), 8; for 2002, Goskomstat Rossii, *Chislennost i migratsiia naseleniia Rossiiskoi Federatsii v 2002 godu* (Moscow: Goskomstat Rossii, 2003), 9. For population data for Ukraine, for 1992–99, Derzhavnyi komitet statystyky Ukrainy, *Statystychnyi shchorichnyi Ukrainy za 1998 rik* (Kyiv: Tekhnika, 1999), 327; for 2000–2, "Richna statystychna informatsia: Naselennia," http://www.ukrstat.gov.ua/richna/richna.html. For migration data for Russia for 1992–99, Goskomstat Rossii, *Rossiiskii statisticheskii iezhegodnik. Statisticheskii sbornik* (Moscow: Goskomstat Rossii, 1999), 101; for 2000, Goskomstat Rossii, *Chislennost i migratsiia naseleniia Rossiiskoi Federatsii v 2000 godu* (Moscow: Goskomstat Rossii, 2001), 32; for 2001–2, Goskomstat Rossii, *Chislennost i migratsiia naseleniia Rossiiskoi Federatsii v 2002 godu*, 15. For migration data for Ukraine: for 1991, Olena Malynovska, "Repatriation to Ukraine," *Migration Issues* 4, no. 11 (1999): 17–29; for 1992–97, Derzhavnyi Komitet u spravakh natsionalnostei i mihratsii, "Mihratsiina sytuatsiia v Ukraini," *Bizhentsi ta mihratsiia: Ukrainskyi chasopys prava i polityky* 2, nos. 3–4 (1998): 207–21; for 1998, Mykhailo Romaniuk, *Mihratsiia naselennia Ukrainy za umov perekhidnoi ekonomiky:metodologiia i prak-tyka rehuliuvannia* (L'viv: Vydavnytstvo Svit, 1999), 76; for 1999, Derzhavnyi komitet statystyky Ukrainy, "Rozpodil mihrantiv za natsionalnistiu ta krainamy v'izdu/ v'izdu/vyizdu u 1999 rotsi (Forma M-8)," 1999; for 2000, Derzhavnyi komitet statystyky Ukrainy, "Rozpodil mihrantiv za natsionalnistiu ta krainamy v'izdu/vyizdu u 2000 rotsi (Forma M-8)," 2000; for 2001, Derzhavnyi komitet statystyky Ukrainy, "Rozpodil mihrantiv za natsionalnistiu ta krainamy v'izdu/vyizdu u 2001 rotsi (Forma M-8)," 2001; for 2002, Derzhavnyi komitet statystyky Ukrainy, "Rozpodil mihrantiv za natsionalnistiu ta krainamy v'izdu/vyizdu u 2002 rotsi (Forma M-8)," 2002. For ethnic kin data for Russia, for 1992–97, International Organization for Migration, *Resettlement of "Refugees" and "Forced Migrants" in the Russian Federation* (Geneva: International Organization for Migration, 1998), 23; for 1998–99, Goskomstat Rossii, *Rossiiskii statisticheskii iezhegodnik: Sta-tisticheskii sbornik*, 354; for 2000, Goskomstat Rossii, *Chislennost i migratsiia naseleniia Rossiiskoi Federatsii v 2000 godu*, 90; for 2001, Goskomstat Rossii, *Chislennost i migratsiia naseleniia Rossiiskoi Federatsii v 2001 godu*, 81; for 2002, Goskomstat Rossii, *Chislennost i migratsiia naseleniia Rossiiskoi Federat-sii v 2002 godu*, 76. For ethnic kin data for Ukraine, for 1992–99, Nikolai Shulga, *Velikoie pereselenie: Repatrianty, bezhensty, trudovyie migranty* (Kyiv: Insti-tut Sotsiologii NAN Ukrainy, 2002), 80; for 2000–2, from sources for migration data cited above.

laws were adopted in Russia and Ukraine in the late Soviet period, lawmakers had little to no awareness of the international refugee legislation and the linkage between citizenship status and eligibility for refugee status contained in the international refugee law. A mismatch between the sociopolitical domestic and international legal understanding of who is a refugee (and thus deserves assistance from the state) was thus created. Whereas international law ruled that co-ethnics and other former Soviet migrants for the most part were not refugees but foreigners from developing-world countries were, domestically in Russia and Ukraine the perception was exactly the opposite: Needy former Soviet co-citizens, not foreigners from the developing world, were considered *bezhentsy* (refugees), and worthy of state assistance.[15]

The above reality makes our empirical puzzle all the more intriguing. Given the similar nature of the refugee problem in Russia and Ukraine (the predominance of migrants from the former Soviet republics, most of them nontraditional refugees and co-ethnics of the titular group), the comparable magnitude of the refugee problem (relative to the national populations; see table 7.1), and a similar domestic perception of who is and is not a refugee, one could expect to see similar refugee admission policies. It would not have been surprising, for example, if both states proved to be more receptive to the former Soviet refugees than to those from the developing world, and/or if both privileged co-ethnics of the titular ethnic group over refugees belonging to the ethnic "other."

Indeed, this is what happened in Russia. In Russia, the overwhelming majority of those recognized under the laws "On Refugees" and "On Forced Migrants" are former Soviet citizens. By the end of 2000, only 450 developing-world refugees received refugee status (2.1 percent of the total registered refugees).[16] Former Soviet citizens in Russia also benefited from the law "On Forced Migrants" adopted in addition to the law "On Refugees." The forced migrant law provided for a more generous regime (in terms of both status acquisition and the social and economic benefits associated with it) for those in a refugee-like situation who were eligible for Russian citizenship. The majority of those recognized under the law were ethnic Russians.[17] In Ukraine, conversely, there was neither legislation nor practice benefiting either ethnic Ukrainians or former Soviet citizens in general. Instead, 69 percent of the refugees recognized in the period 1997–2000 in Ukraine were from developing-world countries (mainly Afghanistan).[18]

Why did Russian and Ukrainian refugee policies turned out to be so different? To understand why similar post-Soviet countries responded differently to a similar refugee problem, we have to understand how the politics of refugee policy in new states is intertwined with and shaped by the politics of nation building; how the politics of nation building creates different constraints and opportunities for the international actors lobbying for a receptive and nondiscriminatory domestic refugee policy; and how these actors' response to the constraints imposed by the politics of nation building enables or impedes the materialization of a nondiscriminatory domestic refugee regime.

The Politics of Nation Building and Refugee Policy in the Post-Soviet Context

The relationship between the refugee problem and the problem of nation building sets the post-Soviet states apart from Western states. Unlike Western states, which faced the modern refugee problem in the aftermath of World War II as established nation-states, the post-Soviet states faced the refugee problem *at the same time* they faced the challenge of state and nation building. In post–World War II Western Europe, established nation-states faced flows of foreign refugees. In post–Cold War Eastern Europe, new states faced a flow of refugees, many of them co-ethnics of the titular group, as they were still trying to define the boundaries of their nations. This simultaneity created an intimate link between the politics of refugee policy and the politics of nation building.

The politics of nation building in the post-Soviet region is not simply about treating co-ethnics of the titular group as "us" and the rest as "other." In many, if not most, of the newly independent states, the very question who is "us" is itself a matter of much debate. Scholars of identity, whose work Arel surveys in the introductory chapter, draw our attention to the fact that contestation over a category of identity is a multidimensional process, and that different dimensions of this contestation need to be taken into account if one hopes to use identity as a variable affecting social and political actions. The Russian and Ukrainian cases reveal the importance of the *degree* of domestic consensus on the question who is "us."

Certain legal acts, most notably citizenship legislation, define what can be called the "official" nation of a given state. We can thus determine the content of the category "nation" from the law.[19] However, without looking at the debates that preceded the adoption of the legislation, we cannot know the degree of agreement among main political actors over the official definition. The degree of agreement (or of contestation) matters greatly for the content of refugee policies, as we are about to see.

The Politics of Refugee Policy in Russia

The Russian case demonstrates that when there was a high degree of domestic consensus over the definition of "us," those who were defined as belonging to the nation received preferential treatment in refugee policy. The Russian case also shows that international actors may be able to liberalize state policy toward foreign refugees, but only if they are aware of how the politics of nation building determines domestic politics of refugee policy and assist refugees who are perceived as belonging to the nation, even if they do not fit the international legal definition of refugee.

The National Question and Refugee Policy

In Russia, all the main political forces (Communists, nationalists, and liberals) shared the idea that the "true" Russian nation transcends the borders of the Russian Federation and embraces Russians and "Russian speakers" in the former Soviet republics.[20] Reflecting this prevalent domestic sentiment, the 1991 citizenship law defined the "official" Russian nation to include all former Soviet citizens by extending the right to Russian citizenship to them.[21] The politics of nation building thus defined Russia's "us" as ethnic Russians and the Russian speakers from the former Soviet republics, and this definition reflected a domestic consensus.

In the refugee policy area, the consensus that Russians and Russian-speaking migrants from the former Soviet republics are "us" rather than "other" translated into a unique legal precedent of Russia adopting in February 1993 two laws to regulate the refugee situation: the law "On Refugees" and the law "On Forced Migrants." The forced migrant law applied to those who were eligible for Russian citizenship (i.e., to the former Soviet citizens recognized as belonging to the "us") and was more generous than the refugee law.[22] The preferential approach to the former Soviet refugees was also evident in practical applications of the law "On Refugees." Formally, anyone who was not a citizen of Russia could apply for refugee status under this law. A citizen of Uzbekistan and a citizen of Somalia, for example, were to be treated equally under the law. In practice, however, in the first half of the 1990s, applications from developing-world asylum seekers were simply not accepted, while arrivals from the former Soviet republics received refugee or forced migrant status virtually automatically.[23]

As a result, by the end of 1993, there were 447,900 recognized refugees and forced migrants in Russia, all of whom were former Soviet citizens; none was from the developing world.[24] At the end of 1994, 702,500 refugees and forced migrants were officially registered, but only 33 (0.007 percent) of them were from the developing world. The 33 developing-world refugees recognized in 1994 were less than 0.1 percent of the 85,800 refugees recognized in Russia that year.[25] By the end of 2002, there were still only 400 recognized developing-world refugees—3 percent of the 13,800 registered refugees.[26]

This refugee policy outcome was predetermined by a strong domestic sense that the former Soviet citizens are part of the "us," and thus ought to be privileged in state policies. Arrivals from the former Soviet republics were readily recognized as refugees and forced migrants, while the developing-world refugees remained in legal limbo. The irony was that the developing-world refugees were "real" refugees (fitting the international legal definition of refugee), whereas most of the post-Soviet migrants were not. This irony, however, had its logic as a product of the consensual politics of nation building that defined the priorities of the government policy toward different groups of refugees.

The politics of nation building can explain why the Russian-speaking migrants from the former Soviet republics were assisted more readily than refugees from developing-world countries, but it cannot explain the evolution of Russia's policy toward developing-world refugees. As table 7.2 shows, the share of developing-world refugees among recognized refugees increased progressively starting in 1998. Starting in 1999, the majority of refugees recognized were from developing-world countries rather than the former Soviet republics.

To be sure, the post-1998 liberalization in Russia's policy toward developing-world refugees was not dramatic. In absolute terms, very few applicants are recognized, and since 2000, these numbers have been declining. Nevertheless, it is a significant change, given that before 1994 no developing-world refugees were recognized at all. The politics of nation building did not change much from the first to the second half of the 1990s. Something else thus has to explain this change in refugee policy. This other factor, the second key source of post-Soviet refugee policies, is the strategy of the UNHCR.

Table 7.2. Refugees Recognized in Russia under the Law "On Refugees," 1994–2002

Year	Recognized Given Year (Persons)	Former Soviet Union		Developing World	
		Persons	Percent of Total	Persons	Percent of Total
1994	85,800	85,700	100.0	30	0.0
1995	46,400	46,350	99.9	50	0.1
1996	19,800	19,720	99.6	80	0.4
1997	5,800	5,690	98.1	110	1.9
1998	500	360	72.0	140	28.0
1999	400	170	42.5	230	57.5
2000	300	140	46.7	160	53.3
2001	130	10	7.7	120	92.3
2002	51	5	9.8	46	90.2

Sources: 1994–96 data for developing-world refugees supplied by the UNHCR Moscow; for 1997, Federal Migration Service of the Russian Federation, "Chislennost bezhentsev po stranam iskhoda po sostoianiu na 01.01.98 g.," 1998; for 1998, Office of the UN High Commissioner for Refugees, "Number of Refugees by Countries of Origin Recognized by FMS of the Russian Federation (Till the End of 1998)," 1998; for 1999–2000, Goskomstat Rossii, *Chislennost i migratsia naseleniia Rossiiskoi Federatsii v 2000 godu* (Moscow: Goskomstat Rossii, 2001), 116; for 2001–2, Goskomstat Rossii, *Chislennost i migratsia naseleniia Rossiiskoi Federatsii v 2002 godu* (Moscow: Goskomstat Rossii, 2003), 138.

The Role of the UNHCR

Refugee policy formation in the post-Soviet region differs from refugee policy formation in post–World War II Western Europe in the greater role played by international actors, specifically by the UNHCR. The UNHCR is an international humanitarian organization mandated by the UN to promote the ratification of the 1951 Geneva Convention on the Status of Refugees and its 1967 Protocol (the international legal instruments that set standards for refugee treatment) and to supervise their application.[27] Although the UNHCR is a central component of the international refugee regime, refugee regimes in Western states evolved without the UNHCR. After its establishment in 1951 and until the end of the Cold War, the UNHCR worked mainly in developing countries, not in Western states.[28] In the post-Soviet region, however, refugee regimes emerged under the scrutiny of the UNHCR.

The UNHCR has had a permanent local presence in Russia since 1992. By virtue of its institutional "modus operandi" (operating through a permanent local office), it was well positioned to influence domestic refugee policies, arguably better than international actors that operate by sending periodic delegations. The novelty of the refugee issue and the lack of domestic expertise further strengthened the UNHCR's position in the post-Soviet states as the resident expert on the subject. In short, the situation in which the UNHCR found itself in the post-Soviet region may be characterized as the "exceptional circumstances" to which Andrew Moravcsik refers, when a "window of opportunity" exists for international organizations' officials to influence national policies.[29] In Russia, however, the UNHCR was initially unsuccessful in its efforts to encourage the government to establish a receptive and a nondiscriminatory refugee regime—to make the Russian authorities extend legal protection to the developing-world refugees. This was because the UNHCR's strategy was not sensitized to the domestic politics of refugee policy in Russia.

The UNHCR in Russia initially acted squarely within the universe of meaning defined by international refugee law. It thus concerned itself exclusively with those who fit the international legal definition of refugees, that is, with the developing-world asylum seekers, and did not assist the "nontraditional" former Soviet refugees because they were not refugees under international law. The conflict of priorities of the UNHCR and the Russian authorities was apparent. The UNHCR focused on the situation of traditional developing-world refugees who fit the international legal definition of a refugee, and it criticized Russia for not assisting them.[30] As far as the UNHCR was concerned, Russia was failing to live up to the international obligations it undertook when it ratified the 1951 Convention and its 1967 Protocol. As far as the Russian authorities were concerned, Russia's refugee problem was first and foremost about the former Soviet nontraditional refugees. They were "true" refugees deserving of UNHCR assistance.

The Russian authorities thus resented the UNHCR's criticism, and for their part attacked the international organization for failing to assist the former Soviet refugees. When Russia became the first post-Soviet state to ratify the 1951 Geneva Convention and its 1967 Protocol in November 1992, it hoped that this would bring international assistance to Russia to deal with the influx of former Soviet citizens.[31] As it became clear that the international assistance was not forthcoming because the former Soviet migrants were not refugees in the sense of international law, the Russian authorities expressed their anger in no uncertain terms. As Viacheslav Bakhmin, the head of the Foreign Ministry's Directorate of International Humanitarian and Cultural Cooperation and, in 1992, one of the main supporters of the ratification of the Geneva Convention by Russia, put it: "We signed [the Convention] so that international community would actively help with refugees—but international help has been very weak. Our position is that the Russian refugees in Russia are refugees in the international sense, and we want the same kind of help that other states get. . . . It is a strategic mistake on the part of international organizations to deal only with non-CIS refugees."[32]

The politics of nation building determined the meaning of the term "refugee" and the priorities of the Russian government. As long as the UNHCR took its cues only from international law, the UNHCR and the Russian authorities were talking past each other. Only in the mid-1990s, when the UNHCR began to change its strategies, did the deadlock that defined the UNHCR–Russia relations in the first half of the 1990s begin to break, and Russia's policies toward developing-world refugees begin to change.

An examination of the evolution of the UNHCR's strategy allows us to speak of a learning process. By the middle of the 1990s, the UNHCR came to realize that the complex nature of forced migration in the wake of the collapse of a multinational state necessitates a nontraditional response on its part. Sadako Ogata, the UN high commissioner for refugees from September 1991 until December 2000, acknowledged that the UNHCR had learned. She describes the UNHCR's activities in the former Soviet Union as "learning on the job" and affirms that when the UNHCR got involved in the former Soviet Union it was "operating in an entirely unfamiliar environment" and had to adjust its strategies and objectives "as it went along."[33] This learning process took time. Only in 1994 would UNHCR headquarters in Geneva employ its first full-time expert on the post-Soviet region.[34] By the middle of the 1990s, in the UNHCR's words, its "evolving strategic thinking" led it to "recognize . . . that an effective and relevant framework for action could not, in this non-traditional environment [i.e., that of the former Soviet Union], be based solely on an asylum-centered strategy."[35]

The changes in the UNHCR's strategy took time to evolve but became evident by the mid-1990s. In late 1994, the UNHCR started its first project to benefit former Soviet refugees in Russia. A total of $4 million was earmarked to assist some 14,000 refugees from Georgia in Russia's Krasnodar region.[36] The onset of hostilities in Chechnya in early 1995 for the first time created a large category of involuntary migrants in Russia who fit an international legal category ("internally displaced persons," or IDPs) and whom the UNHCR could thus assist within the framework of its mandate.[37]

The UNHCR's evolving strategic thinking and deepening involvement with nontraditional migrants in Russia and in other former Soviet states was put on a formal footing by the CIS Conference held at UNHCR headquarters in May 1996.[38] Activists have criticized the CIS Conference for "squandering an important opportunity and producing a document [Program of Action] that was overly general and non-binding,"[39] as well as for failing to adopt a broadened regional refugee definition.[40] At the same time, the conference had an important affect on the UNHCR's operations in the region and formally extended the UNHCR mandate in the CIS region to cover a larger category of involuntary migrants.[41]

Changes in the UNHCR strategy brought changes in Russian refugee policy. As the UNHCR began assisting nontraditional Russian-speaking refugees in Russia, the group of primary concern for the Russian government, the government became more inclined to reciprocate and to recognize developing-world refugees. As table 7.2 shows, the share of developing-world refugees among recognized refugees in Russia increased progressively, starting in 1998. Even though today's Russian policy toward developing-world refugees cannot be described as liberal,[42] there is no longer the deep gap between state policy toward the developing world and toward the CIS refugees that existed in the first half of the 1990s. The securitization of migration and the refugee policy debate that followed President Vladimir Putin's rise to power resulted in a more restrictive approach to all migrants and refugees, including those from the CIS.[43] This further narrowed the gap in the treatment of former Soviet and developing-world refugees.

In sum, a change in the UNHCR's strategy (its decision to begin assisting nontraditional refugees in Russia) produced a liberalization of Russia's policy toward developing-world refugees. At the same time, the politics of nation building—which firmly designated the former Soviet migrants, in particular Russians and "Russian speakers," as "us" and thus the priority group for the government—continues to set limits on how receptive Russia's policy toward other refugees can be. As we are about to see, in Ukraine the situation was different. A result of the conflictual politics of Ukrainian nation building—domestic disagreement on the question of who is "us"—was that no refugee group could be singled out for preferential treatment. This created domestic political space for a nondiscriminatory refugee policy. Such a policy materialized shortly after the UNHCR began operating in Ukraine, which it approached with a different strategy from the start.

The Politics of Refugee Policy in Ukraine

As discussed above, Ukrainian refugee policy differed from that of Russia in two puzzling ways. First, Ukraine did not privilege either ethnic Ukrainians or CIS migrants in its policy. Second, Ukraine's policy toward the developing world was more receptive that Russia's. The first of these two differences can be attributed to the different politics of nation building. The second is due to a different strategy on the part of the UNHCR.

The National Question and Refugee Policy

Unlike in Russia, in Ukraine there was no domestic consensus on the definition of the Ukrainian nation. The two main political forces—the left (Communists and their allies) and the right (nationalists and national-democrats)—held conflicting views on the national question and on the question of Ukrainian statehood. The Ukrainian Communists, just like the Russian Communists, subscribed to the Soviet version of historiography that portrayed the Russians, Ukrainians, and Belarusians as three branches of the same people and the Soviet Union as the "correct" state formation uniting fraternal nations into a single Soviet people. The right, for its part, held Ukrainian independence as the highest goal and understood the Ukrainian state as a multinational state but with an ethnic Ukrainian "core."[44]

Given their divergent views on the national question, the left and the right differed on what group or groups are to be privileged in state policy. The right wanted state legislation to single out ethnic Ukrainians for preferential treatment in state policies. The left, given its objective to have a union state with Russia, focused its energies on opposing measures that underscored the separateness of Ukraine as a state. The left thus opposed any measures that would single out ethnic Ukrainians as the group toward which the state has special responsibility, while trying to institutionalize policies (e.g., dual citizenship and two state languages) that had the potential to foster political unification with Russia.[45] In the end, neither the left nor the right had enough political power to achieve its objectives. The left's dual citizenship proposals were defeated, but so were the right's proposals to accord preferential treatment to ethnic Ukrainians. A compromise was a territorial definition of the "official" nation in the citizenship law: Those with family origins from the territory of Ukraine, regardless of their ethnic, linguistic, and other characteristics, were made eligible to acquire Ukrainian citizenship under a simplified procedure.[46]

The polarized politics of nation building that resulted in a compromise territorial definition of the "official" nation in citizenship law had several consequences for refugee policy. First, it precluded preferential treatment for ethnic Ukrainian refugees. The 1993 refugee law did not include any provisions aimed at ethnic Ukrainian returnees, although the right and the center-right members of Parliament advocated such measures during the debate.[47] Second, measures to benefit refugees who fell under the territorial definition of the "official" nation were also minimal. The entirety of Ukraine's preferential treatment of refugees who fell under this compromise definition of the nation were one provision of the 1993 refugee law and one parliamentary resolution. Article 3 of the refugee law exempted this group from the "safe third country" exclusion clause during application for refugee status.[48] The December 1993 parliamentary resolution grated some additional socioeconomic rights to refugees who were eligible for Ukrainian citizenship.[49] In practice, however, the resolution made those eligible for Ukrainian citizenship actually worse off than "foreign" refugees;[50] and by 2000, just 333 individuals were able to receive assistance under this resolution.[51]

If we recall that in Russia there was an entirely separate law "On Forced Migrants" that created a preferential refugee regime for those who were eligible for Russian citizenship, and that the practical application of the law "On Refugees" also privileged this group, the difference with Ukraine is striking. This difference was a product of the different politics of nation building. In Russia, a high degree of domestic consensus that ethnic Russians and Russian-speaking migrants from the former Soviet republics are "us" rather than "other" mandated a preferential policy toward refugees from the former Soviet republics. In Ukraine, where the territorial definition of the "official" nation was not the first choice of either the left or the right, there was little political will to promote policies favoring this group. The conflictual politics of nation building in Ukraine precluded ethnic Ukrainians (or any other post-Soviet refugee group) from being designated for preferential treatment in state policies; but at the same time, it created a political space for a nondiscriminatory refugee policy. Because no single group was designated for preferential treatment in state policies, all refugee groups could potentially be treated equally.

A policy that is politically feasible may not become a reality, however. Even though a nondiscriminatory refugee regime was politically feasible in Ukraine, there was little domestic interest in it. Public and elite perception of developing-world refugees was as negative in Ukraine as in Russia, and no political force advocated liberal policies toward this group. The Ukrainian refugee law was adopted in 1993 but, until 1996 it remained unimplemented. Developing-world refugees thus had no way to legalize their stay in Ukraine, and, as in Russia, were in the same position as illegal migrants.[52] When the implementation of the 1993 law began in early 1996, however, the results were striking. First refugee cards were handed to Afghan refugees, and for the next several years developing-world refugees continued to be a majority among recognized refugees. As we can see from table 7.3, from 1996 to the end of 2000, 3,540 cases (4,720 persons) were granted refugees status in Ukraine. A total of 84 percent of them were from developing-world countries and 56 percent from Afghanistan.[53]

Table 7.3. Refugees Recognized in Ukraine, 1996–2001

Year	Recognized Given Year (Cases)	Former Soviet Union		Developing World		Main Countries of Origin
		Number of Cases	Percent of Total	Number of Cases	Percent of Total	
1996	1,161	n.a.	n.a.	1,161	More than 90	Afghanistan
1997	844	61	7	783	93	Afghanistan, Congo, Angola
1998	553	117	21	436	79	Afghanistan, Sudan, Azerbaijan
1999	476	65	14	411	86	Afghanistan, Russia (Chechnya), Azerbaijan
2000	506	298	59	178	35	Afghanistan, Russia (Chechnya), Armenia
2001	274	98	36	176	64	Afghanistan, Azerbaijan, Russia (Chechnya)

Note: n.a. = Not available. Data refer to cases, not persons (one case can be several persons, e.g., a family). Of the 1,161 cases recognized in 1996, 995 were from Afghanistan; Oleg Shamshur, "Migration Situation in Ukraine: International Cooperation Related Aspects," *Migration: European Journal on International Migration and Ethnic Relations,* nos. 29–31 (1998): 29–44 (the citation is on 32).

Sources: Official data of the State Committee of Ukraine for Nationalities and Migration. Cited after the following: for 1996 and 1998, Olena Malynovska, "Some Statistic Data on Refugees in Ukraine," *Migration Issues* 3, no. 10 (1999): 28–33; for 1997, Derzhavnyi Komitet u spravakh natsionalnostei i migratsii, "Zvit pro osib, iaki zvernulysia iz zaiavamy pro nadannia statusu bizhentsia v Ukraini stanom na 1.01.1998," 1998; for 1999, Derzhavnyi Komitet u spravakh natsionalnostei i migratsii, "Zvit pro osib, iaki zvernulysia iz zaiavamy pro nadannia statusu bizhentsia v Ukraini stanom na 1.01.2000, Forma 1 (Bizhentsi)," February 3, 2000; for 2000, Derzhavnyi Departament u spravakh natsionalnostei i migratsii, "Zvit pro osib iaki zvernulysia iz zaiavamy pro nadannia statusu bizhentia v Ukraini stanom na 1.01.2001," 2001. For 2001, Derzhavnyi Komitet u spravakh natsionalnostei i migratsii, "Zvit pro osib, iaki zvernulysia iz zaiavamy pro nadannia statusu bizhentsia v Ukraini stanom na 1.01.2002, Forma 1 (Bizhentsi)," January 28, 2002.

If we take into account that thousands of developing-world refugees had been present in Ukraine since early 1990s, and that until 1996 their situation was no better than that of developing-world refugees in Russia, one cannot help but wonder why Ukraine's policy toward developing-world refugees improved so quickly starting in 1996. Ukraine began granting status to developing-world refugees within months after the UNHCR established a permanent local presence in the country in August 1995. This was not a coincidence. The emergence of a receptive refugee regime in Ukraine was a product of the UNHCR's strategy, which from the outset was different from the one it pursued in Russia.

The Role of the UNHCR

By the time the UNHCR got involved in Ukraine, it had learned from its experience in Russia that a strategy centered on the strict application of international refugee law was not very effective in the post-Soviet environment. As discussed above, by the middle of the 1990s the UNHCR was growing increasingly aware of the particularities of the refugee problem in the post-Soviet space, and it began to turn its attention to nontraditional refugees. Since December 1994, the UNHCR had also been preparing to host a conference on the forced migration problem in the former Soviet space (the 1996 CIS Conference). If the decision to hold a conference on the peculiarities of the post-Soviet refugee problem was evidence of the UNHCR having learned on the overall organization level, its activities in Ukraine evidenced such learning at the local level.

In Russia, as we saw above, the consensual politics of nation building made the government primarily concerned with Russian speakers from the former Soviet republics. The conflictual politics of nation building in Ukraine did not generally make Ukrainian, Ukrainian-speaking, or former Soviet migrants a priority group for the Ukrainian government. However, the nature of the forced migration problem in Ukraine placed one group of involuntary migrants in the government spotlight for political, economic, and social reasons. The group in question was the Crimean Tatars.

The Crimean Tatars were deported from Crimea on Stalin's orders in 1944, and since the late 1980s, they had begun to return back en masse. By the mid-1990s, some 250,000 had returned, and the sheer number of returnees made the challenge of their accommodation and integration daunting. Furthermore, Crimea's political sensitivities made the Crimean Tatars a political concern to the Ukrainian authorities. On the one hand, the

Crimean Tatars, who supported Ukraine's independence and opposed the transfer of Crimea to Russia, were an important counterbalance to the threat of Russian separatism on the peninsula. On the other hand, the Crimean Tatars themselves demanded national-territorial autonomy. This demand raised the political temperature on the peninsula, and the central authorities also eyed it with concern.[54]

The question whether to assist the Ukrainian authorities with the integration of the Crimean Tatars and other formerly deported peoples (FDPs)[55] presented a dilemma for the UNHCR. From the point of view of international refugee law, the legal status of FDPs in Ukraine was as ambiguous as the status of the post-Soviet migrants in Russia. In the late 1980s, the Crimean Tatars' return started as an *internal* migration within a single state (the USSR); after 1991, it continued as an *international* migration from other newly independent states to Ukraine. The vast majority of the FDPs were thus neither "refugees" nor "internally displaced persons" in the sense of international law, and therefore not under the UNHCR mandate. Instead of falling back on its mandate restrictions and shunning involvement with the FDPs in Crimea, the UNHCR in Ukraine made a strategic decision to find a way to aid the Ukrainian government with their resettlement.

Starting in April 1995, the UNHCR dispatched a series of fact-finding missions to Crimea to identify groups of FDPs that would fall under its mandate. In July 1995, the Ukrainian government formally requested the UNHCR to assist with the resettlement and integration of FDPs.[56] By early 1996, the UNHCR had identified two groups of FDPs that it could assist under it mandate: several thousand FDPs who had fled conflict areas in the former Soviet republics and who were in a refugee-like situation; and tens of thousands of legally stateless FDPs who had arrived in Ukraine after the 1991 citizenship law entered into force.[57] Once mandate justification for the UNHCR involvement was found, the UNHCR in Ukraine quickly proceeded with concrete assistance, such as financing housing construction for returnees.[58] These shelter rehabilitation projects provided tangible results rather quickly, and they established for the UNHCR a reputation as the international organization that actually "delivers."[59] This reputation was strengthened in the following years. In the period 1997–2000, the UNHCR conducted a massive "citizenship campaign"—its largest in the world—in which it invested $2 million, and which helped nearly 100,000 Crimean Tatars acquire Ukrainian citizenship.[60]

When refugee status determination began in Ukraine in early 1996, it immediately benefited developing-world refugees. The Ukrainian authorities' willingness to grant refugee status to developing-world refugees was in no small measure a reciprocal act for the UNHCR's assistance with the resettlement of FPDs in Crimea. The UNHCR's assistance in Crimea had positive "spillover" effects for refugee protection in all of Ukraine. The UNHCR was also aware of this effect of its engagement with FDPs on refugee policies: "There are side benefits to UNHCR in Kyiv for any assistance policy in the Crimea," a July 1996 UNHCR report noted.[61] Ukrainian government officials likewise acknowledge that the UNHCR's "good will" with the problems of FDPs in Crimea was reciprocated by "good will" on the part of the Ukrainian government with regard to developing-world asylum seekers.[62]

In another departure from its approach in Russia, the UNHCR in Ukraine decided initially not to put too much emphasis on the ratification of the Geneva Convention by Ukraine but instead to concentrate on what it termed a "step-by-step approach."[63] This difference in strategy also can be attributed to the UNHCR's learning experience. Russia ratified the 1951 Geneva Convention and its 1967 Protocol as early as 1992, and it had a liberal refugee law on the books by early 1993, but these legislative developments did not translate into a receptive policy toward developing-world refugees. If there was a clear lesson from the Russian case for the UNHCR, it was that in an environment of the weak rule of law, the mere act of ratification of international instruments or adoption of liberal legislation does not necessarily translate into policies in line with formally declared legal principles and obligations. The UNHCR Kyiv office thus devised a "step-by-step" strategy. The head of the office was himself a national of a postcommunist state (Hungary) who was well aware of the limited power of the letter of the law in the postcommunist context in the absence of authorities' desire and capacity to implement it. The UNHCR Kyiv office got Geneva to back this novel approach.[64]

The essence of the "step-by-step" approach was to emphasize and reward authorities' gradual practical progress in refugee policy, rather than strive for legislative perfection.[65] The primary goal of the "step-by-step" strategy was to encourage the authorities to accept and process refugee applications in a nondiscriminatory manner, even when the national legislation remained suboptimal relative to international standards. In line with this strategy, the UNHCR provided targeted material and technical assistance to the relevant central and regional government agencies. Both the Ukrainian authorities and the UNHCR acknowledge that material and technical assistance provided by the UNHCR enabled and encouraged the authorities to address the

problems of refugees in Ukraine that might otherwise have remained ignored due to the lack of local capacity and resources required to implement
the refugee law.[66] As one senior Ukrainian refugee policy official put it succinctly: "Without UNHCR, we [the Ukrainian migration service] would
have perished."[67]

The second half of the 1990s saw quick progress in refugee protection in
Ukraine. The implementation of the 1993 refugee law began in February
1996, when the first refugees were recognized by the Kyiv City Migration
Service. By the end of 1996, the refugee status determination procedure was
being implemented in fifteen of Ukraine's twenty-seven regions. By the end
of 1999, the procedure was being implemented in all regions of Ukraine.[68]
The UNHCR provided migration services with material, technical, and expert assistance, and it was also generous in its praise of Ukraine's refugee
policies as "an example for the CIS region."[69] Ukraine finally ratified the
1951 Geneva Convention and its Protocol in January 2002, after adopting
a revised refugee law in June of the previous year.

A paradox of the nondiscriminatory refugee policy in Ukraine was its
adverse effects for former Soviet migrants, and especially ethnic Ukrainian (usually referred to as "repatriates") in Ukraine. This was because a
nondiscriminatory refugee policy benefited whoever was a refugee under
international law. In Ukraine, developing-world refugees were the ones
who unambiguously met the refugee definition under international law
(they crossed an international border and were not citizens of Ukraine).
Ethnic Ukrainian repatriates and other former Soviet migrants generally
did not meet the refugee definition because of their migration experience
and/or citizenship status, and thus they could not benefit from a refugee
policy that respected the international legal definition of a refugee. The situation whereby "foreign" refugees are apparently better off than Ukrainian repatriates is frequently lamented in Ukraine, including by government
officials.[70] As one newspaper headline crudely summarized this sentiment,
"If you want to be a refugee in Ukraine, you are better off if you are
black."[71]

Despite the legislative and practical progress achieved in the 1990s, the
Ukrainian refugee regime remains fragile, as events of the most recent years
show. Frequent restructurings of the state administrative organs negatively
affect the functioning of refugee law. In 2001, the main government body
dealing with refugees was re-created and restaffed for the seventh time in
eight years. This restructuring halted the refugee recognition process from
mid-2001 until the end of 2002, and only two refugees were recognized dur-

ing this period.[72] Financial assistance from the UNHCR, which has been an important incentive for the cash-strapped Ukrainian authorities, declined after 2001, when the UNHCR citizenship campaign in Crimea came to an end and the UNHCR Kyiv office saw budget cuts.[73] In 2003, the European Commission began financing the UNHCR-implemented project "Strengthening the Asylum System in Ukraine."[74] It remains to be seen if the resulting increase in the UNHCR Kyiv office budget, and thus of its ability to provide material incentives to the Ukrainian authorities, will lead to an increase in refugee recognition rates in the coming years,[75] and if Ukraine will amend its refugee law in line with UNHCR recommendations.[76]

To sum up, the result of the different politics of nation building and different strategies of international actors in Russia and Ukraine was a relatively more receptive policy toward developing-world refugees in Ukraine in comparison with Russia, and a significantly more receptive refugee policy toward co-ethnics in Russia than in Ukraine. Though one should not overlook the fact that developing-world refugees experience many economic and legal hardships in Ukraine as well, the difference with Russia is still significant. In Ukraine, developing-world asylum seekers generally had a way of legalizing their stay and thus receiving at least minimal protection, whereas in Russia they generally did not. The difference in the treatment of the co-ethnics in the two countries has been even more striking.

Conclusion

The evolution of Russian and Ukrainian refugee policies illustrates how the politics of nation building and the strategies of the international actors shaped refugee policy outcomes in states where the challenges of nation building and of refugee protection are intertwined. The different ways in which Russia and Ukraine responded to the similar challenge of refugee protection had to do with the different politics of nation building and different strategies of the UNHCR. Russian and Ukrainian refugee policy story contains several larger implications that reach beyond the issue of refugee policy.

The first of these implications is for scholars of identity and of nation building. The story told in this chapter underscores what Arel emphasized in his introduction: To understand how identity matters, researchers must investigate the political process that gives meaning to categories of identity; rather than simply assuming that certain objective markers, such as passport ethnicity, language, or territory, will have the same importance (and thus produce similar policies) in different domestic settings. Indeed, it is the politics over the labeling, recognition, and meaning of identity categories that makes a certain cleavage salient (or not) in a particular domestic context. In Russia and Ukraine, as we have seen in this chapter, what mattered for inclusion and exclusion in the nation (and thus for the preferential treatment and for discrimination in refugee policy) was not simply ethnicity (or any other objective characteristic). The relative strength of political forces that "imagined" the nation differently determined how the "us" and the "other" were defined in the law. Whether or not the "us" would then receive preferential treatment in refugee policy further depended on the degree of domestic consensus over the definition of the "us."

The second lesson of the Russian and Ukrainian refugee policy story is that a polarizing politics of nation building may have unintended "liberal" consequences. As the Ukrainian case illustrates, a "weak" national identity and the conflictual politics of nation building can open a political space for a liberal policy in another issue area that would not have existed otherwise. This finding is in line with that of the scholars of democratization who have shown how in states with weak civil societies and no history of democracy elite fragmentation enables a degree of political pluralism and serves as an obstacle to authoritarian consolidation.[77] The fact that the territorial definition turned out to be a compromise definition of the nation in Ukraine also suggests that the default equilibrium outcome of a polarized politics of nation building in terms of state policies may be a civic nation-building project—an intriguing possibility that deserves further research.

Finally, the Russian and the Ukrainian cases both testify to the potential of international actors in the postcommunist region to promote policies respectful of human rights. This implication has an important caveat, however—the evidence from Russia and Ukraine clearly shows that the success of international actors depends on how well they understand the domestic politics of the issue they are trying influence, and how able they are to adjust their strategies to fit domestic constraints.

Notes

1. These are UNHCR statistics for refugees and other categories of displaced persons "of concern" to the UNHCR, as reported in UNHCR, *The State of the World's Refugees: Fifty Years of Humanitarian Action* (Oxford: Oxford University Press, 2000), annex 2, 306–9.

2. The 1977 Soviet Constitution (article 38) provided for the granting of asylum to "foreigners persecuted for defending the interests of the working people and the cause of peace, or for participation in the revolutionary and national-liberation movement, or for progressive social and political, scientific, or other creative activity." However, decisions to grant such asylum were made on an individual basis by the Presidium of the Supreme Soviet of the USSR, and no refugee or asylum legislation existed.

3. UNHCR, *State of the World's Refugees,* annex 2, 306–9.

4. Article 1 (2) of the 1951 Convention reads: "[T]he term "refugee" shall apply to any person who, as a result of events occurring before 1 January 1951 and owning to well founded fear of being persecuted for reasons of race, religion, nationality, membership of a particular social group or political opinion, is outside the country of his nationality and is unable or, owing to such fear, is unwilling to avail himself of the protection of that country; or who, not having a nationality and being outside the country of his former habitual residence as a result of such events, is unable or, owing to such fear, is unwilling, to return to it." According to the 1951 Convention, the term "refugee" applied only to those who fitted this refugee definition "as a result of events occurring in Europe before 1 January 1951." The 1967 Protocol Relating to the Status of Refugees removed the time limit and the geographical limitation set in the 1951 Convention. Thus, since 1967, under the international law the refugees are those who fit the definition of the 1951 Convention, regardless of when and where the events that made them refugees occurred. The text of the 1951 Convention and its 1967 Protocol are in Division of International Protection, UNHCR, *Collection of International Instruments and Other Legal Acts Concerning Refugees and Displaced Persons* (Geneva: UNHCR, 1995), 10–45.

5. UNHCR Russian Federation, "UNHCR Moscow Registration of Asylum Seekers (Till the End of December)," January 28, 1998. Other main countries of origin were Iraq (9 percent), Somalia (8 percent), Angola (3 percent), and Sri Lanka (3 percent). UNHCR registration statistics from 1992 to January 1999 in UNHCR Russian Federation, "1998–2000 Country Report and Operations Plan (CROP) Narrative," 5.

6. Grigory Sereda, "The State Department for Nationalities and Migration: A New Working Strategy," *Citizen,* no. 28 (October 2000): 7–9, 8.

7. Other main countries of origin of refugees from the developing world in Ukraine were Angola, Iraq, Somalia, Sudan, and Sri Lanka.

8. Thus, a 1997 UNHCR survey of 352 refugees in Ukraine, 84 percent of them Afghans, found that 54 percent wanted to remain in Ukraine (23 percent wanted to move to a Western country, and 23 percent to return home); see UNHCR Ukraine, National Institute of Ukrainian-Russian Relations, Institute of Sociology of the Ukrainian Academy of Sciences, *Refugees in Ukraine* (Kyiv: UNHCR, 1997), 56–79. In 1992, Afghan students in Russia created an organization with a purpose to help themselves "remain in Russia." (According to one of the organization's founders; author's interview, Moscow, August 11, 1998.) The desire of many Afghans to remain is understandable, given that most of them were associated with a Soviet-backed Najibullah regime and came to study or train in Soviet civilian and military institutions. They had time to adjust linguistically and culturally to the new environment.

9. Calculated from the UNHCR country statistics for 1999 as reported in UNHCR, *State of the World's Refugees,* annex 2.

10. The term "ethnic unmixing" is Rogers Brubaker's, and describes the return of ethnic minorities to their "ethnic homelands." Rogers Brubaker, *Nationalism Reframed:*

Nationhood and the National Question in the New Europe (New York: Cambridge University Press, 1996).

11. Figure cited after Arthur Helton, "Lost Opportunities at the CIS Migration Conference," *Transition* 2, no. 13 (June 28, 1996): 52–54; the quotation is on 53.

12. By the end of the 1990s, more than 9 million people had moved from one former Soviet republic to another in one of the largest mass migrations in recent European history. Arthur Helton and Natalia Voronina, *Forced Displacement and Human Security in the Former Soviet Union: Law and Policy* (Ardsley, N.Y.: Transnational Publishers, 2000), ix.

13. Under the February 1992 Russian citizenship law (article 18, paragraph 4), all former Soviet citizens were eligible to acquire Russian citizenship virtually automatically, simply by expressing the desire to become a Russian citizen. The November 1991 Ukrainian citizenship law (article 17, paragraph 2) made those who were born, or at least one of whose parents or grandparents was born, in the territory of Ukraine eligible for Ukrainian citizenship under a simplified procedure. For the texts of the laws, see International Organization for Migration, *Sbornik zakonodatelnykh aktov gosudarstv SNG i Baltii po voprosam migratsii, grazhdanstva i sviazannym s nimi aspektami* (Geneva: International Organization for Migration, 1995), 280–95, for the Russian law; and 388–98 for the Ukrainian law.

14. As noted above, under the international refugee law, eligibility for citizenship in a receiving state makes one ineligible to be defined as refugee.

15. On this mismatch between international legal and sociopolitical domestic understanding of who is a refugee in the post-Soviet context, see also Adriano Silvestri and Olga Tchernishova, "The Legal Framework Regulating Asylum in the Russian Federation," *International Journal of Refugee Law* 10, no. 1 (1998): 184–99.

16. See official statistics in Goskomstat Rossii, *Chislennost i migratsia naselenia Rossiiskoi Federatsii v 2000 godu* (Moscow: Goskomstat Rossii, 2001), 116.

17. In 1993, ethnic Russians were 58 percent of those granted forced migrant status. In 1998, ethnic Russians were 76 percent; International Organization for Migration, *Resettlement of "Refugees" and "Forced Migrants" in the Russian Federation* (Geneva: International Organization for Migration, 1998), 22. In 2001 and 2002, ethnic Russians were 66 percent; Goskomstat Rossii, *Chislennost i migratsiia naseleniia Rossiiskoi Federatsii v 2002 godu* (Moscow: Goskomstat Rossii, 2003), table 3.9.

18. This was calculated by the author from official statistics obtained from the State Committee of Ukraine for Nationalities and Migration.

19. To be sure, the definition of the nation in the law is indicative only of the "official" content of the category "nation." The majority of the public in a given state may or may not "imagine" the nation the way it is defined in the law.

20. For a detailed analysis of how main Russian political forces "imagine" the Russian nation in the post-Soviet period, consult Yitzhak Brudny, "Politika identichnosti i post-kommunisticheskii vybor Rossii," *Polis,* no. 1 (2001): 87–104; Vera Tolz, "Conflicting "Homeland Myths" and Nation-State Building in Postcommunist Russia," *Slavic Review* 57, no. 2 (1998): 267–94; Tolz, "Forging the Nation: National Identity and Nation Building in Post-Communist Russia," *Europe-Asia Studies* 50, no. 6 (1998): 993–1022; Tolz, *Russia* (Oxford: Oxford University Press, 2001), chapter 8; and Oxana Shevel, "National Identity and International Institutions: Refugee Policies in Post-Communist Europe." Ph.D. dissertation, Harvard University, 2002, chapter 3.

21. Although the 1991 citizenship law made no explicit mention of ethnic Russians

or Russian speakers, during discussion in the parliament, the chairman of the parliamentary commission on citizenship, Yurii Zaitsev, affirmed that the provision was aimed at this group: "Simplified procedure, i.e., registration procedure, applies to USSR citizens (of course, we have in mind the Russian-speaking population, although this is not stated anywhere in the law) who reside on the territories of the union republics." Verkhovnyi Sovet Rossiiskoi Federatsii, Chetvertaia sessia Verkhovnogo Soveta Rossiiskoi Federatsii, *O proekte zakona o grazhdanstve RSFSR: Povtornoie pervoie chtenie,* November 15, bulletin 12 sovmestnogo zasedania Soveta Respublik i Soveta Natsionalnostei (Moscow: Verkhovnyi Sovet Rossiiskoi Federatsii, 1991), 12.

22. Forced migrant status was easier to obtain than refugee status, because one did not have to prove individual persecution. Persecution against family members, for example, was grounds for granting forced migrant—but not refugee—status. Forced migrant status could also be granted to those who feared "violations of public order or other circumstances significantly violating human rights"; such fears would not have qualified one for a refugee status. Both laws were rather generous, in fact more generous than the 1951 Convention itself, in terms of the social and economic rights they granted. Forced migrant status carried with it greater socioeconomic benefits that were to be guaranteed by the state. In particular, under the forced migrants law, one was entitled to housing (including during the application procedure), to social payments and medical care, and to compensation for property left in the previous place of residence. The Russian state guaranteed a compensation for lost property to forced migrants if they could not obtain it from the state they left. Refugees were not guaranteed such compensation but only the Russian state's assistance in securing compensation from the state they left. Refugees were entitled to three months of free housing in a refugee accommodation center, while there was no such time limit on the right to free housing in the forced migrant law.

23. For arrivals from the former Soviet republics the procedure was one of registration, not of recognition: without individual status determination procedure (although the 1993 laws envisaged individual examination of the claims); with proof of individual persecution usually not required; and with the decision often made the same day. Thus, November 25, 1993, decree 2775 of the Federal Migration Service, "On Recognizing and Registering Forced Migrants on the Territory of the Russian Federation," ruled (article 2.2) that one has to present proof of persecution only "if necessary" (*pri neobkhodimosti*). The decree also recommended (article 2.5) that recognition decisions are to be made on the day of application "if possible," or within five days—time limits not conducive to a thorough examination of applications on the merit of each individual claim.

24. Goskomstat Rossii, *Rossiiskii statisticheskii iezhegodnik: Statisticheskii sbornik* (Moscow: Goskomstat Rossii, 2000), 101.

25. These are 1994 developing-world refugee recognition data provided to the author by UNHCR Moscow. Overall 1994 refugee recognition data are cited after Federal Migration Service of the Russian Federation, "Svedenia o bezhentsakh i vynuzhdennykh pereselentsakh 1992–1996," 1997.

26. Goskomstat Rossii, *Chislennost i migratsia naselenia Rossiiskoi Federatsii v 2002 godu* (Moscow: Goskomstat Rossii, 2003), 138.

27. See Statute of the Office of the UNHCR in Division of International Protection, UNHCR, *Collection of International Instruments and Other Legal Acts Concerning Refugees and Displaced Persons* (Geneva: UNHCR, 1995), v. I, part 1, 3–9.

28. Charles Keely notes that after the displaced persons of World War II were set-

tled, the UNHCR in Europe "had virtually no role. The European desk in the UNHCR was more and more attenuated . . . UNHCR . . . quickly became an agency operating in the third world." Keely, "The International Refugee Regimes: The End of the Cold War Matters," *International Migration Review* 35, no. 1 (2001): 303–14; the quotation is on 307.

29. Andrew Moravcsik argues for the primacy of national governments and domestic politics, rather than international organizations' officials, in all but "exceptional circumstance" that create a "window of opportunity" for supranational actors." Moravcsik, "A New Statecraft: Supranational Entrepreneurs and International Cooperation," *International Organizations* 53, no. 2 (1999): 267–306; the quotation is on 285. These circumstances, according to Moravcsik, are when issues are novel, constituencies unorganized, and governments mired in old policy models—a description well suited to postcommunist refugee policymaking.

30. For examples of UNHCR criticism of Russia, see UNHCR spokesperson, as quoted in Agence France-Press, "UNHCR Accuses Moscow for Failing to Handle Asylum Seekers," October 9, 1997; Adriano Silvestri, "Situatsia grazhdan iz dalnego zarubezhia, ishchushchikh ubezhishcha v Rossiiskoi Federatsii," 1997 (the author was protection officer in the UNHCR Moscow office); and Russia Section of Lawyers Committee for Human Rights, *Critique: Review of the U.S. Department of State Country Reports on Human Rights Practices for 1996* (New York: Lawyers Committee for Human Rights, 1997), written by a former UNHCR Moscow protection officer.

31. This expectation was expressed during the parliamentary debate on the ratification. Deputy Foreign Minister Sergei Lavrov assured the members of Parliament that there will be no financial costs to bear as a result of the ratification of these international documents; that Convention ratification will bring international assistance to Russia for coping with migration from the former Soviet republics; and that it would also ensure that developing-world refugees will be resettled to other counties. See Lavrov's comments in Verkhovnyi Sovet Rossiiskoi Federatsii, Piataia sessia Verkhovnogo Soveta Rossiiskoi Federatsii, *O prisoiedinenii Rossiiskoi Federatsii k Konventsii o statuse bezhentsev ot 1951 goda i k Protokolu, kasaiushchemusia statusa bezhentsa ot 1967 goda*, November 13, bulleten 18 sovmestnogo zasedania Soveta Respublik i Soveta Natsionalnostei (Moscow: Verkhivnyi Sovet Rossiiskoi Federatsii, 1992), chast 1, 7–9.

32. Bakhmin is quoted in Jan Cienski, "Chilly Reception for Refugees in Russia," *Refugees*, no. 4 (December 1994): 10–12; the quotation is on 10, 13.

33. Interview with the author, Cambridge, Mass., October 24, 2001. In a 1996 interview with the Russian daily *Izvestia*, Sadako Ogata likewise admitted that when the UNHCR established its presence in Russia in 1992, for UNHCR Russia was "an unknown territory" and that "for the most part the international community had no knowledge about the scale and the specificities of migration processes [in Russia and the former Soviet space]." Ogata as quoted in Vladimir Mikheev, "OON beret pod svoie krylo bezhentsev Rossii," *Izvestia*, October 16, 1996.

34. Bohdan Nahaylo (senior policy adviser for the newly independent states) was the first area expert employed at the UNHCR Geneva headquarters.

35. UNHCR, *State of the World's Refugees*, 200.

36. Cienski, "Chilly Reception"; also see UNHCR, *The Activities of the United Nations High Commissioner for Refugees in the Newly Independent States* (Geneva: UNHCR, 1994), 27. For more details on the beginning of the UNHCR involvement with

nontraditional refugee groups in Russia, see Shevel, "National Identity and International Institutions," chaps. 4 and 5.

37. The IDPs are victims of armed conflicts, persecution, or a breakdown in law and order who flee their homes but, unlike refugees, do *not* cross an international border. The UNHCR mandate does not refer to IDPs explicitly, but it allows the UNHCR to "engage in such activities . . . the General Assembly may determine." Policy directives for UNHCR involvement with IDPs specify consent of host state, approval of the UN secretary general, and availability of resources as criteria for UNHCR involvement with IDPs. See UNHCR, "Information Note: UNHCR's Role with Internally Displaced Persons," November 20, 1998. In Russia, the first Chechen war created the first large group that was unambiguously IDPs. North Ossetia was another region of Russia where there were IDPs (40,000–50,000 displaced as a result of North Ossetian–Ingush conflict in 1992, i.e., after Russia became an independent state). In October 1994, the Russian authorities formally requested the UNHCR to assist in North Ossetia, and within months, the first Chechen war broke out.

38. The formal title of the conference was "Regional Conference to Address the Problems of Refugees, Displaced Persons, Other Forms of Involuntary Displacement in the Countries of the Commonwealth of Independent States and Neighboring States." It was attended by representatives of all fifteen former Soviet republics and seventy-two other counties, as well as twenty-nine international organizations. For an overview of events leading to the May 1996 CIS Conference, see Helton and Voronina, *Forced Displacement and Human Security,* 67–76.

39. U.S. Committee for Refugees, *1997 Country Reports: Russian Federation,* http://www.refugees.org/world/countryrpt/europe/1997/russian_federation.htm.

40. For activist criticism of the CIS Conference, see Arthur Helton, "Lost Opportunities at the CIS Migration Conference," *Transition* 2, no. 13 (June 28, 1996): 52–54; Helton, "Written statement of Arthur C. Helton, Esq., Director of the Forced Migration Projects of the Open Society Institute on Forced Migration in the Newly Independent States of the Former Soviet Union for the Regional Conference to Address the Problems of Refugees, Displaced Persons, Other Forms of Involuntary Displacement and Returnees in the Countries of the Commonwealth of Independent States and Relevant Neighbouring States," May 31, 1996; and Helton and Voronina, *Forced Displacement and Human Security,* 67–80.

41. Besides internationally accepted categories such as "refugees" and "internally displaced persons," the CIS Conference Program of Action introduced five categories "applicable to situation in the CIS countries" to which the UNHCR mandate in the region was formally extended. These new categories were: involuntarily relocated persons (those who fled general unrest and resettled in their country of citizenship), persons in refugee-like situations (war refugees), formerly deported peoples (who were deported from their historic homeland in the Soviet period), repatriants (who have voluntarily moved to their country of citizenship for permanent residency), and ecological migrants. For full definitions of each category, see annex 2 of the CIS Conference Program of Action reprinted in Helton and Voronina, *Forced Displacement and Human Security,* 212–14.

42. In the late 1990s, the UNHCR continued to criticize many elements of Russia's policy, in particular low recognition rates, the denial of status to many developing-world asylum seekers that the UNHCR considers genuine refugees, and a backlog of cases resulting in long waits (in 2001, in Moscow the wait period before one could apply for

refugee status was as long as two years). For recent criticisms, see UNHCR, *State of the World's Refugees.*

43. The reversal of an "open door" policy toward former Soviet migrants began in the middle of the 1990s. The new editions of the laws "On Forced Migrants" and "On Refugees," adopted in late 1995 and mid-1997, respectively, rolled back what had come to be regarded as overly generous social and economic rights granted to refugees and forced migrants (e.g., guaranteed free housing and compensation for property left abroad). In 1997, the Federal Migration Service also began to deregister previously recognized refugees (some 300,000 were deregistered in 1997–98 alone), and stopped the practice of virtually automatic granting of refugee and forced migrant status to the arrivals from the former Soviet republics. The view that the open-door policy toward migrants from the former Soviet Union undermines Russian security and places an undue economic burden on the Russian state continued to gain currency in official circles, and under President Putin the securitization of refugee policy debate progressed further. In 2000, the Federal Migration Service was liquidated, and in 2001 its functions were transferred to the Ministry of the Interior. A slue of migration legislation adopted in 2001–2 further tightened the rules for the former Soviet citizens who moved to Russia from other former Soviet republics. For more detailed discussion of these developments, see Shevel, "National Identity and International Institutions," chap. 5.

44. For a more detailed discussion of the national identity conceptions embraced by the Ukrainian left and right, see Oleksii Haran and Oleksandr Maiboroda, eds., *Ukrainski livi: Mizh leninizmom i sotsial-demokratieiu* (Kyiv: KM Academia, 2000); Oleksiy Haran, "Can Ukrainian Communists and Socialists Evolve to Social Democracy?" *Demokratizatsiya* 9, no. 4 (2001): 570–87; Taras Kuzio, "Defining the Political Community in Ukraine: State, Nation, and the Transition to Modernity," in *State and Institution-Building in Ukraine,* ed. Taras Kuzio, Robert S. Kravchuk, and Paul D'Anieri (New York: St. Martin's Press, 1999), 213–44; Joan Barth Urban, "The Communist Parties of Russia and Ukraine on the Eve of the 1999 Elections: Similarities, Contrasts, and Interactions," *Demokratizatsiya* 7, no. 1 (1999): 111–34; Andrew Wilson, *The Ukrainians: Unexpected Nation* (New Haven, Conn.: Yale University Press, 2000); and Wilson, "Reinventing the Ukrainian Left: Assessing Adaptability and Change, 1991–2000," *Slavonic and East European Review* 80, no. 1 (2002): 21–59.

45. For a discussion of how in post-Soviet Ukraine dual citizenship and state language are issues that bear on the question of state independence, see Oxana Shevel, "Nationality in Ukraine: Some Rules of Engagement," *East European Politics and Societies* 16, no. 2 (2002): 387–413. For evidence on how the dual citizenship question, the question whether ethnic Ukrainians abroad are to be made eligible for simplified citizenship acquisition, and the question whether knowledge of Ukrainian is to be a requirement for citizenship acquisition dominated the debate of the draft citizenship laws in 1991, 1997, and 2001, consult Shevel, "Nationality in Ukraine," and Shevel, "Citizenship and Nation-Building in Ukraine," paper presented at the Tenth Annual Convention of the Association for the Study of Nationalities, Columbia University, New York, April 14–16, 2005.

46. For a detailed analysis of the politics of citizenship policy in Ukraine since 1991, see Shevel, "Citizenship."

47. During the first reading of the refugee law on April 21, 1993, the absence of any provision aimed at returning ethnic Ukrainians was lamented by the national-democrats. As one member of Parliament (MP) put it, "There is not a hint in this law

about Ukrainians who live beyond the borders of Ukraine and who, in essence, do not feel support of their fatherland." MP Romaniuk, Verkhovna Rada Ukrainy, Sioma sessia Verkhovnoi Rady Ukrainy XIIgo sklykannia, *Zakon Ukrainy pro bizhentsiv—pershe chytannia,* April 21, 1993, Bulletins 28 and 29 (Kyiv: Verkhovna Rada Ukrainy, 1993), 14. Another MP from western Ukraine, Bondarchuk, called to include in the definition of refugees "our Ukrainian brothers" arriving to Ukraine from the former Soviet countries. Verkhovna Rada Ukrainy, Sioma sessia Verkhovnoi Rady Ukrainy XIIgo sklykannia, *Zakon Ukrainy pro bizhentsiv—pershe chytannia,* 5.

48. See article 3, paragraph 4, of the December 24, 1993, law "On Refugees" (no. 3818-XII); the text of the law is found in Ukrainska pravnycha fundatsia, Upravlinnia Verhovnoho Komisara OON u Spravakh Bizhenstiv, Ukrains'kyi Tsentr Prav Liudyny, *Pravovyi zakhyst bizhentsiv v Ukraini: zbirka documentiv* (Kyiv: Polihraf-SVK, 1998), 42–48.

49. The December 24, 1993, resolution of the Presidium of the Ukrainian Parliament, "On Implementing the Law on Refugees," granted citizens of Ukraine who arrived to Ukraine fleeing persecution, as defined in article 1 of the refugee law, rights equal to those of refugees. Those who applied for Ukrainian citizenship but who had not yet received citizenship were granted the same rights as applicants for refugee status (a more limited set of rights). Resolution 3819-XII, text in Ukrainska pravnycha fundatsia, *Pravovyi zakhyst bizhentsiv v Ukraini,* 49.

50. In practice, the resolution hurt refugees eligible for Ukrainian citizenship relative to those who were not because the citizenship acquisition procedure could last up to a year while decisions on refugee applications were generally made within one month. This meant that those eligible for citizenship had to wait up to a year before they could acquire full set of refugee socioeconomic rights, while "foreign" refugees acquired these rights after a few months—as soon as they received refugee status. These unintended consequences of the 1993 resolution are explained in Olena Malynovska, "Repatriation to Ukraine," *Migration Issues* 4, no. 11 (1999): 17–29.

51. Derzhavnyi Komitet u spravakh natsionalnostei i mihratsii, "Zvit pro statevo-vikovyi sklad osib z pravom na sproshchenyi poriadok nabuttia hromadianstva Ukrainy, iaki zhidno z postanovoiu Verkhovnoi Rady Ukrainy vid 24.23.1993 r. No. 3819-XII "Pro poriadok vvedennia v diiu Zakonu Ukrainy "Pro bizhentsiv" do pryinattia rishennia pro nadannia iim hromadianstva maiut prava, preredbacheni statteiu 9 tsioho zakonu, forma 3 (zvedena), stanom na 1 sichnia 2000," February 3, 2000; Derzhavnyi Komitet u spravakh natsionalnostei i mihratsii, "Zvit pro statevo-vikovyi sklad osib z pravom na sproshchenyi poriadok nabuttia hromadianstva Ukrainy, iaki zhidno z postanovoiu Verkhovnoi Rady Ukrainy vid 24.23.1993 r. No. 3819-XII "Pro poriadok vvedennia v diiu Zakonu Ukrainy "Pro bizhentsiv" do pryinattia rishennia pro ponovlennia iim hromadianstva maiut prava, preredbacheni statteiu 12 tsioho zakonu, forma 4 (zvedena), stanom na 1 sichnia 2000," February 3, 2000.

52. The number of developing-world refugees present in Ukraine in the first half of the 1990s is unknown because the authorities were not registering them and the UNHCR did not establish a permanent presence in the country until mid-1995. Ukrainian government experts put the estimate at some 5,000 asylum seekers from more than twenty developing-world countries, 4,500 of them in Kyiv. See Government of Ukraine, "Doklad Ukrainy na konferentsii po problemam bezhentsev, repatriantov, peremeschennykh lits i migrantov na territorii byvshego SSSR," 1995, 8, and Olena Malynovska, *Mihrat-*

siina sytuatsiia ta mihratsiina polityka v Ukraïni (Kyiv: Natsionalnyi Instytut Strate-hichnykh Doslidzhen, 1997), 24. In 1994, the UNHCR dispatched a "care and mainte-nance" mission to Kyiv, which registered 6,000 cases of developing-world refugees, 60 percent of them Afghans, 10 percent Angolans, 8 percent Iraqis, and 8 percent Ethiopi-ans; see UNHCR Moscow, "Country Operation Plan for Russia, Ukraine and Belarus," n.d., section of the report on Ukraine. For detailed analyses of the formation of the refugee regime in Ukraine in the 1990s, see Olena Malynovska, *Bizhentsi u sviti ta v Ukraini: Modeli vyrishennia problemy* (Kyiv: Heneza, 2003); Malynovska, *Mihranty, mihratsiia ta Ukrainska derzhava: Analiz upravlinnia zovnishnimy mihratsiiamy* (Kyiv: Vyd-vo NADU, 2004); Blair A. Ruble, O. A. Malynovs'ka, and O. Braichevs'ka, *"Ne-tradytsiini" immihranty u Kyievi* (Kyiv: Stylos, 2003); Shevel, "National Identity and International Institutions," chap. 6; and Nikolai Shulga, *Velikoe pereselenie: Repatri-anty, bezhensty, trudovyie migranty* (Kyiv: Institut Sotsiologii NAN Ukrainy, 2002).

53. This calculation is from the State Committee for Nationalities and Migration sta-tistics cited in table 7.3.

54. For an analysis of politics in and around Crimea in the 1990s, see Jane Dawson, "Ethnicity, Ideology and Geopolitics in Crimea," *Communist and Post-Communist Stud-ies* 30 (1997): 427–44; Gwendolyn Sasse, "Conflict-Prevention in a Transition State: The Crimean Issue in Post-Soviet Ukraine," *Nationalism and Ethnic Politics* 8, no. 2 (2002): 1–26; Oxana Shevel, "Crimean Tatars and the Ukrainian State: The Challenge of Politics, the Use of Law, and the Meaning of Rhetoric," *Krymski Studii* 1, no. 7 (2001): 109–29; Brian Glyn Williams, *The Crimean Tatars: The Diaspora Experience and the Forging of a Nation* (Boston: Brill, 2001); and Andrew Wilson, "Politics in and around Crimea: A Dif-ficult Homecoming," in *The Tatars of the Crimea: Return to the Homeland: Studies and Documents,* ed. Edward Allworth (Durham, N.C.: Duke University Press, 1998), 281–322.

55. In addition to the Crimean Tatars, a smaller number of other nationalities (Ar-menians, Bulgarians, Greeks, and Germans) were deported from Crimea in the 1940s. Some descendants of these deportees returned in the 1990s. Although politically and numerically Crimean Tatars were the main concern, the term "formerly deported people" was coined in Ukraine as a politically more neutral term.

56. For details on UNHCR involvement in Crimea, see UNHCR Ukraine, *Overview of UNHCR's Citizenship Campaign in Crimea* (Simferopol: UNHCR, 2000); UNHCR Ukraine, "How UNHCR Got Started in Crimea," *Beyond Borders* 5 (May 2005): 11, and Shevel, "National Identity and International Institutions," chap. 4.

57. For findings of these UNHCR missions, see UNHCR Ukraine, "Mission Report on Crimean Tatar Situation (7–11 April 1995)," May 18, 1995; UNHCR Ukraine, "UN-HCR Mission to Crimea: Preliminary Summary," February 1996; and UNHCR Ukraine, "UNHCR in Ukraine," 1999.

58. UNHCR Ukraine, "Summary Mission Report: Assistance to Formerly Deported Peoples, 3 June–31 July 1996, Crimea, Ukraine," August 5, 1996. Shelter rehabilitation projects were chosen as an activity that produces tangible results rather quickly. By 1998, the UNHCR has launched eight shelter rehabilitation projects; Oleg Shamshur, "Migration Situation in Ukraine: International Cooperation Related Aspects," *Migra-tion: European Journal on International Migration and Ethnic Relations* 29–31 (1998): 29–44. By 1999, it financed and oversaw renovations of thirty hostels, three schools, and two clinics in Crimea; UNHCR Ukraine, "UNHCR in Ukraine."

59. This assessment of the UNHCR was echoed by officials from various Ukrainian

government agencies (the Ukrainian Presidential Administration, State Committee for Nationalities and Migration, Ministry of the Interior, and the Parliament) interviewed by the author in May–June 1998. Many officials contrasted the UNHCR with other international agencies and the Western community in general, which in their opinion had offered little practical help.

60. For a description of specific activities UNHCR undertook within citizenship campaign, see UNHCR Ukraine, *Overview of UNHCR's Citizenship Campaign;* and Hans Schodder, "Assisting the Integration of Formerly Deported People in Crimea: Ten Years of UNHCR Experience," *Beyond Borders* 5 (May 2005): 12–17. For an analysis of the formerly deported people citizenship problem and the role of international institutions in solving it, see Oxana Shevel, "International Influence in Transition Societies: The Effect of UNHCR and Other IOs on Citizenship Policies in Ukraine," Working Paper 7, Rosemary Rogers Working Paper Series of Inter-University Committee on International Migration, August 2000.

61. UNHCR Ukraine, "Summary Mission Report." UNHCR officials confirm that they have "capitalized on the positive results of cooperation with the authorities on the citizenship issue to obtain cooperation on issues of refugee policy." Author's interviews, UNHCR Kyiv, April 15 and June 2, 1998.

62. Author's interviews, Ukrainian Presidential Administration and State Committee for Nationalities and Migration, May–June 1998.

63. The term was coined by the senior protection officer of the UNHCR Ukraine office. See Christoph Bierwirth, "Pravova diialnist Upravlinnia Verkhovnoho Komisara z pytan bizhenstiv OON v Ukraini: Dosiahnennia i trudnoshchi, shcho zalyshaiutsia," *Bizhentsi ta mihratsiia: Ukrainskyi chasopys prava i polityky* 2, nos. 3–4 (1998): 23–35.

64. Author's interviews, UNHCR Kyiv, April 1998; and author's interview with Sadako Ogata, the UN high commissioner for refugees, Cambridge, Mass., October 24, 2001.

65. The "step-by-step" strategy was described as follows by the senior protection officer of the UNHCR Ukraine office: "UNHCR has offered targeted assistance and advocated a step by step approach. . . . It has focused its efforts on the development of national legislation and administrative structures, rather than 'pushing for accession' to the Convention." Bierwirth, "Pravova diialnist Upravlinnia Verkhovnoho Komisara z pytan bizhenstiv OON v Ukraini," 24.

66. As a UNHCR senior protection officer noted, "The initial hesitation on the part of the State Committee of Ukraine for Nationalities and Migration resulting in the absence of status determination was overcome by specifically targeted material assistance (technical aid, training, advice) to local migration services such as the Kyiv City Migration Service. This positive initial experience proved to have a decisive impact on the nationwide policy of the State Committee for Nationalities and Migration." Bierwirth, "Pravova diialnist Upravlinnia Verkhovnoho Komisara z pytan bizhenstiv OON v Ukraini," 24.

67. Author's interview, State Committee of Ukraine for Nationalities and Migration, June 23, 1998.

68. Olena Malynovska, "Mihratsiina sytuatsia v Ukraini v 1998 rotsi," 1999; UNHCR Ukraine, "UNHCR in Ukraine."

69. Andrew Harper, UNHCR Kyiv program officer, presentation at a December 1998 seminar; UNHCR Ukraine and Creative Center Counterpart, eds., *Informatsiia pro mizhnarodni ta ukrainski instytutsii, shcho zaimaiutsia problemamy bizhentsiv: Ukrainska*

zakonodavcha basa stosovno bizhentsiv, 21–22 hrudnia 1998 roky (Kyiv: UNHCR and Counterpart, 1998), 11. UNHCR positively commented on Ukraine's refugee policy on numerous occasions. See, e.g., the 1997 speech by Sadako Ogata, UNHCR high commissioner in Kyiv, reprinted in *Bizhentsi ta mihratsiia: Ukrainskyi chasopys prava i polityky* 3, no. 1 (1997): 7–10. Also see Sadako Ogata's letter to President Kuchma; Sadako Ogata, UN high commissioner for refugees, "Letter to His Excellency Mr. Leonid Kuchma, President of Ukraine," September 28, 2000; and articles by Christoph Bierwirth, the UNHCR Kyiv senior protection officer: Bierwirth, "The Need for a Consolidated Ukrainian Migration and Refugee Policy," *Ukrainskyi chasopys prav liudyny* 1, no. 1 (1997): 13–18; and Bierwirth, "Pravova dialnist Upravlinnia Verkhovnoho Komisara z pytan' bizhenstiv OON v Ukraini."

70. E.g., Mykola Shulha, minister of Ukraine for nationalities and migration in 1994–95, noted as "symbolic" the fact that Ukraine's first refugee certificate was issued to an Afghan rather than a Ukrainian. Shulha notes with dismay that of Ukrainians who fled to Ukraine from conflict zones in the former Soviet states "only a few individuals received refugee status," while the rest are "left to fend for themselves." Shulha, "Immihratsiia v Ukrainy etnichnykh grup u 1991–1996 pp," *Bizhentsi ta mihratsiia: Ukrainskyi chasopys prava i polityky* 3, no. 1 (1999): 11–23; the quotation is on 15. In a 1998 paper, Oleh Shamshur, then deputy head of the State Committee for Nationalities and Migration, likewise lamented the absence of policies to assist ethnic Ukrainian returnees: "One has to acknowledge that, unfortunately, problems of the repatriates (with the exception of Crimean Tatars) remain on the periphery of government activities. Sometimes the repatriates are worse off than refugees and asylum seekers who can count on some aid from the UNHCR and other international organizations. It can hardly be considered a normal situation, especially given worrying demographic trends in Ukraine." Shamshur, "Rehuliuvannia mihratsiinykh protsessiv v Ukraini: Suchasni tendentsii," 1998 (unpublished manuscript).

71. *Pravda Ukrainy,* December 3, 1997. In Ukrainian: "Iakshcho vzhe buty bizhentsem v Ukraini, to krashche—v shkuri nehra."

72. UNHCR Ukraine, "Refugees and Asylum Seekers in Ukraine," January 1, 2002.

73. At the height of the citizenship campaign in 1998, the UNHCR Kyiv office annual budget was $4 million. Its budget for 2002–3 dropped by almost 50 percent, to $2.5 million for two years. UNHCR Ukraine, "Diialnist UVKB OON ta ioho vykonavchykh partneriv," 2004, http://www.unhcr.org.ua.

74. The European Commission earmarked 1.4 million euros for the project in 2003–4, and for 2005 the UNHCR Kyiv office budget was increased to $2.1 million (with $390,000 coming from the European Commission). With increased budgetary capacity, the UNHCR is financing construction of additional housing facilities for asylum seekers in different regions of Ukraine during 2004 and 2005. UNHCR Ukraine, "Diialnist UVKB OON."

75. In the first half of 2004, the refugee recognition rate stood at 14 percent—a significant increase in comparison with the 3 percent rate for the period from the fall of 2002, when refugee status determination procedure resumed in Ukraine, and until the end of 2003, but still much lower than 50 percent recognition rate for 1996–2001. UNHCR Ukraine, "Basic Facts about Refugees and Asylum Seekers in Ukraine," *Beyond Borders* 3 (September 2004): 4.

76. For UNHCR opinion on the 2001 Ukrainian refugee law and amendments it de-

sires to see, see Guy Ouellet, "Ukrainian Legislation and the Refugee Problem," *Beyond Borders* 2 (May 2004): 4–6.

77. For this argument, see Lucan Way, "Authoritarian State Building and the Sources of Political Liberalization in the Western former Soviet Union, 1994–2004," *World Politics* 57 (January 2005), 231–61.

Part III

Changing Attributes

8

Explaining the Appeal of Evangelicalism in Ukraine

Catherine Wanner

After the Soviet Union collapsed in 1991, many scholars across disciplines were taken by surprise when a religious renaissance flourished throughout the former Soviet Union. The espoused atheist ideology of the Soviet regime made religious communities and religious practice anathema to the Bolsheviks' vision of modernity and a "bright future" enlightened by science and freed from superstitious belief. Yet repressive measures against the expression of religious sentiment in the public sphere did not necessarily eradicate religious belief and practice and produce secular worldviews among Soviet citizens, as most Western analysts thought. Rather, such state policies produced ignorance of religious practice and displaced the expression of religious sentiment out of the public sphere and into private domains from where it was easily retrieved when political conditions permitted.

Many scholars studying political and cultural change in the final years of Soviet rule focused on the rise of nationalism, including religious nationalisms, and the practices of nationalizing states. In Ukraine, a commitment to religious pluralism was incorporated into the very idea of the Ukrainian nation, at a minimum to accommodate the cohabitation of the various Orthodox churches and the Ukrainian Greek-rite Catholic Church, all of whom claim to be indigenous national institutions. In addition, the granting of a variety of rights and privileges to minority religious communities, beginning but hardly ending with Jews and Muslim Crimean Tatars, became part of the bedrock of the new post-Soviet Ukrainian social order. This created an entirely different role for religion and religious communities in the politics of identity as they evolved in Ukraine after the fall of the Soviet Union.

Ukraine was called the "Bible Belt" of the former Soviet Union because more Protestants lived in Ukraine than in any other republic. When the USSR collapsed in 1991, numerically speaking, it was home to the second largest Baptist community in the world after the United States. In addition, approximately 350,000 Pentecostal Soviet citizens were officially registered as residing in Ukraine. These communities provided a base from which evangelicalism could grow and spread once political conditions changed. When I speak of evangelicals, I am referring primarily to Baptist and Pentecostal believers, and I will limit my discussion to these two groups, although there have always been, of course, Lutheran, Adventist, Mennonite, and other Protestant denominations in Ukraine and in the USSR.

Baptist and Pentecostal communities in Soviet Ukraine can be described as fundamentalist to the extent that they espoused a literal reading of an inerrant Bible, a general suspicion of worldliness that resulted in strict codes of personal morality, and a belief in the imminent return of Jesus Christ. More recently, a phenomenal number of charismatic and neo-Pentecostal churches have been created in Ukraine. These churches offer a charismatic means of expressive, even ecstatic worship, the observance of Pentecostal doctrine, and a relaxation of fundamentalist prescriptions on individual behavior. All these denominations have had to contend with a vast popular outpouring of curiosity to explore things religious, a tremendous influx of foreign missionaries, and massive outmigration.[1] I will use the term "evangelical" to refer to the broad spectrum of conservative Protestants, Baptists, Evangelical Christians, Pentecostals, and neo-Pentecostals who call Ukraine home.

Reflecting the changes in state and popular attitudes toward organized religion, there has been a spectacular rise in the number of religious groups. There were approximately 4,500 registered religious communities in Ukraine in 1990. A decade later there were nearly 20,000, one quarter of which were Protestant.[2] Moreover, by 2000 in the southeast of the country, the number of Protestant churches nearly equaled Orthodox churches.[3] By

2005, the total number of Protestant communities registered nationally in Ukraine rivals that of the combined number of Orthodox communities.[4] Furthermore, because of the relatively tolerant political and legal environment in Ukraine, evangelical organizations envision Ukraine as a center of evangelical seminary training and publishing serving Protestants throughout the former Soviet Union. Currently, hundreds of Ukrainian missionaries travel annually to Russia and to other regions of the former Soviet Union to evangelize. These staggering changes have largely taken root in the last fifteen years, thanks to sweeping political and legal change that has allowed Western missionary organizations to offer extensive assistance to nascent evangelical communities to help them grow.

In this chapter, I offer an explanation as to why a religious revival emerged in Ukraine and why it has worked to the favor of evangelicals. I analyze what the implications are for identity, community membership, and cultural change more generally when individuals turn away from historically Ukrainian national denominations and join faith-based communities perceived as nontraditional and "foreign." I argue that evangelical religious communities in Ukraine are introducing fundamentally new attributes of individual identity that largely hinge on shared understandings of morality and how these moral understandings should inform the social contract and economic exchange more generally. In particular, evangelical religious communities increasingly challenge identity categories that symbiotically link religion and nation-state as an organic unity. Rather, the dimensions of the religiously based identity they advocate are simultaneously operative on highly local and global levels and ultimately serve to deterritorialize identity by recasting it as a morally empowering choice.

Political and Legal Reform and Its Effects on Religious Communities

Whether one speaks of the Revolution of 1905, the Revolution of 1917, or the collapse of the USSR in 1991, during each of these periods of political reform, widespread social change and extensive moral questioning also led to the repositioning of the Orthodox Church. In each instance, demands for political reform triggered extensive legal reform concerning the status of minority religious organizations. Given the historic partnership of the Orthodox Church and the state in this part of the world, these social and political crises powerfully affected religious communities and were to some degree predicated on alienation from established religious authorities. Legal reform and the search for alternative moral communities have led to a proliferation of new religious communities as often as they have led to disillusionment with organized religion and the spread of secular worldviews.[5]

At these key historic junctures of political change, some individuals cast aside their religious heritage and chose to identify with another faith that carries decisively different political and national implications. Over time, those who converted to evangelicalism chose to construct cosmologies, philosophies of life, and worldviews as self-conscious traditionalists who, like everyone else in the greater society, were obliged to adapt to changing social and political realities. Yet they chose to do so as practicing evangelical Christians within the confines of fundamentalist religious communities that were branded as "foreign."

Evangelicals were persecuted, initially under the Russian Empire, and subsequently under the Soviet regime, because they were accused of embodying alien worldviews and values. Beermann, among others, has noted that there are striking similarities between the attitudes of the pre-1905 Imperial government and the Soviet authorities with regard to "foreign faiths" or religious minorities.[6] Especially during the Soviet period, accusations of illegitimate financing from the exploitative capital of "Brother Rockefeller" served as the justification to stigmatize and persecute evangelicals. The Soviet authorities clearly recognized the "ideological provocation" evangelicalism represented and the power of religion to transgress state boundaries, even formidable ones, such as those that the Soviet Union constructed, to forge bonds of allegiance among coreligionists of different national and social backgrounds and political systems.[7] Religiously motivated migratory practices to missionize and evangelize underlined the greater community to which evangelical believers were enjoined and sought to expand. At the same time, missionizing exposed comparatively small and isolated communities to practices and values embraced by other communities.[8]

The Religious Renaissance of the 1990s

Amid growing demands for political reform in the late 1980s, the millennium of Christianity in Kyivan Rus' was commemorated in 1988. The series of commemorations unleashed vast popular interest in religion and prompted a sea change in Soviet religious policy.[9] In October 1990, one of the primary goals of Soviet ideology, to establish a scientific atheistic worldview, was abandoned when the Supreme Soviet adopted legislation that guaranteed freedom of conscience and a legal status for all religious communities. Legalizing overt religious practice propelled the emerging religious renaissance into a resurgence. With less fear of state retribution, some clergy and religious institutions used their moral authority to overtly lend support to nationalist movements as oppositional forces to Soviet rule.

A religious and national resurgence occurred simultaneously because political opposition leaders positioned religion as a key attribute of Ukrainian nationality. Evoking a nation's right to self-determination and an individual's right to freedom of conscience became twin pillars of opposition to Soviet rule in the late 1980s. The fusion of religion and nationality took on new relevance when it could be mobilized to advance the goals of a political opposition aimed at remaking, if not dismantling, the Soviet system.

Orthodoxy in Ukraine, as in Russia, is widely considered the foundation of national traditions, aesthetic forms, and other elements of a unique sociocultural matrix. Yet many factors distinguish Ukraine's religious traditions from those its neighboring countries, in spite of a shared Orthodox tradition: the origins of Orthodoxy in Kyivan Rus'; the cohabitation of Orthodox and Greek Catholic religious traditions, both of which are embraced as unique and indigenous national institutions; and Ukraine's geopolitical location as a "borderland" among empires, which over time strengthened the multiethnic and multiconfessional cultural attributes of the Ukrainian population. Perhaps most important of all, religious participation and the number of religious institutions have historically been higher in Ukraine than they have been in Russia.[10]

Although "religious nationalisms" are a fundamental component of nation building in much of the former Soviet Union, the same cannot be said of Ukraine. Rather, the splintering of the Orthodox Church into several denominations after independence has inadvertently weakened the status of Orthodoxy in Ukraine. The three Orthodox churches—the Ukrainian Orthodox Church–Kyiv Patriarchate, the Ukrainian Autocephalous Orthodox Church, and the Ukrainian Orthodox Church–Moscow Patriarchate—each offer a different political vision based on the links each one offers, respectively, to Ukraine, to Ukraine and the diaspora, or to Russia. Although church leaders in each of the denominations attempt to position their church as *the* Ukrainian Orthodox Church, their failed efforts have ultimately brought an end to the state-backed monopoly status of Orthodoxy in Ukraine. When a single church cannot dominate and influence political policy, de facto there are greater freedoms for other faiths to exist and for individuals to worship as they choose.[11] As the national churches compete among themselves for dominance, a new space is opened up for nontraditional faiths and new religious movements to establish roots in Ukraine.

The history of active religious participation and confessional diversity in Ukraine has combined to create a political and cultural climate that is more favorable to a spectrum of denominations, especially when compared with Russia and Belarus. The suspension of most legal restrictions on foreign religious organizations' activities in Ukraine and the lifting of most prohibitions on forms of assistance (financial, material, technical, etc.) that foreign religious organizations are allowed to offer coreligionists and others in Ukraine has greatly strengthened the presence of nontraditional religious communities. The resulting religious pluralism, especially when combined with a nominal commitment to an Orthodoxy that is often more cultural than religious in nature among large sectors of the population, has made Ukraine one of the most active and competitive religious marketplaces in Europe, if not the world.[12]

Recent surveys in Ukraine note that religious institutions are the most trusted institutions in Ukraine, with almost half, or 47 percent, of all respondents claiming they trust the church and 45 percent claiming that religion should be part of political life.[13] Forty-one percent of Ukrainians maintain that their president must be a religious person.[14] Religion has become an institutional mechanism facilitating the formation of communities that attempt to challenge—or secure—the growing uneven distribution of capital in all its forms—financial, social, and cultural. Religion has returned to play a key part in the twin political projects of protesting and perpetuating new forms of political and economic inequality. By extension, it plays a role in challenging or establishing political legitimacy for the emerging economic order in moral terms. No longer seen as the "opium of the people," religion in Ukraine is now considered a moral and national bulwark, regaining its historic role as the key institution defining and defending Ukrainian language and culture, and by extension, the Ukrainian people. The "transition" is understood in many ways: as a process of economic vandalism; as a new form of soft imperialism; or, as the most radical reformers would argue, as a necessary and painful step in the process of economic advancement. Regardless of how one understands the nature of the sweeping changes that have beset Ukraine since independence in 1991, there is widespread agreement that one of the initial and most powerful results has been the reemergence of religion as a salient part of political, communal, and individual life.

Conversion to Evangelicalism

Conversion is a complex process culminating in religious change that gives life new meaning by changing the way an individual perceives reality and the intellectual and social tools he or she has to respond to it.[15] Today, 3 percent of the Ukrainian population has made the decision to convert to evangelicalism and undergo full-body baptismal immersion. The impact of these communities is greater than their numbers would suggest because these congregations tend to have active memberships engaged in a variety of intracongregational activities, charitable initiatives, and outreach programs.

One of the sources of confessional conflict in Ukraine today is that the Orthodox Church considers Orthodoxy an attribute of Ukrainian nationality; that is to say, a Ukrainian is by definition Orthodox. A significant exception is made for Ukrainian Greek-rite Catholics, who for historic reasons belong to a different, albeit related, national denomination. An Orthodox identity is geographically defined and automatically inherited. In the eyes of Orthodox clergy, there is no need for missionizing because all Ukrainians have a religious identity, whether or not they choose to act on it.

This understanding of religiosity is dramatically different from the "born again" conscious experience of adult conversion upon which an evangelical identity is predicated. For evangelicals, anyone who has not been "saved" through repentance and conversion inspires proselytizing. Evangelicals actualize their faith by acting on the moral obligation to save the unsaved, to help church the unchurched.

Conversion can be a swift means to redefine concepts of self and other through cultural appropriation of new values and practices. This new collective identity and group membership are marked by subsequent behavior modifications as public manifestations of inner spiritual change. By becoming an evangelical in post-Soviet Ukrainian society, one redefines fundamental cultural categories, such as familiar and foreign, space and time, power and agency, and gender and class. One rewrites autobiography into preconversion and postconversion periods, giving in to the frequent temptations to see signs retrospectively of the impending conversion in one's deep past and thereby affirming the righteousness of the Christian life one has adopted. I have argued elsewhere that evangelical faiths derive a good bit of their appeal from propagating a "complete break with the past" and a "new beginning as a different (and morally superior) person."[16] Just as the Ukrainian nation was "born again" in 1991, conversion offers the believer an experience of erasure and renewal.

The faith of evangelicals is manifest through a strict interpretation of the Bible as the Word of God, which dictates how one should live. In addition to adult full-body baptismal immersion, which all evangelicals practice, Pentecostals subscribe to the baptism of the Holy Spirit, which is manifest in the practice of speaking in tongues or glossolalia; prophecy, as revealed in visions or dreams; and faith healing. Conversion to any of the evangelical faiths constitutes a total lifestyle change, with belief and behavior, family and community, ideally merging into one. Communal life is characterized by a doctrine of the "priesthood of the believer" and features extensive lay participation. For men and women alike, congregational life often offers possibilities for assuming positions of responsibility, status, and prestige, which may or may not elude them in the secular world.

The family is understood to be the core of a believer's life, and the dynamics of family life are superimposed on the congregational, national, and global levels. This explains the evangelical support for biblically grounded prohibitions against divorce, sexual license, birth control, and abortion, all measures designed to strengthen the family, and extensive congregational programs designed for children. The family metaphor is to this day reinforced by discursive practices. Believers refer to each other as "brothers and sisters," drawing on the assumption that fellow church members have similar levels of conviction, and this binds them together in a family-like community.

When an individual converts to evangelicalism and departs from hereditary and national understandings of an Orthodox identity, however he or she understands and practices them, conflicts almost always arise between the convert and kin and neighbors. Dispensing with common cultural practices, such as drinking, smoking, and dancing, alienates the convert from his or her kin. When home is sanctified by icons and nationality is understood in religious terms, a convert to evangelicalism is willfully rejecting established patterns of lifestyle and identity. As Ruth Marshall-Fratani has written, "Friends, family and neighbors become 'dangerous strangers,' and strangers, new friends. The social grounds for creating bonds—blood, common pasts, neighborhood ties, language—are foresworn for the new bond of the brother or sister in Christ."[17]

Indeed, the exclusivity of evangelical cultural practices contributed, especially during the Soviet period, to widespread perceptions that evangelical communities are "sects," in some way separate from and outside of mainstream religious life. This perception was further enhanced by the faith-as-lifestyle orientation of evangelical doctrine and the extensive commitments to communal life that official members are obliged to make, such as attending several services a week, each of which lasts more than two hours; participating in the numerous activities the church sponsors; and tithing 10 percent of one's income. The decision to become a practicing evangelical quickly becomes a fundamental attribute of identity, a primary influence on social relationships, and a significant factor structuring everyday life. For many converts, evangelicalism begins to overshadow, but not necessarily reject, the importance previously invested in other factors informing identity. Conversion and the "born again" do not erase the importance of other forms of social identity. Rather, they become the primary organizing principle assimilating, mediating, and subsuming them.

The popular perception of the dichotomous choice of a national or foreign faith is largely a false one. As Ranger writes of the widespread coexistence of various religious groups in Africa, "We should see mission churches as much less alien and independent churches as much less African."[18] The same could be said of religious life in Ukraine. The national Ukrainian churches have links to institutions and hierarchies located abroad, be it the Vatican or the Moscow Patriarchate, and themselves react by adapting to the religious pluralism surrounding them. Second, although the choice to convert to an evangelical faith in Ukraine today exerts appeal because it opens up access to new zones of contact, many of the imported doctrines and practices are rapidly adapted to local cultural mores and quickly take on a Ukrainian cast. In this way, all religious communities are forced to negotiate the local or national contexts in which they wish to situate themselves as well as the links they offer individuals, communities, and institutions beyond Ukrainian borders. Visiting preachers, missionaries, and dignitaries from abroad simultaneously underline the global dimensions of religion today and serve to locate Ukraine within it.

Communal Membership and Individual Identity

In numerous interviews conducted with converts to evangelicalism in northeastern Ukraine from 2000 to 2005, most responded to open-ended questions concerning self identification by saying that they were either "believers" or "Christians." Other attributes, such as nationality, residence, profession, gender, or social roles (mother, elderly, etc.), were cited only secondarily after they noted the fact that they lived a religious life. The defining attribute of their identity was that they were "believers." They use the term "believers" according to its original meaning, namely, to indicate quite simply conviction, faith that rests on a trust in God. Reference to a particular denomination or a specific body of doctrine, as we would expect belief to be defined in most Western societies, is largely absent.[19] After decades of an official state policy of atheism, the key issue is whether one has faith or not, and hence the widespread use of the term "believer" to self-identify among adherents to a variety of religious denominations.

The response of Ludmilla, a forty-five-year-old librarian from Kharkiv, to the question of identity was rather typical: "I am first and foremost a Christian, saved by the blood of Jesus Christ and by the grace of God. I endeavor to live by the Word of God. I am also a beloved mother of three children and a wife." I learned later that her nationality is in fact Ukrainian, as are her husband's and children's. She considers her native language Russian *and* Ukrainian because she was raised in a *surzhyk*-speaking village. Today she speaks Russian at home and prays in Russian. Many evangelical believers, even some in more western regions of Ukraine, pray in Russian because the few Bibles, hymnals, and other religious literature that were available during the Soviet period were almost exclusively in Russian. Therefore, most sermons, Bible study, and preaching was, and certainly in eastern Ukraine continues to be, in Russian. However, given the reliance on informal, even underground, means of transmitting an oral tradition of religious practice, there were nonetheless poems recited and hymnals sung across Soviet Ukraine in Ukrainian. Indeed, in the village where Ludmilla was raised, there were ten to fifteen Baptists who met quietly in private homes. One of them taught her several religious poems in Ukrainian when she was a child.

When asked why she does not call herself a Baptist, she explains, "We try to call ourselves 'believers' or 'Christians' because the word 'Baptism' is frightening to many people. But when someone asks what the official name of my faith is, I say 'Evangelical Christian-Baptist.' The name is only secondary. The most important thing is to live by the Word of God." Living according to their beliefs, as revealed in the Bible, is a key attribute of evangelical believers. Pivotal changes in behavior and values are expected to accompany conversion and church membership. Acceptance of belief triggers this transformation, and community membership sustains it. Although there is little disapproval of people who have begun to practice religion, virtually all Protestant faiths remain to a degree popularly stigmatized. Abandoning one's "natural" and national faith for evangelicalism is widely considered "not right."

There are other reasons explaining the overall preference for a general term such as "believer" or "Christian." Especially during the Soviet period, when meeting space was often unavailable, many communities made home churches or met in a church of a related denomination. Although there were meaningful doctrinal differences among categories of believers, such as Baptists, Evangelical Christians, and Pentecostals, there was extensive intermarriage among members and considerable denominational switching, often driven more by circumstances than by choice, further diluting the meaning of the denominational differences among evangelical faiths in the region.[20] Thus, the dimensions of a religious identity ultimately collapse into two categories of people: believers and nonbelievers. Language, nationality, and even socioeconomic status as attributes of believers in post-Soviet Ukraine fail to emerge in any kind of systematically important way.

Ludmilla never practiced religion until 1979, when she was twenty-three years old and already a mother. As is often the case, her conversion was precipitated by a crisis that left her powerless to control her fate. Her son fell terribly ill and lost consciousness. After several days in the hospital, he showed no signs of improvement, and the doctor, who she notes was an elegant Jewish man, told her: "Only God can save your son." "I was so surprised," she said, "that such an educated person would speak of God. I went home and cried for a long time. As best I could, I turned to God, and said, 'God, if you exist, please save my child!' In several days, the crisis was over. It was the grace of God. After that, I wanted to read the Bible." At this point in her life, she was religiously inclined and began to attend an Orthodox Church in spite of the fact that in 1979 there were still some risks involved in overtly practicing religion.

However, as she explains, her attitude toward the Orthodox Church gradually changed. "I didn't really like that people came one after another to kiss icons. Then you had to buy a candle. I didn't regret spending the money. I had money. But I didn't like that you had to do it. It's one thing if you want to, but this was totally different. And I really needed someone to explain the Word of God to me, and they don't have that there. My soul just wasn't satisfied." She asked one of her mother's Baptist neighbors to take her to a Baptist church the next time he came into the city. So began her membership in the oldest Baptist church in Kharkiv, a community that dates its foundation to 1892.[21]

Conversion and Connections

Conversion is frequently a response to crisis, a coping strategy that enables an individual to overcome difficulties by reordering a relationship to higher, more powerful forces, and by creating relationships within a new community. Svetlana explains how church membership has affected her sense of identity and how it has begun to repair a shattered sense of home and homeland. Now a refugee in Kharkiv, she is an Armenian who fled her home in Baku, Azerbaijan, in 1988 as a result of ethnic tensions and political instability. When she first left Baku, she settled in Yerevan and in 1998 relocated once again to Kharkiv. She claims, "I am a person without a homeland. My heart doesn't lie anywhere. If I had the possibility, I would emigrate again. I'm not proud of that, but if there was such a possibility, why not?" In other words, at this point in Svetlana's life, a sense of belonging is not in any way tied to place or to a particular national way of life. Although she could choose to see herself as part of the Armenian diaspora, she does not. Rather, she embraces, church membership as a quick and effective way to reestablish a sense of stability, community, and access to a forum with possibilities for self-realization. Conversion narratives and testimonies reorder autobiography in a teleological fashion leading up to the moment of finding faith. As such, they restore order and logic to lives that have been disrupted by traumatic events.

Svetlana remembers her earliest exposure to religion as coming from her neighbors in Baku who were Russian Molokans: "They were real believers, and we were just Christians." Again, she ignores all denominational differences and their related national implications and explains the difference between "believers" and "Christians" by noting that "my family believed in God, or at least that's what they called it. Every Sunday we went to an Orthodox Church and lit candles. We didn't know any prayers, but my mother would always bring home a prayer sheet and we would put it under our pillows." She contrasts this pro forma religious practice with the caring relationships she observed among the Molokan. "On Saturday and Sunday, they didn't work. They went to church. They knew their faith well and helped each other. There were no elderly or children who were ignored." Svetlana understood the warmth of their interpersonal relationships as a manifestation of faith, and this impressed her.

While she was living in Yerevan and working as a hairdresser, one of her favorite clients took her to a Baptist church. Again, as with the Molokan, she was impressed by how kind people were to one another, how they seemed to know one another, and how warmly they welcomed her. At the time, she had almost no friends. Few had fled from Baku to Yerevan. Most left for Russia or America or simply stayed behind in Baku. In 1994, in rather quick succession, she repented, was christened, and became an official member of the church in Yerevan, participating in many of its activities, including prayer groups, visiting the sick, and attending several services a week.

After her daughter and her family moved to Kharkiv, Svetlana and her husband decided to relocate, too. Thanks to a letter from her pastor attesting to her membership in good standing in Yerevan, she was able to transfer her membership to a church near her new home in Ukraine. Birgit Meyer claims that the success of evangelical communities in Africa can be attributed to their dual recognition of the experience of marginalization and of being forgotten, all the while situating believers in a meaningful way within "the wider world." Conversion delivers membership in a local community of "brothers and sisters" and assures believers a place in a transnational organization. Meyer writes, "The mass appeal of PCCs [Pentecostal charismatic churches] can be explained, at least in part, against this backdrop. Adopting a strategy of extraversion, which deliberately develops external links and promises connection with the world, PCCs nevertheless have to address a politics of identity and belonging, in which fixed markers govern processes of inclusion and exclusion, both in Africa and in the diaspora."[22] Not only for Africans but also for other diasporic peoples, such as Armenians and Ukrainians, membership in a community that is at once local and global is appealing. In this way, Svetlana belongs to another type of "imagined community." Most likely, wherever she moves, she will be able to find other believers and be accepted into their community in spite of where she is from and where she might move to next.

A great deal of mobility in the former Soviet Union is, of course, economically driven. In a similar vein, writing on the spectacular rise of Pentecostal communities in Latin America, where many members are rural migrants who have relocated to the cities in search of work, David Martin claims that religious communities cater to the "mobile self" by enhancing the "portability of charismatic identity."[23] This, he argues, makes Pentecostalism a postmodern religion par excellence. Participation in church communities can provide a sense of continuity in the face of radical disruption through the repetition of rituals, prayers, and other daily activities. For believers such as Svetlana, the "portability" of certain religious identities has played a crucial role in softening the negative effects of relocation, and hence they have become more meaningful.

Starting over again in Kharkiv has not been easy. "I believe in God," she explains, "and I have given over to him all my struggles and I know that he will never leave me. He will always help. . . . I never complain and I never ask people for help. I only ask God knowing that he will help me through other people." She gave an example of how she believes her faith and prayer have helped her resettle: "When we arrived here, we had to pay to get a place to live. We didn't have any money. I asked one of the sisters [a female member of the church] to lend me some money. She also didn't have much money, but she evidently spoke to the members of the church because the next time I came to church, the pastor received me and gave me the money as an interest-free loan. To this day, I give back a little each month, about ten hryvnia. But I never asked for it and I will never ask for money." In the face of a crumbling state social service sector, some church communities attempt to provide a safety net of sorts for members. In this effort, they are often assisted by coreligionists abroad, who send shipments of humanitarian aid to Ukraine and rely on particular congregations to distribute it to the needy. Svetlana and her family, for example, get their clothes this way.

Although Svetlana has experienced tremendous disruption in her life over the past decade, many of her daily practices and her church membership have remained a constant. Particularly for the displaced, church membership provides a ready-made community that offers regular and frequent face-to-face encounters; activities for children; and, as we see in Svetlana's case, a pronounced commitment and ability to assist those in need.[24] Although she has been deracinated, her nationality rendered a burden, and her homeland inaccessible, she has found community membership in Kharkiv, which confers an identity as a moral person, provides an ongoing sense of belonging, and assures that she will not suffer alone. In an era of increased and often unwanted mobility, the stability and adaptability of a religious identity based on this kind of omni-sited community membership exerts mounting appeal. Although the embrace of a national identity can mean living in exile or in the diaspora, there are no believers in exile. Individual believers mediate the negative effects of social change and the disruption of mobility by recasting their identity through conversion to relocate the focuses of daily life to a local community and simultaneously to reach beyond state or territorial borders by enjoining the individual to a global community of believers.

Western Missionaries and the Growth of Evangelicalism

Evangelicalism has become a motivation for and a means to greater mobility. As believers circulate in search of converting others to actualize their faith, the isolation brought on by the Iron Curtain and a secular Soviet public sphere is rapidly replaced by the interconnections that international agencies, transnational religious communities, and individual non-Ukrainian believers offer at a critical moment to religious communities forming in Ukraine.

With the fall of the Soviet Union, it became possible for a wide spectrum of missionary and other religious organizations to participate in the religious resurgence that was occurring throughout the region. Their role is complex and multidirectional in furthering conversion to a religious lifestyle among the religiously curious. By 2001, there were 1,681 long-term foreign missionaries supported by seventy-seven different missionary organizations from twenty-two different countries working in Ukraine.[25] The overwhelming majority of them were American. Mission to the World and send are among the most active agencies in Ukraine that are based in the United States. Missionary organizations from Canada, South Africa, and Germany all support between ten and twenty missionaries in Ukraine.

Initially, foreign missionary organizations pioneered a two-pronged approach to providing assistance. They sent clergy and lay leaders to assist in garnering converts and providing leadership for emerging congregational communities. They also provided vital financial assistance at a critical moment to establish the necessary infrastructure to maintain growing evangelical communities. There are now three evangelical seminaries in Kyiv alone; a Christian university in Donetsk, the former capital of the "cradle of the proletariat" region; and a significant evangelical theological center in Odesa, in the south of the country, which is also home to the largest Christian publishing house in Ukraine and the sponsor of a major initiative to chronicle on cd-rom archival documents of the evangelical experience under Soviet rule.

Of course, the process of creating evangelical infrastructure reveals sharp power differentials that are fueled by money from the West coming to cash-strapped believers and communities in Ukraine. Therefore, the interconnectedness that this collaboration cements occurs against a background of stark inequality. Nonetheless, I do not wish to suggest that this renders Ukrainians powerless or passive. Each of these institutions relies to some degree on foreigners to staff them but is nonetheless led by Ukrainians.

The missionary group SEND claims that its ministry strategy is "simply to help the Ukrainian Church with the tools and people to reach their own country for Jesus Christ, and to launch a missionary movement from Ukraine into the former Soviet nations. Whenever SEND enters a country where there is a small church presence, we seek to partner with the local church."[26] In other words, missionary organizations, in word and often in practice, recognize the importance of linguistic and cultural competence for effective missionizing and therefore prioritize the development of local leadership to lead churches, seminaries, and Bible institutes, and of local missionaries to evangelize other locals. The assistance of international agencies is largely infrastructural in nature, driven by the goal of establishing, localizing, and nationalizing the institutions created as soon as possible in a step-by-step process to overcome the very cultural barriers that often impede proselytizing leading to conversion. This is a strategy that proved tremendously successful in Latin America. Initially, North Americans missionized there with little success. After World War II, the locuses of proselytizing shifted to locals evangelizing other locals. Especially in several countries, such as Guatemala and Brazil, the result of this shift has been dramatic. In these two countries, evangelicals are mounting a formidable challenge to the historic dominance of Catholicism in the region.[27]

The interconnectedness to the West and to global Christian communities that foreign missionary assistance offers Ukraine simultaneously serves to tie it to the former USSR. Within the former Soviet Union, other power differentials are operative that are conducive to making Ukraine a base for theological training for the entire former Soviet bloc. Nearly all Ukrainians have at least passive fluency in Russian, and about one-third of the 48 million Ukrainians are native Russian speakers. With a population that possesses imperial "cultural capital," Ukraine is an ideal location to train missionaries and clergy destined to serve in other parts of the former Soviet Union. Thus, as evangelical initiatives tie Ukraine into a global community of believers, those same initiatives also reinforce Ukraine's ties to its Soviet past.

A clear indicator of the depth of religious sentiment in a particular region, according to missionary organizations, is the number of communities needed to support a single full-time missionary. This reveals how robust local communities are and how committed their membership is to evangelization. In the case of Ukraine, in spite of a less than enviable economic situation, it takes 6.4 communities to support a single missionary. This contrasts sharply with levels of support in evidence in surrounding countries: 16.9 for Russia; 92 for Belarus; 24.5 for Hungary, 57.4 for Slovakia, and 62.6 for Romania. Only Poland, which requires 9.7 communities to support a missionary, at all approximates the level of commitment to outreach that is exhibited by Ukrainians.[28] Furthermore, almost 400 Ukrainians were serving abroad as full-time missionaries, and more than 500 more were working "cross-culturally" within Ukraine. None of the aforementioned countries came close to supporting that many missionaries. Although the population of Ukraine is three times *less* than that of Russia, as of 2001 there were 914 Ukrainian evangelical missionaries as compared with 396 from Russia. Nearly all the Ukrainian missionaries were serving in the Russian Federation.[29]

Clearly, religious communities are becoming an increasingly prominent domain, not only where frequent face-to-face contact among local members occurs but also where disparate people and places encounter one another, where occurrences abroad or in other regions are increasingly felt at home. During Baptist and Pentecostal services, for example, time is allotted for visitors from other congregations or those who have traveled to other congregations to individually stand and offer greetings. Anthony Giddens refers to this overall phenomenon of bringing people from disparate places together as the creation of "distanciated relations." He claims that this is a unique and relatively recent dynamic of social life and a key characteristic of globalization. He understands the reorganization of time and space as largely hinging on the stretching of social life to span great distances. He writes, "larger and larger numbers of people live in circumstances in which disembedded institutions, linking local practices with globalized social relations, organize major aspects of day-to-day life."[30] Religious communities are indeed laden with social relations that span great distances, be they evangelical, Orthodox, or of another denomination. They are increasingly the sites where the local and global interlock in a powerful way to shape the consciousness and everyday practices and identities of individual believers.

A Church for People of All Nations

The largest evangelical church in Europe today is located in Kyiv. In many ways, it illustrates a number of growing trends in global Christianity, and in particular how they are operative in Ukraine. Known as the Embassy of the Blessed Kingdom of God for All Nations, or the Embassy of God, to its nearly 20,000 members, the church was created in 1994. It calls itself a "Full Gospel" church and draws on a Pentecostal-charismatic tradition of expressive worship. As of 2004, the Embassy of God had opened thirty-eight daughter congregations. Eighteen of them are abroad, including four in the United States and two in Germany. As the activities of this church demonstrate, the interconnections among believers embedded in religious institutions are multidirectional and often are quite vibrant among regions that otherwise have had little previous historical interaction and little current political collaboration.

The Embassy of God was founded by a Nigerian, who came to Soviet Belarusia to study journalism in 1989. After the collapse of the USSR, Pastor Sunday Adelaja created the Word of Faith Church in Belarus and after encountering severe difficulties with the authorities there, relocated to Kyiv in 1993, where he began a Bible study group with seven others. The following year he founded a church, the Word of Faith, with 50 members. His goal was to convert 100 people a month and make them members of the church.[31] After one year, the church had more than 1,000 members. In 2002, the name of the church was changed to its current one as its membership continued to soar. In 2004, the Embassy of God purchased a large parcel of land in downtown Kyiv with plans to build a Ukrainian Spiritual Cultural Center, which will seat 50,000 people.

It is not just the enormous size, the rapid growth, and the leadership of this church that are distinctive. The vibrant evangelical communities taking root in Ukraine are remaking the historic patterns of missionary dynamics and integrating Ukraine and Ukrainians in the world in a different, albeit meaningful way. When a Nigerian opens a church in Ukraine that sends Ukrainian believers to the United States, Germany, and elsewhere to save the unsaved and church the unchurched, it is no longer a case of core exerting influence on the periphery. Rather, the interconnections and the cultural flow of ideas, objects, and people are also significant among non-Western regions and from the so-called Third World to the West. With cultural and linguistic fluency, the colonized missionizes the colonizer, as hundreds of Ukrainians have been doing in Russia for more than a decade now. The Embassy of God is a highly innovative example of a religious community going global, and yet its heart and roots are in Ukraine. Using this particular church as a lens, I now consider why so many Ukrainians are choosing to embrace evangelicalism at this particular historic juncture.

One of the more interesting aspects of this church is the dual way it negotiates nationality. The word "embassy" in the name of the church has obvious political and state connotations and is meant to suggest that all believers are ambassadors of God. The symbol of the Embassy of God is a globe with Africa, where the church founder is from, positioned in the center. The globe has a golden crown and cross on top. Just below the crown is a light emanating from Ukraine and shining throughout Europe and the

Middle East. There is nothing particularly Nigerian or even African about the services the Embassy of God offers, although the doctrine espoused by its leader draws on trends in theology that are well developed there, such as an emphasis on faith healing, civic involvement, and the evangelization of Muslims.[32]

Having a foreigner at the helm, and a man of color yet, does indeed signal that this community is particularly open to all newcomers and a likely destination for visiting foreign preachers. Among the Embassy of God's daughter congregations is an English-language church run by the pastor's wife. About 200 people—Africans, foreigners living in Kyiv, and Ukrainians striving to improve their English-language skills—gather every Sunday morning in a rented meeting room at an Intourist Hotel.

The main church is actually a rented sports arena, the only location capable of accommodating the crowds Pastor Adelaja draws. The sports hall is converted into a church by adding a sweeping stage and preaching platform up front, which is flanked on all sides by dozens of state flags. When the music and movement begins, parishioners come to the front, and with swaying flags in hand, create a colorful, animated effect. The Ukrainian flag is *always* the first flag chosen. After the Ukrainian flag, usually the American, Israeli, or German flag comes next, followed by the Russian flag and an assortment of others. Usually within minutes, the large area to each side of the preaching platform and the wide side aisles are filled with national flags swirling in the arms of enthusiastic worshipers. In this way, national differences and state borders are recognized and celebrated even as they are as they are subsumed under a higher religious authority, as it is recognized by followers from around the world gathered in the Embassy of God.

Prosperity Theology

The Embassy of God's most famous member is Leonid Chernovet'skyi of the Verkhovna Rada. He was the first Parlamentarian to lend his very vocal support to Pastor Adelaja when the State Committee of Religious Affairs was trying to have him deported. Other Parlamentarians, including former Ukrainian president Leonid Kravchuk and former prime minister Yevhen Zviahil'skyi, also signed the petitions to the Ministry of Internal Affairs to protest the government's efforts to revoke Adelaja's residency permit. Chernovet'skyi explains how and why he converted:[33]

I was around 46 when I came to the Word of Faith Church and now I'm 53. Before then I searched for God for many years, went to Orthodox churches, prayed to different icons while I was imagining God, lit candles. But, to speak honestly, I never had the feeling of communicating with God. I wanted to hear the Word of God, but no one there said anything about this in any of those churches. . . .

My actual turning to God is connected with my political ambitions, when in 1995 or 1996, I already don't remember exactly, in a really exhausting campaign, I tried to become a deputy of the Supreme Soviet. It wasn't working because, according to the election law of the time, at least 51 percent of the population had to vote. But in the Darnitsa district, where one of the largest radioelectronic factories in all of Ukraine shut down, no one wanted to vote. Twice I tried to do it with different [public relations] campaigns to get people to vote but they didn't believe in anything. They only spoke to me about sausage and other daily problems and they weren't at all interested in politics. And, I have to say, I was very far from thinking about how to protect people. That's why, through one of my former partners, I met Pastor Sunday who, in the presence of a huge number of people, prayed for me. I stipulated that my joining the church was dependent on a large number of people who would campaign for me—and I was really afraid of this because I didn't trust churches. And a miracle! Around one thousand of my future voters prayed for me and I saw in their eyes the fire of faith and happiness.

Unashamed of the raw exchange of membership-for-votes-deal he has made and admits to here, Chernovet'skyi joins a large legion of politicians the world over who have long recognized that religion is politics by other means. Churches offer a highly efficient platform from which to spread a political message, especially when it is endorsed by the moral authority of clergy, and build a popular base of support. Chernovet'skyi was one of the first politicians in Ukraine, however, to openly ally himself in partnership with a nontraditional Protestant denomination.

Continuing to stress the instrumental value of conversion and church membership, Chernovet'skyi describes the many other "surprising events" that occurred in his life after he came to God. Although the "devil had attacked our family with terrible problems," he claims his newfound faith provided the strength, patience, and hope necessary to overcome adversity. The "terrible problems" he opaquely refers to are rumored to be his children's drug use while they were at boarding school in Switzerland.

Perhaps most important of all, Chernovet'skyi credits God with "saving him from a moral fall." As a highly successful politician, businessman, and co-owner with his wife of one of Ukraine's largest banks, he is an icon of the "health and wealth" Gospel message of prosperity theology advocated by the Embassy of God. Older, more traditional Pentecostal churches in Ukraine stress a doctrine of "holiness," antimaterialism, and withdrawal from the world—and certainly from politics. As a result, those churches appeal primarily to the poor and disenfranchised. Newer ones, such as Embassy of God, in sharp contrast, prefer to situate themselves squarely in the "world." They have recast the meaning of wealth and material pleasures. Rather than an antagonistic view of money as a corrupting force, they see personal wealth and success as evidence of a blessing from God bestowed upon those that lead a truly Christian life. This doctrine stresses the importance of a "morally controlled materialism" as it encourages entrepreneurial and political engagement.

Chernovet'skyi explains how his conversion has contributed to a new sense of morality and how this influences his politics and the legislation he proposes:

In my opinion, the basis for the current crisis in Ukraine is the destruction of the spiritual core of the nation, the destruction of the markers of morality and justice in society. As a politician and believer, I am deeply convinced that the choice of a democratic government and the choice of a market-based economy are directly connected with Christian ideology, which is conducive to simple people living comfortably and politicians acting morally. Not long ago I began to think seriously about creating a new political party for Ukraine—a Christian liberal party based on Christian values, the principles of economic liberalism and Western European democracy.[34] The ideas and programmatic goals of this party will support ever more people with moral values, independent of whatever faith they practice. . . . I am certain that God wants all people to be free and materially provided for—but the most important thing is moral provision. I would build on this model: God wants to see all people morally prosperous, and then they will be materially prosperous.

In this way, Chernovet'skyi's initiatives blend a religious basis for morality with economic goals and political reform—all in the name of fulfilling God's plan for Ukraine. Chernovet'skyi is a magnetic illustration of the potential harvest prosperity theology may yield. By advocating such an ideologically infused theology, he neatly equates his staggering wealth with moral purity. He found God, began to live a moral life as an observant Christian, and from that pivotal moment all blessings have flowed. He, and this theology in general, offers little guidance, solace, or explanation to other "good Christians" who live a moral life and yet are denied material comfort and financial stability. Specifically as concerns Ukraine, he offers little in the way of guidance as to how a believer should navigate the harsh and corrupt world of money, where each business interest often adheres to its own moral order of right and wrong over anyone else's and certainly over the law.[35] Attempting to do business in Kuchma's Ukraine inevitably presented moral quandaries involving lying, cheating, and other behaviors that are supposedly not becoming of believers. Prosperity theology suggests that if each believer resists corruption and deceit and goes against the current by adhering to a biblically based morality, the believer will be rewarded in this life with wealth and in the next with salvation. Judging by the cheering crowds at the Embassy of God, these guidelines for coping with the complexities of political and economic life are welcome and understood as viable prescriptions for reform.

Morality and Materialism

Peter Berger asserted in his landmark study *The Sacred Canopy* that religion simultaneously commands a "world-maintaining" and "world-shaking" power.[36] It is this multiplex "double function" of religion for individuals, for social groups, and even for the political order that I would like to focus on in this last section. This double function, I believe, holds the key to the broad reemergence of religion in postsocialist societies across socioeconomic groups and is yet another key to explaining the appeal of evangelicalism. The duality of religious experience gives religion its unique power: It can be effective on the individual and communal levels by creating unique moods and motivations and on the national and global levels as it engages the dynamics of political economy with clear ramifications for perceptions of political legitimacy.

Chernovet'skyi is a living fulfillment of the ideals of prosperity theology. For the overwhelming majority of converts, however, Marx and Engels' oft repeated citation is more applicable: "Religious distress is at the same time the expression of real distress and the protest against real distress."[37] In a Marxian vein, religion does, of course, provide a source of comfort, an otherworldly explanation for suffering, and promises of distant redemption which diverts attention from altering the source of one's suffering in the here and now. Evangelical communities have proven themselves particularly adept at flourishing amid poverty, deprivation, and social instability.[38] Arguably, they help believers accommodate these deplorable conditions, rather than strive to change them. Many Ukrainians are still reeling from ongoing social and political change, during which many lost their social status and profession. The majority of converts to evangelicalism the world over are poor. Many converts, especially in Latin America and Africa, are migrants like Svetlana and welcoming of time-intensive involvement in communities delivering ecstatic experience and moral prescriptions for behavior amid a relatively egalitarian, communal ethos. Yet this is only a beginning explanation for the appeal of the variety of evangelical faiths that have growing numbers of adherents in Ukraine.[39]

Religious communities function as social support networks, offering votes to some, and companionship, information, and needed goods and services to others.[40] This explains in part the powerful gender component of religious participation.[41] Those who have become disenfranchised are able to trade in forms of social and political exclusion for membership in inclusive communities. The mission statement of the Embassy of God claims that it is committed to the "salvation and restoration of the individual" through faith healing and the rehabilitation of individual moral agency by realigning the disjuncture between what "is" and "what ought to be" in an individual believer's life. In a break with evangelical tradition in Soviet Ukraine, this church connects the sources of individual problems to greater social problems to the extent that it stresses the believer's moral obligation to be civically engaged in resolving political and social issues. In this way, religion responds to perceived identity threats, marginalization, and poverty, with community and allegiance building at the local level that increasingly has repercussions politically and economically.

Religious organizations share a renunciation of things worldly, and especially of the worldly desires of consumption. Members retain a sharp distinction between the moral recalcitrance of the outside world and the redeemed enclave of the believing community. Evangelical churches retain the suspicion of great wealth due to the temptations it poses and condemn excesses of all kinds, particularly sexual promiscuity and the hedonism of consumer capitalism. In other words, they offer a transition from economic disenfranchisement to divine empowerment, a release from ascribed categories to a transformative mode leading to healing and eventual salvation.

Yet religious communities are themselves vehicles for displaying inequalities, and their very survival dependents on the ability and willingness
of their members to tithe 10 percent of their income. Believers, such as
Chernovet'skyi, who are in a position to financially sustain the community
and its activities, of course, gain status and respect, which may or may not
elude them in the wider society. Sascha Goluboff's study of a Moscow synagogue is a particularly poignant illustration of these tensions.[42] She documents how the synagogue's life changed when significant class divisions
emerged among its members after 1991 that overlapped with ethnic differences, conflating the two sources of tension.

Many studies have noted the sharp differences between the poor and elite
in terms of religious affiliation, interpretation of religious doctrine, and
community activities. The popular churches in Latin America, for example,
tend to downplay consumption and celebrate discipline, responsibility, and
trust.[43] David Martin has written that the reaction to American goods ad-
vertised on television has been to equate them with "the evils of moral
chaos, family break-up, and consumer hedonism."[44] The insatiable desire
conjured up by the postmodern marketplace is feared, condemned, and redirected to salvation in the afterlife. Religious communities that serve the
poor confront frustrated consumer desires by reaffirming the righteousness
of the "spiritual war" against materialism and corruption—yet the desire to
possess is in evidence with the books, calendars, tapes, and other trinkets
for sale at nearly every service.

Overall, Martin, much like Chernovet'skyi, argues that churches create
a "free space" and a "cultural logic" that has strong, albeit latent, potential for democratization that awaits political conditions that will allow it
to emerge. Martin writes, "The framework of moral controls set by the
strict rules of the believing congregation and the need to render individual accounts to God and to the brethren together enable the believer to internalize a self-control which can survive the buffeting of the corrupt
world in which he or she has to earn a living, often outside corporate structures altogether."[45]

Indeed, most evangelical churches offer members alternative structural
supports to help earn a living and advance career ambitions that draw on
biblical principles. Some individual prayer groups are organized according to profession; that is, a group of musicians, computer programmers,
journalists, and the like meet weekly to study the Bible, discuss career-
and business-related problems, and provide each other with opportunities
to strengthen one's networks, an essential resource in entrepreneurial life.

The Embassy of God has also organized the Christian Business Leadership Fellowship, designed to advance "Christian principles" as a basis for doing business, over the "*po poniatiiam*" or "by understanding," meaning not by the criminal-based legal code for conducting business. In other words, religious belief and affiliation at the Embassy of God play a role in articulating boundaries of the acceptable and unacceptable, honorable and dishonorable, and this boundary work potentially softens the challenges of doing business in Ukraine. It also establishes alternative means for evaluating self-worth independent of material success and social hierarchies, which becomes especially important in the event of failure.

Deacons, lay preachers, and volunteer leaders play a key role in running evangelical churches. The emphasis on local lay leadership not only offers a source of direction and self-worth for members but also makes for highly active and engaged congregants. An active membership, in turn, maximizes the number and types of activities a church can offer, reinforcing the fundamental allure and benefit of membership in the first place.[46] The Embassy of God further distinguishes itself by giving formidable and highly visible leadership positions to women. Two powerful women preachers are the deputies to the senior pastor, Sunday Adelaja, and each runs their own congregations with memberships in the thousands. Given the patriarchy that is palpable in the greater Ukrainian society and permeates so many religious institutions, the prominence of numerous women leaders is another key component explaining the phenomenal success of this particular church and evangelicalism more generally.

Conclusion

The role of organized religion as a legitimator of the status quo has deep historical roots in this region of the world. Yet the religious pluralism that has been institutionalized in Ukraine has led to a flourishing of religious activity, and it has allowed religious communities, in all their guises, to offer competing visions of a desired moral order. The churches play a key role in articulating the type of commitments one should have to others and what the reciprocal obligations and expectations should be between a state and its citizenry, thereby laying the foundation for a remake of the social contract. Although evangelicals are usually accused of "political quietism," within Ukraine they have been vocal participants in this public dialogue of morality and polity.

Religious institutions in Ukraine today play a role in shaping political alignments and institutional structures, forging transnational connections and reinfusing political action with religious symbolism. As the symbolic boundaries between religion, politics, and morality fluctuate during this transformative period, religion holds sway over believers—and politicians—in that it offers a repertoire of values and practices from which to foster collective action to realize a political worldview.

Sharp economic differences remain not only within formerly socialist societies but also between the societies that experienced socialism and those that did not. Yet those differences remain largely misunderstood and are readily used to further structure the inequality between the "new" and "old" Europe. Evangelicalism provides an institutional base from which believers can detach themselves from nations mired in economic distress and political turmoil and enter larger, supranational religious communities.[47] In this way, in spite of the nationalist revival throughout the region, the nation-state is not necessarily the primary or even logical unit of social and political analysis when studying change in the former USSR. The salience of residence in a fixed territory is eroding as an attribute of identity, and by extension the connection between a culture being rooted in a particular place is also weakening. Religious knowledge, as a form of cultural knowledge, is free floating. Tied to doctrine, it is independent of a particular place or specific institution, and as a result it can be easily introduced into new contexts and new cultural environments. This basic dynamic holds whether one speaks of a religious organization from Littleton, Colorado, establishing a base in Ukraine or a Ukrainian church establishing a base in Sacramento.

The changes in the political power of organized religion, which took root before the collapse of the Soviet regime and has only continued to grow, challenge our previous assumptions about the nature of secularization in the former Soviet Union and our understandings of the ideological battles that were fought there. The imposed secularism in the former Soviet Union has proven incomparably less tenacious than the voluntary secularism of Western Europe. Religion is unlikely to recede as a force shaping the dynamics operative in this transformative period and as a factor influencing identity politics. Rather, as this profile of burgeoning evangelical communities shows, especially given the absence of respected legal codes, religion will continue to operate at multiple levels, forging intersections between the local and transnational and the political and cultural. Since the collapse of the Soviet Union, religious institutions, and evangelical communities in particular, have proven themselves to be among the most adept at shaping individual and group identities in Ukraine by creating unique motivations for change and allegiances to those who promise to actualize those aspirations.

Notes

1. The 1989 Lautenberg Amendment made it possible for practicing evangelicals who could prove a history of past discrimination to emigrate to the United States with refugee status, much as Soviet Jews had. Through the Family Reunification Act, many more evangelicals were able to join their families in the United States. Today there are an estimated 500,000 Soviet evangelical believers living in the United States.

2. Patrick Johnstone and Jason Mandryk, eds., *Operation World* (Waynesboro, Ga.: Paternoster Publishing, 2001), 644–45.

3. Nicholas Mitrokin, "Aspects of the Religious Situation in Ukraine," *Religion, State and Society* 29, no. 3 (2001): 173–96.

4. John Marone, "Protestants in Power," *Ukrainian Observer* 57, no. 6 (2005): 24–27; the citation here is on 24.

5. For an analysis of how legal reform in Ukraine has shaped the religious landscape differently than it has in Russia, see Catherine Wanner, "Missionaries of Faith and Culture: Evangelical Encounters in Ukraine," *Slavic Review* 63, no. 4 (Winter 2004): 732–55. The adoption of certain laws either allows or thwarts the creation of new social institutions, which in turn foster cultural differences in values and practices between Ukrainians and Russians. In other words, legal reform is the catalyst that has triggered sweeping change in multiple domains.

6. The official ideological position of the Soviet state, of course, was to promote an atheistic worldview. For depictions of early Soviet policies and actions to eradicate religious belief and practice, see R. Beermann, "The Baptists and Soviet Society," *Soviet Studies* 20, no. 1 (1968): 67–80; the citation here is on 68–69; Daniel Peris, *Storming the Heavens: The Soviet League of the Militant Godless* (Ithaca, N.Y.: Cornell University Press, 1998); William B. Husband, *"Godless Communists": Atheism and Society in Soviet Russia, 1917–32* (DeKalb: Northern Illinois University Press, 2000); and Daniel E. Powell, *Antireligious Propaganda in the Soviet Union: A Study of Mass Persuasion* (Cambridge, Mass.: MIT Press, 1975).

7. Evangelical communities were hardly the only religious communities targeted for repression because of the links and connections they were capable of forging. Serhii Plokhy has rightfully, in my opinion, made the argument that the fierce repression of the Ukrainian Greek Catholic church and its eventual outlawing in 1946 were primarily motivated by Stalin's concerns that the Vatican might exert influence over post–World War II reconstruction in Eastern European countries with significant Catholic minorities. The accusations of Nazi collaboration, of assisting the underground nationalist movement, and of overall sympathy to the nationalist project were, of course, additional factors that did not earn the church favor in the Kremlin. See Serhii Plokhy, "In the Shadow of Yalta: International Politics and the Soviet Liquidation of the Ukrainian Greek Catholic Church," in *Religion and Nation in Modern Ukraine,* ed. Frank Sysyn and Serhii Plokhy (Edmonton: Canadian Institute of Ukrainian Studies, 2003), 59.

8. The obligation among believers to evangelize motivated Ukrainian immigrants who left the Russian Empire for the United States to return to their homeland to prose-

lytize in the 1920s. These returning immigrants were some of the most successful preachers responsible for garnering new converts. Similarly, in the 1990s, religiously persecuted Ukrainian refugees who settled in the United States returned to their homeland to play a critical role in missionary efforts to spread Pentecostalism and Baptism in Ukraine today.

9. For a discussion of the impact of the millennium celebrations on the growth of religious participation, see Michael Bourdeaux, "Glasnost and the Gospel: The Emergence of Religious Pluralism," in *The Politics of Religion in Russia and the New States of Eurasia,* ed. Michael Bourdeaux (Armonk, N.Y.: M. E. Sharpe, 1995). The anniversary was initially commemorated in Moscow, followed by "regional" commemorations in Kyiv. To Ukrainians, this underlined the colonial nature of the relationship of Ukrainians, their history, religion, and language, to Russians and served to advance the national and religious resurgence that was under way. See Catherine Wanner, *Burden of Dreams: History and Identity in Post-Soviet Ukraine* (University Park: Pennsylvania State University Press, 1998), 140–69.

10. Wanner, "Missionaries of Faith and Culture," 736.

11. For a full analysis of the political ramifications of the divergent statuses the Orthodox Church has come to assume in Ukraine and Russia, see M. Tataryn, "Russia and Ukraine: Two Models of Religious Liberty and Two Models for Orthodoxy," *Religion, State and Society* 29, no. 3 (September 2001): 155–72.

12. José Casanova speculates that Ukraine is likely to go the way of America; that is to say, the religious landscape will become highly pluralistic, and this pluralism will generate competition among denominations for adherents, which will yield active communities, and ultimately high levels of religious participation. José Casanova, "Between Nation and Civil Society: Ethnolinguistics and Religious Pluralism in Independent Ukraine," in *Democratic Civility: The History and Cross-Cultural Possibility of a Modern Political Ideal,* ed. Robert W. Hefner (New Brunswick, N.J.: Transaction Publishers, 1998).

13. Both surveys were posted by the Religious Information Service of Ukraine at http://www.risu.org.ua, and can also be found at http://www.socis.kiev.ua.

14. Alexei Krindatch, "Religion in Post-Soviet Ukraine as a Factor in Regional, Ethno-Cultural and Political Diversity," *Religion, State and Society* 31, no. 1 (2003): 37–73; the citation here is on 37.

15. Lewis R. Rambo, *Understanding Religious Conversion* (New Haven, Conn.: Yale University Press, 1993).

16. For an analysis of what conversion narratives reveal about attitudes toward the Soviet past, see Catherine Wanner, "Advocating New Moralities: Conversion to Evangelicalism in Ukraine," *Religion, State and Society* 31, no. 3 (September 2003): 273–87. Conversion allows an individual to break with values and practices that are no longer considered appropriate as well as to reject the cultural values held by the greater society. In this way, conversion narratives can be read as another prescription for revolutionary change in post-Soviet society. A similar analysis for the conversion narratives of Russian Baptists in the 1920s is offered by Heather J. Coleman, *Russian Baptists and Spiritual Revolution, 1905–1929* (Bloomington: Indiana University Press, 2005).

17. Ruth Marshall-Fratani, "Mediating the Global and Local in Nigerian Pentecostalism," in *Between Babel and Pentecost: Transnational Pentecostalism in Africa and Latin America,* ed. André Corten and Ruth Marshall-Fratani (Bloomington: Indiana University Press, 2001), 86.

18. Terence O. Ranger, "Religion, Development and African Christian Identity," in *Religion, Development and African Identity,* ed. K. Holst Petersen (Uppsala: Scandinavian Institute for African Studies, 1987), 31.

19. Malcolm Ruel analyzes how the understanding of belief has evolved over time among Christians. He argues that the use of the term "believer," as I am indicating Ukrainians employ it, is indeed the earliest meaning of Christian belief. This understanding of belief and of being a believer, he argues, has evolved in a highly individualistic way to where "belief as doctrine has *almost* become the honest opinion of anyone who declares himself to be a Christian." Malcolm Ruel, "Christians as Believers," in *Anthropology of Religion,* ed. Michael Lambek (Malden, Mass.: Blackwell, 2002), 109.

20. Walter Sawatsky, *Soviet Evangelicals since World War II* (Scottdale, Pa.: Herald Press, 1981); William C. Fletcher, *Soviet Charismatics: The Pentecostals in the USSR* (New York: Peter Lang, 1985); S. N. Savinskii, *Istoriia Evangel'skikh Khristian–Baptistov Ukrainy, Rossii, Belorussii (1917–1967)* (Saint Petersburg: Biblia dlia Vsekh, 2001).

21. P. A. Datsko, *Tserkov' Preobrazhenie: Kratkii Istoricheskii Ocherk* (Kharkiv: Evangel'skoe Sluzhenie, 2002).

22. Birgit Meyer, "Christianity in Africa: From African Independent to Pentecostal-Charismatic Churches," *Annual Review of Anthropology* 33 (2004): 447–74; the citation is here is on 468.

23. David Martin, *Pentecostalism: The World Their Parish* (Oxford: Blackwell, 2002).

24. Roger Lancaster, *Thanks to God and the Revolution: Popular Religion and Class Consciousness in the New Nicaragua* (New York: Columbia University Press, 1988); David Martin, *Tongues of Fire: The Explosion of Protestantism in Latin America* (Oxford: Basil Blackwell, 1990); John Burdick, *Looking for God in Brazil: The Progressive Catholic Church in Urban Brazil's Religious Arena* (Berkeley: University of California Press, 1993).

25. Johnstone and Mandryk, *Operation World,* 750.

26. Quoted from the SEND Web site at http://www.send.org/ukraine/lives.htm.

27. Karla Powe, ed., *Charismatic Christianity as Global Culture* (Columbia: University of South Carolina Press, 1994).

28. Johnson and Mandryk, *Operation World,* 750.

29. Ibid.

30. Anthony Giddens, *The Consequences of Modernity* (Stanford, Calif.: Stanford University Press, 1990).

31. In time, he also incurred the wrath of Ukrainian authorities. Efforts to deport him from Ukraine, however, were definitively blocked by thirty-one members of the Ukrainian Supreme Soviet, who intervened on his behalf. They petitioned the State Committee for Religious Affairs in protest of the way Adelaja was treated by the Ministry of Interior Affairs. His growing and increasingly vocal following also took to the streets in protest. In 2004, Pastor Sunday Adelaja was granted permanent resident status.

32. Meyer, "Christianity in Africa"; André Corten and Ruth Marshall-Fratani, eds., *Between Babel and Pentecost: Transnational Pentecostalism in Africa and Latin America* (Bloomington: Indiana University Press, 2001).

33. All quotations from L. M. Chernovet'skyi are cited from an interview published in the Embassy of God's own full-color magazine. This particular issue doubled as a ten-year anniversary commemorative publication. Vadim Chernets, "L. M. Chernovetsky: Blagodaria Bogy, . . ." *Posol,* no. 1 (2004): 6–7.

34. Chernovet'skyi did indeed create such a party, and in the spectacular elections of 2004 he was its candidate for president. In the runoff elections between Viktor

Yushchenko and Viktor Yanukovych, Chernovet'skyi threw his support—and by extension that of his voters and a large part of the membership of the Embassy of God—to Viktor Yushchenko, the eventual winner in the Orange Revolution election.

35. For an analysis of how conflicting moralities, when compounded by a weak legal system, complicate economic transactions, see Catherine Wanner, "Money, Morality, and New Forms of Exchange in Post-Soviet Ukraine," *Ethnos* 71, no. 4 (2006): 515–37.

36. Peter Berger, *The Sacred Canopy* (New York: Doubleday, 1967).

37. Karl Marx and Friedrich Engels, *On Religion* (New York: Schocken Books, 1964), 42.

38. R. Andrew Chesnut, *Born Again in Brazil: The Pentecostal Boom and the Pathogens of Poverty* (New Brunswick, N.J.: Rutgers University Press, 1997); Martin, *Pentecostalism;* Martin, *Tongues of Fire;* Anna Peterson, Manuel Vasquez, and Philip Williams, eds., *Christianity, Social Change, and Globalization in the Americas* (New Brunswick, N.J.: Rutgers University Press, 2001).

39. Elsewhere, I have written of the broader sociopolitical (Wanner, "Missionaries of Faith and Culture") and psychocultural (Wanner, "Advocating New Moralities") factors that have prompted increased religious participation just before and after the fall of the Soviet Union.

40. The independent Ukrainian state has thus far refused to cast its lot with one of the three competing Orthodox churches in Ukraine today. The resulting pluralism, and the growing success of denominations that engage in outreach by offering social services, is pushing the Orthodox Church to do the same.

41. This double function of religion is especially visible concerning gender dynamics. If religious institutions are so patriarchal, why are their memberships so overwhelmingly female? Many authors have argued that religious institutions simultaneously preach "submission" and empower women by creating a space for self-actualization and leadership positions that elude them elsewhere.

42. Sascha Goluboff, *Jewish Russians: Upheavals in a Moscow Synagogue* (Philadelphia: University of Pennsylvania Press, 2003).

43. Martin, *Pentecostalism;* Burdick, *Looking for God in Brazil;* Lancaster, *Thanks to God and the Revolution;* Peterson, Vasquez, and Williams, *Christianity, Social Change, and Globalization.*

44. Martin, *Pentecostalism,* 35.

45. Martin, *Pentecostalism,* 80.

46. Roger Finke and Rodney Stark, *Acts of Faith: Explaining the Human Side of Religion* (Berkeley: University of California Press, 2000).

47. Gediminas Lankauskas's (2002) study of evangelical communities in Lithuania illustrates this point with his focus on the choice of beverage at wedding ceremonies: traditional Lithuanian spirits, with their concurrent rituals, or the Western-imported Coca-Cola of teetotaling evangelicals. In spite of widespread nationalist sentiment, grounded in part in Catholicism, many young people are choosing to embrace a religious ideology, such as evangelicalism, that promotes values and practices seen as "modern" which are predicated on a rejection of the traditional.

9

Soviet Nationalities Policy and Assimilation

Dmitry Gorenburg

In recent years, students of Soviet and post-Soviet nationalism have developed a consensus that Soviet nationalities policy unwittingly strengthened ethnic identity among minority populations in the Soviet Union. This view overly simplifies the actual thrust of Soviet nationalities policy in the post-Stalin period. The Soviet government pursued a dual course toward its minorities, enacting assimilationist policies at the same time as it maintained and even strengthened the ethnic institutions that were established in the 1920s. The slogan "national in form, but socialist in content" symbolizes this dual approach. The national "forms" of ethnic republics, titular control of regional governments, and separate political and academic institutions for these republics all acted to reify and maintain ethnic identities.

At the same time, the Soviet government enacted policies that favored the use of Russian. Officially, Russian was labeled the language of interethnic communication, but speaking Russian became an essential element of participating in Soviet society. Because language use is generally a zero-sum decision, promoting one central language inevitably led to a decline in use of competing national languages. And because language, in turn, is a key component of ethnic identity, the shift in language use away from national languages led to an increase in ethnic assimilation of members of non-Russian minorities.

Although the institutionalization of ethnicity did reinforce ethnic identity among certain segments of the minority population, the assimilation policy had a remarkable effect in a relatively short period of time. The ethnic institutions established by Soviet policies strengthened the ethnic identity of many members of groups that had official homelands within the Soviet Union by privileging ethnic identity attributes over those of class, location, or religion.[1] The effects of these policies were variable, depending on location and type of homeland region. These institutions operated locally, within the homelands, so that members of minority groups who lived elsewhere in the Soviet Union were particularly vulnerable to assimilation.

The number and strength of ethnic institutions within the Soviet ethnic republics also varied depending on the republic's status in the Soviet Union's four-tiered ethnofederal hierarchy.[2] The inhabitants of union republics, which had the most extensive networks of ethnic institutions, were on average less vulnerable to assimilation than the inhabitants of autonomous republics, provinces, or districts, which were permitted to have progressively fewer ethnic institutions. Finally, the extent to which ethnic institutions prevented the assimilation of particular individuals depended on the extent to which these institutions played a significant role in people's lives. For example, native language education and native language print media were more prevalent in rural than in urban areas. Theaters and academic institutes catered to city dwellers, but they were used primarily by those with a connection to the countryside.[3]

Other than variation in the extent of ethnic institutions, the factors that influenced the extent of variation in the level of assimilation included the number of Russians in the region and their settlement patterns, the extent to which Russian was known and used among that nationality before the nationwide shift in favor of Russian language education and use, and the extent of linguistic differences between Russian and the national language of the republic.

This chapter begins with a critical discussion of the consensus that has recently emerged in the scholarly community on the impact of Soviet assimilation policies and goes on to develop an alternative perspective that links Soviet nationality policies and trends in the assimilation of minorities.

In the following two sections, I develop a model of the assimilation process and present data that demonstrate the extent of assimilation in the Soviet Union by 1989 and describe the trends in assimilation from 1959 to 1989. I conclude by discussing the political consequences of assimilation during the late Soviet period.

Identity Promotion, Assimilation, or Both?

The views of Western scholars on Soviet nationality policies have changed over time. In the 1970s and 1980s, most scholars believed that the Soviet government was engaged in an extensive and deliberate program of Russification that was aimed at destroying minority languages and cultures.[4] This viewpoint was consistent with the dominant paradigm of the Cold War, which portrayed the Soviet Union as first and foremost a repressive state that aimed to eradicate all differences among its citizens in its efforts to create a "new Soviet man."

With the end of the Cold War and the concurrent explosion of nationalism in the Soviet Union and throughout the former communist world, this dominant view was replaced by its opposite. The current dominant perspective among Western scholars is that not just the policies but even the very structure of the Soviet state strengthened ethnic identity among Soviet minorities. In this section, I show that this new conventional wisdom has gone too far in neglecting the extent to which the Soviet state was successful in assimilating part of its non-Russian population even as it strengthened the ethnic identities among other non-Russian Soviet citizens. I argue that scholars must recognize the tension between identity promotion and assimilation that was an inherent part of Soviet nationality policy throughout the Soviet Union's existence.

First, however, let me set out the argument of those who see the Soviet state as predominantly engaged in the promotion of ethnic identity. In the words of Ronald Suny, the Kremlin "foster[ed] the development in many republics of native cultures, encouraging education in the local languages, and promoting, through a peculiar form of affirmative action, cadres from the dominant nationality."[5] This argument was initially formulated by Suny and by Yuri Slezkine, and it is perhaps must succinctly articulated by Rogers Brubaker.[6] Suny argues that the policies of nativization strengthened the national identities of the dominant ethnic groups in the Soviet ethnic republics.[7] This outcome was not the intended consequence of Soviet policy, but it did result in making national identity the most important form of identity for Soviet citizens.

This situation came about because Bolshevik efforts to create a federation that was national in form but socialist in content resulted in the institutionalization of ethnicity through ethnic republics and passport identification. This institutionalization, it is argued, strengthened ethnic identification among minorities by forcing a single and unchangeable ethnic identity upon each person and by establishing incentives for individuals to identify as members of a minority ethnic group within their titular republic. The personal ethnic identity was enshrined in the internal passport, which listed nationality. Personal nationality was noted in almost all official transactions, was transmitted by descent, and was formally unchangeable across generations except for the offspring of interethnic marriage, who could choose either of the parents' nationalities when they received their passports at the age of sixteen years.[8] The incentives provided by ethnic republics included preferential treatment in education and employment, native control of most ethnic republics, and policies designed to promote native cultures.[9]

These scholars argue that as a result of this combination of personal and territorial institutionalization of ethnicity, minority ethnic identities were strengthened throughout the Soviet Union. Brubaker notes that the Soviet state "established nationhood and nationality as the fundamental social categories."[10] Similarly, Suny argues that "identification with nationality was for most non-Russians a far more palpable touchstone than the eroded loyalty to social class."[11] This view that the Soviet Union fostered ethnic identification by institutionalizing ethnicity represents the new conventional wisdom among students of Soviet nationalities policy.

Scholars who follow this line of reasoning tend to underestimate the success of Soviet efforts to assimilate minorities. Brubaker, for example, argues, "The regime had no systematic policy of 'nation-destroying.' It might have abolished national republics and ethnoterritorial federalism; . . . it might have ruthlessly Russified the Soviet educational system. . . . It did none of the above."[12] Suny, while aware of the policies that "pulled non-Russians toward acculturation, even assimilation," argues that Soviet nativization policies on the whole strengthened minority ethnic identities.[13] Another recent study argues that minorities "experienced little linguistic Russification during the postwar period," despite presenting census tables that provide contradicting evidence.[14]

As I suggested above, the processes of linguistic assimilation, linguistic reidentification, and ethnic reidentification actually affected a large number of non-Russians in the Soviet Union. Why has the extent of these processes been neglected by recent scholarship? I argue that there are three reasons why the academic literature has underestimated the extent of assimilation. Most important, the emergence of strong nationalist movements throughout the Soviet Union in the late 1980s fostered the belief that if national identity among Soviet minorities was strong enough to generate demonstrations of hundreds of thousands of people in a few regions and tens of thousands of people in many others,[15] then it must have been relatively unaffected by the government's assimilation policies.

In addition, the relatively short period of time that the assimilation policy was in place meant that its effect was just starting to be felt when the Gorbachev regime's liberalization led to the end of Soviet Russification efforts. As I describe below, the Soviet government did not begin its wholesale Russification campaign until the late 1950s. Assimilation is a slow, multigenerational process, so that statistics on language and identity change were only starting to reflect the extent to which individuals who grew up in the new environment had switched their primary language of communication to Russian.

Finally, the construction of census questions on language and ethnicity resulted in the underestimation of linguistic Russification among Soviet minorities. The census language question asked respondents to state their native language rather than the language they used most frequently or were most comfortable speaking. In addition, this question immediately followed the census question on nationality. Both Russian and Western demographers believe that many respondents restated their nationality as their native language despite being far more fluent in Russian.[16]

For these reasons, the extent of assimilation in the Soviet Union has been understated in recent works. Yet demographers and political scientists writing in the 1970s and early 1980s, before the emergence of nationalist movements throughout the Soviet Union, detected the first signs of assimilation and published data documenting its progression and variation across ethnic groups.[17] In the Soviet Union, policies that promoted ethnic identity existed side by side with policies that encouraged assimilation. The interaction between these policies played a key role in creating the environment that led to the nationalist mobilization that undermined Gorbachev's reform program and led to the collapse of the Soviet Union. In the next section, I discuss the ideological tension that caused the Soviet government to pursue mutually contradictory policies toward its minorities.

Soviet Nationalities Policies and
Their Impact on Assimilation

Although the Soviet government's policies toward its ethnic minorities varied over time, there was always a tension between the goal of showing the world that the Soviet Union treated its ethnic minorities better than any other country in the world and the goal of hastening the future merging of nations into a single communist mass. This tension originated with Lenin's belief that minorities could only be brought to support socialism once they no longer felt oppressed by the Russian majority and were given the right to use their native language. Lenin summarized this position as follows:

> Having transformed capitalism into socialism, the proletariat will create an *opportunity* for the total elimination of national oppression; this opportunity will become a *reality* "only"—"only"!—after a total democratization of all spheres, including the establishment of state borders according to the "sympathies" of the population, and including complete freedom of secession. This, in turn, will lead *in practice* to a total abolition of all national tensions and all national distrust, to an accelerated drawing together (*sblizhenie*) and merger (*sliianie*) of nations which will result in the withering away of the state.[18]

This contradiction drove Soviet nationality policy for the next seventy years. The establishment of ethnofederalism, indigenization, and native language education were paired with efforts to ensure the gradual drawing together of nations for the purpose of their eventual merger. Though changes in Soviet nationality policy over time resulted from minor shifts toward one or the other of these poles, at no time during the Soviet period was one of these poles completely removed from the ideology of the Soviet government.

Soviet nationalities policy from 1917 through the 1930s has been brilliantly described by Terry Martin.[19] This was the golden age of nationalities, when the ethnoterritorial federalism and its concomitant ethnic incentive structure that came to characterize the Soviet Union were established. During this period, the Soviet government established ethnic territorial units from the republic to the village levels, promoted members of ethnic minorities to leadership positions in these units, developed literary languages for ethnic minorities, and organized native language education in those languages. During this period, Russification was condemned as Great Power chauvinism and rejected by the state. The governing ideology stated that members of ethnic minorities could only develop socialism when they reached equal status with the majority Russians. As Slezkine noted, this period represented "the most extravagant celebration of ethnic diversity that any state had ever financed."[20]

By the mid-1930s, this policy was in retreat. Ethnic autonomy was curtailed, and most village- and district-level ethnic units were abolished. Though large ethnic regions were retained, minority political and cultural leaders were accused of nationalism and repressed during the Great Terror of 1936–38. Native language education and the promotion of minority cultures were largely, but not entirely, eliminated in areas outside the remaining ethnic homelands. The government also launched some initial efforts at increasing Russian language knowledge among the minority population.[21]

The trend toward Russification continued during and after World War II. Stalin's toast to the Russian people at the conclusion of the war endorsed the Russian majority's position as primus inter pares among the various Soviet nationalities.[22] The official histories of minority groups were revised to take this relationship into account; many historians were condemned for "bourgeois nationalism" as a consequence. The entire populations of several ethnic groups, including the Volga Germans, Crimean Tatars, Chechens, and many others, were exiled en masse to Central Asia and Siberia.

Stalin's death allowed some of these groups to return to their homelands, but it did not change the overall trend toward Russification, which continued until the mid-1980s. The most significant step in this regard was the school reform of 1958. Khrushchev introduced the concept of Russian as the language of interethnic communication throughout the Soviet Union. By the mid-1960s, government policies and statements made it clear to the population that in the Soviet Union, socialism spoke Russian. As part of the campaign to ensure that all Soviet citizens were fluent in the Russian language, ethnic regions were instructed to introduce Russian-language instruction in first grade and expand it to all schools under their control. Most critically, the Communist Party adopted a resolution that gave parents the right to choose the language of instruction for their children. In many regions, parents were then strongly encouraged to send their children to Russian-language schools. Local authorities organized meetings where parents spoke out in favor of Russian-language instruction for their children. Previously, members of minority ethnic groups were required to send their children to national schools, where the minority language was usually the language of instruction.[23]

The new rules were portrayed as democratic because they allowed parents to choose their children's language of instruction. And, in truth, many minority parents, especially in urban areas within the autonomous republics and regions of the Russian Soviet Federated Socialist Republic (RSFSR), did prefer to send their children to Russian language schools because of the perception that fluency in Russian was the key to a successful career. As enrollments in schools with native language education declined, many ethnic regions dropped native language education entirely in favor of Russian-language education with the native language taught as a subject.[24]

By the 1980s, the majority of non-Russian children throughout the RSFSR and in several other union republics were being educated in the Russian language, even in their homeland regions.[25] The assimilationist policies introduced by Khrushchev were retained for thirty years and were pursued simultaneously with policies that encouraged the perception that ethnic regions were designed to foster the development of minority ethnic groups. As I show in the following sections, this dual policy both encouraged assimilation and promoted the growth of nationalist attitudes in these regions, leading to the formation of nationalist movements after Gorbachev's liberalization program allowed the formation of nongovernmental organizations.

The Assimilation Process

Assimilation is a concept with multiple meanings. In the aggregate sense, it refers to a change of ethnic identity, usually from a minority or subordinate group to a majority or dominant group, resulting in the "blending into one of formerly distinguishable sociocultural groups."[26] For an individual, assimilation implies a shift of identity from one ethnic group to another. In the literature, linguistic assimilation refers to the change of language from one's traditional national language to that of a different ethnic group. Linguistic assimilation does not always indicate a change of ethnic identity.[27] It is also unclear what criteria should be used to determine whether an individual has changed his or her language. Changes in language use may not be accompanied by changes in people's perception of which language they consider native. As I will show below, language use and language identity were often at variance in the Soviet context. To avoid confusion, I refer to a change of language use as "linguistic assimilation" and to a change of language identity as "linguistic reidentification."

Linguistic assimilation and reidentification in the Soviet Union were promoted by a combination of two factors, urbanization and the reduction of native language education. Because Russians who lived in the Soviet Union's ethnic regions were usually concentrated in urban areas, individuals who moved to cities were more exposed to Russian language and culture than their peers who stayed behind in the (usually monoethnic) villages. At the same time, urbanization brought a loosening of ties to traditional values and customs. City dwellers were also more likely to learn Russian because of their career aspirations. Most of the more prestigious careers in urban areas required not just knowledge of Russian but also fluency in it. City dwellers were also less likely than rural non-Russians to have access to native language education. In the wake of the 1958 school reform, urban native language schools were largely eliminated in the autonomous republics of the RSFSR, eastern and southern Ukraine, and Belarus. They were also reduced in number in Moldova and Kazakhstan. As a result, Brian Silver finds that even as early as 1959, 18.2 percent of urbanized non-Russians considered Russian to be their native language, versus only 3.5 percent of the rural non-Russians.[28]

Native language education was also almost entirely absent for non-Russians living outside their homeland region. Though minority students attending Russian-language schools in their homelands were usually given the opportunity to study their native language as a subject, this type of instruction did not fully offset the lack of native language education. In many regions, particularly outside the union republics, such courses were considered electives or were additional to the regular school program. In such cases, children did not take these courses seriously, particularly if they rarely used their ethnic group's language outside school. Even where such courses were required, they were not sufficient to counteract the overwhelmingly Russian-speaking environment found in almost all Soviet cities.[29] Members of Soviet ethnic groups who did not have the opportunity to attend schools that were taught in their native language were much more likely than those who attended such schools to switch to Russian as their primary language.[30]

The impact of both urbanization and native language education on linguistic assimilation and reidentification was connected to the relative prestige of Russian and the local language. In areas where urban elites primarily used Russian, members of the native group often sought to send their children to Russian-language schools to increase their likelihood of being accepted at a prestigious Russian-language university and thereafter finding a good job. In areas where urban elites spoke the minority language (the Baltic republics and the Caucasus) and where the labor markets were ethnically segregated (most of Central Asia), minority parents felt more secure in sending their children to national language schools.

Of course, ethnic identity does not change just because one adopts the dominant language. Many Russian-speaking members of ethnic minorities continued to identify themselves as members of the group in documents such as internal passports, but they did not see this category as playing an important role in their lives and shared few if any of the cultural character-istics of the group, a process known as acculturation.[31] For these people, the Russian language and the Soviet civic identity had replaced ethnicity as the most salient identity categories. These people were more likely to re-port Russian as their native language in census interviews and sociological surveys. Most important, such people were far more likely than other mem-bers of the ethnic group to marry outside their group. During the Soviet pe-riod, the children of such intermarriages generally identified themselves as Russian.[32] This two-generation assimilation process developed over sev-eral decades and had just begun to have a significant demographic impact in the 1980s.

The Extent of Assimilation

Assimilation in the Soviet Union can be measured in two ways. Linguistic reidentification occurs when individuals change their native language while retaining their ethnic identity. This type of assimilation may also be called Russification. A second form of assimilation occurs when individuals change both their native language and ethnic identity. In this section, I use Soviet census data to present some initial findings on the extent of both lin-guistic Russification and complete ethnic assimilation for Soviet minority ethnic groups.

Claiming Russian as One's Native Language

The most straightforward method of measuring Russification is to look at the number of people who declare Russian to be their native language while retaining their ethnic identity. The total number of non-Russians claiming Russian as their native language rose from 10.2 million (10.8 percent) in 1959 to 18.7 million (13.3 percent) in 1989. Kaiser interprets these num-bers to mean that "considering the privileged status . . . [of the Russian lan-guage], surprisingly little Russification took place during [this period]."[33]

Yet if we consider the low likelihood that individuals will change their native language during the course of their lifetime, as well as the high rates of assimilation among many ethnic groups, then we can see that linguistic reidentification among non-Russian minorities in the late Soviet period was actually quite rapid.

The percentage of members of each ethnic group that declared Russian as their native language is shown in table 9.1. The highest overall rates of Russification in 1989 were among several groups without an ethnic homeland, such as Jews, Greeks, Germans, and Koreans, as well as among Karelians and Mansi. Other highly Russified groups included peoples of the far north and the traditionally Russian Orthodox ethnic groups with autonomous republic homelands. Of the twenty-five least assimilated groups, twenty live predominantly in Central Asia or the Caucasus. The most Russified group from either of these regions (Ossetians) ranked thirty-fourth overall out of sixty-three groups. With the exception of Belarusians and Ukrainians, groups with their own union republics also had relatively low rates of Russification.

To measure the impact on Russification of changes in Soviet nationalities policy after the 1950s, we can look at the increase in the percentage of minority members claiming Russian as their native language from 1959 to 1989. Once again, we find that Central Asian and Caucasian ethnic groups had the smallest increase in Russification, as did Kalmyks, Tuvans, and the three Baltic groups. The highest rates of increase in Russification were found among ethnic groups that started with the highest rates—peoples of the far north and traditionally Russian Orthodox ethnic groups with autonomous republic homelands. Most of the groups without an ethnic homeland also had high increases in linguistic reidentification, although Gypsies and territorially concentrated and predominantly rural groups such as Romanians and Hungarians were exceptions. Among the union republic nationalities, Belarusians, Ukrainians, and Moldavans had relatively high increases in the rate of Russification.

Members of Soviet minorities were far more likely to become Russified if they lived in urban areas or outside their homeland. Looking at data from 1959, Silver found that these two factors have a multiplicative effect, so that minorities living in urban areas outside their homeland were particularly likely to become Russified.[34] Though overall rates of Russification increased substantially between 1959 and 1989, only a few groups showed much evidence of Russification in rural areas within their homeland (see table 9.2). Those with rates above 10 percent in 1989 included Karelians,

Table 9.1. Linguistic Russification by Ethnic Group, Entire Soviet Union, 1959–89

Group	1959	1970	1979	1989	Change, 1959–89
Jewish	76.4	78.2	83.3	83.6	7.2
Mansi	40.4	47.4	50.3	62	21.6
Finnish	35.7	42.5	50.3	54.6	18.9
Karelian	28.5	36.8	44.1	51.8	23.3
Greek	46.1	49.5	56.8	51.4	5.3
German	24.2	32.7	42.6	50.8	26.6
Korean	20.5	31.3	44.4	50.1	29.6
Koriak	8.9	18.2	30.6	46.4	37.5
Khanty	22.3	30.5	31.8	38.8	16.5
Mordvin	21.8	22.1	27.4	32.7	10.9
Udmurt	10.7	17.2	23.4	30	19.3
Komi-Permiak	12.1	14.1	22.8	29.7	17.6
Komi	10.5	17.2	23.7	29.5	19
Bulgarian	18.2	24.4	29.1	28.8	10.6
Polish	14.7	20.7	26.2	28.6	13.9
Evenk	8.7	16.5	20.7	28.5	19.8
Belarussian	15.3	19	25.4	28.5	13.2
Chukchi	5.7	16.9	21.2	28.3	22.6
Khakass	13.9	16.3	19	23.6	9.7
Chuvash	9	13	18.1	23.3	14.3
Mari	4.6	8.6	13	18.8	14.2
Ukrainian	12.2	14.3	17.1	18.8	6.6
Nenets	5.5	9	14	18.1	12.6
Dolgan	n/a	9.9	9.8	15.9	6
Tatar	7	10.2	13.2	15.6	8.6
Altai	11.2	12.6	13.5	15.5	4.3
Buriat	5.1	7.3	9.8	13.6	8.5
Bashkir	2.6	4.5	7.1	11.2	8.6
Gypsy	23.5	16.7	14.9	10.8	-12.7
Gagauz	4	4.9	8.6	10.6	6.6
Armenian	8.3	7.6	8.4	7.6	-0.7
Moldovan	3.6	4.2	6	7.4	3.8
Kalmyk	7.2	5.9	5.9	7.3	0.1
Ossetian	4.9	5.4	6.6	7	2.1
Cherkess	6.7	5.4	5.9	6.3	-0.4
Sakha	2.4	3.7	4.6	6.1	3.7
Rumanian	2.4	3.6	4.8	5.6	3.2
Balkar	2.2	2.3	2.7	5.4	3.2
Adygei	3.2	3.4	4.2	5.1	1.9
Latvian	4.6	4.6	4.8	5	0.4
Abkhaz	3.1	3.1	4.1	4.9	1.8
Lezgin	3	3.7	4.7	4.8	1.8
Kurd	2.9	3.8	4.8	4.5	1.6
Estonian	4.7	4.4	4.5	4.4	-0.3
Uyghur	2.3	2.8	3.6	3.9	1.6
Hungarian	1.8	2	2.6	3.3	1.5

Table 9.1. Continued

Group	1959	1970	1979	1989	Change, 1959–89
Ingush	1.9	2.4	2.5	2.8	0.9
Karachai	1.5	1.6	2	2.7	1.2
Kabardin	1.9	1.8	2	2.6	0.7
Kazakh	1.2	1.6	2	2.2	1
Kumyk	1.4	1.2	1.5	2.1	0.7
Avar	0.8	1	1.3	1.9	1.1
Dargin	0.9	1.2	1.4	1.9	1
Lithuanian	1.2	1.5	1.7	1.8	0.6
Chechen	1	1.2	1.3	1.7	0.7
Azeri	1.2	1.3	1.8	1.7	0.5
Georgian	1.3	1.4	1.7	1.7	0.4
Tuvin	0.8	1.2	1.2	1.4	0.6
Karakalpak	0.3	0.4	0.5	1	0.7
Turkmen	0.6	0.8	1	1	0.4
Tajik	0.5	0.6	0.8	0.8	0.3
Uzbek	0.5	0.5	0.6	0.7	0.2
Kirgiz	0.3	0.3	0.5	0.6	0.3
Averages					
SSRs	4	4.4	5.5	5.9	1.9
ASSRs	5.7	7.5	9.6	12.1	6.4
AOs	7.3	7.9	8.9	10.6	3.3
Aokrug	14.8	20.6	25.2	33.5	18.7
Other	21	24.1	28.6	29.7	8.7

Note: SSR = Soviet socialist republic. ASSR = autonomous Soviet socialist republic. AO = autonomous oblast.
Source: Robert J. Kaiser, *The Geography of Nationalism in Russia and the USSR* (Princeton, N.J.: Princeton University Press, 1994), 266–68.

Komi, Udmurt, Khakass, and all groups with autonomous district-level homelands except the Dolgans. Groups with a greater than 10 percent change in Russification between 1959 and 1989 included Karelians, Koriak, Evenk, Chukchi, Khanty, and Mansi.[35] Rates of linguistic reidentification above 10 percent among urban homeland residents were found among all of the groups with high rates of rural Russification, plus Ukrainians, Belarusians, Moldovans, Buriats, Mari, Mordva, Chuvash, Sakha, Altai, and Dolgan. Rates of change above 10 percent were found among Komi, Karelians, Udmurt, Chuvash, Komi-Permiak, and several northern ethnic groups. However, close to half the groups had negative rates of change in urban Russification between 1959 and 1989, due to migration by native language speakers from rural to urban areas within the homeland.

Table 9.2. *Russian Native Language by Population Type, Entire Soviet Union, 1989 Census*

Type	Homeland Rural	Homeland Urban	Outside Rural	Outside Urban
Mansi	54	76	45	65
Khanty	38	59	24	53
Koryak	43	57	34	61
Karelian	35	56	41	67
Chukchi	25	52	22	50
Komi	11	42	42	56
Evenk	22	41	23	39
Udmurt	12	39	29	51
Dolgan	7	37	24	47
Komi-Permiak	11	36	46	53
Nenets	11	31	39	55
Chuvash	1	31	19	42
Belarusian	3	30	52	64
Khakass	12	26	46	49
Altai	9	26	33	46
Mari	5	23	16	37
Mordva	4	23	25	51
Ukrainian	2	19	50	57
Buriat	4	18	20	38
Sakha	2	15	36	32
Moldovan	1	11	11	36
Bashkir	1	10	10	27
Kalmyk	2	6	17	35
Tatar	1	5	9	25
Cherkess	0	5	11	29
Abkhaz	1	4	17	29
Latvian	1	3	43	56
Adygei	1	3	9	20
N. Karabakh[a]	0	3	n.a.	n.a.
N. Ossetian	1	3	7	22
Tuvin	0	3	13	14
Kazakh	1	3	4	9
Lezgin	0	2	2	12
Balkar	0	2	14	33
Kabardin	0	2	15	28
Karachai	0	2	7	18
Turkmen	0	2	1	13
Avar	0	2	3	18
Dargin	0	2	2	16
Estonian	0	2	42	61
Tajik	0	2	1	4
Kumyk	0	1	3	16
Uzbek	0	1	1	5
Kyrgyz	0	1	1	7
Azeri	0	1	3	16
Ingush	0	1	5	11

Table 9.2. Continued

Type	Homeland Rural	Homeland Urban	Outside Rural	Outside Urban
Karakalpak	0	1	2	13
Chechen	0	1	3	12
S. Ossetian[b]	0	0	n.a.	n.a.
Georgian	0	0	17	33
Lithuanian	0	0	23	38
Armenian	0	0	9	30
Averages				
SSR	1	5	18	31
ASSR	4	13	15	30
AO	3	9	21	33
Aokrug	26	49	32	53

Note: n.a. = not available. SSR = Soviet socialist republic. ASSR = autonomous Soviet socialist republic. AO = autonomous oblast.
[a]Armenians outside the homeland exclude those in Nagorno-Karabakh autonomous oblast and are listed under Armenia.
[b]Ossetians outside the homeland are listed under the entry for North Ossetia.
Source: Robert J. Kaiser, *The Geography of Nationalism in Russia and the USSR* (Princeton, N.J.: Princeton University Press, 1994), 276–80.

Among non-Russians living outside their homeland, Russification was far more common. Only four groups had less than 10 percent Russification rates among members living in urban areas outside their homeland. These included the Uzbek, Kazakh, Kirgiz, and Tajik groups, many of whose members lived in cities in other Central Asian republics, rather than in Russia. Rates for groups such as Ukrainians, Latvians, Estonians, Belarusians, and Mordva were higher than 50 percent. At the same time, few groups experienced significant changes in rates of urban linguistic reidentification outside their homeland during the 1959–89 period, because members of most groups living in such locations were already highly Russified by 1959. Only among Lithuanians, Bashkirs, Balkars, Tatars, and most autonomous district nationalities did the rate of linguistic reidentification increase by more than 10 percent during this period.

For non-Russians living in rural areas outside their homeland, linguistic reidentification rates were low for Central Asian and Caucasian ethnic groups, and high for all others. The only exceptions were Georgians, Kabardin, Balkar, Abkhaz, and Cherkess—Caucasian ethnic groups with linguistic reidentification rates of 10 to 16 percent in 1989, and Tatars, who had a rate of 8.5 percent. Rates of change were relatively low, averaging 5 to 7 percent for all groups except inhabitants of autonomous districts, who had rates averaging 14 percent.[36]

Although the overall proportion of non-Russians claiming Russian as their native language increased by only a few percent between 1959 and 1989, there were large increases in Russification among most ethnic groups living outside the Caucasus, Central Asia, and the Baltic republics. Though further analysis would be needed to determine the reasons for this difference, it seems likely that resistance to Russification is increased by a combination of factors such as linguistic distance, religious difference, and higher status of a particular ethnic group in the Soviet ethnic hierarchy.[37] A more nuanced view of the extent of linguistic assimilation and reidentification is provided in the next section by introducing the knowledge of Russian as a second language into the analysis.

Four Categories of Linguistic Assimilation

The extent of linguistic Russification may be estimated with measures developed by Silver. He describes four categories that distinguish the extent of linguistic assimilation. The assimilated are those who list Russian as their native language and do not list their ethnic group's native language as a second language. Assimilated bilinguals are people who list Russian as their native language and their ethnic group's native language as a second language. Unassimilated bilinguals are people who list their ethnic group's native language as their native language and list Russian as a second language. Finally, the parochial group includes individuals who list their ethnic group's native language as their native language and do not claim any knowledge of the Russian language.[38] In this section, I use these categories to examine the extent of Russian language knowledge within the RSFSR.

In table 9.3, I show the trends in these four categories for the republic nationalities of the RSFSR / Russian Federation from 1970 to 1994. For most ethnic groups, the overwhelming majority of the population fits in the unassimilated bilinguals category in all four censuses; these are the people who consider their ethnic group's language as their native language but also speak Russian. The only exception are the Karelians, most of whom are in either the fully assimilated or assimilated bilinguals categories by 1989. For several other groups, including the Khakass, Komi, Mordva, and Udmurt, more than 25 percent of the population is in these two categories by the end of the time period. Few people place themselves in the assimilated bilingual category, showing that most non-Russians who know their national lan-

Table 9.3. Silver Linguistic Assimilation Categories, 1970–94

Group	Category	1970	1979	1989	1994
Adygei	Parochial	28.9	19.3	13.2	10.3
	UB	68	76.9	82.2	85.6
	AB	1.1	1.1	1.1	0.7
	Assim	1.9	2.8	3.6	3.2
Altai	Parochial	32.8	18	19.6	15.7
	UB	55.1	69.2	65.6	73.4
	AB	2.7	2.2	1.9	0.9
	Assim	9.2	10.6	13	10.1
Avar	Parochial	58.6	35.7	32.8	20.1
	UB	40.1	62.8	65	77.3
	AB	0.1	0.1	0.1	0.2
	Assim	0.9	1	1.5	1.7
Balkar	Parochial	24.8	20	15.3	11.3
	UB	73.5	78.1	80.1	87
	AB	0.3	0.3	0.3	0.1
	Assim	1.2	1.7	4	1.5
Bashkir[a]	Parochial	43.2	29	17.3	14.7
	UB	52.9	64.9	72.6	75.1
	AB	1.3	0.7	1.8	1.3
	Assim	2.5	5.4	8.3	9.1
Buriat	Parochial	26	18.3	14.3	10.2
	UB	66.8	72.1	72.4	77.1
	AB	2.6	2.4	2.5	1.8
	Assim	4.5	7.2	10.9	11
Chechen[b]	Parochial	32.4	22.9	24.9	N/A
	UB	66.9	76.4	74	N/A
	AB	0.2	0.2	0.2	N/A
	Assim	0.5	0.6	1	N/A
Cherkess	Parochial	24.2	23.2	16	10.3
	UB	69.3	69.6	75.6	85.8
	AB	0.5	0.4	0.4	0.3
	Assim	4.2	4.2	4.9	3.5
Chuvash	Parochial	29.4	17.6	11.7	9.6
	UB	58.5	65.4	65.8	68.8
	AB	3.8	4.1	4.4	3.8
	Assim	8.2	13	17.9	17.6
Dargin	Parochial	56.5	34.9	30.3	17.2
	UB	42.2	63.8	67.8	80.5
	AB	0.1	0.1	0.1	0.2
	Assim	0.9	1.1	1.4	1.8
Ingush	Parochial	27.9	18.7	18	10.9
	UB	70.9	80	80.2	87.1
	AB	0.4	0.3	0.2	0.2
	Assim	0.9	1.1	1.4	1

(*continued*)

Table 9.3. Continued

Group	Category	1970	1979	1989	1994
Kabardin	Parochial	26.9	20.2	19.6	16.9
	UB	71.5	78.1	78	81.2
	AB	0.3	0.3	0.2	0.3
	Assim	1.1	1.5	2	1.7
Kalmyk	Parochial	11.5	8.4	6.2	2.4
	UB	83.2	86.2	86.9	92.8
	AB	1.1	0.7	0.9	0.5
	Assim	4.2	4.7	6	4.4
Karachai	Parochial	30.9	22.5	18.1	9.3
	UB	67.9	76	79.8	89.1
	AB	0.3	0.3	0.4	0.2
	Assim	0.7	1.3	1.8	1.4
Karelian	Parochial	3.9	4.4	2.4	1.4
	UB	59.9	52.2	46.2	41.4
	AB	14.6	12.6	13.5	12.4
	Assim	21.6	30.9	37.7	44.6
Khakass	Parochial	18.3	12.9	9.5	2.3
	UB	65.7	68.6	67.2	71.1
	AB	3.1	2.8	2.8	2.9
	Assim	12.7	15.7	20.3	23.8
Komi	Parochial	20	11.9	8.3	5.6
	UB	63.5	65	62.8	65.1
	AB	5.1	5.4	5.6	4.4
	Assim	11.4	17.7	23.4	25
Kumyk	Parochial	41.3	25.9	23.3	11.3
	UB	57.1	72.6	74.5	86.8
	AB	0.1	0.1	0.1	0.1
	Assim	0.9	1.2	1.7	1.6
Lak	Parochial	41.5	23.4	17.8	6.6
	UB	55.2	73.1	77.3	87.8
	AB	0.3	0.2	0.2	0.2
	Assim	2.4	2.7	3.7	4.6
Lezgin	Parochial	54.2	32.3	26.1	17.5
	UB	43.2	64	68	77.9
	AB	0.2	0.3	0.4	0.2
	Assim	2.2	2.9	4.2	3.8
Mari	Parochial	29.4	17.4	12.6	7.5
	UB	62.5	70.3	69.4	75.1
	AB	2.4	2.5	3.2	2.3
	Assim	3.8	9.6	14.7	14.9
Mordva	Parochial	12.7	7.3	4.8	2
	UB	67	67.3	64.3	57.7
	AB	7.5	7.2	8	7.9
	Assim	12.8	18.2	23	32.2

Table 9.3. Continued

Group	Category	1970	1979	1989	1994
Ossetian	Parochial	20.5	13.3	10.2	9.8
	UB	74.6	80.7	83	83.3
	AB	1.4	1.2	0.9	1
	Assim	3.4	4.6	5.5	5.5
Sakha	Parochial	54.7	30.5	29.1	28.6
	UB	41.7	65	65	67.7
	AB	1	1	1.3	0.7
	Assim	2.7	3.5	4.7	3
Tabasaran	Parochial	68.1	39.4	34.7	19.6
	UB	31.2	58.5	62.1	78.4
	AB	0	0.1	0.2	0.2
	Assim	0.6	1	2.3	1.7
Tatar	Parochial	28.4	19.5	13	9.6
	UB	62.1	68.6	72.6	75.9
	AB	3.7	3.4	3.5	2.7
	Assim	5.6	8.3	10.7	11.4
Tuvan	Parochial	60	39.5	39.5	35.1
	UB	38.8	59.3	59.1	63.4
	AB	0.3	0.1	0.2	0.2
	Assim	0.8	1.1	1.2	1.3
Udmurt	Parochial	19.9	12.5	8.6	7.3
	UB	63.6	65.2	62.2	65.3
	AB	4.9	4.6	5.3	4.3
	Assim	11.4	17.8	23.7	22.9

Note: UB = unassimilated bilingual, AB = assimilated bilingual, Assim = assimilated.
[a]Bashkirs who consider Tatar their native language are included with those who consider Bashkir their native language for the purposes of this table.
[b]The 1994 microcensus was not conducted in Chechnya.
Sources: Calculated from Russian and Soviet census publications.

guage declare it their native language during the census. Only a few groups have sizable percentages that speak only the national languages. These are primarily Caucasian groups such as the Avars and Chechens, as well as the Sakha and the Tuvans.

Turning to trends over time, the dynamic is similar for virtually all the groups. Between 1970 and 1979, we see a sharp shift from parochial to unassimilated bilingual, followed by a continuing gradual decline in the number of parochials through 1994. The percentage of each ethnic group in the unassimilated bilingual category is fairly stable from 1979 to 1989 and then increases in 1994, often partially at the expense of the assimilated category. The assimilated bilingual category remains relatively stable over time for most groups. After increasing gradually from 1970 to 1989, the percentage of the population in the assimilated category declines for most nationalities from 1989 to 1994, showing a return to the national language for at least a small percentage of the minority population in the post-Soviet period.

Although these data confirm our hypothesis that the number of non-Russians who considered Russian their native language was steadily increasing during the Soviet period, they also show that the vast majority of members of Soviet minority groups retained their national language as their native language as they learned Russian. However, the understanding of native language as an aspect of identity meant that many people listed their national language as their native language, even though Russian was their language of daily use or the language they learned first. In the next section, I examine the lack of correspondence between native language and language of use in Russia.

Native Language versus Language Use

The 1994 Russian microcensus shows the extent to which the census question on native language exaggerates the actual extent of language use.[39] Whereas 70 percent of non-Russian respondents declared their ethnic group's native language to be their native language, only 46 percent declared their ethnic group's native language to be the language they used at home. Even fewer respondents used their native language at work or at school. The difference between reporting of native language and language of use varied by nationality. Ethnic groups that have territorial homelands within the Russian Federation had the highest rates of retention for both native language and language of use, as well as the lowest difference between the two indicators. Ethnic groups that did not have a homeland in Russia (including the titular nationalities of the other former Soviet republics) tended to use the Russian language at home while often still declaring their ethnic group's language as their native language (see table 9.4). Kalmyks, Chukchi, Moldovans, Lithuanians, Georgians, and Uzbeks had particularly high differences (more than 40 percent) between these two rates.

The microcensus also shows that few members of minority groups in Russia use their native language at work or in school. Unfortunately, Goskomstat did not publish raw numbers for these two categories, so it is impossible to determine the overall percentage of non-Russians that use their native language at work or in school. The breakdown by ethnicity, however, shows quite clearly that these numbers are quite low. The native language is used in school by more than half of respondents only among

Table 9.4. Native Language and Language of Use, Russian Federation, 1994 Microcensus

Ethnic Group	Native Language	Language of Home Use	Language of School Use	Language of Work Use
Tuvan	99	96	70	70
Ingush	98	96	16	20
Kabardin	98	93	28	39
Karachai	98	91	1	16
Tabasaran	98	90	8	42
Balkar	98	90	7	19
Kumyk	98	90	4	26
Dargin	98	89	8	34
Avar	97	91	15	46
Sakha	96	91	75	77
Adygei	96	86	23	25
Lezgin	95	84	14	40
Rutul	95	82	1	19
Kalmyk	95	35	2	2
Lak	94	72	4	10
Ossetian	93	75	7	16
Altai	89	74	50	57
Nogai	88	75	3	16
Buriat	87	65	27	27
Roma	86	72	2	6
Tatar	86	61	14	21
Kazakh	86	50	1	5
Kirgiz	83	56	14	16
Mari	83	53	12	26
Cherkess	81	70	2	19
Turkmen	81	59	6	6
Azeri	80	47	1	3
Chuvash	78	51	24	31
Bashkir[a]	74	56	20	26
Udmurt	73	42	15	26
Khakass	73	42	1	9
Komi	71	40	24	25
Tajik	71	37	9	8
Komi-Permiak	70	45	21	30
Dolgan[a]	67	49	3	19
Armenian	65	35	1	3
Georgian	65	23	0	1
Veps	63	43	9	20
Nenets	61	26	0	6
Chukchi	61	5	0	2
Khanty	60	27	1	10
Mordva	60	24	2	10
Moldovan	58	13	1	1
Uzbek	56	16	2	1

(continued)

Table 9.4. Continued

Ethnic Group	Native Language	Language of Home Use	Language of School Use	Language of Work Use
Shor	54	22	2	3
Even[a]	53	20	7	19
Lithuanian	51	10	1	0
Nanai	47	11	2	3
Karelian	43	15	0	3
Latvian	40	6	2	1
Estonian	39	10	0	1
German	36	13	0	3
Greek	36	12	0	1
Ukrainian	33	5	0	1
Korean	32	11	1	1
Finn	30	7	1	2
Mansi	30	4	0	0
Belarus	29	2	0	0
Koriak	21	3	1	4
Evenk[a]	15	6	1	1
Jews	11	4	0	0

[a]High number assimilated to other language (Bashkir to Tatar, others most likely to Sakha).
Source: Goskomostat Rossii, *Raspredelenie Naseleniia Rossii po Vladeniiu Iazykami* (Moscow: Goskomstat Rossii, 1995).

three Siberian groups (Sakha, Tuvan, and Altai). Among forty-four of the sixty-one groups, fewer than 10 percent of respondents use their native language in school. Use of the native language at work is slightly more prevalent, with three Dagestani groups (Avar, Tabasaran, and Lezgin) scoring more than 40 percent in addition to the same three Siberian groups registering over 50 percent. Nevertheless, fewer than 10 percent of respondents use their native language at school among twenty-nine ethnic groups.

The microcensus data confirm the findings of Soviet researchers, who showed that large numbers of people who claimed the language of their ethnic group as their native language in census reports actually preferred to use Russian both at home and in public. Sociologists conducting surveys in the Soviet period made similar findings. Thus, whereas 69.5 percent of urban Udmurts declared Udmurt to be their native language in 1979, only 15 percent spoke Udmurt at home.[40] This was also true in major cities outside Russia. Even in Erevan, one of the most monoethnic non-Russian cities in the Soviet Union, 20 percent of Armenians surveyed in 1979–81 stated that they knew Russian better than Armenian, while 11 percent said they predominantly spoke Russian at home.[41] In Georgia, almost 10 percent of urban Georgians used Russian at home in the 1970s.[42] These data confirm that the extent of linguistic assimilation, as measured by the use of Russian in the home, is much greater than the extent of linguistic reidentification, as measured by the native language question in the census.

Ethnic Reidentification

So far, I have focused on linguistic assimilation and reidentification. Yet most Soviet ethnic groups also lost population to ethnic reidentification between censuses. The extent of this kind of reidentification in the Soviet Union was relatively limited, because rules prohibited individuals from changing the ethnic identity inscribed in their passports and required children to declare the nationality of their parents unless their parents were of different ethnic backgrounds.[43] The census, however, allowed individuals to state their ethnicity freely, without checking whether it matched the ethnicity listed in the respondent's passport.[44] Nevertheless, the official listing of ethnicity in one's passport had a socializing effect on respondents so that they became accustomed to identifying themselves according to their passport nationality.

The listing of ethnicity in numerous official documents limited individuals' freedom to change their ethnic identities and ensured that ethnic reidentification in the Soviet Union was a gradual process. However, though difficult, individual ethnic reidentification was not impossible. Surveys conducted in 1993 in urban areas in several former Soviet union and autonomous republics showed that ethnic identity and the ethnicity listed in one's passport did not match for 1.5 to 7.2 percent of total respondents, depending on the republic.[45] There are numerous reports of individuals having the ethnicity listed in their passports changed, most often to ease promotion within the Communist Party hierarchy. Such situations occurred fairly frequently in Bashkortostan, where many Tatars beginning a career in the Communist Party were encouraged to have their passports changed to list them as Bashkir and were assisted in doing so by party apparatchiks. Some people were able to change their passport ethnicity when having their passports replaced or after marrying a spouse of a different nationality.[46] Nevertheless, these individuals were the exception rather than the rule.

Despite the limits on reidentification described above, Anderson and Silver found extensive shifts to Russian ethnic identity between the 1959 and 1970 censuses at an aggregate level among several non-Russian ethnic groups. These shifts occurred primarily, but not exclusively, among the children of intermarried couples who chose Russian as their ethnic identity. The overall rate of ethnic identity change for non-Russians during this period was only about 1 percent.[47] Anderson and Silver show that the groups with the largest shift in identity are the "[autonomous Soviet socialist republic]–level nationalities with official homelands in the RSFSR and with an Orthodox Christian religious background."[48] These groups include the Karelians, who lost 17 percent of the population under the age of thirty-eight years; the Mordva, who lost 15 percent; and the Chuvash, Komi, Mari, and Udmurt, who each lost about 8 to 9 percent (table 9.5).

Finally, the Sakha shifted to Russian identity at a rate of about 6 percent, lower than the groups of Orthodox background but higher than those of Muslim background. Significant population losses among a few other groups, such as the Tuvans and the Bashkirs, were probably not the result of a shift to the Russian identity. Tuvans were most likely emigrating to neighboring Mongolia, while Bashkirs shifted to a Tatar identity at a rate of about 7 percent.[49] Most union-republic nationalities, as well as the Tatars and Buriats, lost population at a rate of 0 to 3 percent, with Armenians, Georgians, and Russians gaining from these shifts at a rate of 1 to 2 percent. The actual identity shift rate for Tatars was probably somewhat higher due to population gains of Bashkirs shifting to a Tatar identity. Despite the low rate of identity shift among Ukrainians and Belarusians, their large total population means that the bulk of the Russian group's population gain (357,000 out of 600,000) comes from these Slavic groups.[50]

Anderson and Silver's analysis shows that the highest rates of identity shift are found among the nine-to-eighteen-year-old age cohort. This is the age range during which individuals had to declare their nationality for official documents. Groups with high overall rates of identity shift had even higher rates among this age cohort, with Karelian youth reidentifying at a rate of 31 percent, Mordovians at 28 percent, and the other Orthodox autonomous Soviet socialist republic groups at between 18 and 24 percent. Bashkirs changed their identity at a rate of 24 percent, but again primarily to Tatar rather than Russian. Other groups of Muslim background shifted to Russian identity at rates of 7 to 13 percent, as did Sakha and Buriats. The lowest rates of identity shift were found among ethnic groups from western union republics, such as Estonia and Ukraine (table 9.5).

As Anderson and Silver point out, these rates of ethnic identity shift largely parallel the rates of linguistic Russification for each ethnic group.[51] This parallel lends support to my hypothesis that linguistic Russification was the first stage of a multigenerational process that culminated in the assimilation of some members of Soviet minority ethnic groups into the Russ-

Table 9.5. Ethnic Reidentification by Ethnic Group, Percent Reidentifying, Entire Soviet Union, 1959–70

Group	Age 9–18 Years	Age 0–38 Years
Belarusian	1.7	0
Moldavian	5.9	1.4
Ukrainian	1.5	1.1
Estonian	–0.1	2.4
Latvian	1.8	1.2
Lithuanian	0.7	–0.1
Armenian	6.2	–1.2
Georgian	4.3	–1.4
Azeri	13.4	1.1
Kazakh	2.9	–0.3
Kirgiz	11.6	3.0
Tajik	8.0	2.1
Turkmen	8.7	1.3
Uzbek	8.3	0.1
Buryat	8.8	3.5
Chuvash	19.7	8.2
Karelian	31.6	17.3
Komi	17.9	8.3
Mari	24.2	7.8
Mordva	28.6	15.2
Tuvan	3.9	5.1
Udmurt	23.2	9.2
Yakut	13.0	6.1
Bashkir	24.3	7.0
Tatar	7.0	2.0
Russians	–2.0	–0.8
Non-Russian Slavs	2.8	1.2
Non-Slavs	3.8	0.8
All Non-Russians	2.9	1.0

Source: Barbara A. Anderson and Brian D. Silver, "Estimating Russification of Ethnic Identity among Non-Russians in the USSR," *Demography* 20, no. 4 (1983): 461–89.

ian majority. The groups that were most susceptible to assimilation pressures were those that had their homelands within the RSFSR and shared the Russian Orthodox religion.

The Consequences of Assimilation

In this section, I sketch some hypotheses on the impact of Soviet assimilation policies on Soviet politics, and specifically on the rise of nationalist movements that led to the division of the country into its constituent republics. As assimilation accelerated in the second half of the twentieth century, it had two contradictory consequences for Soviet politics. On the one hand, the adoption of the Russian language and Soviet culture by an ever-increasing number of minority group members created the perception that the Soviet policy of ethnic integration (*sblizhenie*) was bearing fruit. On the other hand, as linguistic assimilation accelerated, minority cultural leaders began to fear that their ethnic groups' cultures were about to die out. Some of them took advantage of the political liberalization of the late 1980s to launch cultural revival movements that later became full-fledged nationalist organizations.

As the data presented in this chapter show, a large and increasing number of young people in most minority ethnic groups were declaring Russian as their native language. The 1994 microcensus shows that, at least within the Russian Federation, an even larger number were switching to Russian as their primary language to communication. For some ethnic groups, the switch to the Russian language was combined with a switch to Russian ethnic identity, primarily but not exclusively among the children of mixed marriages. By the early 1980s, both linguistic assimilation and linguistic reidentification in the Soviet Union were on an accelerating trajectory, and it seems quite likely that had Soviet nationality policies remained in place for another twenty to thirty years, many of the Soviet Union's minority ethnic groups would have become almost entirely Russophone, while a large number of their members would have reidentified as Russian. Given this context, it is not surprising that as late as the early 1980s, Soviet policymakers firmly believed that they had "solved the nationality problem" by integrating the minorities and the Russian majority into a single Soviet people (*Sovetskii narod*). This perception was proven false by the rapid growth in minority nationalism that started almost immediately after Mikhail Gorbachev announced his perestroika program.

The institutionalist theory that the rise of nationalist movements in the Soviet Union was the result of Soviet nationalities policy underplays the role of grievances in determining the character of the newly established movements' demands. Though the ability of minority nationalists to take advantage of the new political opening to launch powerful mass movements was the result of the Soviet state's provision of organizational resources to ethnic groups and regions,[52] many of the nationalist leaders got involved in the movements because they feared that their group's culture and language were being destroyed by Soviet nationalities policies—the same policies, ironically, that created conditions that allowed the nationalist movements to flourish and, in some cases, to successfully challenge the Soviet state.

These concerns were not always about linguistic assimilation directly. In the Baltic states, where linguistic assimilation was rare and reidentification almost unheard of, activists worried about the rapidly increasing population of Russian migrants, who did not learn the local languages and insisted that locals address them in Russian. Public space became dominated by the Russian language, creating the perception that titular languages were being relegated to the private sphere and had no future. For this reason, concerns about linguistic and cultural issues played a dominant role in the early stages of nationalist mobilization, even in areas where members of the titular groups overwhelmingly used their national languages among themselves.[53] The nationalists' top priority was to ensure the survival of their ethnic group through a revival of native language use in the public sphere, as well as an increase in the resources given to local cultural needs. The political demands came later, when activists in many Soviet regions decided that greater sovereignty, or even independence, would enable local authorities to begin a local cultural revival and local authorities realized that they could use the nationalist movements to gain more power for themselves vis-à-vis Moscow.

Conclusion

In this chapter, I have tried to show that Western scholars have tended to underestimate the success of the Soviet government's Russification policies, which were enacted in the late 1950s. I show that by the time these policies were repealed under Gorbachev, they had had a significant effect on the linguistic and ethnic identities of Soviet minorities, especially among younger cohorts who had grown up in a Russian linguistic environment and were much more likely than their elders to claim Russian as their native language or to change their ethnic identity to Russian.

Although these policies occasionally led to changes in individual ethnic labels, they were more likely to result in a shift in the salience of particular identity categories, from ethnicity and culture to language and belonging to the Soviet people. The success of these policies played an important role in the character of the nationalist movements that were formed during the perestroika movement. These movements' initial focus on cultural and language demands was not a cover for still impermissible political demands. Nationalist activists feared that their ethnic culture and language were on the way to extinction unless they launched a cultural revival and persuaded the government to restore native language education. Political demands came later, when these activists decided that sovereignty and/or independence for their ethnic region was the best way to ensure that a cultural revival did take place.[54]

Soviet nationalities policy continually oscillated between the two poles of Russification and ethnophilia. Recent Western scholarship has tended to focus on the Soviet promotion of ethnicity and dismiss the effectiveness of Soviet assimilation policies. In this chapter, I have shown that given the relatively short period of time these policies were in effect, they were quite successful in getting members of ethnic minority groups to assimilate to the Russian linguistic community and even to the Russian ethnic group. Had the Soviet Union retained such policies for another one to two generations, it is not unlikely that a large percentage of minority group members would have declared Russian as their native language or switched their ethnic identity to Russian. I have also sketched some preliminary hypotheses for the impact of these assimilationist policies on the explosion of nationalist sentiment in the Soviet Union in the mid-1980s. Future studies should further explore the interaction between the two sides of Soviet nationalities policy and its impact on late Soviet and post-Soviet politics.

Notes

1. For more on identity categories, and the attributes that make up these categories, see Arel's introduction to this volume.

2. Dmitry P. Gorenburg, *Minority Ethnic Mobilization in the Russian Federation* (New York: Cambridge University Press, 2003).

3. Gorenburg, *Minority Ethnic Mobilization.*

4. Robert Conquest, *The Last Empire: Nationality and the Soviet Future* (Stanford, Calif.: Hoover Institution Press, 1986).

5. Ronald Suny, *The Revenge of the Past* (Stanford, Calif.: Stanford University Press, 1993), 155.

6. Yuri Slezkine, "The USSR as a Communal Apartment, or How a Socialist State Promoted Ethnic Particularism," *Slavic Review* 53, no. 2 (1994): 413–52; Rogers Brubaker, *Nationalism Reframed: Nationhood and the National Question in the New Europe* (New York: Cambridge University Press, 1996).

7. Suny, *Revenge of the Past,* 166–56.

8. Brubaker, *Nationalism Reframed,* 31.

9. Brubaker, *Nationalism Reframed;* Slezkine, "USSR as a Communal Apartment"; Suny, *Revenge of the Past,* 155.

10. Brubaker, *Nationalism Reframed,* 23.

11. Suny, *Revenge of the Past,* 121.

12. Brubaker, *Nationalism Reframed,* 37.

13. Suny, *Revenge of the Past,* 125, 155.

14. Robert J. Kaiser, *The Geography of Nationalism in Russia and the USSR* (Princeton, N.J.: Princeton University Press, 1994), 295. Kaiser's tables clearly show extensive Russification among all non-Muslim minorities within the Russian Federation, as well as among urban Ukrainians, Belarusians, and Moldovans living in their home republic (pp. 276–78).

15. Mark Beissinger, *Nationalist Mobilization and the Collapse of the Soviet State: A Tidal Approach to the Study of Nationalism* (New York: Cambridge University Press, 2002).

16. Brian Silver, "The Ethnic and Language Dimensions in Russian and Soviet Censuses," in *Research Guide to the Russian and Soviet Censuses,* ed. Ralph Clem (Ithaca, N.Y.: Cornell University Press, 1986); M. N. Guboglo, *Sovremennye Etnoiazykovye Protsessy v SSSR* (Moscow: Nauka, 1984).

17. Brian Silver, "The Status of National Minority Languages in Soviet Education: An Assessment of Recent Changes," *Soviet Studies* 26, no. 1 (1974): 28–40; Isabelle T. Kreindler, ed., *Sociolinguistic Perspectives on Soviet National Languages: Their Past, Present, and Future* (New York: Mouton de Gruyter, 1985).

18. V. I. Lenin, "Itogi diskussii o samoopredelenii," in *Voprosy Natsionalnoi Politiki i Proletarskogo Internatsionalizma* by V. I. Lenin (Moscow: Politizdat, 1965 (orig. pub. 1916), cited in Slezkine, "USSR as a Communal Apartment," 419.

19. Terry D. Martin, *An Affirmative Action Empire: Nations and Nationalism in the Soviet Union, 1923–39* (Ithaca, N.Y.: Cornell University Press, 2001).

20. Slezkine, "USSR as a Communal Apartment," 414.

21. Peter A. Blitstein, "Stalin's Nations: Soviet Nationality Policy between Planning and Primordialism, 1936–1953," Ph.D. dissertation, University of California, Berkeley, 1999.

22. The text of the first part of the toast reads as follows. "I would like to raise a toast to the health of our Soviet people and, before all, the Russian people. I drink, before all, to the health of the Russian people, because in this war they earned general recognition as the leading force of the Soviet Union among all the nationalities of our country." Available at http://www.cyberussr.com/rus/s-toast-e.html.

23. Yaroslav Bilinsky, "Education of the Non-Russian Peoples in the USSR, 1917–1967, an Essay," *Slavic Review* 27, no. 3 (1968): 411–37.

24. Silver, "Status of National Minority Languages."

25. Rasma Karklins, *Ethnic Relations in the USSR: The Perspective from Below* (Boston: Unwyn Hyman, 1986). Native language education remained the norm in the Baltic republics, the Caucasus, and in Central Asia except for Kazakhstan. Russian language education was dominant throughout the autonomous republics, in eastern Ukraine, and in Belarus, as well as in urban areas in Ukraine, Moldova, Kyrgyzstan, and Kazakhstan.

26. Jorgen Elklit and Ole Tonsgaard, "Elements for a Structural Theory of Ethnic Segregation and Assimilation," *European Journal of Political Research* 12 (1984): 89–194.

27. Walker Connor, "Nation-Building or Nation-Destroying?" *World Politics* 24 (1972): 319–55.

28. Silver, "Status of National Minority Languages," 96.

29. The Baltics, the Caucasus, and parts of Central Asia present an exception to this tendency. But these were precisely the regions where children of the titular ethnic group were least likely to receive Russian-language schooling.

30. A. P. Galstian, "Nekotorye aspekty armiano-russkogo dvuiazychiia," *Sovetskaia Etnografiia* 6 (1987): 81–91.

31. Herbert Gans, "Symbolic Ethnicity: The Future of Ethnic Groups and Cultures in America," *Ethnic and Racial Studies* 2 (1979): 1–20.

32. Karklins, *Ethnic Relations in the USSR,* 37–39; A. Volkov, "Etnicheski sme-shannye sem'i v SSSR: Dinamika i sostav," *Vestnik Statistiki* 8 (1989): 8–24 (the citation here is on 13–15). This was true except for the Baltic, Central Asian, and Caucasian union republics, where children of marriages between members of the titular ethnic group and Russians chose the titular nationality more frequently. Children of marriages between members of the titular ethnic group and members of another non-Russian group generally adopted the titular ethnic identity. In future work, I plan to examine patterns of identity choice among children of mixed marriages in the Soviet Union and the interaction between these patterns and Soviet nationalities policy.

33. Kaiser, *Geography of Nationalism,* 262.

34. Silver, "Status of National Minority Languages," 101.

35. Kaiser, *Geography of Nationalism,* 276–77.

36. Kaiser, *Geography of Nationalism,* 279–81.

37. In "Elements for a Structural Theory," Elklit and Tonsgaard provide a theoretical justification for these factors' positive impact on resistance to assimilation.

38. Brian Silver, "Methods of Deriving Data on Bilingualism from the 1970 Soviet Census," *Soviet Studies* 27, no. 4 (1975): 574–97; the citation here is on 584.

39. The microcensus was conducted in February 1994 in all regions of the Russian Federation except Chechnya. Five percent of the population (7.3 million people) were interviewed. The data are considered representative for all but the smallest ethnic groups. For more information, see Goskomostat Rossii, *Raspredelenie Naseleniia Rossii po Vladeniiu Iazykami* (Moscow: Goskomstat Rossii, 1995).

40. L. M. Drobizheva, "Natsionalnoe samosoznanie: Baza formirovaniia i sotsialno-kulturnye stimuly razvitiia," *Sovetskaia Etnografiia* 5 (1985): 3–16; the citation here is on 7.

41. Galstian, "Nekotorye aspekty armiano-russkogo dvuiazychiia," 81–83.

42. Drobizheva, "Natsionalnoe samosoznanie," 7.

43. Victor Zaslavsky and Yuri Luryi, "The Passport System in the USSR and Changes in Soviet Society," *Soviet Union / Union Sovietique* 6, no. 2 (1979): 137–53.

44. Silver, "Ethnic and Language Dimensions."

45. The survey was conducted in Estonia, Latvia, Kazakhstan, Ukraine, Bashkortostan, and Tatarstan by David Laitin and Jerry Hough as part of the Language and Nationality in the Former Soviet Union Project. It was designed to represent the most ethnically mixed environments and is not necessarily representative for the entire republic. The correlations between self-identification and passport nationality were 94.5 percent in Bashkortostan, 98.5 percent in Tatarstan, 92.8 percent in Ukraine, 96.4 percent in Kazakhstan, 95.7 percent in Estonia, and 95.3 percent in Latvia. For more information on the survey and its results, see David Laitin, *Identity in Formation* (Ithaca, N.Y.: Cornell University Press, 1998), for the former union republics; and see Gorenburg, *Minority Ethnic Mobilization,* for Bashkortostan and Tatarstan.

46. Karklins, *Ethnic Relations in the USSR,* 34.

47. All rates listed in this section are the means of a range of about 2.5 percent. The actual number depends on the cohort survival assumption used. For more detail, see Barbara A. Anderson and Brian D. Silver, "Estimating Russification of Ethnic Identity among Non-Russians in the USSR," *Demography* 20, no. 4 (1983): 461–89.

48. Anderson and Silver, "Estimating Russification," 475. Anderson and Silver's analysis did not include ethnic groups without homelands or with homelands below the autonomous Soviet socialist republic level. It seems likely that these groups assimilated at a rate equal to or higher than the Karelians.

49. Anderson and Silver, "Estimating Russification," 476.

50. Anderson and Silver, "Estimating Russification," 481.

51. Ibid.

52. Gorenburg, *Minority Ethnic Mobilization.*

53. I am indebted to Dominique Arel for this point.

54. In Dmitry P. Gorenburg, "Regional Separatism in Russia: Ethnic Mobilization or Power Grab?" *Europe-Asia Studies* 51, no. 2 (1999): 245–74, I develop the argument that leaders of republics within the Russian Federation systematically pursued cultural revival policies even when such policies alienated segments of their electorate.

10

The Influence of Tatar Language Revival on the Development of Divergent Referential Worlds

Helen M. Faller

On the basis of fifteen months' anthropological field research with Tatarstan children and adults conducted from 1997 to 2001 mostly in Kazan, the capital of Tatarstan, this chapter addresses the question of what the social effects of a political movement for sovereignty have been on the people living there. It demonstrates that reintroducing the Tatar language into what Kazanians classify as public domains—one of the results of Tatarstan's sovereignty movement—has altered the boundaries of the discursive worlds people there inhabit. Though Russian president Vladimir Putin has rendered Tatarstan sovereignty politically unviable since coming to office in 2000, follow-up interviews I conducted as recently as August 2004 confirm that the movement's social effects persist.

In Tatarstan, people whose primary language of identification is Tatar are increasingly coming to perceive the world differently from those who identify with the Russian language. I demonstrate the existence of this difference in four different spheres of social organization. First, I describe the cultural norms for speaking Tatar, as opposed to speaking Russian, in Kazan.

Second, I illustrate how these conventions came to be contested in late 1990s Kazan. Third, I reveal how early 1990s newspaper discourses were bounded by linguistic conventions in Tatarstan letters to the editor. And fourth, I show the divergence in worldviews in connection to the political opinions held by Tatar speakers vis-à-vis Russian monoglots concerning Chechnya and Chechens.

The divergence in worldviews among Tatarstan people based upon linguistic affiliation can be seen as a shift in identities caused by sweeping political changes. These changes have caused identities among people in Tatarstan vis-à-vis the state to shake out into three loose clusterings: monoglot Russian-speaking ethnic Russians with affiliations to the Russian state and its seat in Moscow; bilingual ethnic Tatars possessing varying feelings of loyalty toward the Russian state, but for whom Kazan has political and cultural saliency; and russophone ethnic Tatars whose allegiance tends toward Russia but is nevertheless in flux due to their lack of fit with pro-scribed Soviet-period views regarding the relationship between language and nation. Thus, though my study focuses upon the microprocesses of linguistic interactions, those interactions both reflect and influence large-scale political actions.

Tatarstan Sovereignty

Tatarstan's government declared sovereignty in 1990 before the Soviet Union collapsed. Since then, Tatar nation builders have been attempting to make sovereignty a reality by trying to establish the political authority Tatarstan would require to realize their aims for building a society more equitable than the one in which they attained adulthood. The Tatarstan sovereignty movement has encouraged the revival of local national cultures through the promotion of national languages, especially the Tatar language, and religious activity. Pointing to high rates of church attendance in the United States, which they consider an equitable and free society, Tatar nation builders assert that increasing religiosity will help to make for a more moral society in Tatarstan. Two effects of increasing linguistic and religious activity among the Tatarstan people have been to encourage both a shift in the ways people in Tatarstan conceive of the worlds they inhabit and a multiplication of the republic's publics.

The primary mechanism through which these transformations have been effected is the divergence of the domains in which Kazan's inhabitants speak Tatarstan's two government languages, Tatar and Russian. Specifically, an elevation of the status of the domains in which Tatar is spoken, as well as an increase in the number of those domains, has caused the discursive worlds occupied by bilinguals in Russian and Tatar to become different from those occupied by people who are monolingual in Russian.[1] This is not because language somehow iconically indexes a particular culture, or world, in my parlance. Rather, the linguistic conventions for speaking particular languages encourage certain kinds of cultural practices and conventional ways of thinking about the world.[2] These include conventions for discussing certain kinds of topics and expressing certain kinds of opinions. Moreover, repeated practice allows room for the development of more particularized practices and conventions. That is, part of the emergent quality of changes in Tatar ethnic identity is that the longer and more frequently Tatars speak Tatar, the more they generate a shared Tatar world, inaudible to monoglot Russian speakers.

Soviet Nationalities

Until the mid-1990s (former) Soviet citizens had to choose a single official nationality upon attaining the age of sixteen years. The state inscribed people's nationality in their internal passports, along with their name and date of birth, and Soviet people were required to produce these passports at every bureaucratic encounter. Thus, for example, every time a Soviet citizen purchased a train ticket or checked a book out of a library, he or she had to produce his or her passport, the particulars of which were duly noted down, and thereby both demonstrate and be reminded of his or her nationality. The resulting habitus was one in which state bureaucratic institutions made people highly aware of nationality as a pervasive social category.[3] In theory, adolescents chose the nationality of one of their biological parents. In practice, young people in Russia sometimes chose to inscribe themselves as "Russian," even when neither of their parents was a member of that nationality.

Following upon the presumption that every individual belongs to a single nationality is one asserting that members of a nationality possess as their native language the standardized version of the language attributed to that nationality. This latter presumption results in an ideology of personhood whereby individuals are perceived most saliently in terms of their membership in the collective of a nationality and their official national culture must occur in the nationality's official language. On the ground, people recognize that nationality is not a person's only salient attribute and likewise that everyone straddles certain kinds of boundaries between nationalities.

Despite this, however, following in Soviet footsteps, the government of Tatarstan treats the republic's nationalities as if they were self-contained, nonoverlapping units whose members' native languages are their national languages. Furthermore, in the former Soviet Union, people tend to cluster the attributes considered to define a nationality, so that when they speak about identity groups, they shift between indexes like nationality category, national language, and ascribed national religion without marking a change in footing.[4] One result of this tendency to cluster indexes is that speaking Tatar has become associated not only with Tatar culture, but also with Muslim religious identity and Muslim worldviews.

The Sociolinguistic Field

One of the problems with treating Russia's inhabitants as if they belonged to self-contained units in the form of nationalities is that there is a fundamental asymmetry of knowledge between people who are monolingual in Russian (hereafter, "Russian speakers" or "Russophones") and people who are bilingual in Russian and another language.[5] To illustrate, Tatar speakers living in Kazan are all functionally bilingual in Russian. Thus, they have access to things occurring in the Russian language, whether or not they turn their attention to it, whereas people who are monoglot Russian speakers, regardless of their nationality, do not have access to the growing spheres of Tatar-language activity occurring in Tatarstan.

Most Tatarstan people who do not speak Tatar have some passive knowledge of the language and use a few words of Tatar vocabulary.[6] Furthermore, Tatarstan's monoglot Russian speakers have relatives or coworkers or acquaintances who are Tatar speakers. Certainly, some aspects of Tatar culture can be adequately translated into Russian, and not all cultural information is conveyed linguistically. Nevertheless, a lack of linguistic knowledge can and does create barriers to cultural understanding. Moreover, linguistic conventions create discursive boundaries between speech communities and hence between the discursive worlds members of these communities inhabit.

Although Kazan has been a dominantly Russian-speaking city since the end of World War II, in 2001 Tatar speakers reported that speaking Tatar previously had only been acceptable in Kazan domains tagged as rural, like the city's bazaars and its Agricultural Institute. After 1945, speaking Tatar was increasingly considered to be "barbaric" and doing so publicly limited one's access to career advancement. Consequently, Tatars living in Kazan more often than not attempted to "forget their Tatar" and to refrain from speaking it in front of their children.

By the beginning of perestroika in 1986, Kazan reportedly had become almost completely Russophone; the only people who are said to have been speaking Tatar in public domains were women past retirement age for whom not being assimilated could no longer negatively affect their lives or career trajectory.[7] Subsequently, more and more people have begun speaking Tatar in public domains (on public transportation, on the streets, and in businesses).[8] The following example illustrates how some Tatar speakers living in Kazan first experienced being differently positioned from the city's monoglot Russophones.

Hayat *apa,*[9] who tells this story, migrated from a Tatarstan village to Kazan in the early 1970s to take her university entrance exams. Her account is typical of reports from other Tatar speakers likewise involved in Tatarstan's nation-building efforts:[10]

I graduated from a Tatar school; I grew up in a Tatar village. When I came to Kazan and wanted to get into university, they said to me, "Take your [oral] history exam in Russian." I had never studied history in Russian. It's as if *you* were told that you had to take an ethnography exam in Tatar. I didn't speak Russian until I was 17.[11] It was completely unnecessary in my village. I had good teachers, but they didn't teach us how to speak Russian.

"You don't know Russian, then go to the Agriculture Institute." O-ho, Tatars were so afraid of higher education institutes! A lot of them went to the Agriculture Institute because you could speak Tatar there. [Somehow, Hayat got admitted to Kazan University, but she added] the first years were so difficult. They required that you know Russian, but they didn't teach it. So, I moved in with a Russian grandmother.[12] I rented a room from her and started speaking Russian with her.[13]

The story of how Hayat migrated to Kazan arose out of a conversation about Russian chauvinism, which itself was sparked by her asking me what Americans thought about the most recent war in Chechnya. Echoing statements Tatar speakers made to me innumerable times during my research about being chastised, shamed, ridiculed, or beaten for speaking Tatar in public, Hayat described her early reception in Kazan, "For speaking my own native language in my own city, they kicked me off the tram [*vygoniali iz tramvaia*]. They made an example of me and I was forced to go on foot."[14]

Although incidents like this ceased to occur some time after 1990 when Tatar was made an official language—I never observed any—Russian speakers are still reported to require Tatars to speak Russian to each other in their presence. Moreover, there is a tacit understanding in linguistically mixed settings that speaking Tatar in the presence of Russians is barely tolerable and that doing so for too long is not acceptable. Occasionally, Tatar speakers told me, their Russian coworkers still demanded that they cease speaking Tatar in their presence. By contrast, speaking Russian in a Tatar context is acceptable.

Expanding Tatar-Speaking Domains

A statement by Amina xanym, a *käräshen* Tatar old-age pensioner, clearly illustrates the shift in the status of Tatar language. She told me over drinks one blistering hot summer afternoon, "Before, my son used to say to me, 'Mama, why are you speaking that barbaric tongue? Stop cursing right now!' Now, he asks me why I didn't teach him Tatar."

The revival of the Tatar language, as well as the introduction of a number of other languages,[15] has caused a structural shift in the political economy of language in Kazan.[16] The result of this shift has entailed a significant change in the norm for accommodating people who do not speak Tatar language. Previous to 1986, Tatar speakers reported to me, it was normative to use Russian language outside a domestic environment, even with other Tatar speakers. Since 1986, however, the ability to speak Tatar provides individual speakers with increased benefits. These benefits include an advantage in quotidian negotiations with Tatar speakers—for example, lower prices for food and clothing purchased at local bazaars; the ability to advance in republic bureaucracies, like the police force, higher educational institutions and museums, and the school system; and improved status in private enterprise, where bilingual businessmen are perceived to be working for the good of the people of Tatarstan. The structural shift in linguistic political economy has consequently not only affected the ways that languages are used but also had a transformative effect on speakers of languages and the ways in which they position themselves in the worlds they inhabit.

Thus, sovereignty has meant that Tatar speakers and others are freer to use a language other than Russian in public in Kazan. Nonetheless, pressures to use Russian still persist, though not, as before, because daring to use another language is discouraged through petty acts of ostracism or actions as serious as imprisonment on charges of bourgeois nationalism.[17] Rather, promoting bilingualism complicates Kazan's sociolinguistic field. Despite changes in the sociolinguistic field, it is frequently easier not to insult an unknown person and thereby lose face by using the default language of Russian in conversations with strangers. At the same time, sticking to speaking Russian does not guarantee speakers the access to special privileges of intimacy so necessary to negotiating everyday life in the states of the former Soviet Union.[18] Therefore, though the linguistic accommodation practiced in Kazan bears some similarity to that observed in other bilingual cities,[19] in each of these cases, the motivating factors for accommodation are fundamentally different.

Tatar-Only Domains

In certain domains marked as ethnically Tatar speaking, Russian is considered inappropriate. These domains include the building that houses the Tatar Social Center, the acronym for which is either TOTs or TIU, and the city's mosques. In the TOTs building, university-aged Tatars sometimes suffer performance anxiety regarding their ability to speak Tatar fluently.[20] In mosques, the language to speak—except while praying—is Tatar. However, the international Muslim community (*umma*) is supposed to supersede nation. Thus, even though Islam is considered iconic of Tatarness, rules for code choice in mosques are not rigid. And consequently, despite outrage from some Tatars, in order to gain new converts, Russian has become acceptable among the Islamic hierarchy as a language for teaching about Islam.

Tatar: The Language of Secrets

An additional social effect of speaking Tatar is that Tatar speakers can pass along potentially sensitive information they do not want people without knowledge of Tatar to understand. This is not a new phenomenon in Kazan —indeed, it has been one of Russians' primary complaints when they chastise Tatars for speaking the Tatar language in their presence.

On more than one occasion when Tatar speakers introduced me to new people, the new acquaintances praised my speaking ability in Tatar and half-joked, "We won't be able to keep any secrets from her." This illustrates that part of Tatar's role as a language of intimacy and creating solidarity entails a function as a code for keeping secrets from outsiders. These kinds of exchanges can be somewhat malicious, as when I observed two friends of mine, who usually spoke Russian to each other almost exclusively, switch into Tatar at a tram stop to gossip about a man dressed in an Orthodox priest's habit. Or they can be used as a kind of private aside, as when a Tatar university administrator who otherwise insisted on speaking Russian with me switched to Tatar to tell me not to lose heart when my fiancé was hospitalized. Most frequently, though, using Tatar seems to grant a person certain license to ask favors. It allows people to extend village mores for interaction into an urban terrain.

I observed an example of this pragmatic use of Tatar on a trolley bus in June 1998. A woman boarded the bus to find that there were no vacant seats. She was rather corpulent and needed both hands to hold onto the bar above her head so she would not be tossed about as the bus dipped in and out of potholes. However, she held a plastic pail in one hand and had difficulty grasping its handle and the bar at the same time. The standing woman noticed that two seated women were conversing between themselves in Tatar and appealed to them in that language to take her pail onto their laps. At first, they looked affronted and were only willing to cram the pail into the space between their seats and the filthy wall of the bus. But the standing woman insistently explained that the pail was clean, and the two seated women finally acquiesced to hold the pail on their laps and risk soiling their clothes, as if the woman making the request deserved neighborly consideration. The standing woman was successful in extending village mores into her urban environment by using Tatar where strangers usually speak Russian among themselves.

Choosing a Code

Knowing what language to use in Kazan is something bilinguals (whether complete or partial) constantly have to negotiate on a daily basis. In fact, figuring out which language is appropriate to speak in any particular situation can be stressful, at least for outsiders and partial bilinguals, who are just learning the rules for multiple code interactions. These, in turn, are changing, in part as a result of the introduction of new speakers into the social field of bilingual interactions. Because the Soviet Union's centralized economy was highly bureaucratic and promoted a culture of rudeness among people with any institutional power, not knowing how to approach a post office clerk, bank teller, salesclerk, or bus driver can make for feelings of anxiety.

Code choice for bilingual speakers can be understood in a hierarchy of decision-making criteria regarding what languages to use. These criteria are represented in a code choice tree (see figure 10.1) based upon observations of bilinguals' speech patterns and checked with native experts for accuracy. However, this model does not adequately account for all observed behavior, both because individual agency is unpredictable, and more important, because the rules for interaction are in flux. Instead, it captures a synchronic moment in which Soviet and post-Soviet linguistic conventions coexisted. The hierarchy in the tree nevertheless reflects salient criteria: the location of an interaction; the formality of the situation; the level of intimacy between interlocutors; and, finally, that the age cohort(s) to which interlocutors belong influences how they choose which language to use.

How bilinguals approach encounters with strangers reflects negotiation of a Tatar-held linguistic ideology in which Tatar is the language of intimacy and solidarity—similar to the situation in Catalonia.[21] In contradistinction, Russian has been perceived as the nonintimate, external language that becomes differently inflected depending upon the situation. Thus, Russian can connote authority, status, power, or even brutality. Introducing bilingual education and encouraging speaking Tatar has consequently unseated this ideology and created a great deal of uncertainty in Kazanians' everyday interactions.

Besides their work environments, two public domains through which almost all Kazanians have to move on a regular basis are public transportation and shopping in stores and markets.[22] Though the number of private vehicles is growing, most families only have one. This means that everyone has some experience with riding public transportation, which almost always entails communication with strangers. In addition, in 1999–2001, self-service grocery shopping remained a relatively rare practice among people in Kazan. This is primarily because the commodities sold in self-service stores were pricey for all except New Russians.[23] The more conventional, Soviet-type shops require that patrons ask clerks for items that are kept behind counters out of customers' reach, which in turn requires that patrons and clerks converse.

When I first began conducting group interviews with bilingual urban teenagers in Kazan in 1999, I asked them what languages they use with whom. Though asking bilinguals what languages they speak with whom constitutes an unreliable source of data regarding actual language use, it is valuable in revealing speakers' language ideologies. In other words, because Tatar speakers feel that speaking Tatar creates bonds of intimacy between interlocutors, which language they report speaking reflects their affective

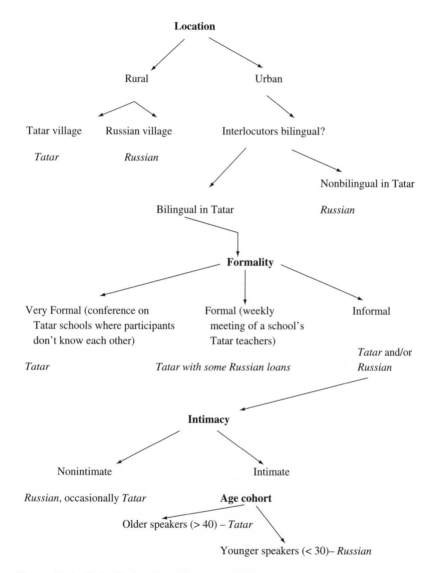

Figure 10.1. Code Choice Tree, Tatarstan, 2000

relations to the people they are speaking with. Though the bilingual teenagers' responses demonstrate that Tatar is the language associated with the
people to whom they have the strongest emotional bonds, their responses
also reveal that Kazan's linguistic field is full of unknowns.

Supporting the ideology Tatar speakers articulate regarding the link between Tatar language and intimacy, the bilingual teenagers responded that
they use Tatar or Tatar and Russian with their parents.[24] With people outside their homes, they said, it depended. Choosing shopping as the sphere
of activity in which they needed to decide which language to use with
strangers, their assumption was that, if a seller spoke Tatar, that was the language they should use. Thus, the question of code choice became one of trying to discern a person's nationality based upon visible indexes.

The teenagers explained that figuring out who was Tatar was much easier in stores and indoor markets, where the clerks wear name tags, than at
outdoor markets, where they do not. "If there is a Tatar name written on the
clerk's name tag, then it is a safe bet that she speaks Tatar," although, they
added, "It happens that a person has a Tatar first and last name and doesn't
know a word of Tatar." What these teenagers mean by a "Tatar name,"
however, is a Muslim name. But, in addition to Muslim Tatars, there are
a significant number of Christian Tatars (Kereshen) who almost always
have names indistinguishable from the "Russian" names of other Orthodox
Christians.[25] In my own visits to markets and shops, I frequently encountered women who appeared to be Russian, judging by their name tags, but
who spoke Tatar, as well as women with Muslim names who could or would
not speak Tatar with me.[26] Thus the first problem with regard to deciding
what language to use with strangers is that one can never be entirely sure
who is Tatar. Neither phenotypes nor markers of "authentic" identity like
names provide absolutely reliable information.

The rules for code choice in these domains are changing and uncertain,
and this uncertainty can be described as a threefold problem. The first is that
people in Kazan cannot always be sure who is an ethnic Tatar. A second and
related problem is that approximately half of ethnic Tatars are not functionally bilingual in Tatar.[27] In stores and in the markets, the chances that
ethnic Tatars speak Tatar are greater simply because these are jobs requiring minimal training and therefore often held by migrants from the countryside with little education. All the same, one has to be careful not to use
Tatar with strangers who do not feel comfortable speaking the language.
Despite the fact that pressures were put on non-Russian Soviets not to speak
their "barbaric" languages in the presence of Russians during the Soviet pe-

riod,[28] non-Russians ironically now feel shame for knowing their "native tongues" inadequately. Therefore, making the mistake of speaking Tatar to an ethnic Tatar who does not feel comfortable speaking the language can elicit reactions of embarrassment or anger. Likewise, making the mistake of speaking Tatar to an ethnic Russian can cause offense.

Beyond this, however, speaking Tatar to an ethnic Tatar who is fluent in the language can also be considered inappropriate behavior. There are two interrelated reasons for this. The first is that, perhaps from the 1930s on, speaking Tatar or other non-Russian Soviet languages in public marked a person as a rural migrant, that is, as unsophisticated and bad mannered, in Hayat *apa*'s words, but also as uneducated and an outsider in Kazan. As a result, people confined speaking Tatar to their intimates. Therefore, speaking Tatar to a Tatar-speaking stranger may not only express solidarity but also can be construed as an affront because it presumes intimacy.[29] The second of these interrelated reasons is that Russian has historically been used as the language of authority, and thus individuals may interpret a stranger's use of Tatar with them as an attempt to undermine their institutional authority.

For example, the following interaction, which I observed in 1997, demonstrates the usage of Russian as the language of authority. Two elderly women were speaking Tatar between themselves as they stood at a tram stop. Some boys, who were also speaking Tatar among themselves, were monkeying around at the tram stop. One of the elderly women interrupted what she was saying in Tatar to her companion, turned to the boys, and scolded them in Russian. She then turned back to her companion and resumed speaking Tatar. This illustrates how bilingual speakers can employ Russian as the language of authority.

Moreover, how speaking Russian reinforces institutional authority in post-Soviet Kazan may be seen, for instance, in the behavior of a woman who worked in the photocopy room in one branch of the National Library. She insisted on speaking Russian with me, despite the fact that we both knew Tatar.[30] In our first encounter, I had not followed protocol when presenting her articles I needed photocopied, and she began to chastise me in Russian for not knowing how to do things correctly. I countered that I was a foreigner and did not know how things worked and that the library's method for making photocopies was far from universal. Once I realized, after having heard her address someone else in Tatar, that she was a Tatar speaker, I tried to ameliorate my relations with her by conversing with her in that language. She refused to acknowledge my code shift and maintained Russian in all her subsequent exchanges with me. Eventually our relations broke down to the point that she refused to make me any more copies.[31] Had our interactions taken place in Tatar, it might have been harder for her to assert this refusal.

Another incident in which refusal to speak Tatar was employed to maintain distance inclines me to make this interpretation. The final conversation I had with one of my research assistants, Elvira, was a falling out. After a few months of acquaintance, Elvira attempted to cheat me out of a thousand dollars by involving me in a pyramid scheme. On a later occasion, Elvira spent money I had given her to obtain a visa invitation for a subsequent visit to Kazan and then denied that I had ever given her any money, so I stopped telephoning her from the United States. When I arrived in Kazan in July 2001, after acquiring an invitation through other means, I still did not contact her. However, she tracked me down and telephoned me one evening shortly before my departure. Her tone was bullying and aggressive: How dare I not call her when she was my friend? During this half-hour-long argument, Elvira rebutted all my efforts to converse in Tatar, which I knew better than she did by then, and she repeatedly used Russian to respond to my Tatar utterances.

Although Elvira's refusal to switch to Tatar differed significantly from our usual speech pattern of moving back and forth between the two languages, I would argue that there was more at play in this situation than linguistic proficiency. Because Tatar was a language Elvira used only with her closest family members, it constituted the most intimate code in her repertoire. That is, Tatar was a language through which she expressed solidarity and love rather than status or authority.[32] Therefore, I believe that she felt too vulnerable to put up a good fight when speaking Tatar because she found it difficult to maintain distance in the language she associated with her closest family members. Her code choice reflects the language ideology, possessed by many urban Tatars, according to which Tatar language is marked emotionally as the language of kindness and generosity, as opposed to Russian, which is deemed cruel and authoritative. This ideology may explain why the woman in the National Library's photocopy room refused to speak Tatar with me; speaking Russian allowed her to be rude and arbitrary as in making decisions that impeded my archival research.

Contested Conventions

The following four examples present evidence for the expansion of Tatar's functional domains beyond the intimate sphere. These examples of expansion occurred when bilinguals policed people who speak Russian in public by demanding that they recognize the status of Tatar as a government language.

The first example occurred in 1998 in a food store with the Tatar name Bäxät (Happiness). A man approached the sausage counter and greeted the shop clerk standing behind it in Russian with the standard "Zdravstvujte [Hello]." (In this section, italics indicate *Tatar* and regular type indicates Russian.) With a broad smile on her face, the clerk proclaimed in response loudly enough for everyone to hear, "*Isenmesez!* Zdravstvujte ne ponimaem [*Hello!* (in Tatar). We do not understand the word "zdravstvujte" (in Russian)]." Thus, the shop clerk asserted her right to be addressed in her native language. Her behavior represents the expansion of Tatar-speaking domains into the public sphere, but was not nationalist,[33] for the clerk switched to the hegemonic language of Russian to make herself understood.

On another occasion, in 2000, I was waiting in the reception office of a Tatar-dominant government-funded research institute. The institute is Tatar dominant in two ways: First, it houses researchers who only work on topics pertaining to Tatar language and culture; and second—unlike similar institutes—both the Tatar and Russian languages are used in formal exchanges such as dissertation defenses. In other similarly positioned institutes, the business of official meetings takes place in Russian, whereas utterances in a lower register of formality, such as telling latecomers to "take a seat," occur in Tatar. People working in the latter kind of academic institutes have explained to me that they still find using Tatar at work difficult, even when everyone present is a Tatar speaker, both because they have received their intellectual training in Russian and because they were so well-trained not to use Tatar in the public sphere.[34]

As I sat waiting to see the director of the institute, a television crew from the local Tatarstan Republic Television station entered the room. A member of the crew greeted the people in the reception area with the Russian Dobryi den' (Good day), to which one of the members of the institute staff responded in Tatar, "*Tatarcha söyläshä*" [Speak in Tatar (second person, singular imperative form)]. The staff member who policed the television crew member was a generation older than the crew member. The wisdom attributed to age gives the elder license to dictate the younger man's linguistic behavior, and, apparently, to use a familiar (second person, singular) form of address with him. Indeed, greeting people in Tatar is now considered almost obligatory in Tatar intellectual and Tatarstan government institutions, after which the rest of a conversation may occur in Russian.[35]

A third interchange similar to the one described above demonstrates that the authority that elder Tatars wield over younger ones does not depend on the status conferred by occupation. As is the case with many low-status jobs, the women who operate the food concession stands located in the lobby of the main building of Kazan State University speak Tatar publicly. On one occasion when I was purchasing some food from one of these vendors, the vendor instructed a male student who ordered his lunch in Russian to speak Tatar, using me as an example to shame him. The entire text of the interchange is as follows:

The woman (x) who sells savory pastries, ice cream, and drinks was having a conversation with another woman in Tatar. She turns to me:

| x. | Chto vam? | *What do you need?* |
| me | *Su,* pozhalujsta. | *Water,* please. |

She tries to give me juice, which in Russian is called sok:

me	*Su, su.*	*Water, water.*
x.	*Salkynmy?*	*Cold [water]?*
me	*Äie.*	*Yes.*
x.	*Sez kaidan?*	*Where are you from?*
me	*Min Amerikadan kildem.*	*America.*
x.	*Tatarcha soiläshäsezme?*	*You speak Tatar?*
me	*Beraz tatarcha soiläealam.*	*I can speak a little Tatar.*
x.	*Bashka ber Amerikadan kilgen keshe bar.*	*There's another person from*
	Ul da tatarcha bilä. Any biläsezme?	*America. S/he knows Tatar too. Do you know him/her?*
me	*Iuk. Mondamy?*	*No. Is s/he here?*
x.	*Monda.*	*Yes, here.*

A male student [st.] approaches and orders something in Russian:

| x. | *Tatarcha soilä.* | *Speak Tatar.* |

The boy answers in Russian. The vendor continues in Tatar:

x.   *Bu keshe Amerikadan kilde.*   *This person is from*
                                           America.
      Tatarcha bilä.   *She knows Tatar.*

st.   Ia ponimaiu, no govorit' ne mogu.   I understand, but I
                                           cannot speak.

x. (to me) Zdes' ne umeiut razgovorivat'. They don't know how
                                             to talk here.

Incidents like this interchange are common and embarrassing reminders to young Tatars that they are unequipped to meet their elders' expectations. But they likewise represent a shift in the expectations for conversational interactions from those of late socialism. The next interaction demonstrates how old attitudes are still held, even if they are no longer hegemonic.

This incident involved a Russian ticket inspector I encountered on a Kazan tram. The Kazan city government estimates that at least 10 percent of public transport riders travel *zaitsem,* that is, without paying their fares.[36] As a result, there is an extremely aggressive campaign to catch transgressors: Teams of ticket inspectors swarm trams and buses at central stations and escort people without valid tickets to a waiting bus, where they are held until they pay a fine. In December 1999, a middle-aged, female ticket inspector stopped me at Kazan's central tram stop. I had just been having a conversation in Tatar with a couple of old women and so, when the inspector asked for my ticket, I responded with the Tatar word *xäzer,* meaning "just a moment." The inspector sneered at me and responded in Russian, "Chto eto znachit, '*xäzer*'?" (What does that mean, "*xäzer*"?) I retorted, "Eto znachit 'seichas' po-tatarski, v odnom iz vashei gosudarstvennykh iazykov" (It means "just a moment" in Tatar, in one of your government languages). The woman took fright and returned my ticket to me without examining it properly.

These four examples illustrate changes in the rules for interactions between strangers in Kazan and simultaneously point out the tensions that arise when it is unclear to interlocutors in an exchange which language should be used. Moreover, in the last and possibly the first example, the policed interlocutors did not possess the necessary linguistic repertoire required to maintain the interaction.

Since perestroika's beginning in 1986, many ethnic Tatars have activated previously passive linguistic repertoires, while others feel freer to "be Tatar," as they put it, because the stigma attached to speaking Tatar has been lifted. Greater freedom of unstigmatized expression in languages other than Russian has consequently caused a shift in Kazanians' social networks such that they are likely to maintain closer and more frequent ties with people with whom they share a native language or religious practice.

Iman nury: The Light of Faith

The second indicator of Tatarness named by bilingual adolescents during the interviews mentioned above was something harder to read than a name tag. They said, "Tatars have a different look about them. Their eyes are different; their gaze is different somehow." I subsequently started asking adults about this gaze. People informed me that the gaze was the light of faith (*iman nury*). Although Sveta *apa,* a devout Muslim, considers that all religious people, no matter what their faith, possess *iman nury,* everyone else I spoke to asserted that it was a quality possessed by Muslims. For example, Dilbara, one of my research assistants, said of my then-fiancé that as soon as she saw him, "I knew he wasn't from Germany or a country like that. I knew . . . I don't know how to say it in Russian." I told her she should say it in Tatar and I would try to understand. She continued,

Feyzie *apa*[37] says, *in the faces of Muslims there is a light.*
(*I understand.* I responded.)
So when I saw him I knew that he was from a Turkish country, or maybe an Arab, from that world. It comes from speaking Tatar. Russians don't have that light.
(*Does this light come to a person through Tatar language?*)
Yes. If you keep on speaking Tatar, you will have that light too.

One of the most interesting things about this interchange is Dilbara's insistence that speaking Tatar is a Muslim practice and her presumption that Muslims, for she glosses all Turks and Arabs as Muslim, speak Tatar.

Indeed, the assumption not only that Muslim and Tatar are synonymous terms but that all Muslims speak Tatar is common among Kazan Tatars. For example, Liutsia hanim, the only person I met who insisted she could always differentiate Tatars from Russians, informed me when I asked her how she picked out Tatars, "I can always tell a Muslim." This statement is interesting for two reasons. First, it reproduces the perceived iconic relation between Islam and Tatars. When I asked Liutsia hanim about Christian Tatars (*käräshennär*), she asserted that they were Russians. Second, not all Muslims, especially at the bazaar, where Liutsia hanim says she tries to speak as much Tatar as possible,[38] are Tatars. A lot of bazaar merchants are Uzbeks and Azeris, that is, speakers of other Turkic languages, but some of them are also Tajiks, who speak a language closely related to Farsi and therefore not Turkic at all. So, even though Liutsia hanim frequently expresses disdain for Islam, she constructs the boundary between Tatar and Russian as one between Muslims and non-Muslims.

In the case of my then-fiancé, however, religious background did indeed coincide with linguistic ability. He was originally from Turkey and spoke something close to standard literary Tatar. Therefore, despite the fact that Dilbara's comment revealed her provincial perspective regarding the kinds of people who inhabit the planet, the particular case did bear out her observation. What I think may have been more important, however, with regard to her perception of my fiancé was his absolute ignorance of the Russian language. Consequently, in the estimation of Dilbara and other bilingual Tatars, he was cut off from the world ideologized as external to intimate relations, where the light of faith can be extinguished.

Bounded Discourses

In 1991, the Kazan newspaper *Respublika Tatarstan* published a translation of an article written by the Tatar nationalist Fauzia Bayramova for the Tatar-language newspaper *Shaxri Kazan*. In it Bayramova made a number of ideological statements, some of which are not uncommonly made in Tatar. For example, she bemoaned the fact that Tatars are ashamed of their language and culture, and instead adopt the lowest-grade cultural material from another nation, namely, Russians; she pointed out that the area of Tatar land, that is, land occupied by ethnic Tatars, extends far beyond the boundaries of the Republic of Tatarstan;[39] and she complained of Russian chauvinism with regard to other national cultures.[40] Although Tatars frequently make all these statements in both speech and writing, they usually are careful not to do so in Russian. The letters to the editor printed in *Respublika Tatarstan* in reaction to Bayramova's article, from both Russians and Tatars, lambasted her on all counts.

By presenting Bayramova's opinions in the Russian language to a nationally mixed audience used to conversations about peaceful international relations, the newspaper made a strawman of her. The alarmist expression of condemnation of Bayramova's nationalism by both Russians and Tatars helped to create a feeling of solidarity among them. This clash concretely illustrates which discursive boundaries between Tatarstan's languages cannot be bridged. More generally, however, analysis of letters to the editor published in both the Russian-language *Respublika Tatarstan* mentioned above and Tatarstan's Tatar-language Communist Party organ newspaper *Vatanym Tatarstan* between 1990 and 1993 demonstrates what the conventional boundaries are, as well as how peace is maintained in Tatarstan.[41] These letters simultaneously reveal the nonequivalence of the worlds inhabited by Russian- and Tatar-writing writers and editors, in effect documenting their divergence by comparison with letters published during late socialism.

Differences in how writers make their cases in letters to the editor in each language arise in the devices used to legitimate their opinions as somehow representative of other people, in how they imagine homeland and its relationship to the polity in which they live, and in whether they use alarmist tactics or selective memory to represent their concerns. Significant differences in the scale of the demands writers make likewise exist, with Russian writers usually showing more concern for the political sphere, while Tatar writers tend to focus more on the mundane or the ideological.[42] Though letters printed in different languages depict sometimes irreconcilably different worlds, those published in the Russian-language newspaper seem to accept the terms of a single debate, no matter what the ascribed nationality of their writers. Indeed, the claim can be made that maintaining an international dialogue in letters to the editor printed in the Russian-language newspaper *Respublika Tatarstan,* even if it is occasionally a heated one, encourages peaceful social relations in Tatarstan. For even if readers disagree with letter writers' ideas, the government sees to it that they are made aware of them; those ideas thus have been made part of the public debate. Moreover, the anti-Soviet and anti-Russian opinions expressed in *Respublika Tatarstan* are milder than some of those printed in the Tatar-language *Vatanym Tatarstan;* that is, the former do not function outside an ideological framework recognizable to Russians.

Although many of the letters published by *Vatanym Tatarstan* represent an extreme departure from received political institutions, Russians do not have the linguistic ability or desire to read them. Furthermore, people acculturated to Tatar linguistic practices are trained not to give in to expressions of anger but rather to keep the peace.[43] Children are taught at an early age the importance of using persuasion to convince their potential opponents to comply with their wishes. Thus, I would argue that, though the maintenance of a dialogue in the Russian-language newspaper encourages feelings of inclusive nationalism among Tatarstan's inhabitants, the pressure to use persuasion, as opposed to alarmism, among Tatarstan's Tatar speakers helps the monoglot Russian population feel included in and rewarded for participating in nation-building processes.

Unbounded Borders and Multiple Publics

Letters to the editor most clearly demonstrate the nonequivalence and effective divergence of Tatar and Russian writers' worlds in where they locate their imagined political frameworks. Writers' imagined political frameworks are made apparent by the use of terms denoting birthplace (*tugan yak* in Tatar and *rodina* in Russian), country (*il* in Tatar), or foreign place (*chit* in Tatar; *za rubezh* in Russian).[44] Nearly all the references made to homeland, either directly or implicitly by reference to foreignness, occur in *Vatanym Tatarstan* and draw the boundaries of that homeland around the territory of Tatarstan.

These boundaries are made most salient in a cluster of letters concerning military service printed under the framing title, "If We Don't Protect [Them], Who Will?" (*Bez yaklamasak, kem yaklar?*). In these letters, several mothers of soldiers complain that their sons have to perform their military service in foreign (*chit*) oblasts and republics, that is, beyond the borders of Tatarstan. In addition to letters from soldiers' mothers, a letter from a soldier serving in Siberia alludes to the hazing taking place in his military company and makes the following request, "Now that our republic is a sovereign government [*möstäkyil' däülät*], I would like to finish my tour of duty in my own birthplace [*tugan yak*]."[45]

Demonstrating similarly imagined borders, although providing evidence that they may not be newly so, is a letter from a woman living in Uzbekistan. Complaining of the prohibitory inflation of *Vatanym Tatarstan*'s price, she writes, "Although I live abroad [*chit*], I have subscribed to *Vatanym Tatarstan* for many years. Every time I take the paper in my hand, I become happy, as if I were returning to my native country [*tugan il*]."[46] This letter suggests that, even if Tatarstan's 1990 Declaration of Sovereignty acts as a performative by imbuing the republic with new political authority, the boundary between Central Asia as *chit* and Tatarstan as *tugan il* may predate perestroika in Tatar imaginings.[47]

Other letters suggest that less potentially permeable boundaries divide *chit* from *tugan il.* In a letter the newspaper editors title "Where O Where Is [the] Tatar?" (*Tatar kaida da tatar?*) a man writes from Zelenodol'sk[48] complaining that people coming from foreign (*chit*) regions, namely neighboring Chuvashia, Udmurtia, and Kirov oblast', buy up "our wealth" of food stuffs "in broad daylight" and take them away. This hoarding for the homeland motif appears in other letters,[49] which, while similarly fixing the boundaries of homeland at Tatarstan's borders, imply different locations for *chit.* Another writer, whose letter is printed on the same page as the previous one, marvels that the head of the delegation to the All-World Tatar Congress (*Koryltai*) from Ulyanovsk is a Tatar-souled man (*tatar janly eget*), even though he grew up in a "foreign place," the Republic of Georgia, and only came to Tatarstan for the first time as a young adult.[50]

Writers supporting sovereignty seem to locate *chit* in Moscow, the seat of the Soviet Union's and subsequently Russia's centralized governments. For example, one Tatar-speaking woman writing from the Tatarstan city of Älmät about the Soviet past laments, "Throughout [our] life the wealth we acquire has been taken from our very mouths," which wealth Moscow did not subsequently redistribute equitably to the rest of the country.[51] Likewise voicing this view and simultaneously demonstrating the real-life messiness of the relationships between language communities and political opinion, Kharitonov, a self-identified lawyer, advocates in Russian that the people of Tatarstan should vote "yes" in Tatarstan's referendum, in part, so that Tatarstan can retain its wealth and therefore govern itself effectively.[52] Thus, though the letters about military service, as well as the one from the woman in Uzbekistan, do not seem to fix the borders between homeland and elsewhere concretely at the edges of Tatarstan, these latter letters do.[53]

The relationship between letters' place of origin and where their writers fix the center of the polities in which they live is not transparent. For example, the Tatar woman living in a small Tatarstan city and complaining that their wealth was seized from their mouths juxtaposes the Tatar term for country (*il*)[54] with the word for homeland (*tugan yak*). The last paragraph of her letter begins as follows. "For the sake of our country [*il*] and our land 20 million people lost their lives in the Great Patriotic War. But, we do not know the value [*kader*] of our homeland [*tugan yak*], we sell it," from which it is not clear whether *il* and *tugan yak* refer to the same territory or not.[55] There appears, nonetheless, to be a tendency for Tatar writers residing in Tatarstan to fix the boundaries of the polity around Tatarstan and to include other Tatar speakers in it.[56] External Tatars may imagine the homeland to be Tatarstan, while the larger polity they imagine themselves inhabiting, that is, the Soviet Union, may no longer exist. Like Russian-oriented writers, external Tatars may find themselves occupying a liminal state in which what and who constitute the polity is unclear. The lack of clearly defined, political borders among Tatarstan's letter writers indicates the existence of a multiplicity of publics,[57] as opposed to the single public imagined by both Jürgen Habermas and Benedict Anderson.[58]

Parting Words

I conducted the interviews drawn upon in the following section over the course of a year and a half with both Tatar- and Russian-track classes attending the Lab School, a progressive feeder high school for Kazan University.[59] Like those in most Kazan schools, children at this school socialize together in the hallways and at school events like celebrations of Teacher's Day, International Woman's Day, and Halloween, and occasionally date across national lines. My conversations with the children demonstrate that, even though they attended a school organized according to progressive principles, their primary language of identification nevertheless strongly influenced the boundaries of the thought worlds they inhabited.

As in all Kazan schools, the Tatar-track classes contained only Tatar children, whereas the children in the Russian classes were not necessarily Russian. Nonetheless, labels of language instruction iconically index ethnic identification and assumed political affiliation. Therefore, in the mid-1990s, many parents of Russophone Tatar children or children of mixed parentage chose Tatar classes for their children. However, when they realized their children could not function in all-Tatar environments, they moved them to Russian classes. Decisions regarding which classes children should study in are not without political implications. Enrolling one's child in a Tatar class shows support for Tatarstan sovereignty, while withdrawing children from Tatar classes implies withdrawal of that support.

Despite efforts to increase the status and domains of use of the Tatar language, the political economy of Tatar and Russian remains decidedly asymmetrical. Not only is Russian more widely used in schools, media, and other public domains, but it is also effectively the sole language spoken in Russia outside Tatarstan. Therefore, the overwhelming majority of media consumed by children, even those studying in Tatar classes, is exclusively in

Russian. Moreover, the introduction of new Tatarstan ideologies complicated an already-existing two-tiered system of national identification,[60] so
that children can now identify with nations as peoples, for example, Tatars
or Russians, as well as with territorial governments, that is, Tatarstan or
Russia, or indeed, some combination of these.

In 2001, Russian remained the hegemonic language, even in Kazan's
Tatar classrooms. Although their Tatar teachers delivered their lessons to
the children in Tatar, most conversations among Tatar children at the Lab
School occurred in Russian. All the same, when speaking Russian to each
other, children inserted phrases and made jokes in Tatar. These speech patterns created a certain kind of solidarity among them that they could not
share with their Russian monoglot schoolmates.

Many children in the Russian-track class described themselves as ethnically mixed or even as Tatar, but they did not speak Tatar at home. Indeed,
the fact that they moved through a world indexically configured in the Russian language seemed to imply unwavering identification with the Russian
nation both as a collective of people and as the occupants of a territorial
polity. Among children fifteen and sixteen years old, home language seemed
crucial to how they interpreted competing ideologies of nationhood. The reactions of Tatarstan adolescents to Tatarstan's bilingual education policies
in the context of growing Russian government conservatism can generally
be divided into two types: ethnically Tatar children proud of speaking Tatar
and hoping to create a pluralist, bilingual society on Tatarstan territory; and
everyone else. The children in the former group embrace, if loosely,
Tatarstan's policies of multiculturalism, and they reject exclusionary Russian nationalism, while many non-Tatars dismiss Tatarstan ideological pluralism as a mask for Tatar ethnic nationalism.[61]

The divergence in worldviews by language of identification became evident during conversational English lessons in 1999 with the Lab School's
Tatar- and Russian-track eleventh-grade classes. At our first meeting, the
Russian class asked me what Americans thought about the war in Chechnya. I responded that those Americans who know where Chechnya is were
appalled by reports that Russian troops were committing atrocities there.
The class claimed ignorance of these reports. So I brought to our next meeting some articles from U.S. news sources, which reported that Russian
troops were raping and murdering unarmed Chechen civilians. The children
responded to these allegations with outrage and anger, which they directed
toward me. One girl in particular, who identified as half Tatar and half Russian, exclaimed that it was insulting to the young men who were dying to de-

fend the country from terrorists to entertain the possibility that atrocities were being committed. After this meeting, the whole class stood me up, and that was the thankful end to their conversational English practice, although we continued to spend time together less formally.

When the class teacher of the eleventh-grade Tatar class learned of the articles I had given the Russian-identified children, she requested that I give her class the same materials, for, she explained, they have to receive information from as many sources as possible. The class and I read through the articles together. The girls in the class, much less likely to talk about sexual matters than their Russian-identified counterparts, expressed no shock whatsoever at the articles' content. They told me they were not surprised to learn that Russian soldiers were raping and murdering girls younger than themselves. The boys remained silent.

Apparently reproducing opinions expressed by their parents, as well as Russian-language Moscow media sources, Russian-speaking children said that the war is a just struggle against terrorists and that any criticism of Russian troops, including reading foreign-press articles claiming that Russian soldiers have been committing atrocities, is unacceptable. Tatar speakers in Tatarstan, by contrast, express no surprise that Russian soldiers should be committing acts that violate decency; these adolescents, like their parents, consider the war in Chechnya and general discrimination against Chechens to be acts of violence by Russia against its own people and yet another example of Russian imperialist aggression against Muslims.

Along with the increasing conservatism of media broadcasts from Moscow, non-Russian language media sources likewise influence the divergence of Tatarstan's publics. Because very few Russian-identified people consume any media broadcast in the Tatar language,[62] the debates taking place in the Tatar media are external to the boundaries of Russians' referential worlds. The Russian government has increased content censorship of media broadcast in the Russian language. However, this censorship has not been extended to Tatar-language media. Therefore, with the tacit support of the Tatarstan government, Tatar-language media continue to proliferate information quietly critical of Russocentric national ideologies. For instance, official Tatar-language sources frame the question of Chechnya in terms of the unnecessary loss of life the war causes both Chechens and Russia's sons drafted to fight there. I therefore propose that the two groups of children to which I showed news items on Chechnya reacted differently because the Russian-identified pupils perceive themselves as part of a single group in solidarity with the "Russian" soldiers (who in fact come from every ethnic group living in Russia) represented in the Moscow media, while the Tatar-identified children feel alienated from the "we" projected by the Russian government.

Parallel to this shift is one in the speech of Russia's president. When the Soviet Union split up, it became necessary for the first time since before the 1917 Revolution to find a way to talk about Russian nationhood. Thus, the imperial-period term "*rossiiskoe*," meaning related to the territory of Russia, was revived and employed by President Yeltsin and others to refer to the nation. By contrast, Putin, almost immediately after assuming office, began to use the word "*russkoe*," which Tatars disdain because they feel it refers only to people of Russian ethnicity. The increasingly exclusionary quality of official Russian national ideology has been creating feelings of widening social distance among Tatar speakers from people they identify as Russian. And the expression of irreconcilably different views about the war in Chechnya has made this decreasing solidarity painfully obvious to some.

Thus, as ideologies projected by the government in Moscow about who belongs in the Russian nation have shifted from including the inhabitants of Russian territory to excluding non-Russians, a parallel shift has occurred among Russia's population. Those for whom standard Russian is their language of national identification ally themselves with exclusionary nationalist ideologies, while those who speak another language at home seem inclined to feel distanced from these ideologies. The result of Moscow's attempts to unify a Russian public around the cause of war against a terrorist enemy has in fact served to make more concrete divisions in public opinion among Russia's inhabitants.

As a result of the second war in Chechnya since the Soviet Union's collapse, Tatars have begun to see their differences with "Russians" as irreconcilable. This is most saliently demonstrated by attitudes toward Chechens, as described above. However, it is not only linguistic ability but also contexts and patterns of language use, that influence people's attitudes. For example, Tatar speakers I interviewed in Moscow and Saint Petersburg, who do not share Tatarstan Tatars' fear of a Russian military invasion, and are not deeply enmeshed in broad Tatar-speaking networks, express little sympathy for the plight of Chechens.

All the same, Chechnya is pivotal to understanding the political field of perceived possibilities for national belonging in Russia. If the recent increase in "Chechen" terrorist acts over the course of the past several years can teach us anything, it is how desperate the question of who belongs to the Russian nation has become. U.S. news sources have asserted that the

Russian government cannot allow Chechnya to secede, for secession could incite other Russian regions to break away from the crumbling state. This presupposition implies that military action against Chechen rebels must continue to maintain Russian statehood. However, such statements ignore how the national ideologies projected by Russia's government have changed since Putin became president in 2000. When Yeltsin was president, Russian national ideologies projected a relatively inclusive vision of the state. Now, by contrast, the Russian government suggests that ethnic Russians are the state's only true citizens. So, while Chechen rebels do not have the option of seceding from the Russian Federation, individual Chechens no longer have any place in it. And Kazan's Tatar speakers, who feel a connection to Chechens through their shared religion and aspirations for sovereignty, also feel less and less as if the Russian state is willing to accommodate them as full-fledged citizens.

The war against the people of Chechnya, as Tatar speakers tend to perceive it, has brought the divergence of Kazan's language communities to their attention. Speaking to me in the summer of 2000, one Tatarstan intellectual explained, in Tatar, the recent changes thus. She said that before Tatars and Russians had all been part of one homogenous society, but now it seemed that they were on two separate paths because the Tatars want to develop a more humanitarian society based on pluralism. She noted that she used to have Russian friends, but that she does not anymore; the breaking point was the Chechen war. Their opinions are too different. Her well-read, intelligentsia Russian friends thought that it was necessary to annihilate the entire Chechen people, not just the terrorists, but all of them. "Before," she concluded, "we Tatars lived with Russians because we wanted to do so, but now we live with them because we have no choice, because we are afraid of Moscow."

Conclusions

In this chapter, I have illustrated that changes in political opinion occur through social practices. In particular, I have demonstrated how the increase in the social practice of speaking the Tatar language in the Republic of Tatarstan, a result of a political movement for sovereignty, has produced changes in political attitudes. I examine the social and cultural resonance of speaking Tatar in terms of four kinds of linguistic practice. These include explaining the cultural conventions for code choice in Kazan; illustrating how Tatarstan's sovereignty movement caused these conventions to become contested; revealing how newspaper discourses are bounded by linguistic conventions; and, finally, describing how changing linguistic practices have influenced the expression of political opinions that indicate increasing social distance between Kazan's two primary language communities. These changes in patterns of speech behavior and the ways in which they are linked to the sociolinguistic field may not be unique to Tatarstan. Indeed, I assert that, although such changes in linguistic practices represent a localized phenomenon of differentiation, they may serve as a prediction for processes that will eventually take root throughout the Russian Federation and the surrounding states, as people there become increasingly post-Soviet.

Notes

1. When I use the term "Tatar speaker," I am referring to bilingual Tatar-Russian speakers. When I use the term "Russian," I am referring to Tatar speakers' perception of the category of "Russian." These include people who self-identify as Russian, as well as (sometimes) Russian monophones of non-Russian nationality and people professing confessions other than Islam, even if they are ethnically Tatar (Kereshen, who are Christian Tatars) or otherwise Turkic (Chuvash). Although I do not subscribe to the notion that religion or language determines national culture, I do perceive that the worlds people inhabit, at least in Tatarstan, are differently configured depending upon whether Tatar or Russian is their primary language of orientation—because the cultural space through which people move consists of different referential and experiential worlds; see James Fernandez, "The Mission of Metaphor in Expressive Culture," in *Persuasions and Performances* (Bloomington: Indiana University Press, 1986), 28–70.

2. Roman Jakobson, "Boas' View of Grammatical Meaning," in *On Language*, ed. Linda R. Waugh and Monique Monville-Burston (Cambridge, Mass.: Harvard University Press, 1990), 324–31; Edward Sapir, "The Psychological Reality of Phonemes," in *Selected Writings of Edward Sapir* (Berkeley: University of California Press, 1933), 46–60.

3. Rogers Brubaker, *Nationalism Reframed: Nationhood and the National Question in the New Europe* (New York: Cambridge University Press, 1996).

4. Erving Goffman, "Footing," in *Forms of Talk* by Erving Goffman (Philadelphia: University of Pennsylvania Press, 1981).

5. Because it is the most widely spoken indigenous language after Russian in Tatarstan, I will focus on Tatar here. However, the sociolinguistic field is more complex than what I represent; there are, e.g., native speakers of Chuvash who are fluent in both Tatar and Russian and native speakers of Yiddish who are fluent in Russian and have acquired some knowledge of Tatar.

6. In 2001, only 3 percent of "Russians" in Tatarstan admitted to knowing Tatar (Iskhakov, personal communication), up from 1.5 percent in 1989; Jean Robert Raviot, "Tipy natsionalizma, obshchestvo i politika v Tatarstane," *Polis* 5/6 (1992): 42–58. How they define knowing Tatar is unknown, as is the question of what is contained in the category of "Russian."

7. Evidence from my interviews with surviving Volga Germans—as well as in Eu-

genia Semyonovna Ginzburg's *Journey into the Whirlwind* (New York: Harcourt, 1967) —reveals that multilingual German pharmacists and Ginzburg herself may have been exposed to especial scrutiny by the NKVD for having learned how to speak Tatar. See also Venera Yakupova, *100 istorij o suvernitete* [One hundred stories about sovereignty] (Kazan: Idel-Press, 2000).

8. This is based upon my own observations, likewise confirmed by other frequent visitors to Kazan.

9. *Apa* is a Tatar kin term meaning "aunt" or "older sister," used in conjunction with a person's name to show both affection and respect.

10. After reading an article I wrote on this topic, the Tatar ethnographer Damir Iskhakov informed me that, at least in the 1960s, there was a cadre of Tatar academics who helped channel Tatar children seeking to gain admittance to Kazan University through the exam process by allowing them to take their exams in Tatar. However, he added that, after being admitted, it took two to three years to adapt so as to be able to perform adequately in university seminars.

11. In another conversation about this, Hayat *apa* says that she had no speaking of knowledge of Russian when she migrated to Kazan at the age of sixteen years in 1960; i.e., it took her a year to learn to speak Russian.

12. Hayat uses the Russian kin term "*babushka*" here, which constitutes a general way of referring to women of one's grandmother's generation and does not indicate that she is somehow related to the woman from whom she rented the room.

13. *Ja zakonchila tatarskuiu shkolu i vyrosla v tatarskoi derevne. Kodga ia priexala v Kazan' i khotela postupit', mne skazali: sdavaite istoriiu na russkom iazyke. Ia nikogda ne izuchala istoriiu po-russkii . Eto kak esli vam skazali, chto nado sdavat' ekzamen po etnografii na tatarskom iazyke. Ia ne govorila po-russkii do 17 let. On byl sovershenno ne nuzhen v moei derevne. U menya byli xoroshie uchiteli, no oni ne nauchili russkii.*

Ne znaite russkii, idi togda v sel'skokhoziastvennii institut. O-o tatary tak boialis' VUZov. Mnogo iz nikh khodili v Sel'skokhoziastvennii institut potomu, chto tam mozhno bylo govorit' po-tatarski. [I somehow convinced them and got into Kazan State University.] A pervij god ucheby bylo tak tiazhelo. Tak [they require it] i ne obuchaet.

Ia perekhala zhit' c russkoi babushkoi, snimala u nee komnatu i s nei nauchilas' govorit' po-russki.

During this period the door to the hallway is opened quite frequently. We hear voices and sometimes someone in the room, on the other side of the bookcases. This makes H nervous. She looks up every time she hears a sound and asks who it is.

14. *Za to, chto ia govorila na svoem rodnom iazyke v svoem gorode, menia vygoniali iz tramvaia. Delali zamechanie i mne prishlos' khodit' peshkom.*

15. Besides the ubiquitous English, German, French, Arabic, Turkish, Hebrew, and Polish, less widely spoken indigenous languages, such as Mari and Chuvash, have become part of the linguistic landscape for Kazan's inhabitants since 1989.

16. For an explanation of similar phenomena in other places, see Judith Irvine, "When Talk Isn't Cheap: Language and Political Economy," *American Ethnologist* 16 (1989): 248–67.

17. Helen M. Faller, "One Nation Divisible: The Unmaking of Soviet People in Tatarstan, Russia," Ph.D. dissertation, University of Michigan, 2003.

18. Caroline Humphrey, *The Unmaking of Soviet Life: Everyday Economics after Socialism* (Ithaca, N.Y.: Cornell University Press, 2002).

19. See, e.g., Kathryn Woolard, *Double Talk: Bilingualism and the Politics of Ethnicity in Catalonia* (Stanford, Calif.: Stanford University Press, 1989).

20. For more on performance Tatar as a speech genre, see Suzanne Wertheim, "Linguistic Purism, Language Shift, and Contact-Induced Change in Tatar," Ph.D. dissertation, University of California, Berkeley, 2003.

21. Woolard, *Double Talk.*

22. There are certainly many other public domains. E.g., Kazanians have to navigate government institutions, like the post office, and private ones, like banks.

23. "New Russian" is a term applied to people who have profited from the collapse of the Soviet Union's socialist system. For more on New Russians as a social category, see Humphrey, *Unmaking of Soviet Life.*

24. The written responses they gave on a matched guise test on language attitudes corroborated this oral evidence.

25. Before the 1917 Revolution, some 10 percent of Tatars were Kereshen; Paul W. Werth, "From 'Pagan' Muslims to 'Baptized' Communists: Religious Conversion and Ethnic Particularity in Russia's Eastern Provinces," *Comparative Studies in Society and History* 42, no. 3 (2000): 497–523. Because Kereshen have not been a separate census category since the 1920s, it is impossible to know how many of them have assimilated into larger Russophone culture. In 2002, there was a controversy between some Muslim-identified Tatars and the Russian government, which has been proposing to separate Kereshen as a nationality in the upcoming census. Tatars object that this is an attempt to diminish the credibility of Tatar calls for pluralism by artificially diminishing their numbers.

26. On one such occasion, I asked a merchant with a "Russian" name printed on her tag if she were Tatar and she replied, "Yes, I am a Muslim."

27. Wertheim, "Linguistic Purism."

28. For numerous accounts of this, see Yakupova, *100 istorij o suvernitete.*

29. Roger Brown and A. Gilman, "The Pronouns of Power and Solidarity," in *Style in Language,* ed. Thomas A. Sebeok (Cambridge, Mass.: MIT Press, 1960), 253–76. For a similar situation among a community of New York Puerto Ricans, see Bonnie Urciuoli, *Exposing Prejudice: Puerto Rican Experiences of Language, Race, and Class* (Boulder, Colo.: Westview Press, 1996); and Urciuoli, "The Political Topography of English: The View from a New York Puerto Rican Neighborhood," *American Ethnologist* 18, no. 2 (1991): 295–310.

30. Her behavior differed from that of most Tatar-speakers I met, who happily engaged in Tatar conversations with me when I initiated them.

31. She complained that her work collective could no longer make my photocopies (despite the fact, someone else informed me, they received a commission for doing so) because it was too much work. She said, "We do not even have time to drink tea [*My dazhe chai pit' ne uspevaem*]."

32. Woolard, *Double Talk.*

33. See Ralph Fasold, *The Sociolinguistics of Society* (Malden, Mass.: Blackwell, 1987).

34. Like all workplaces in Kazan and reflecting the social networks described above, even though this research institute is Tatar-dominant, not all its employees are. Thus, I was surprised to discover that the institute's librarian did not know any Tatar when I asked her where the toilet was in that language.

35. When initiating conversations in noninstitutional domains, however, Tatar speakers are not always aware whether they are speaking Tatar or Russian. E.g., I overheard a woman on a tram say to her fellow travelers, "*Anda barabyzmy* ili *monda*

barabyzmy? Davai, poshli. [*Do we go that way* or *this way?* All right, let's go]." Regular type indicates speech in Russian. For an analysis of "Tatar on-stage" style, in which the author argues that everyday code mixing indicates nonawareness of code choice, see Wertheim, "Linguistic Purism."

36. Literally, bunny style.

37. Feyzie *apa* is Dilbara's aunt who lives in the United States. Because Feyzie *apa* never lived under Soviet rule, her family in Tatarstan considers her an authority on authentic Tatarness.

38. The reason she gives for this is that bazaar workers have been traditionally looked down upon for being Tatar.

39. E.g., 1.5 million self-identified Tatars live in neighboring Bashkortistan.

40. *Respublka Tatarstan,* October 25, 1991, 2.

41. For a detailed explication of the former, see Faller, "One Nation Divisible," chap. 5.

42. The mundane includes small-scale demands, which ask that particular things within the existing system be fixed, while the political refers to larger-scale demands requesting that the existing system be modified; ideological demands appeal to an alternative system of values for social organization. The letters to the editor published in the Russian-language newspaper generally tended to propose that the system needed to be fixed, while the letters to the editor in the Tatar-language newspaper frequently focused upon problems that needed to be fixed within the system or made appeals to an alternate system of values.

43. Faller, "One Nation Divisible."

44. The only example of a letter I have that employs *za rubezh* places it at the edge of the Soviet Union's territory. *Respublika Tatarstan,* March 13, 1993, 10.

45. *Vatanym Tatarstan,* July 1, 1992, 2.

46. *Vatanym Tatarstan,* January 19, 1993, 2.

47. On the performative, see J. L. Austin, *How to Do Things with Words* (Cambridge, Mass.: Harvard University Press, 1975) (orig. pub. 1962).

48. A Tatarstan city of about 100,000 people.

49. Caroline Humphrey alludes to this as a generalized feeling among ex-Soviets in the early 1990s; Humphrey, *Unmaking of Soviet Life.*

50. He came to Kazan to study at the Kazan Aviation Institute; *Vatanym Tatarstan,* July 11, 1992, 2.

51. *Vatanym Tatarstan: Alai tügel, bolai ul,* April 28, 1993, 2.

52. *Respublika Tatarstan,* March 18, 1992, 1.

53. However, the imagined political framework may be differently engendered for some Tatar speakers living outside Tatarstan. One example of this occurs in a *Vatanym Tatarstan* letter that does not fit the editorial frame in which it is placed, "Let our sons do their [military] service on Tatarstan territory!" The letter, sent from Samara district [*ölke*], by the mother of at least three boys, one of whom served in Mongolia and another in the Baltic Republics, states that "wherever the country [*il*] sends them, that's where men should do their service" (*Vatanym Tatarstan,* July 1, 1992, 2). Although this woman is a Tatar speaker, her "country" appears to be the Russian Federation, and perhaps even (still) the Soviet Union. One would expect this to be generally the case for apparent Tatars sending letters to the Russian-language newspaper, *Respublika Tatarstan,* and indeed it is. The one exception to this an excerpt from a letter written by a Tatar woman who has been living "outside the borders of Tatarstan" since 1953 writing in to

support Tatarstan sovereignty. She writes, "Ia tatarka, s 1953 goda zhivu za predelami Tatarstana" (*Respublika Tatarstan*, March 18, 1992, 1).

54. In Tatar speech recorded during my fieldwork in 1999–2001, *il* seemed to refer to Tatarstan, while *tugan yak* usually meant the particular rural region of a person's origin. In these letters, however, it appears to refer to the Soviet Union.

55. *Vatanym Tatarstan: Alai tügel, bolai ul,* April 28, 1993, 2.

56. An exception to this is a letter about the writer's Russian friends (*Vatanym Tatarstan*, April 11, 1992, 2). The fact that its writer felt compelled to compose it, as well as the newspaper's editors' decision to publish it, however, indicates its likely remarkability.

57. Susan Gal and Kathryn A Woolard, eds., *Languages and Publics: The Making of Authority* (Northampton, Mass.: St. Jerome Publishing, 2001).

58. Jürgen Habermas, *The Structural Transformation of the Public Sphere: An Inquiry into a Category of Bourgeois Society* (Cambridge, Mass.: MIT Press, 1989); Benedict Anderson, *Imagined Communities* (London: Verso, 1991).

59. Age cohort likewise affects the sense that Tatarstan children make of the conflicting messages they receive about what nation they are part of. I spent more time with adolescents than with younger children, and therefore I cannot make any generalizations about the latter's attitudes.

60. Helen M. Faller, "Repossessing Kazan as a Form of Nation-Building," *Journal of Muslim Minority Affairs* 22, no. 1 (2002): 81–90; Faller, "Transforming Soviet Language Ideologies into post-Soviet Language Policies in Tatarstan," *Anthropology of East Europe Review* 18, no. 1 (2000): 81–86.

61. However, Russian-identified people in Tatarstan are not as extreme in their views as Russians who live in places where they are the ethnic majority, and at the same time are more provincial in their perspectives than either Russians from Russia's capital cities or Tatars from Kazan.

62. Zaituna Askhatova Iskhakova, "Tatarsko-russkoe gorodskoe dvuiazychie v Tatarstane v 1980–90-e gody" [Tatar-Russian urban bilingualism in Tatarstan in the 1980s–90s], candidate of philosophical science dissertation, Institute of Language, Literature, and Art of the Tatarstan Academy of Science, 1999.

Conclusion:
Unending Transition

Blair A. Ruble

The formation of identities is a complex, interactive, and often highly contested process, as Dominique Arel argues in the introduction to this volume. State institutions, civil society broadly defined, and individuals—from both within and beyond a given set of political boundaries—constantly make choices that affect cultural markers, alter the definition of categories of identity, and change the social and political significance of dimensions of identity. The previous chapters of this volume demonstrate the complex processes whereby identities within the present-day Russian Federation and Ukraine are being perpetually recalibrated through the filters of long-standing social, political, economic, and cultural legacies in response to changing external environments. How human beings conceive of who they are in Russia and Ukraine, as elsewhere, is no more fixed than the space occupied by galaxies in an expanding universe.

The complex and fluid processes of identity change in Russia and Ukraine are not only of interest to scholars developing theories of identity formation. The case studies in this volume have important and wide-reaching implications for anyone who is concerned with the future political, economic, and social development of these states. The most important implication is the idea that transition is not a finite period of national development. During periods of political transition, reconstituted state institutions interact with broader social and cultural environments to catalyze the process of identity renegotiation. The consequent redefinition of identity is never complete. Instead, "transition" is a natural state of being.

The suggestion that identity transition is perpetual is an important one for those who think about public policy or are charged with the custodianship of the state. Such a stance renders meaningless declarations of missions accomplished, graduations completed, and stages of development surpassed. The successful renavigation of identity only opens up opportunities for further negotiation; the legacies of previous negotiations only deepen the ambiguities and complexities of the processes through which people come to place themselves within social and political space. Identities "rebound" rather than becoming "resolved."

In the context of an unending transition, this volume suggests four specific areas that are important for scholars and policymakers interested in Russia and Ukraine to consider: the connections between state security and individual belief, the importance of language as an attribute of identity for the region, the significance of the societal differences between Russia and Ukraine, and the danger of recentralization for post-Soviet Russia.

State Security and Individual Belief

Indeterminancy is hardly unique to the post-Soviet transition, though the upheavals of state collapse necessarily amplify the need to reconfigure identity. Human beings forced to reconsider who they are naturally turn to previous identity cues for guidance. The past furnishes a repertoire of identity categories, which remain readily at hand. Consequently, conversations, practices, modes of thought, and institutions resurface even as the present becomes the past. Such consciously—and unconsciously—recurring identity patterns may be seen in the strikingly similar ways that very different Russian governments have approached religious practice.

Paul Werth's analysis of the Imperial Russian state's "deep implication in the Russian Empire's religious affairs" recounts Tsarist policies and practices that regulated "foreign faiths" (non-Orthodox religions and confessions). The confessional choice of an Imperial subject determined life opportunities because "Russia had not constructed a civil order in which rights and obligations were universally shared by the entire citizenry, and religious confession represented one of the principal sources of the society's division into particularistic components." Religious beliefs regarded as deeply personal in other societies were subject to formal state regulation in Russia. Moreover, Saint Petersburg's bureaucrats maintained a hierarchy of religious acceptability.

This general pattern of state regulation extended beyond the religious reforms promulgated in response to the upheavals of the 1905–7 Revolution. As Werth concludes, "religion continued to represent a fundamental source of morality and stability, and it therefore represented something that the state could never afford to regard with indifference."

A century later, Russian officialdom continues to consider individual religious belief to be too important a matter to be left to individual conscience. Werth's contribution reveals that the issue of state control over religion extends well beyond the more recent Soviet-era effort to eradicate religion. Post-Soviet Russia nurtures space for religious belief and for religious institutions to prosper. As in Imperial Russia, the domain of religious belief continues to be considered a legitimate sphere for state regulation, as revealed in Katherine Graney's discussion of "Russian Islam."

Graney explicates the attempt of the contemporary Russian state to create "a realm of official, state-sanctioned 'Russian' Islam." For early-twenty-first-century Russian policymakers, post-Soviet Russia confronts the task of creating "a more democratic and productive relationship between different religious confessions and the state." Such preoccupation with state security stands at the core of the 1997 Law on the Freedom of Conscience and Religious Association in Russia, which establishes official principles and state institutions to regulate religious practice. Contemporary Russian religious legislation is markedly reminiscent of the Imperial laws discussed by Werth, with the notable addition of non-Christian creeds (Islam, Judaism, and Buddhism) to the ranks of Russia's officially sanctioned "traditional" religions.

Similitudes in state policies, institutional configurations, and concepts of the state revealed in the chapters by Werth and Graney illustrate an important lesson for both policymakers and social scientists. State collapse does not create a "clean slate" on which a new system may set forth its own principles. Identities, institutions, policy inclinations, and fundamental attitudes concerning the relationship between state and society persist, thereby circumscribing the arena for policy action. Lines once firmly etched by previous legislation, administrative hierarchy, and governmental custom and practice constitute identity fault lines even as they become submerged under the declarations of a new regime. Their demarcation need not be metaphorical for, as Steven Seegel demonstrates, metaphorical boundaries become drawn on maps.

Seegel's cartographers—together with the ethnographers and census officials standing behind their efforts—created identity by establishing categories according to which reality would be described. Official Romanov and Hapsburg mapmakers drew lines around territories and ethnic settlements so as to bring representational order to the chaotic legacies emerging from the collapse of the early modern Polish-Lithuanian Commonwealth (*Rzeczpospolita obojga narodów*). They simultaneously defined their empire's new territories as inherently "Russian" and "Austrian" by drawing new administrative units with differently shaded pencils, and by linking towns and villages to their own imperial settlement hierarchies.

Reflecting a growing preoccupation with ethnos and language, Vienna's and Saint Petersburg's cartographers similarly traced patterns of ethnic settlement. Differently colored areas became associated with various national, linguistic, confessional, and cultural communities. Once having identified an area as home to one group or other, maps rendered the region's cultural complexity comfortably evident (except for those unfortunate residents who either carried an identity different from the mapmaker's expectation or belonged to a group—such as Jews and Roma—unrecognized by imperial geographic societies).

Having been set firmly on paper, official maps provided grounds for subversive discourse. Lines drawn in the drafting office of one empire could be placed anew by the drafting office of another. Opponents of one imperial regime could convert mapmaking to subversive purpose. Polish maps from the period reveal pretensions to an empire that, in fact, never existed; maps produced from a Ukrainian perspective established a homeland *ex nihilo*.

The act of producing a map imposed novel representational realities as regimes emerged and collapsed. The publication of an atlas recalibrated identity. Legacies need not be centuries old to become potent markers in the renegotiation of identity under a new regime. Official cartographers from Vienna and Saint Petersburg—followed by their later counterparts from Moscow, Warsaw, Prague, Berlin, and Kyiv—produced a representational reality that communicated a certainty and clarity often absent in the minds of the human beings living in the lands covered by their maps. Such disjuncture between cartographic and psychological reality ultimately transformed the lands of the collapsed Polish-Lithuanian Commonwealth into a twentieth-century European heart of darkness.

As Arel argues in the introduction, the state plays a critical, but not hegemonic, role in the construction of identity. Policy decisions made in the interest of strengthening central control over diverse populations have had profound and long-lasting effects on how those populations understood their own identities. In some cases, these policies have helped produce nationalist discourses that act against the interests of the state.

Speaking Identity

Official religious policies and imperial geographic societies negotiated identity from without. Individual human beings confront the question of identity from within every time they open their mouths to speak. As Dmitry Gorenberg argues, to be "Soviet" meant speaking Russian in public. Presentation of self as "Tatar," according to Helen Faller, necessitates using the Tatar language in an expanding array of public settings. Being a citizen of contemporary Ukraine, Alexandra Hrycak suggests, requires parents to send their children to Ukrainian-language schools.

Gorenburg's work runs counter to a conventional wisdom that has come to view Soviet nationalities policy as having encouraged the strengthening of ethnic identity among the minority populations of the Soviet Union. Instead, he argues that post-Stalinist Soviet policies promoted a dual course that simultaneously promoted institutions predicated on national and ethnic distinctiveness and elevated the Russian language to the status of the only officially sanctioned and accepted language for interethnic communication. As he succinctly observes, "socialism spoke Russian." Linguistic Russification thereby encouraged assimilation even as formal institutional arrangements of state authority granted additional status to so-called titular language communities in national homelands. "Soviet nationalities policy," he concludes, "continually oscillated between the two poles of Russification and ethnophilia."

Linguistic Russification not surprisingly became an object of concern to many ethnic communities around the Soviet Union. Nationalist movements during the Gorbachev era frequently used the demise of native language education and an accompanying decline in native language use as a rallying cry against the centralized Soviet state. Not surprisingly, language became a primary means of reidentification among the various peoples seeking sovereignty during the collapse of Soviet power. If socialism spoke Russian, postsocialism would speak many tongues.

Faller charts this linguistic evolution in Tatarstan based on anthropological fieldwork with children and adults in the Tatarstan capital of Kazan between 1997 and 2001. She finds that the Tartar language was used in an increasing number of linguistic domains during the period and, moreover, that these domains were elevated in status. In other words, Tatar was spoken more often, and in more prominent public environments. An ability to speak in Tatar became socially obligatory in certain official contexts. The Tatar language was transformed from "the language of secrets" to one of public discourse. Individual residents of Kazan thus used knowledge of the Tatar language to establish their identity as "Tatar."

Faller contends that "people whose primary language of identification is Tatar are increasingly coming to perceive the world differently from those who identify with the Russian language." For example, Tatar speakers, who have access to a realm of media that monolingual Russian speakers do not, tend to be much more sympathetic toward the cause of the Chechen separatist movement. Language choice reflects and, in turn, shapes identity and political points of view.

Language plays a perhaps even greater role in the renegotiation of identity in post-Soviet Ukraine than in Faller's Tatarstan. Ukrainian became Ukraine's official state language at the outset of independence. However, as Hrycak observes, "the use of Russian remains extensive in many elite domains, particularly in higher education, science, business, and the media. Even today, young people still speak Russian almost universally in informal settings in many Ukrainian cities." The country's sizable Russian minority is, in fact, a majority in a number of regional communities to the east and south. The continuing dominance of Russian in various geographical areas within Ukraine is seen by some as a form of lingering resistance to the Ukrainian state-building enterprise.

Hrycak demonstrates that language issues must be examined from a multigenerational perspective. Schools throughout Ukraine have reintroduced Ukrainian instruction. For Hrycak, language policies in education are "likely to broaden the use of Ukrainian in daily life" in Russified areas. Resistance to the Ukrainianization of education appears to be poorly organized and rather weaker than one might have expected. Such an outcome is especially noteworthy in light of the adoption by Ukrainian "state builders" of a model for nationhood that "makes competence in standard Ukrainian an increasingly important skill."

One reason for the muted response among Russian speakers in Ukraine toward this policy is that language usage across the country does not correspond to ethnic boundaries. Consequently, distinctions that appear so clearly pronounced in Faller's Tatarstan are more blurred in Ukraine. Ethnic Ukrainians are often more proficient in Russian than in Ukrainian, while many ethnic Russians have been able to learn passable Ukrainian. Ukraine increasingly emerges as a society in which everyone has some degree of bilingual competence. Meanwhile, knowledge of Ukrainian has become a necessary precondition for entrance into prestigious institutions of higher learning as well as high-status positions in state administration and the professions.

Hrycak argues that independent Ukraine's language policies have brought about surprisingly little change at the interpersonal level, even as citizens of the Ukrainian state are coming to accept the status of Ukrainian as the language of official transaction. Given this complex linguistic heterogeneity, non-native speakers of Ukrainian are choosing to have their children learn the Ukrainian language at school rather than engage in social protest. Hrycak's future Ukraine becomes a society of complex bilingualism, with varied patterns of linguistic use remaining in place throughout a state predicated on a high degree of decentralization.

Differences between Russia and Ukraine

Faller and Hrycak describe starkly different approaches to statecraft in Russia and Ukraine. These contrasts, which were visible long before the so-called Orange Revolution of 2004, suggest some of the underlying forces that burst forth during Ukraine's contentious presidential elections. Hrycak's Ukraine emerges as a more decentralized state with more fluid and open-ended policies. The politics of political compromise that enabled Ukrainian elites to find peaceful solutions to the political impasse of November 2004 was predicated on such sensibilities. Faller's Russia, by contrast, expresses concern over an increasingly centralist and interventionist state in which language use becomes politicized in a manner reminiscent of Gorenberg's Russian-speaking socialism. To borrow a turn of phrase in vogue in American popular psychological discourse, "Russia is from Mars, Ukraine is from Venus." This was so before Ukraine turned "Orange."

These contrasting images are more starkly posed when recalling that both the Russian Federation and Ukraine emerged from the same hyper-centralized Soviet state. The complex, at times ambiguous, and strikingly fluid processes of identity formation in Russia and Ukraine suggest that both Russia and Ukraine are likely to be very different countries a decade from now than they appear to be at this moment. More important for those concerned with policy issues, both nations are likely to be more different from one another than is presently the case. The Orange Revolution, within this context, becomes an initial bursting forth of deeper processes.

Several of the contributions to this volume portray a Russian Federation and a post-independence Ukrainian state that appear to be heading along different trajectories more than a decade after the collapse of the Soviet Union. In addition to the contributions of Faller and Hrycak, the chapter by Catherine Wanner on religion and post-Soviet moral order as well as Oxana Shevel's chapter on post-Soviet refugee policies indicate that Russia and Ukraine are diverging in profound ways.

Wanner argues that Ukraine's experience with widespread religious resurgence began before the collapse of the Soviet regime. She sees religiosity as unlikely to abate, given the context of ongoing social, political, and economic uncertainty. More significant, the imposed secularization of Soviet society is proving itself to be less robust than the voluntary secularization of Western European societies. Religion matters in Ukraine and other post-Socialist states.

The Ukrainian religious landscape is variegated and divided. Greek Catholicism, Roman Catholicism, Judaism, Islam, Protestant Christianity, and numerous other religious groups compete with Orthodox Christianity for moral authority and believers. And just as important, Wanner notes, though Orthodox "is widely considered the foundation of national traditions, aesthetic forms, and other elements of a unique sociocultural matrix," the Orthodox community in Ukraine is divided into several denominations. The Ukrainian Orthodox Church–Kyiv Patriarchate, the Ukrainian Autocephalous Orthodox Church, and the Ukrainian Orthodox Church–Moscow Patriarchate all claim to be the true Orthodox Church of Ukraine. "As the national churches compete among themselves for dominance, a new space is opened up for nontraditional faiths and new religious movements to establish roots in Ukraine," Wanner writes.

Wanner describes a Ukraine where religious faith is highly divided and contested, and where religion has important consequences for personal identity and for society as a whole. In response, the Ukrainian state has had little choice but to establish a relatively open, tolerant, and liberal legal regime that creates space for a multiplicity of religious practices. This legal system contrasts with the more confined space for religious activities in Russia described elsewhere in the volume by Werth and Graney.

Shevel's explication of state policies toward refugees in Russia and Ukraine renders explicit the contrast between legal regimes implicit in Wanner's, Werth's, and Graney's analyses. Varied domestic politics in Russia and in Ukraine have produced strikingly different refugee policies. The Ukrainian state has proven itself to be much more receptive to accepting international norms than a Russian state intent on demonstrating its peculiarity. Ukraine ultimately endorsed policies favoring neither ethnic Ukrainians nor migrants from other members of the Commonwealth of Independent States. Ukraine also has proven to be more receptive than Russia to hosting refugees from Africa, Asia, and the Middle East.

Shevel argues that the lack of domestic consensus over the definition of the Ukrainian nation undermined legislative proposals and legal norms that privileged or excluded various groups. Ukrainian law could not privilege any single group because Ukrainians could not agree on a definition of the nation that gave preference to an ethnos, a linguistic group, or a confessional community. The Russian Federation, conversely, has increasingly come to view itself as the inheritor of the Soviet regime. Therefore, former Soviet citizens should receive preferential treatment when seeking residency in Russia. Similarly, a stronger consensus on the meaning of "Russianness" and national distinctiveness impinges on the acceptance of international legislative norms.

Wanner's and Shevel's contributions enhance an appreciation of the differences between the Russian Federation and Ukraine following the collapse of the Soviet Union. From a shared starting point of Soviet-era laws and political norms, both states have evolved in different directions. Confronting fragmentation along all the cleavages that may run through a society, the Ukrainian state, long before the Orange Revolution, had begun to retreat into an inclusive legal order that creates the political, social, cultural, and legal space where citizens with expansive differences may coexist. The Russian Federation—as conceived by state-building elites—has sufficient internal coherence to tempt those political leaders with an inclination toward standardization to pursue their centralizing impulses.

Is Recentralization an Answer to Russia's Challenges?

Readers of this volume have undoubtedly become more skeptical about Russia's official claims of internal coherence than they were when first opening its covers. The Vladimir Putin administration evinces a centralizing impulse that runs counter to the diversity reflected in the contributions presented here. The chapters in this volume accentuate a deep complexity within the social, economic, political, and psychological structures of Russian life that does not lend itself readily to one-size-fits-all solutions.

Recentralizing policies have not, as yet, produced a backlash against Russia's present government. A number of the grievances underlying the issues and institutions explored in this book may well be consolidating within Russian society; they have not yet been mobilized behind any political, cultural, or religious agenda. The work of these authors suggests that the present preoccupation of many within and outside Russia with the need for standardized approaches to Russia's various problems may mobilize countervailing dispositions in response. As Mikhail Alexseev and Elise Giuliano demonstrate, such a standardizing and centralizing impulse may eventually set in motion triggers for animating the largely latent grievances described in this book.

Alexseev seeks to identify and measure hostility toward Chinese migrants in the Russian Far East, looking for the manner in which such attitudes find political expression. His puzzle becomes to explain why alarmist sentiments have not found ready expression and acceptance in local political life. He concludes that symbolic threat perception plays a larger role in fostering antimigrant hostility than the actual scale of migration. Perception of threat, rather than actual threat, triggers political action.

Given the fragmented nature of concern over the presence of Chinese migrants in the Russian Far East, politicians wishing to "play the Chinese card" have been unable to mobilize hostility behind their political goals. As Alexseev writes, "As long as the social bases of anti-Chinese mobilization remain fragmented and marginal, and as long as political elites pursue divergent goals, the spillover of hostility into collective action is unlikely." He cautions that symbolic anti-Chinese hostility remains a now-dormant resource for politicians in Moscow and the Far East who chose to exaggerate the "Chinese threat."

Alexseev, in the very specific context of reactions to Chinese migrants in the Russian Far East, posits the existence of breakpoints in the process of political mobilization. The mere existence of widespread grievances need not lead to the politics of protest. Those concerned with policy must avoid making the reductionist assumption that because Russians in the Far East are hostile to Chinese migrants, they will support right-wing politicians who attack the Chinese presence.

Giuliano's sweeping examination of nationalist separatism in Russia sounds a similarly cautionary note at the level of the Russian Federation as a whole. Policymakers in Moscow, Washington, and elsewhere should not assume the existence of separatist sentiment simply because national grievances may be said to exist. Additional triggering mechanisms are necessary before grievances find expression in political action.

Reviewing the existing scholarly literature on sovereignty campaigns during the late Soviet and early post-Soviet era, Giuliano maintains "that nationalism should not be thought of as an idea or set of attitudes that is present or absent, but as a fundamentally *political* phenomenon that develops out of a dynamic interaction between ethnic identity, individual experience, and elites' framing of grievances." In other words, it is a mistake to see increased individual identification with an ethnic group as leading inevitably to a nationalist program or support for separate statehood. Cultural, demographic, and grievance-based explanations for ethnic mobilization remain insufficient for explaining the complex processes that unraveled the Soviet Union. "The journey from ethnic group member to nationalist supporter," Giuliano writes, "is longer and less direct than generally believed."

Understanding Statecraft in Complex States

The picture of Russian and Ukrainian society that emerges from this volume points to larger lessons for those concerned with policy. Russia and Ukraine are complex, fragmented, diverse states in which a variety of often contradictory identity cues from the past retain powerful salience. Post-Soviet Russia and Ukraine are societies in which old grievances continue to fester even as new grievances emerge. Identities rooted in the past may rebound to shape the future in unexpected ways.

Readers of this volume will come to understand that the problem of identity is especially troublesome in postsocialist states because communist ideology had become so transparently discredited and disbelieved that it had long stopped providing meaningful markers for how people thought about who they were. Other identity labels return to fill the gap left by state and system collapse. However, old and new labels cannot merely be substituted for their Soviet counterparts. Identity formation must be viewed as a more dynamic and iterative process within which individuals, groups, and national institutions recalibrate and renegotiate membership.

The post-Soviet transition presents a particularly complex instance of identity re-formation because the Soviet experience provided such a poverty of guiding principles for charting the complex reality of identity. Soviet-style socialist ideology demanded an identity of interest between the totality of society and the Communist Party–dominated state. In its purist form, no legitimate interests existed apart from those of the party-based regime. This is why the Hungarian Communist Party leader Janos Kadar's shift in rhetoric during the 1960s from the notion of a regime believing that "those who are not with us are against us" to one recognizing that "those who are not against us are with us" proved to be a transformative alteration in Hungarian politics. The denial of multiple interests in society necessitated the denial of multiple identities.

The contributors to this volume demonstrate that societies were and remain far more complex than Soviet-speak and Communist Party rhetoric suggested. As Arel notes in the introduction to this volume, the principle of nationality, however potent as a mobilizing force, is deceptively simple. Multiple interests and multiple identities existed and exist throughout the Soviet and post-Soviet world. The inability of communist regimes to create concepts, language, institutions, and identities predicated on the reality of such diversity ultimately contributed to their implosion across a dozen time zones. The question of the moment is whether or not postcommunist regimes can rise to the challenge of redefining how citizens think about their identity, an issue that proved so vexing for their shared Soviet predecessors.

The authors represented here argue that sustaining democratic institutions requires a transformation of ingrained habits of thought and action. Citizens of democratizing regimes must begin to think differently about the nature of the political game and the nature of power. They and their leaders must move beyond concepts of politics and identity predicated on "zero-sum" solutions toward more compromise-oriented and inclusive political mechanisms. Those who observe post-Soviet societies from afar similarly must accept complexity and remain humble in analyzing transitional polities where new identities are being formed and old identities are rebounding.

Contributors

Mikhail A. Alexseev (Ph.D., University of Washington, 1996) studies threat assessment in interstate and internal conflicts, with an emphasis on migration, ethnic group relations, and post-Soviet Russia. He is the author of *Immigration Phobia and the Security Dilemma: Russia, Europe, and the United States* (Cambridge University Press, 2005); and *Without Warning: Threat Assessment, Intelligence, and Global Struggle* (St. Martin's Press, 1997). He is the editor of *A Federation Imperiled: Center–Periphery Conflict in Post-Soviet Russia* (St. Martin's Press, 1999). He is currently the principal investigator for a multiyear international research project on migration and ethnoreligious violence in Russia funded by the National Science Foundation and the John D. and Catherine T. MacArthur Foundation. He has published extensively in academic journals and in the mainstream media, including the *New York Times, Newsweek, Toronto Globe and Mail, USA Today,* and *Seattle Times.* He is a member of the Carnegie/MacArthur-sponsored Program on New Approaches to Russian Security of the Center for Strategic and International Studies in Washington.

Dominique Arel is associate professor in the School of Political Studies and chair of Ukrainian studies at the University of Ottawa. He received his Ph.D. from the University of Illinois at Urbana-Champaign in 1993 and was affiliated for seven years with the Thomas J. Watson Center for International Studies at Brown University. He is completing a collaborative manuscript on the identity politics of the 2002 Russian Census and is the coauthor of *Census and Identity: The Politics of Race, Ethnicity, and Language in National Censuses* (Cambridge University Press, 2002). His articles on census politics have been published in the *Oxford Handbook of Contextual Politics, Population, Post-Soviet Affairs,* and the *Canadian Review for Studies in Nationalism.* He has written extensively on language politics in Ukraine, and his analyses of the Ukrainian Orange Revolution have appeared in English, French, Russian, and Ukrainian. Since 2004, he has served as president of the Association for the Study of Nationalities.

Helen M. Faller received her Ph.D. in anthropology from the University of Michigan in 2003, and her B.A. from Bryn Mawr College in Russian language and Soviet political science in 1992. She spent half of 1993 living in Saint Petersburg teaching English and working as a translator and editor for an English-language newspaper. After having made several trips to Russia, she started graduate school in anthropology at the University of Wisconsin in 1995. During the year she spent in Russia, she had the opportunity to start learning about Central Asian and Russian Turks. In 1996, she transferred to the University of Michigan. She conducted dissertation research funded by both Fulbright-Hays and International Research and Exchanges Board fellowships in Kazan, Tatarstan, from 1999 to 2001. Before going to do fieldwork, she had been able to study several Turkic languages (Kazakh, Uzbek, and Turkish), which made it possible for her to learn Tatar in Kazan and allowed her to conduct research on how the referential worlds of Tatar-Russian bilinguals and Russian monophones are differently configured. Her dissertation research focused on emerging linguistic, ethnic, and religious communities in post-Soviet Tatarstan.

Elise Giuliano is a political scientist (Ph.D., University of Chicago, 2000) and an assistant professor at the University of Miami. In 2005–6, she was a visiting fellow at Harvard University's Davis Center for Russian Studies, where she completed a manuscript examining the conditions under which nationalist movements win and lose popular support. Understanding the demobilization of ethnic populations—an undertheorized phenomenon in social science—has important implications for grasping how political stability and accord can supersede interethnic violence. She examines these questions with regard to Russia and the former Soviet states during the late Soviet and early post-Soviet period. The manuscript builds on her doctoral dissertation field research in the Republic of Tatarstan, portions of which have been published in *Comparative Politics* and *Nationalism and Ethnic Politics.*

Dmitry Gorenburg is the executive director of the American Association for the Advancement of Slavic Studies and a visiting lecturer in the Department of Government at Harvard University. He is also a research analyst and director of Russian and East European Studies at the Center for Strategic Studies of the CNA Corporation, where he has worked since 2000. During the 2003–4 academic year, he was a fellow at the Woodrow Wilson International Center for Scholars. He holds a Ph.D. in political science from Harvard University and a B.A. in international relations from Princeton University. His current work focuses on the evolution of Soviet policies toward minority ethnic groups from 1953 to 1991 and the impact of these policies on ethnic identities in the region during and after the Soviet collapse. He is the author of *Nationalism for the Masses: Minority Ethnic Mobilization in the Russian Federation* (Cambridge University Press, 2003). He has also published several articles on minority nationalism in Russia that have appeared in journals such as *World Politics, Ethnic and Racial Studies,* and *Europe-Asia Studies.*

Katherine Graney received her B.A. from the College of the Holy Cross. She received her M.A. and Ph.D. in political science from the University of Wisconsin–Madison. Since 1999, she has held the position of associate professor of government at Skidmore College. Her research interests include sovereignty and nation-state building, and the role of gender and Islam in these processes. She was also a participant in an earlier Kennan Institute workshop on gender in the former Soviet Union. Her publications include articles in *Europe-Asia Studies* and *Problems of Post-Communism,* and several book chapters. She is currently working on an edited volume about "Europe" as seen from different vantage points in the former Soviet Union.

Alexandra Hrycak is associate professor of sociology at Reed College and vice president of the American Association for Ukrainian Studies. She received her B.A. in mathematics from Rutgers University and her Ph.D. and

M.A. in sociology from the University of Chicago. Her dissertation, "From the Iron Fist to the Invisible Hand: Writers, Artists and the Nation in Ukraine," examined the construction of Ukrainian national identity. It was based on several years of ethnographic and archival research on Ukrainian theater. Her current work focuses on gender and politics in Ukraine. Since 2001, she has investigated the formation of women's associations in the cities of L'viv, Kyiv, and Kharkiv. In 2005, she conducted interviews and focus groups on the role women in these three cities played in the 2004 elections and the Orange Revolution. She has contributed articles to the *American Journal of Sociology, Harvard Ukrainian Studies, Journal of Ukrainian Studies, Problems of Post-Communism,* and *East European Politics and Societies.*

Blair A. Ruble is currently director of the Kennan Institute of the Woodrow Wilson International Center for Scholars in Washington. He also serves as director of comparative urban studies at the Woodrow Wilson Center. He received his M.A. and Ph.D. degrees in political science from the University of Toronto (1973, 1977), and an A.B. degree in political science from the University of North Carolina at Chapel Hill (1971). He has edited more than a dozen volumes. His book-length works include a trilogy examining the fate of Russian provincial cities during the twentieth century: *Leningrad: Shaping a Soviet City* (University of California Press, 1990); *Money Sings! The Changing Politics of Urban Space in Post-Soviet Yaroslavl* (Woodrow Wilson Center Press and Cambridge University Press, 1995); and *Second Metropolis: Pragmatic Pluralism in Gilded Age Chicago, Silver Age Moscow, and Meiji Osaka* (Woodrow Wilson Center Press and Johns Hopkins University Press, 2001). His latest book is *Creating Diversity Capital: Transnational Migrants in Montreal, Washington, and Kyiv* (Woodrow Wilson Center Press and Johns Hopkins University Press, 2005).

Steven J. Seegel is a lecturer in the Department of History at the University of Tennessee. In August 2005, he defended his dissertation at Brown University, titled "Blueprinting Modernity: Nation-State Cartography and Intellectual Ordering in Russia's European Empire, Ukraine, and Former Poland-Lithuania, 1795–1917." Interpreting maps as texts rather than mere sources of historical information, his research focuses on the interrelatedness of power and knowledge across borders in Central and Eastern Europe. He has lectured and presented papers in Finland, Poland, Sweden, Russia, Ukraine, the United Kingdom, and the United States. He was active at

Brown University's Thomas J. Watson Center for International Studies in the recent three-year research initiative of Omer Bartov, "Borderlands: Ethnicity, Identity and Violence in the Shatter-Zone of Empires since 1848." He is serving as a contributor to volume 4 of the *History of Cartography* series (ca. 1650–1800), edited by Matthew Edney and Mary Pedley (University of Chicago Press, forthcoming).

Oxana Shevel is an assistant professor in the Department of Political Science at Purdue University. She received her Ph.D. in government from Harvard University in 2002, an M.Phil. in international relations from the University of Cambridge in 1994, and a B.A. in English and French from Kyiv State University in 1992. In 2002–3, she was a postdoctoral fellow at Harvard University's Davis Center for Russian Studies, and in the spring of 2006 she will be a Shklar Fellow at the Harvard Ukrainian Research Institute. Her research addresses issues of nation and state building in postcommunist Europe, and the influence of international institutions on democratization processes in the region. She is currently completing a book manuscript titled *Migration and Nation Building in New Europe* that examines how the politics of nation building and the strategies of international institutions shaped refugee and forced migration policies in Russia, Ukraine, the Czech Republic, and Poland in the 1990s.

Catherine Wanner is an assistant professor in the Department of History and Religious Studies Program at Pennsylvania State University. She received her doctorate in cultural anthropology from Columbia University and is the author of *Burden of Dreams: History and Identity in Post-Soviet Ukraine* (Pennsylvania State University Press, 1998). This book was based on ethnographic research on the rise of nationalism in Soviet Ukraine and how the nationalist paradigm influenced the cultural politics of historiography in everyday life in Ukraine after the collapse of the Soviet Union. She is currently completing a book manuscript on evangelicalism in Ukraine. This study analyzes how Soviet-era evangelical religious practices and communities in Ukraine have changed in response to the introduction of global Christianity since the collapse of socialism.

Paul W. Werth is associate professor of history at the University of Nevada, Las Vegas. He received his B.A. from Knox College (1990) and his Ph.D. from the University of Michigan (1996). In 2002, he published *At the Margins of Orthodoxy: Mission, Governance, and Confessional Politics in the*

Volga-Kama Region, 1825–1905 (Cornell University Press, 2002). His current research project examines discourses and practices of religious tolerance and their relationship to the construction of a modern civil order in Russia from 1772 to 1914. He is currently working on a study concerning the discourses of religious tolerance in Russia from the 1760s through the early twentieth century.

Index